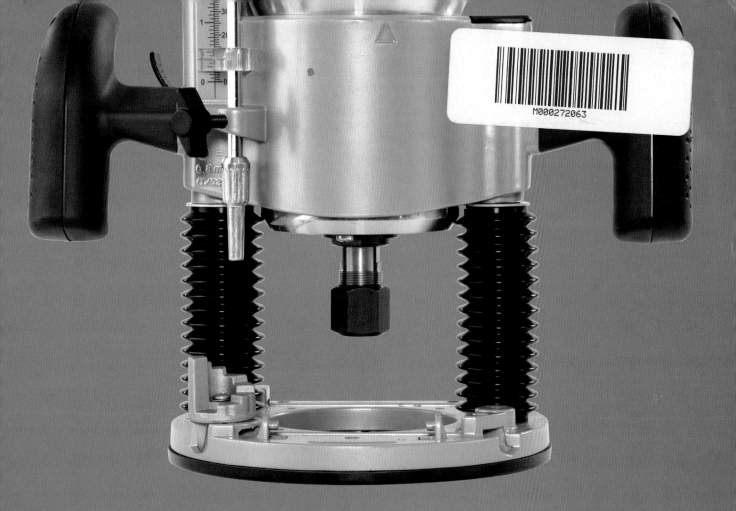

The Complete New
ROUTER
BOOK
for Woodworkers
Essential Skills, Techniques & Tips

The Complete New ROUTER BOOK for Woodworkers
Essential Skills, Techniques & Tips

PRINTED IN 2006.

Tom Carpenter
Creative Director

Heather Koshiol
Managing Editor

Jen Weaverling
Senior Book Development Coordinator

Julie Cisler
Senior Book Designer

Alan Geho
Principal Photographer

Special Thanks to: Terry Casey, Janice Cauley and John Kriegshauser.

Printed in China

Distributed by Landauer Corporation
300 NW 101st Street Suite A
Urbandale, Iowa 50322
800-557-2144: www.landauercorp.com

Landauer ISBN 13: 978-1-890621-94-0
Landauer ISBN 10:   1-890621-94-3

TABLE OF CONTENTS

WELCOME

ABOUT THE AUTHOR

Chris Marshall, a self-proclaimed tool addict, has been working wood since childhood. A former member of the editorial staff at HANDY magazine and book editor for the Handyman Club of America, Chris has authored books on table saws as well as trim carpentry and cabinetry, and has edited numerous volumes on woodworking and home improvement topics.

He is currently a full-time freelance writer, and serves as a contributing editor for Woodworker's Journal magazine, for which he writes woodworking project stories and tool reviews. He also is a regular tool reviewer for HANDY magazine and writes on a variety of shop, woodworking and home improvement topics from his home in Sunbury, Ohio.

Whether used by itself or in tandem with various accessories and jigs, no other woodworking tool can match a router's versatility.

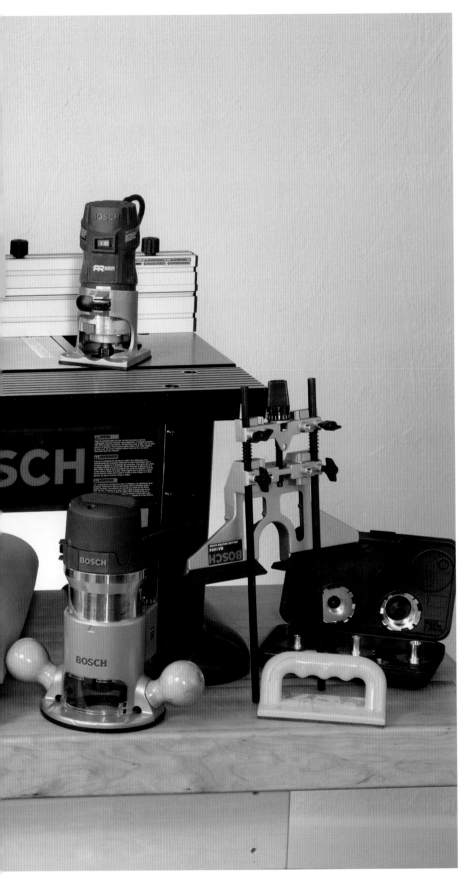

Whether you've been working with wood for a few years or many ages, you know the router's value in getting projects done, and done right. If you're new to woodworking, you're going to soon find out that knowing your way around a router — and knowing how to use it properly — is critical to your success in the shop.

No matter where you fall on the woodworking experience scale, *The Complete New Router Book* is for you. We saw a glaring need for new, fresh updated and reliable information on routers, and you're holding the result of our monumental efforts. It's a huge topic, as you can feel by the heft of this book. There's a lot to know! That's why precise words and gloriously instructive photos guide you to routing success every step of the way.

We guarantee there's nothing else like this book out there. It's that good, fresh and complete. From choosing the router that's right for you to using it safely, efficiently and effectively, here is every detail you're ever going to need to know about your router and how to use it. Plus, we've included ten great projects so you can get right to work!

Success in the workshop revolves around your router and how you use it. That's what *The Complete New Router Book* is all about. So roll up your sleeves and let's get busy!

ONE

INTRODUCTION TO ROUTING

Regardless of what kind of woodworking you do (or would like to do someday!), woodworking really boils down to performing a number of basic operations over and over again. We cut parts to size, flatten or shape the edges or ends and assemble the pieces with many variations of joints. Sometimes we cut curves and holes, and often we need to duplicate regular or unusually shaped parts accurately. When it comes to ornamentation, most square edges can be improved by modifying them with decorative profiles or even an inlay of contrasting wood or veneer. Once you've taken care of this collection of tasks, what's left amounts to sanding and finishing work. In a nutshell, that's woodworking.

If you're the frugal sort — and most woodworkers I know are — what could be better than a single tool that accomplishes most of the above-mentioned tasks with equal skill and ease? If you haven't guessed already, woodworking's wonder tool is definitely the router. More than any other shop machine, the router deserves boasting rights for being the closest "jack-of-all-trades" tool there is. It's a shaping, cutting and joint-making tool, all in one small package. It's the only woodworking tool that has cross capabilities as both a handheld tool and a stationary machine. Even

Adding a router or two to your tool collection will open up a wide range of profiling, cutting and joint-making capabilities to your woodworking. You'll wonder how you ever got along without this useful machine.

better, all of these attributes can be had for much less than you'll pay for most stationary tools — most professional-grade routers sell for around $200.

In my years of using, studying and writing about woodworking tools, I've learned that more research and development goes into improving routers than any other tool type. The reasoning is simple: Manufacturers put their energy and resources into those tools that offer the biggest return on investment. Routers are the second most sought after tool behind cordless drills. Router innovations keep tool designers busy, because we woodworkers love our routers, and we're eager for any new development that makes a great tool even better.

This chapter presumes nothing about your knowledge of routers. Like any good story, we'll start at the very beginning and build your knowledge about routers with each subsequent chapter. If you already own a router and know your way around the tool, jump ahead to other chapters as you like to get right to those techniques or other router information you'd like to learn more about. Maybe you're in the market for a new router to replace a tired tool or to expand your collection. Be sure to read the section in chapter two on new router features and packaging options.

Routers are made in three basics sizes: small, light-duty trim routers (center), mid-sized routers for general work (left) and routers meant for heavy-duty use with large bits (right).

Full-size routers in the 3 hp range are ideal for router table use, but their weight and size makes them less convenient for hand-held use.

Mid-sized routers offer a good compromise between handling and power for general routing tasks.

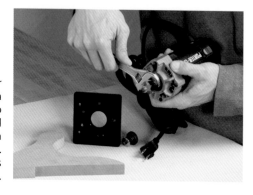

Because of their compact size, trim routers are easier to maneuver over small workpieces than mid-sized routers. The trade-off is limited power.

What Is A Router?

In spite of an impressive list of capabilities, routers are remarkably basic machines. Pare down all the specialized features, and any router is essentially a motor mounted in a base to stabilize it. A bit attaches to the motor shaft, which points down, and spins to cut in a rotating fashion. It's a simple tool that performs a simple function.

There's quite a range of sizes between routers, from trim routers that you can easily hold in one hand to two-handed monster machines rivaling a stationary shaper for power and capability. Size differences aren't just marketing ploys with routers. Tool proportion and weight are directly related to what the routers are intended to do. Small trim routers are designed for lighter-duty trimming tasks, sometimes in awkward or tight spaces where a larger router won't fit. Big, heavy routers spin large bits that cut large profiles, and the operation requires loads of motor power. Medium-sized routers are crossover machines that perform both light- and heavy-duty operations reasonably well. That's why mid-sized routers are the most popular and best-selling models made.

Anatomy Of A Router

Fixed-Base Router

Motor Pack

Power Switch

Depth-Setting Controls

Base

Base Locking Lever

Handles

Collet

Subbase

Plunge Router

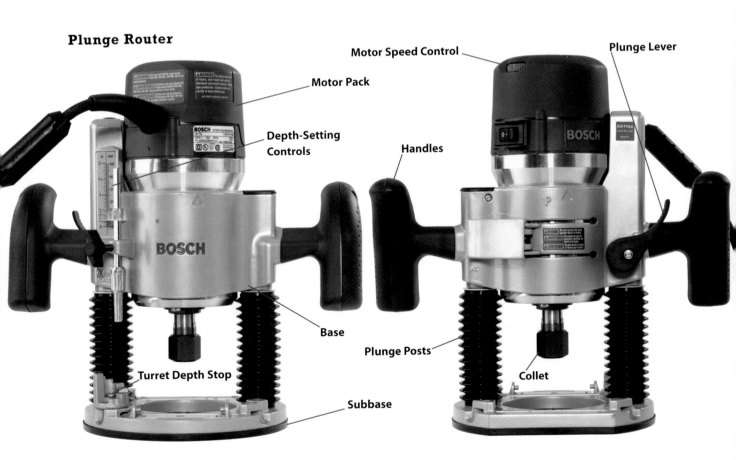

Motor Speed Control

Plunge Lever

Motor Pack

Depth-Setting Controls

Handles

Base

Plunge Posts

Turret Depth Stop

Collet

Subbase

Routers contain universal motors, just like other portable power tools. Universal motors are lightweight and produce substantial horsepower, but they can't sustain this power for extended periods like the motors on larger woodworking machinery.

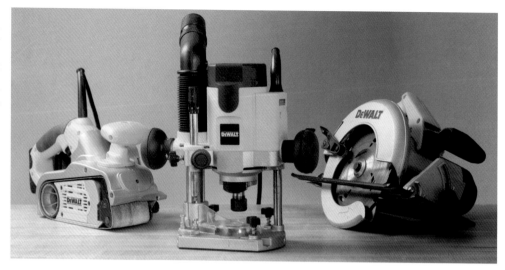

Motor

The heart of a router is its motor, which ranges in size from 3/4 to 3.25 peak horsepower. Like other portable woodworking tools such as drills, circular saws and sanders, router motors are universal style. Universal motors run at high rpm and amperage, which enables them to be powerful without also being heavy. Some routers, particularly older or entry-level tools, have single-speed motors. Once the tool is on, it spins every bit at the same speed. Most new routers have variable-speed control, so you can adjust the motor speed to better suit the bit you're using. Routers operate at dizzyingly high speeds from 8,000 to as much as 30,000 rpm. High speeds provide helpful inertia to get relatively lightweight bits to cut through hard wood at fast speeds. But the biggest benefit to high speed is that bits take smaller bites of wood, leading to smoother cuts.

Low speed settings allow the motor to produce more torque for pushing large bits through the wood without stalling. The slower speed also keeps large bits from spinning faster than is safe for their design.

The motor is contained inside a plastic or metal housing with some of the operator controls and a large cooling fan. The downside to a high energy, lightweight universal motor is that it generates significant heat as it operates. The cooling fan draws fresh air through the housing and exhausts the hot air. It must do this

The heart and soul of a router is its motor. In this case, the motor is contained in a removable motor pack. This style allows the same motor to be used in different types of router bases.

A large cooling fan inside the motor pack reduces heat build-up, but it also contributes to noise levels that will require hearing protection when using a router.

both efficiently and quietly. Depending on the router style, the motor can either be removed from the tool or it can't. Motor removal makes it easier to perform maintenance, change bits or insert it in another router base. In this book, when the motor can be removed, we'll call the motor and its housing a motor pack.

Collet

Part of the versatility of routers is due to the fact that they accept hundreds of different interchangeable bits. To do this, the end of the motor armature shaft is fitted to accept a two-piece collet that grips the bits. On the outside, a collet has a large nut that threads onto the motor shaft. Within the nut is a cone-shaped sleeve that's precisely machined to fit inside a conical hole milled into the end of the motor shaft. The sleeve has from two to as many as eight slits cut partially along its length. When the nut is threaded onto the motor shaft, the slits allow the sleeve to compress as it slides down and nests

into the armature shaft. It closes like a vise all around the bit shank to hold it firmly and evenly. Sleeves with more slits grip more uniformly than those with fewer slits.

The inner sleeves of router collets have slits that allow the sleeve to compress around the bit shank. Sleeves may have from two to eight slits, depending on the design.

Collet sleeves with more slits generally provide better grip than sleeves with fewer slits, because the sleeve can compress more evenly around the bit shank.

Collets fit onto threads on the end of the motor shaft. The inside surface of this opening is tapered, which closes the collet's inner sleeve when it's tightened down on a bit.

Collets are made to accept either ¼-in. or ½-in. bit shanks. Most good-quality routers will come with both sizes of collets for greater versatility.

Collets come in two primary sizes, according to the bit shank size they accept. These days, most bits are manufactured with ¼ or ½-in. shank diameters. Usually, a collet accepts one or the other bit size but not both. This is not always the case, however. On some routers with ½-in. collets, the router comes with a second sleeve that fits inside or replaces the first sleeve for retrofitting the ½-in. collet for ¼-in. shank bits. A third collet size, ⅜-in., also used to be a popular bit option, but bits are seldom sized this way anymore. European routers sold in this country may have metric

collets that accept metric-shank bits instead of imperial sizes. Usually these routers can be fitted with conventional sleeves as accessory items.

Some entry-level routers don't have a sleeve mounted inside the collet nut. Instead, the motor shaft is bored and slit to take the place of the sleeve. On these kinds of collets, the armature will have only two slits that allow it to compress around the bit. The trouble with collets of this sort is that bits are more likely to slip if they aren't tightened securely. Professional routers do not have sleeve-style armatures. They're mainly found on light-duty, low-priced routers.

On many older routers, the collet sleeve and nut are separate pieces. This two-piece collet style is typical on trim routers as well. Here, the sleeve may have only one slit. The sleeve fits inside the armature bore, and the nut compresses the sleeve. When the nut is removed, the sleeve is supposed to come out as well. However, this doesn't always work, particularly if the sleeve is dirty or if it gets tightened in the collet without a bit. A stuck sleeve is difficult to extract, and it can be equally hard to remove a bit from a stuck sleeve. To solve the problem, most routers now have self-releasing collets. The sleeve has a rim that fits on a shoulder inside the nut, and the two act as one piece. Or, the sleeve fits into the collet nut and locks in place with a snap ring. When the nut is loosened, it both pulls the sleeve out of the armature and also opens the sleeve and releases the bit. Bits never get stuck inside the sleeve on self-releasing col-

Not all routers have two-piece collets. The motor armature on this model is machined to form the inner sleeve, rather than having a separate sleeve fitted inside the collet nut.

Routers made more than a few decades ago often had collets with separate inner sleeves. These single-slit sleeves were prone to getting stuck or slipping when gripping bits.

lets, provided the sleeves are kept clean and free of corrosion.

It's crucial to keep a router collet clean and in good condition (for more on router cleaning a collet, see page 79). Eventually, tightening and loosening the collet will cause it to wear and begin to lose its grip on bits. When this starts to happen, a collet should be replaced, both for performance's sake and as a measure of safety. You don't want a bit to work free when it's spinning at 20,000 rpm. The workpiece will be destroyed, the bit will be damaged — and the bit could hurt you, too.

Base

You'll learn in chapter two that general-purpose routers come in two primary configurations: fixed and plunge base. Fixed-base routers have motor packs that separate from the base. The motor on a dedicated plunge router, on the other hand, can't be removed from the base. On fixed-base routers, the base provides a housing that wraps around the motor pack to hold it in place. The housing is formed with a slit though it. A locking turnscrew or a flip lever crosses the slit and squeezes the router base against the motor pack to secure it.

Depth-Setting Controls

On fixed base routers, manufacturers use several different systems for adjusting the vertical position of the motor pack inside the base. This is the principal method for establishing cutting depth. Plunge routers have a different base configuration. Here, the motor can be adjusted up and down by sliding it along a pair of posts on the base. The posts are hollow and fit into sleeves in the motor housing so the motor slides smoothly and accurately. A pair of return springs located either inside or outside the posts raise the motor back up to full height for withdrawing the bit from a cut. There's no automatic return of this sort on a fixed-base router, which is why the router is "fixed" in position during the cut.

Some routers are designed with removable motor packs, while others have motors integrated into the tool housing so they can't be removed.

Setting cutting depth involves making both coarse and fine adjustments. The first setting gets the bit roughly where you want it, and the second dials in the cutter position precisely. Both router styles have provisions for making these macro and micro adjustments, using indexed collars or depth rods and turrets. We'll learn more about the differences between making height adjustments for fixed and plunge routers in chapter two.

Setting accurate bit depth is crucial on a router. On this model, a large depth adjustment ring controls the depth, and a buckle locks the motor in place.

Handles

Aside from motor positioning devices, router bases are outfitted with a pair of handles for controlling the tool during use. Usually, these handles are circular or ball-shaped, but they can also be elongated into grips or horn shapes. There's also a D-shaped handle as one of the base options for many fixed-base routers. Some users prefer this style for use when two-handed operation isn't feasible. One manufacturer even makes routers with a plastic wrap around the motor pack shaped to fit the contour of a hand so the tool can be palm-gripped with one hand instead of with the usual pair of handles. The On/Off trigger and speed control are often located on the handles of a plunge router. For fixed-base routers, these controls are generally on the motor pack instead.

Both fixed-base and plunge-base routers usually have a clear chip shield mounted on the rim of the base for viewing the bit and work during cutting. The other openings around the base provide for chip clearance as well as access to the collet and bit.

Subbase

All routers have a secondary baseplate that attaches to the metal base, called a subbase. The subbase provides two primary functions. It's usually made of plastic or other smooth composite material to provide a low-friction, scratch-free surface for moving the tool over the work. A second and equally important attribute of subbases is that the center bit cutout can be fitted with rub collars (see Chapter Eight for more information on types and applications of rub collars). Subbases attach to the router base with several screws. Sometimes routers are packaged with more than one subbase with different sized bit clearance holes. The smaller hole is typically sized to fit rub collars for doing template work. The larger subbase hole provides clearance for using large bits. It also makes the cutting area easier to see, which can be advantageous in some setups.

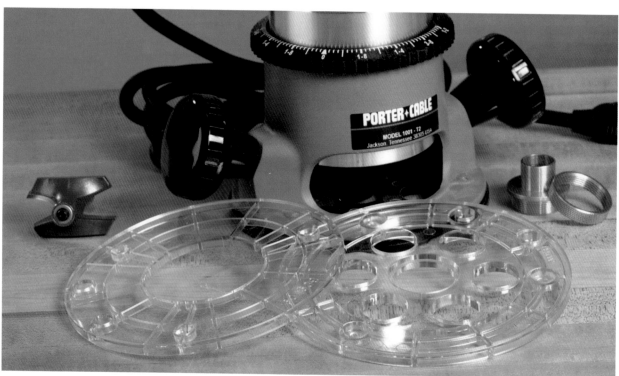

Subbases provide a smooth surface for sliding the router along. Subbases with large holes allow for oversized router bits. Smaller holes are often made to fit removable guide bushings for template routing.

Short History Of Routers

Before electricity was harnessed for household use, woodworking was an entirely human-driven enterprise. The work we now do with electric routers was once the domain of hand planes, handsaws, bit and braces and the like. A trip to any flea market will show you the countless individual hand planes used by our forebears for shaping and profiling work. You can actually still buy a specialized router plane for cutting dadoes and grooves, although the task is much faster and easier with a router and straight bit.

Thanks to the Industrial Revolution, early vertical milling machines and the development of lightweight, high-speed electric motors, technology paved the way for the creation of the first handheld routing machines.

The first motorized routers were developed around the beginning of the last century, but who deserves credit for the "first" electric routers is

Routers perform many of the same edge-shaping functions as wooden hand planes once did. This triple fluted router bit mimics the shape of a fluted plane iron.

Aside from the rise of modern plastics and some modifications in handle style, routers made 50 years ago or so look remarkably similar to the routers we use today.

Porter-Cable's Routo-Jig was marketed as an all-in-one woodworking tool. Among other options, the tool had interchangeable jigsaw, router and planer bases.

still a debatable issue. Around WWI, a patternmaker named R. L. Carter began mass-producing predecessor versions of what we now call fixed-base routers. These early routers were considerably larger, heavier and relatively more expensive to users of that time than what we use now. Shortly after WWII, a German engineer named Eugen Lutz founded Elu, a company that is given credit for inventing the first plunge-base routers. Since that time, routers have remained in the same basic fixed- or plunge-base styles.

During the 50s and 60s, Rockwell/Porter-Cable and Stanley attempted to expand the versatility of routers even further. Routers were packaged with unusual jigsaw and jointer plane bases to convert routers into planers and saws as well as shaping tools. The trend didn't continue, and routers returned to more conventional styling. These days, routers have either fixed or plunge bases only.

As you'll see, both major router base styles continue to have unique advantages that keep each form viable for modern woodworking. New developments and improvements happen almost every year — but innovations improve features such as motor circuitry, dust collection, handle design or cordless power, rather than attempt to turn routers into other tools. These days, there's a dedicated power tool for virtually every purpose, and the scope of router usage doesn't change much.

This vintage Stanley router converted into a jointer plane by mounting the motor pack horizontally into the planer attachment.

What Can Routers Do?

It would be ridiculous to say that routers can do it all. No tool has limitless capabilities. However, a router's range of woodworking applications is impressive, to say the least. While some woodworkers can do without certain tools, based on the emphasis of their woodworking, it's hard to imagine why at least one router doesn't belong in every woodworking shop. In terms of versatility, a router performs at least five primary operations. Here's an overview of what you'll see covered in much more detail later in this book:

Decorative Edge Profiling

As chapter four will illustrate, there are hundreds of different router bits available. The majority of them are designed for cutting decorative profiles into wood. Once upon a time, profiling was done by hand planes with shaped blades or with heavy shaping machines, but now these tasks are accomplished almost exclusively with a router in home workshops. So, profiling is arguably a router's primary function. The operation is fast and easy to do, even if you're just getting started with a router. Whatever woodworking you do or will do as your hobby develops, you'll probably use your router as a profiling tool to some degree on every project you build.

If you're considering buying your first router, chances are you want one to turn those square edges into curved or angular shapes. Decorative profiles, when used with a modicum of restraint, add flair to your work. They turn hard, relatively uninteresting surfaces into eye-catching shapes that are pleasing to the eye and enjoyable to the touch. They can "lighten" the heaviness of thick furniture parts, from a visual standpoint, adding a touch of grace as well as visual interest. Profiling also benefits a project from a safety standpoint. Profiles such as roundovers and chamfers "break" sharp edges and corners so they're less painful to bump up against or grab. When these edges are removed, profiles also improve the wear and tear on a project, because wood is less likely to splinter when it doesn't terminate in a corner or edge.

Profiling with a router usually involves guiding a ball bearing on the end of the router bit along the edge

Dozens of different router bit shapes make it possible to cut all sorts of edge and face profiles. Your creative options are wide open.

Routers mounted in router tables are capable of making a variety of decorative joints for drawer construction.

Joinery

Another significant advantage to a router is that you can use these machines for cutting joints. Of course you can build a number of strong joints with just glue and screws or nails, but eventually you'll want to try building joints where the wood actually locks together. The first joint type that probably comes to mind is the timeless dovetail. With the appropriate setup, you can make dovetail joints with a router. A wide variety of other interlocking joints are possible to make with a router as well, as you'll see in chapter nine. The joints are fun to build, and they'll take your woodworking to a higher level of skill and quality. You can even use routers to build production-style joinery for making raised-panel cabinet doors and windows.

Generally, building joinery involves using the router and appropriate bits or guide collars with a jig. In this configuration, the router is moved in a controlled and repeatable way. Joinery requires this degree of precision, because parts often need to fit together within tolerances measured in thousands of an inch. This degree of accuracy is hard to match using other types of power tools or building joints by hand.

or end of the wood, with the bit's cutter removing a controlled amount of wood. Some types of profiling operations like fluting happen on the face of workpieces rather than along the edges. Either way, routers can be guided by hand to do this work, moving the tool over the wood to cut the profile (see chapter six for more on freehand techniques). Or, the wood can be moved past the router with the router inverted and mounted underneath a router table (see chapters five and seven for much more on router tables and their use).

With the appropriate bits and a large router, your router becomes a makeshift shaper for building doors and other millwork.

With a template and guide collar, a router is capable of duplicating parts precisely. No other home woodworking machine performs this unique function.

Template Work

After profiling and joinery, template routing is another huge benefit of routers. Here, you can use a router and piloted bits run against a template to duplicate parts. Flush-trimming or pattern bits allow the router to follow any shape of template, trimming the wood to match the template exactly. Often, you'll make a template to manufacture parts with shapes that need to match or to perfect an unusual shape before committing it to your actual project wood. Once the template is made and fixed to a workpiece cut to rough size, a router trims the shape quickly and easily to match the template.

You can add decorative or functional inlays to your projects using a router, template and simple inlay kit.

Both parts of the sturdy mortise and tenon joint can be made with a router and a single straight bit quickly and easily.

With a router and the appropriate bits, you can make your own custom moldings in any wood species you choose. You're no longer limited to off-the-shelf home center millwork.

A router outfitted with an edge guide will cut straight, uniform dadoes or grooves, just like a dado blade on a table saw.

In other instances, you can use a template to cut relief areas or holes for mortises. Again, the template controls the router's cutting path and area, which enables it to cut accurately, swiftly and repeatedly. Door installers use routers and hinge mortising jigs all the time to cut hinge mortises with minimal effort and maximum accuracy. Templates also make it possible to use a router for cutting decorative inlays, butterfly

Have you ever wanted to make decorative lettered signs? It's easy to do with a router and signmaking kit.

inserts and even lettered signage. Routers can even be used as drilling devices with a template for boring shelf pin holes in cabinetry. We'll cover the range of template-routing operations in chapter nine.

Trimming And Cutting

Along the same principle as template routing, routers are also great tools for trimming large workpieces to size. If you work with sheets of plywood or other heavy composite sheet materials like medium-density plywood, you know how hard it is to cut large panels accurately when manipulating large sheets over a stationary saw. It's much easier to size down sheet goods with a circular saw or jigsaw first, cutting the pieces to rough size. At this point, a router and straight bit, when guided against a straightedge, can trim those rough edges perfectly smooth, flat and square. Splintering is all but eliminated, and the routed edges are cleaner than what can be done with any sawblade. A router outfitted with a trammel jig can also cut accurate circles,

Plunge routers can drill evenly spaced holes with the proper jig. It's a helpful application for building bookcases and cabinetry.

ovals and arches — a particularly useful skill for building tabletops and picture frames.

Installing plastic laminate is a relatively common cabinetry and woodworking task. Here, it's important that the fragile laminate is trimmed perfectly flush to its substrate material.

Routers make handy trimming tools when run against a straightedge. If a panel is too large to feed over a table saw, use a router to trim it square and smooth.

Precise depth adjustment allows a router to perform flush-trimming tasks without marring the surrounding worksurfaces.

Aside from edge trimming, routers with micro-adjustable depth setting provisions can be used for surface trimming, too. This is useful in cases where a joint is pinned with a dowel or when screw holes are capped with wooden plugs. A router can trim the dowel or plug flush with the surrounding wood faster than you can cut or sand them flat and with perfect accuracy.

Edge Jointing

Forming trued stock, cutting joinery or gluing up boards into larger panels requires workpieces with flat, square and smooth surfaces. The stationary tool for flattening and squaring edges is a jointer, but it's a relatively expensive machine and definitely not one you're likely to purchase unless you're a serious woodworker. Fortunately, a router and router table can be set up to operate like an accurate edge-jointing tool with little difficulty or cost.

Light-duty trim routers or any router outfitted with a flush-trim bit make quick work of this trimming task. Wood veneer can also be trimmed flush this way.

A straight bit in a router table can perform edge-jointing tasks on par with a stationary jointer. It's a helpful function for making edge-glued panels or for squaring up stock.

Routers are relatively inexpensive woodworking tools, but to use them to their full potential you'll still need to invest in numerous bits and related accessories.

Cost Considerations

In light of their many functions, routers are relatively inexpensive tools to purchase, in the big continuum of woodworking machinery. Light-duty routers can be had for less than $100, and most professional-grade routers are priced under $400. You'll find a glut of good models from which to choose in the $125 to $200 price range (for more on the differences between consumer and professional routers, see Chapter Two). Depending on your woodworking needs, a single router may be all you need.

There are other costs involved with getting the full range of capability from your router. Over time, you'll probably spend more money on bits and accessories than you will for the router itself. It seems each new project involves purchasing a bit or two, but eventually you'll amass quite a collection. You don't need to buy an exhaustive set of bits to start with. It's sensible to build a bit collection as the need arises, once you've got a basic set of essential bits (see page 109 for a list of "must have" bits). With care, bits can last for many hours.

The accessories you buy will also depend on what you build and how often you plan to use these devices. You'll need a reliable edge guide for your router and probably a set of template guides. Eventually you'll probably also want to buy a dovetail jig. Other accessories can actually be built from scrap material for reasonable cost. We'll show examples of both manufactured and shop-made accessories throughout this book.

One accessory that no router should be without is a router table. A router table expands the versatility of a router immensely and makes many tasks safer and easier to perform, especially joint-making, shaping with large bits or detailing small workpieces. There are numerous router tables you can purchase, and most are relatively expensive investments. Or, you can build a router table without advanced woodworking skills or significant cost. Chapter ten includes one plan for building a simple and a more elaborate router table.

TWO

CHOOSING A ROUTER THAT'S RIGHT FOR YOU

Among fixed-base, plunge-base and trim routers, there are at least a dozen different models of each type. Most manufacturers offer a few horsepower options in both base styles as well as packaging with different standard accessories. Some routers come with multiple subbases, or an edge guide, while others come with dust collection provisions. Not all fixed-base or plunge routers are built the same, in terms of features, performance or handling. So, the challenge to buying your first router or to replacing one you already have is two-fold: First, do you pick a fixed- or plunge-base tool? Second, which model has the right combination of features, power, accessories and price to suit your needs?

This chapter will help sort through the issues you need to know to pick the right machine (or machines) for you. Use it as

buying guide of sorts before you start seriously shopping. While we won't review specific models — that's the stuff of router reviews in woodworking magazines — we'll put fixed-base, plunge and trim routers under the microscope so you can evaluate their functional differences more carefully. We'll also take a closer look at common features of both fixed-base and plunge routers. Routers are laden with bells and whistles that bear some likeness to one another, and it's important to know what's essential to have on your next tool. Once all this information is under your belt, read some other router reviews in woodworking magazines to gain perspective on particular models and pricing. Then you'll be ready to make an informed buying decision and one you'll be happy with for years to come.

Trim routers were originally designed to trim plastic laminate, but their compact size also makes them convenient for routing small workpieces.

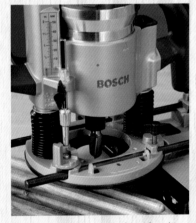

Plunge routers are capable of making edge cuts, like fixed-base routers, but they're also uniquely designed to make internal plunging cuts.

Fixed-base routers are easier to use in a router table than plunge routers, because plunge springs make depth changes more difficult with the router inverted.

FIXED-BASE ROUTERS UP CLOSE

Recall from chapter one that fixed-base routers consist of a motor pack that clamps in the base. Moving the motor up and down inside the base changes the cutting depth of the bit. Once the bit depth is set, it stays there for the cut. The tool has to be shut down and the motor moved in the base to change the bit setting for altering the cutting depth. This impacts the types of cuts you can make, because the bit has to be started at a fixed depth rather than plunged into the work. The usual locations for starting a cut with a fixed-base router are along the edge or end of a workpiece. Or, cuts must begin inside a starter hole large enough to provide clearance for the router bit if the cut happens within the workpiece instead of around the perimeter. In contrast, a plunge router can create its own bit clearance hole by lowering the bit into the work while it's spinning. It's unsafe to do this with a fixed-base machine using it in a handheld way.

Advantages Of Fixed-Base Routers

If you're a novice woodworker and buying your first router, a fixed-base type may be your best choice. It's also a sound buy if your tool budget only allows for one tool. In terms of capability, fixed-base routers have three distinct advantages over plunge routers. First, the subbase on fixed-base routers is round and generally larger than those on plunge routers. Some plunge routers have much smaller subbases with a flat edge, which reduces the tool's stability in some circumstances. The round subbase provides a large and regular footprint for the tool, regardless of how it's positioned on the workpiece. This is particularly helpful when routing smaller parts or feeding the tool along an edge when only half the router base — and sometimes even less — is supported by the workpiece. The more base you can have on the wood, the better control you'll have over the tool, which translates into smoother cuts and improved safety.

Decorative edge profiling adds visual interest to any woodworking project, and fixed-base routers do the job well.

A second advantage to fixed-base design is that the handles are positioned closer to the subbase than on plunge routers. Lower handles help drop the tool's center of gravity so it feels less "tippy" than a plunge router. In contrast, the handles on a plunge router are always straddling the motor, where the tool weight is, regardless of how high the motor is raised on the plunge posts. Low center of gravity is a real benefit if you're just learning to rout and get-

For router table applications, it's generally easier to set bit height with a fixed-base router than a plunge router. Bit changes are also a simple matter of pulling the motor pack out of the base.

A larger subbase on most fixed-base routers provides a more stable platform for guiding the tool than smaller, "clipped" subbases on some plunge routers.

ting comfortable with both tool manners and bit behaviors in different situations. When handles give you a better sense of control over the tool, you'll have one less thing to worry about and feel more confident in your setup and cutting task.

Aside from the ergonomic advantages of large subbases and low handles, fixed-base routers offer a third advantage: They're the best choice for router table use. Since fixed-base routers don't have plunge posts with springs, you don't have to overcome spring compression when pushing the router up to set bit height above the table. The motor simply adjusts up or down in the base, and your only obstacle is the weight of the motor itself. Changing bits is also easier with a fixed-base router in the table. Generally, all you'll need to do is unlock the base and pull out the motor to gain full access to the collet nut. With a plunge router in a router table, bit changes usually mean crouching down under the table to reach the collet or removing the whole tool and insert plate. Either option is less convenient than simply dropping the motor out of its base.

Disadvantages Of Fixed-Base Routers

Fixed-base routers have a few limitations worth considering. Since cutting depth can't be changed without turning off the tool and waiting for the bit to stop, using a fixed-base router for making deep cuts takes longer than plunge routers. This isn't a big issue for hobby woodworking, but it does get tiresome if you have a lot of repetitive routing to do or you're working with large bits that require more than one pass to form the profile.

Another drawback that's somewhat model-dependant is that many fixed-base routers do not come with provisions for dust and chip collection. Routing produces substantial amounts of airborne dust and wood chips. Routers that connect to shop vacuums make routing more pleasant and tidy, while keeping the bit area cleaner so you can see what you're doing as the cut progresses. Keeping the chips clear also prevents the subbase or pilot bearing on a bit from hanging up on the debris and altering the cut. Some fixed-base routers have dust ports, and more models have them every year, but it's still a more typical feature among plunge routers.

Since fixed-base routers don't have plunge posts, the motor remains closer to the worksurface, which also keeps the center of gravity low.

There's a notable size difference between the proportions and weight of full-size, versus mid-sized fixed-base routers. The smaller of the two styles are more convenient for freehand use.

Differences Between Fixed-Base Routers

Within the fixed-base category, models differ in two significant ways: the size of the motor and how the motor packs install and adjust in their bases.

Power Issues

The glut of fixed-base routers falls in the 1 to 2.25 hp range. From there, power jumps to a few big machines in the 3 or 3.25 hp range. Keep in mind that these horsepower estimates are based on peak power limits, not on continuous hp delivery (for more on what horsepower ratings mean, see page 55). Mid-sized fixed-base routers in the 2 hp range are suitable for middle-duty cutting operations, such as edge profiling work, trimming tasks and building joinery. Weighing in at around 7 to 10 pounds, these mid-sized machines are ideally suited for

handheld routing. They're also capable of router table work, although a larger 3 or 3.25 hp machine is the better choice. The heavyweight machines are built for demanding profiling work with large, heavy bits, and they can handle the increased stresses sometimes placed on routers in table-routing applications.

Big routers are also designed to run for longer periods of time without overheating — a real concern in production-routing situations. While 3 or 3.25 hp routers can double as hand-held tools as well as for router table use, their proportions and 12- to 18-lb. weight make them unwieldy for routing small parts. And large panel-raising or shaping bits are unsafe to use for freehand work anyway.

Motor Mounting And Adjustment

All fixed-based routers share the common design of raising and lowering the motor in the base to change bit depth. The differences between different models mostly have to do with how the motor mounts and moves in the base. Across the router industry, the method for holding the

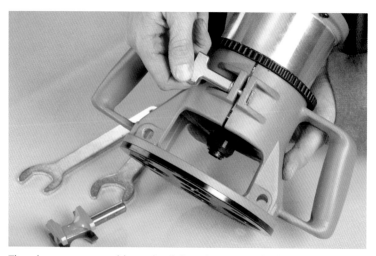

Thumbscrews are an older style of clamping system for fixing motors in bases. They can be harder to tighten down firmly, and the design isn't commonly used anymore.

like an offset cam to draw a bolt that pulls the base tight along its open seam. As the cam wears, a nut on the end of the bolt can be tightened to account for the wear. The nut also makes the clamping pressure variable so you can set it to a comfortable "throw." With the buckle mechanism, making motor height adjustments is a tool-free operation, and it's painless to do.

Fixed-base routers are regularly inverted for router table use, so manufacturers provide a secondary means of holding the motor in the base when the buckle or screw is released. The secondary stop keeps the motor from falling out accidentally and becoming damaged. It also serves as a safety in the event that the motor slips out of clamping pressure while the bit is still spinning. Depending on the tool, the extra stop can be a pocket formed on the motor pack threads. It sidetracks the motor's travel out of the base so you have to manually reengage the motor on the grooves again in order to twist it all the way out. Or, the stop may be

motor in place has undergone some changes in recent years. Many fixed-base routers used to have a thumb-screw or a setscrew stop for tightening the motor in place. A few routers still use this clamp style, but the difficulty with a thumbscrew is that over time, wear and tear on the base and thumbscrew threads means you have to twist harder to tighten the motor securely. It's harder on your fingers, and the typical recourse is to grab a pair of pliers or a wrench to wrangle the extra leverage into the screw.

These days, most new routers have buckle-style flip levers instead of the thumbscrew. Here, the buckle works

A secondary stop on this fixed-base router keeps the motor from falling out of the base, even when the buckle clamp is released. It's a good safety feature for router table use.

Buckle clamps are a newer and emerging standard for locking router bases in place. The lever activates a cam that tightens the base against the motor.

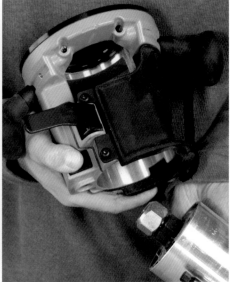

The secondary stop can be a pocket cut next to the threads in the router base or a separate button that must be pressed to remove the motor from the base.

a secondary button that you have to press to release the motor pack. Whatever the method, the secondary stop is a good design feature.

Helical Motor Adjustment

The typical method for raising and lowering the motor pack in its base is to turn the motor like a screw. Sometimes, spiral grooves are milled into the motor pack housing, and it rides on pins in the base. Or, the system can be reversed so the base is threaded instead of the motor pack, and the pins are on the motor. Either style forms a reliable and simple

On this helical-thread design, the pins are inside the base, and they ride on threads cut in the motor pack to move the motor up and down.

Another option for helical motor adjustment is to have the pins on the motor pack and threads cut inside the router base.

HOW TO SET BIT DEPTH ON A FIXED BASE ROUTER

1 Setting bit depth on a fixed-base router involves first lowering the bit until it just touches the workpiece.

2 With the bit touching the wood, rotate the depth adjustment ring to zero.

3 Set the amount of bit depth by rotating the index ring to the desired depth of cut. In this case, the cutting depth will be 1/8 in.

4 Rotate the motor back to the "zero" position on the depth ring without moving the ring to drop the bit to 1/8 in.

method for changing motor height, especially when the router is used conventionally for handheld operations. When the router is mounted in a router table, helical adjustment is less convenient on routers with On/Off switches and speed controls located on the side of the motor pack. Depending on where you have to set the motor and bit under the table, the controls can end up facing away from you and hard to reach, especially in a closed-base router table.

The way to make precise depth settings on a helical-style base is to turn a depth adjustment ring that forms a rim around the top of the base. The ring is graduated into 1/64-in. markings for making small height adjustments accurately.

Depth adjustment rings function differently from model to model. Sometimes the ring simply spins on the base but doesn't engage the motor pack. It's basically a sliding ruler. Making a depth adjustment with this style of ring involves "zeroing" the bit flush with the worksurface and turning the ring so its zero setting aligns with a marker on the motor pack. Once "zeroed out," you pivot the ring to whatever depth setting you want, then turn the motor so its marker aligns with zero again. Swiveling the motor drops the bit the same amount as the ring setting. Other depth adjustment ring mechanisms actually move the motor up or down once the bit is zeroed out on the workpiece.

Other Motor Adjustment Systems

Not all fixed-base routers have depth adjustment rings or helical thread systems for setting bit height. Some motor packs drop straight into their bases and use a rack-and-pinion system or a threaded rod with a depth adjustment knob for dialing in bit depth. The knob allows for micro-adjustment. The process for setting bit depth on this motor adjustment style is similar to routers with ring adjusters. Essentially, you zero the bit to the wood, adjust an indexed ring under the knob and rotate the knob to lower the bit to whatever cutting depth you need.

Generally, these bases will also have a set of preset depth stops or a quick release for the knob so the motor can be brought to coarse adjustment first, then fine-tuned from there. The "drop in" style design is particularly convenient for router table use, because the motor doesn't have to be turned for setting bit height. This way the On/Off and

Some routers don't have depth stop rods to set bit depth. This Bosch router, for instance, uses a micro-adjust knob for adjusting bit depth.

speed controls stay in the same position under the table all the time. Your hands will become accustomed to finding the controls quickly and without looking.

This Milwaukee router has a "drop-in" style motor that moves up and down on a rack-and-pinion thread system. The design provides depth adjustment without twisting the motor.

Another "drop-in" style fixed-base router has three preset notches for setting coarse motor depth. A micro-adjust knob fine-tunes bit depth from there.

PLUNGE ROUTERS UP CLOSE

Plunge routers are manufactured in the same power range as fixed-base routers — $1^1/_2$ to 3.25 hp. The same motors are used in both router styles. Weight-wise, plunge routers tend to be slightly heavier than fixed-bases, due to the extra plunge posts and larger motor/handle housings, but the difference in weight isn't obvious when you're using them.

Fixed-based routers offer a broad range of uses, but sooner or later you'll need the unique capabilities of a plunge router, too. Again, no single router is the perfect all-around tool. Plunge routers have some unique strengths and a few limitations worth considering.

Advantages Of Plunge Routers

The vertical plunging capability is the plunge router's overwhelming design benefit. With a plunge router, you don't need a starter hole to begin a cut when it's inside the perimeter of a workpiece. You also don't need to start your cut from the edge of the workpiece. A plunge router can create its own starter hole by plunging the bit into the wood like a drill. All you have to do is set the bit depth, turn the machine on with the motor and bit raised above the workpiece, press a plunge lever and push the bit down into the wood. Simple. Once the cut is complete, pressing the plunge lever again unlocks the depth setting, and the return springs inside

the plunge posts lift the motor up and out of the cut. There's no need to turn the motor off while doing this. You can proceed immediately with the next plunge cut.

Plunge routers have a turret stop on the base that's stepped off for making incrementally deeper plunge cuts. This stepped capability is another unique advantage to the plunge design. If, for instance, you need to cut a 1-in.-deep mortise, the cut can't be made in a single plunge pass. Doing this will overload the motor and probably break the bit. However, the turret stop allows you to plunge the router into the wood in a series of shallow passes, usually about 1/4 in. deep. Turning the turret to a lower

The primary advantage of plunge routers is the ability to begin a cut in from the edge of a workpiece. Cuts can also be made in increasing depths without ever raising the tool off the wood.

With a turret depth stop on a plunge router, you can make progressively deeper plunge cuts in increments of 1/8 in. by simply twisting the turret. This isn't possible on a fixed-base router.

setting with each pass drops the router bit lower into the wood. So, you can obtain the 1-in. depth you need by stepping off the total cutting depth of cut in manageable passes.

This incremental system prolongs bit and motor life while also providing a fast and easy way to make precise depth cuts. In terms of efficiency, this system is a faster way to make both plunge and profile cuts, because the motor doesn't have to be turned off between each cut. Just change the turret depth and continue with successive cuts.

Versatility is a plunge router's third advantage over fixed-base machines. To some degree, a plunge router can do everything a fixed-base router can do and more. It can be used for template routing, trimming and general profiling while also doing what a fixed-base machine

can't do — plunge cutting for joinery or relief work and signage.

Disadvantages Of Plunge Routers

Despite all this versatility, plunge routers do have some drawbacks. Many plunge routers have smaller bases than fixed-base machines, with one edge flattened for following edge guides. The smaller base can compromise stability when moving the machine over small workpieces. Not all plunge routers have clipped bases, and those with round subbases are more stable for handheld use. Or, you can retrofit a clipped base with a round or oversized base to increase the footing.

The handle position on plunge routers also influences stability. Unlike the low handles of fixed-base routers, plunge router handles move up and down with the motor. When you're using long bits for shallow cuts, the configuration can place the motor near the top of its travel on the plunge posts. The high center of gravity makes the tool harder to handle. Most plunge router designs also have the handles straddling the plunge posts, creating a wide profile for the tool. Fixed-base routers have handles spaced more closely together on the base.

We've already reviewed the inconveniences of using a plunge router in a router table — especially for tables where the router mounts directly to the table and not to a removable insert plate. Bit changes are more tedious, and so is raising the router against the pressure of its plunge springs to set bit depth. One new 3.25 hp router made by Bosch allows the return springs to be deactivated so the machine can be used more easily in a router table. It's a beneficial feature. Or, if you only buy a plunge router and need to use it for router table use, you can also remove the plunge springs from the posts — but this "fix" isn't recommended by manufacturers. It also disables the router from the plunging function.

Differences Between Plunge Routers

Manufacturers design their line of plunge routers with some degree of variation on features. Some changes are an effort to improve on the designs of other tool makers, but there's also a degree of "difference just for differentiation's sake" going on here. Here are a few features where the differences usually appear:

Plunge Levers

All plunge routers will have a lever that controls the plunging motion of the tool. It's usually mounted behind one of the tool handles so you can reach it without taking your hand off the machine while it's running. On one DeWalt plunge router, the left tool handle doubles as a plunge lock in place of a separate lever for this plunging. Twisting the handle engages the plunge mechanism.

Usually the plunge handle is spring-loaded and has to be depressed in order for the motor to move up or down. It's a safety precaution as well as a functional option. You can't accidentally plunge the router down, and if your fingers slip off the lever, the motor stays put. Not all plunge locks work this way. Sometimes, the lever isn't spring-loaded. Or, the plunging action is free until the lever is pressed to lock the setting. Whichever style your plunge router has, you'll probably get comfortable with the function after awhile. Other plunge mechanisms aren't necessarily better than what's on your tool — they're just different than what you're used to.

Plunging Action

Routing in general is a precise task, where cutting smoothness and accuracy are the primary goals. Plunge routing requires slippery smooth plunging action from the

The plunge mechanism on this router is activated by twisting the left-hand knob on the router base. It's an unusual but convenient depth control feature.

tool. This means the posts and bushings must glide almost effortlessly past one another from the top of the plunge travel to the bottom. If the posts hang the tool up while plunging, it can lead to a rough or inaccurate cut. Not all posts and bushings work equally well. On some models, a bit of extra play between these parts makes it possible to literally bind the plunge action, especially if you push down a little harder on one handle than the other one.

The other factor that affects plunge action is post spring stiffness. The springs should offer just enough

The way to activate the plunge feature on most plunge routers is by pressing a spring-loaded lever that releases a lock on the plunge posts.

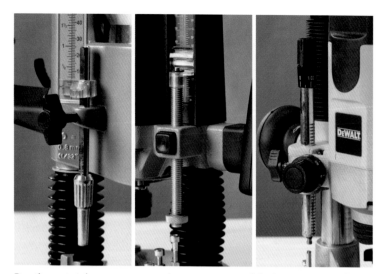

Depth post styles vary among plunge router models. Some consist of a sliding rod with a lock nut to hold position. Other posts are threaded or move up and down on a rack-and-pinion system.

Depth Setting Features

Adjusting and setting the cutting depth on a plunge router is entirely different from a fixed-base router. Here, you'll find a vertical depth scale on the motor head with an adjustable index marker mounted on a sliding post. The post slides up or down for making contact with the turret at any of the turret positions. Raising the post off of the turret stop establishes a gap that sets the depth the bit will cut when the router is plunged downward. Some models have smooth depth-setting posts while others have threaded posts. Either a push button or a lock knob allows you to adjust the post relative to the turret.

If you use your plunge router for indexed plunge operations, you'll want to look for a model with a scale that's easy to read. The most legible scales have large, bright demarcations and a sliding index marker that points clearly to the scale. Most index markers have red hairlines, which tend to be easier to read off the scale than black hairlines.

The adjustable turret below the depth rod on the router's base is the other component of a plunge router's depth setting system. Turrets have the same basic design from one plunge router to another, but there are a couple subtle differences in style. For one, turrets will vary in the number of "steps" they have. More steps are ben-

resistance when compressed to push the motor up to the top of its travel on the posts. Sometimes, manufacturers install springs that are too robust. When the plunge lever is released, the tool almost jumps the motor out of the cut. The best plunge router action is one in which the springs gently lift the motor up and are easy to resist with your arms. The smoother the return action, the more confident you'll feel about withdrawing a spinning bit. Remember, in many cases that bit is just thousandths of an inch away from the edges of the cut you're making.

Some plunge routers will have micro-adjust screws on the turret so you can fine-tune one or more plunge depth settings. Other turret styles have "stepped" fixed stops only.

eficial when you're using the turret incrementally, because they reduce the amount of material being removed with each pass. When turrets have just three or four steps, the depth change from one step to the next may be greater than 1/8 to 1/4 in., which is too deep for any router to cut in one pass. These turrets serve more as coarse depth setting devices than true incremental plunge cutting aids.

Aside from the number of steps, some turrets will also have micro-adjusters on the steps. These amount to screws with lock nuts, with the head of the screw serving as the contact surface of the step. Turning the screw up or down allows you to change step "height" in hundredths of an inch, when needed, to "micro-adjust" your cutting depth.

Despite the minor differences between depth stop rod and turret designs, the process for zeroing out the router and setting cutting depth is basically the same. Presuming the cut you need to make is a plunge operation, the motor must be lowered until the bit touches the workpiece, then locked there. Lower the depth stop rod until it touches the turret, and slide the depth index marker so it lines up with the zero setting on the plunge scale. This "zeroes" the bit on the workpiece. To make a plunge cut of a specific depth, unlock the depth stop post and, without moving the index marker on the post, slide the post up the scale until the pointer reaches the cutting depth of the first pass you want to make. Relock the post and release the plunge lever to move the motor to the top of its travel. When the motor and bit are lowered again, plunging the tool until the depth stop rod and turret make contact will make a cut that matches the setting on the scale. You can use the turret to make incremental depth cuts by "zeroing" the depth rod and bit to a high step on the turret first. Then, each time you move the turret to a lower step, the router will make a deeper plunge cut that matches the height of the step.

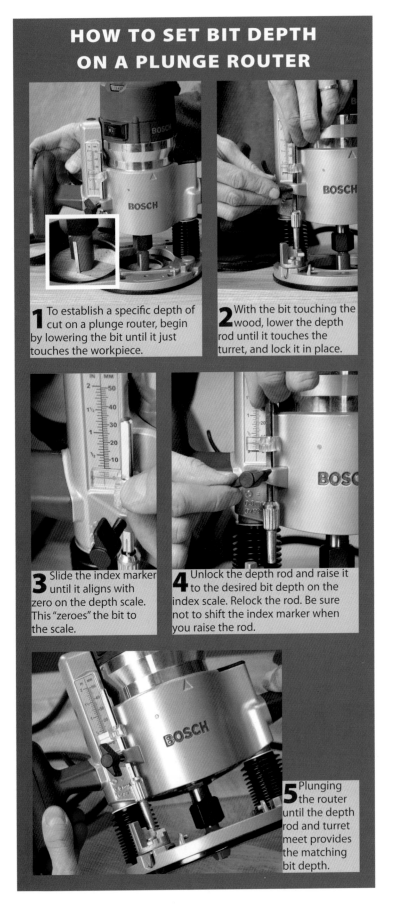

HOW TO SET BIT DEPTH ON A PLUNGE ROUTER

1 To establish a specific depth of cut on a plunge router, begin by lowering the bit until it just touches the workpiece.

2 With the bit touching the wood, lower the depth rod until it touches the turret, and lock it in place.

3 Slide the index marker until it aligns with zero on the depth scale. This "zeroes" the bit to the scale.

4 Unlock the depth rod and raise it to the desired bit depth on the index scale. Relock the rod. Be sure not to shift the index marker when you raise the rod.

5 Plunging the router until the depth rod and turret meet provides the matching bit depth.

The depth post on this plunge router also has a pair of nuts on top for limiting the "up" travel of the plunge range.

A stiff spring around or inside each plunge post provides the "up" travel, unique to a plunge router. Sometimes these springs will be covered with accordion bellows to help protect them from dirt and damage.

Differences In Plunge "Travel"

Plunge routers will vary in terms of the overall amount of travel they're capable of from top to bottom. Most models will have at least 1³⁄₈ in. of travel, and the largest plunge routers will have about 3 in. If you buy a plunge router with only moderate travel, you can sometimes increase the cutting depth by using a longer bit. A plunge router's travel can limit the length of bits you use; the amount of travel must always exceed the bit length so the bit can be completely withdrawn inside the base.

Plunge routers generally do not have adjustable features for changing the upper limit of motor travel, but a few machines do. Those that do will have some sort of knurled knobs and a threaded shaft running through one of the posts for setting the up limiter.

Plunge Posts

All common plunge routers in this country have two plunge posts.

They're made of hardened steel and usually polished to a chrome finish. Some posts are exposed, while others are protected by accordion-style bellows. The bellows offer some prevention from dinging the posts with wrenches when you're changing bits. Dings in the posts can hamper smooth plunge action, so bellows are helpful features. However, if your router doesn't have them, it's not a limitation. Whether plunge routers have bellows or not doesn't seem to matter regarding crud control. The posts and bushings work just as well with sawdust on them as without, although it's always a good idea to try to keep them clean and free of dust.

Operator Controls

Dedicated plunge routers generally have a leg up on fixed-base routers as far as controls are concerned. Since the handles are on the motor head, wires can be run into either handle for outfitting the On/Off switch.

The location of the On/Off switches on plunge routers will vary, depending on whether the motor can be removed from the base. If the motor is an integral part of the tool housing, the switch is usually near one of the handles. When the motor comes out of the base, the switch will be on the motor pack.

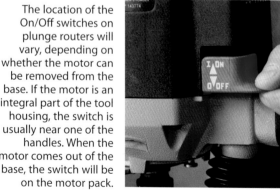

Having the switch on one of the handles is a nice convenience, because you can keep your hands in place for controlling the tool while turning it on or off. On fixed-base routers with removable motors, you'll have to reach for the motor switch or take one hand completely off the handle to turn things on or off. When the On/Off switch is mounted in a plunge router handle, it's usually a squeeze trigger similar to a drill, but it can also be a toggle or slider switch. A lock-on button near the switch is helpful, too, for making long passes or carrying out repetitive cuts without turning off the motor. It's also essential to have a lock-on switch on a plunge router if you use it in a router table — you can't keep your hand on the trigger when the tool is mounted below a table.

Not all plunge routers have On/Off switches in the handle. Sometimes you'll find them on the motor head also, more in keeping with fixed-base routers. On multi-base router kits where a single motor mounts in either a fixed or a plunge base (see page 47), the control switch is always on the motor pack unless the kit comes with a D-handle base (see page 50).

Plunge routers usually have variable speed control these days. The closer this dial is to the On/Off switch, the better. It's a particular convenience for router table use, because you can change motor speed and turn the tool on without crouching down and searching for the speed control dial.

Dust Collection

Not all plunge routers have dust collection features, but those that do offer improved cleanliness during routing. It's easier to see what the bit is doing when chips aren't collecting around it, and a vacuum hook up will help reduce airborne dust as well. The style of vacuum hook up will vary. DeWalt's DW621 plunge router has one oversized plunge post connected to a tunnel in the base that leads to the bit area. The top of the post has a vacuum fitting, so the post actually works like a vacuum attachment for sucking dust and chips up and away. The more typical dust collection system involves attaching a clear plastic shroud around the bit area inside the base. The shroud has a vacuum port molded into the shroud. New styles of dust collection appear from time to time as manufacturers attempt to find the ideal location for the vacuum nozzle. Porter-Cable engineers one popular router with dust collection through a grip handle.

Some form of dust collection is a good benefit to have on a plunge router, but don't expect it to capture all the dust the tool makes. Some styles of dust ports work better than others, but efficiency is also influenced by the vacuum and the size and type of bit you're using. The best way to find how well each style works is to try them out before you buy. When this is impractical, you can often find dust collection information in the router reviews written in woodworking or building magazines.

This DeWalt plunge router has a vacuum port that draws dust up and away through an oversized plunge post.

FIXED-BASE VS. PLUNGE ROUTERS AT A GLANCE

FIXED-BASE ROUTERS	PLUNGE ROUTERS
Low center of gravity for improved stability	Make internal cuts or profiling without a starter hole
Generally larger subbases provide better handling on small workpieces	Can make incremental plunge cuts for mortising, relief work and signage
Easy motor adjustment in a router table	Can function in a router table, but less elegantly than a fixed-base router
Convenient motor removal for bit and base changes	Well suited for edge profiling, template and other guided work
Well suited for edge profiling, template and other guided work	More models with dust collection provisions than fixed-base routers

T rim routers, also called laminate trimmers, are essentially miniature routers. Designed for flush-trimming countertop laminate, trim routers can also be used as crossover tools for woodworking. More than a dozen different trim routers are available, and each weighs less than 4 lbs. The motor packs are designed for one-handed use by gripping the motor, so these tools don't have the usual pair of handles. Their small, lightweight proportions can be a real benefit when you need to balance the tool on narrow edges or work a router into small, confined areas. They're also excellent choices for trimming delicate wood veneer to size after it's mounted to a substrate or for cutting small relief areas, such as tiny hinge leaf mortises. A trim router is even handy for profiling the edges of smaller parts where a larger tool would be difficult or impossible to guide over the workpiece.

Given the popularity and versatility of fixed- and plunge-base routers, they're chock-full of features. Trim routers are designed with almost an opposite mentality. They're virtually feature-free and designed for the workaday needs of a contractor. Basically, you get a motor, a base and sometimes a few optional bases or edge guides. Trim routers are fixed-base routers without plunging features. For laminate trimming, you can buy bits that can be plunged through the laminate, and the small size of the tool makes a plunge cut easy to do by tipping the tool and bit into the work. This technique isn't advisable to do if you're using the tool for wood routing.

Here are the unique features of trim routers and how they differ from their larger cousins:

The perfect tool for cutting hinge mortises on narrow workpieces is a trim router. Small bit sizes make these tools easy to control for making precision cuts.

Trim routers excel at light-duty cutting tasks, such as flush-trimming thin plastic laminate or wood veneer.

Trim routers are also easy to maneuver over small workpieces, where larger router bases could tip or cover up the workpiece.

Motor

Until recently, trim routers were single-speed tools with motors operating at 20,000 to 30,000 rpm. Single speed isn't a limitation for these tools. As you'll see in future chapters, variable speed is necessary on larger routers for working safely with large bits to slow the bit speed down. However, only small bits with 1/4-in. shanks are useful with trim routers, and they're designed to be operated at high speed. Bosch now makes a trim router with variable motor speed, and more models will probably follow suit from other manufacturers. One advantage to this design change is that you can start the tool at a low speed so it produces less of a "kick" at start-up.

Trim router motors aren't usually rated by their developed horsepower, like larger routers. Instead, you'll find that trim routers are categorized by their peak amperage draw — about 3 to 5$\frac{1}{2}$ amps. In terms of horsepower output, this equates to well under 1 hp. If you buy a trim router for light-duty wood routing, buy one on the higher end of the amperage continuum. For laminate or veneer trimming, any amperage motor will do the job for you.

Base

Trim routers have cast-metal bases like larger routers. The base is outfit-

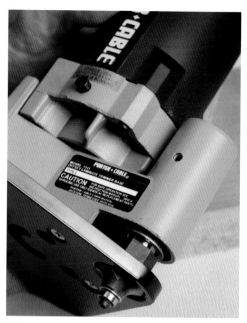

Trim routers are popular for countertop fabrication and installation. This offset base makes it easier to rout into tight countertop corners.

ted with a plastic subbase to safeguard against scratching the work and to provide a smooth surface for sliding the tool along. The subbase measures 3 to 3$\frac{1}{2}$ in. square, so the tool has a tiny footprint, but it's proportionally matched to the smaller size of the machine, so it doesn't seem overly small. On most models the motor attaches to the base with a knurled thumbscrew so it can be

Compared with a full-size router, the base on a trim router seems miniscule, but the tiny proportions come in handy for close-quarter work or for routing tiny workpieces.

hand-tightened in position. A few models have motors that screw into the base like helical-style fixed-base routers or use a buckle to tighten the motor down.

The standard base that comes with a trim router holds the motor and bit perpendicular to the work. Countertop installation often involves more intricate scribing to fit counters against uneven walls. It's also common for installers to have to trim into tight corners or hold the tool at arm's length. So, special bases are available for these application-specific demands. You can buy offset bases in which the motor drives a belt-driven shaft and offset collet. It can be useful for gaining more footprint for the tool on a workpiece or for trimming inside corners in tight spots. Tilting bases are another common base style made for tipping the tool to make bevel cuts. You might find a tilt base useful for chamfering profiles with a straight bit. These sorts of optional bases probably won't be necessary for ordinary woodworking jobs, so they aren't "must have" items when buying a trim router. But they may come as standard accessories with the model you buy.

Depth Adjustment

For laminate trimming, it isn't necessary that these routers have elaborate depth adjustment systems and micro-adjustability. As long as the cutting edge of the bit is set deep enough to cut through the laminate, there's no need for better depth control. This explains why you won't find a depth scale on most trim routers. Even the mechanism for raising and lowering the router in the base is somewhat crude, compared with larger routers: it's usually just a thumbscrew that engages the motor with threads cut into the motor pack. Turning the screw raises or lowers the motor. However, the depth adjustment system is refined enough so you can set and lock the bit where you need it, but don't expect more sophisticated controls here.

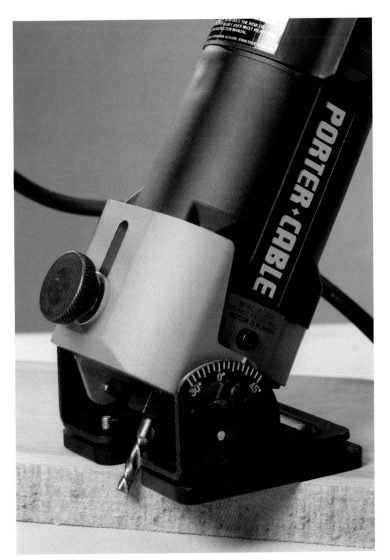

Tilting bases are also available for trim routers for making scribing and bevel cuts.

Most trim routers have a threaded depth adjustment feature with a knurled nut. Revolving this nut changes bit depth.

Unlike larger routers, trim routers have single-slit collet sleeves. The simplified sleeve provides sufficient grip for holding smaller bits.

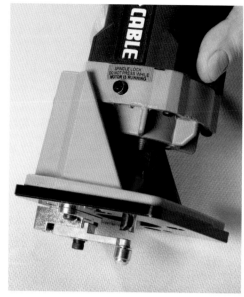

This bearing guide, which mounts to a trim router base, turns an ordinary straight bit into a piloted flush-trim bit.

Collet

Trim routers all have ¼-in. capacity collets for use with ¼-in.-shank router bits. The collet design is similar to larger routers with an inner sleeve that compresses against the bit to hold it and an outer nut that tightens the sleeve. These two parts may be connected so the sleeve comes off with the nut, or the sleeve and nut may be separated. The connected style prevents the sleeve and bit from becoming lodged in the tool — it's a real hassle to remove a stuck bit when this happens. So, the connected sleeve-and-nut collet style is a desirable feature to look for.

Edge Guide Options

For edge profiling or template routing, you can use bits with ball-bearing pilots to serve as edge guides. This is true for all routers. However, some trim routers come with a roller guide that attaches to the subbase to take the place of the bit bearing. The roller guide keeps an unpiloted bit following the edge of the workpiece. Since the guide doesn't spin with the bit, it will last longer than the pilot bearing on a bit spinning at high speed.

In cases where you need to make cuts in from the ends or edges of a workpiece, trim routers can be outfitted with adjustable straightedge guides as well. These work similar to the edge guides on larger routers: the guide clamps to the base and allows the bit to be inset a specific distance from the edge of the workpiece. When the guide is held against the workpiece, the tool will cut a straight dado or groove.

An edge guide can be quite helpful for woodworking, so it's worth buying a trim router that includes an edge guide. If the trim router you buy doesn't come with one, you can also clamp a piece of straight scrap to your workpiece to form a straight-edge that works the same as an edge guide. (For more on routing against a straightedge, see page 156.)

Trim routers can also be retrofitted with an edge guide for making straight cuts in from the edges or ends of a workpiece.

Multi-Base Router Kits

Up until the last ten years or so, buying a router meant choosing one style or the other — dedicated fixed-base or dedicated plunge. So, using routers to their full extent for woodworking meant buying at least one router for handheld operations and usually another router for router table use. This isn't a limitation you have to face anymore. Nowadays, it's possible to buy a hybrid system in which one motor pack fits into both a fixed base and a plunge base. These multi-base kits fall into the 1¾ to 2.25 hp range, aimed at the widest router market and mid-range demand. Some kits even offer a third D-handle base.

Buying a multi-base kit is a wise investment. If you're building a tool collection on a tight budget, a router kit costs less than what you'll pay for two dedicated-base tools. What's surprising, given the relatively low cost of these kits, is that both bases are made to the same quality standards as the bases on other routers — and the interchangeable bases have just as many features. In terms of functional differences, the main issue is one of control placement. Since the motor pack in a multi-base kit has to swap between two bases, the On/Off and speed controls have to be located on the motor pack. If you're a long-time plunge router user and are used to powering up the router with a handle-mounted On/Off control, reach-

Multi-base router kits, like this mid-sized combination from Porter-Cable, provide the convenience of two routers for the price of one.

ing for the switch will take a little getting used to. Otherwise, the motor is generally easy to move from one base to the other. Most kits have a buckle system for locking the motor in the base, so switching between bases is a tool-free operation.

Most woodworkers buy a multi-base router kit in order to mount the fixed base to a router table and use the plunge base for handheld routing. Considering the pros and cons of plunge routers, you'll have to decide if a plunge router is the tool you want to use for all your edge profiling and handheld work. Another option is to buy the kit and a fixed base to mount in the router table. The kit motors are usually standardized within the router brand so you can buy separate fixed bases to fit. This way, the kit provides all the benefits of fixed-base or plunge routing, and you have a permanent mount for switching the motor over to the router table.

The genius of a multi-base system is that the same motor pack fits into either a fixed base or a plunge base. This Hitachi kit has buckle-style locks on both bases for tool-free motor changes.

With a multi-base kit, you can mount the fixed base permanently in a router table and use the plunge base for all of your handheld routing needs.

A Closer Look At Router Features

As we've seen, there are numerous functional and stylistic differences between fixed-base and plunge routers as well as pros and cons of both types. However, there are several common features shared by both styles worth knowing about the next time you're in the market for buying a new router. Here's what to look for:

Soft Start

One significant improvement in router technology over routers made a decade or two ago is soft start. Basically, the motor circuitry is designed to bring the tool up to speed slowly instead of powering up in "jack rabbit" fashion. For novices, soft start makes a router less scary to use. Without soft start, a router will tend to twist or jerk in your hands when you turn it on. It accelerates to full power quickly. This torque-twisting characteristic is especially noticeable with larger bits. Soft start also helps prolong motor life by controlling the initial surge of power that's harder on the motor's circuitry.

Variable Speed Control

Most professional-grade routers and even some of the budget-priced tools come with speed control. Speed control is essential if you plan to use both large and small bits in your router. You'll need to reduce the speed for larger panel-raising or shaping bits to use them safely. If you don't plan to use oversized bits, variable speed isn't a crucial feature to have. Variable speed control also allows you to improve the cutting performance of other bits. Sometimes a slightly slower speed will allow some bits to cut with less burning. Burning is often caused by feeding the tool too slowly along the wood or because the bit is dirty or dull, but at least with variable speed control you can experiment to find the right speed for the work you're doing.

Variable-speed control dials vary among different models and manufacturers. The most helpful styles have a speed chart or an rpm indication right on the dial, so you can set the router's speed to match the bit size.

Electronic Feedback Circuitry

This subtle feature usually comes with a router that has a soft start. Electronic feedback means the router's computer chip senses the amount of torque demanded from the tool and tries to regulate the power needed to meet the demand. In other words, when you push the router hard, electronic feedback will attempt to maintain even power. Be sure the router you use in your router table has electronic feedback control — it's easy to push a router to its limits when it's mounted in a router table and you're pushing hard or making a particularly deep pass. It's easy to tell if a router has electronic feedback the first time you use the tool. If the motor maintains a relatively constant rpm and sound during use, it has EVC. Manufacturers will usually specify this feature on the packaging as well.

Collet Capacities

These days, most bits are available in both 1/4- and 1/2-in. shank sizes. Better routers will generally come with collets in both sizes. In order to take advantage of a full range of bits, you'll want the versatility of having two collets, so avoid buying a general-duty router with only one collet. By the same token, some machines have 1/2-in.-capacity collets that come with a 1/4-in. sleeve insert that fits inside the 1/2-in. sleeve. This is a less desirable arrangement than having two collets because the smaller sleeve is more likely to slip inside the larger sleeve. When this happens, the inner sleeve can score the bit shank and damage it. Worse, the router bit can slide out of position in the collet and ruin the workpiece.

Spindle Lock

Changing bits often requires two wrenches — one to grip the collet nut and one to hold the motor spindle in place. Using the two-wrench method isn't difficult if you do it properly (see page 63), and it's been the standard method for changing bits in

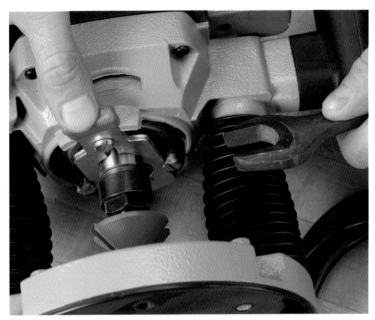

Spindle locks make it easier to change bits. A lever or push button locks the spindle, so it only takes one wrench instead of two to install or remove bits.

routers all along. More and more new routers have a new locking feature that makes bit changing even easier. Depending on the model, a spring-loaded pin or a sliding collar locks the spindle in place, so it only takes one wrench to tighten or loosen bits instead of two.

Critics of spindle locks contend that some spindle lock designs aren't foolproof. Most spindle lock designs will have a strong return spring to pull the locking mechanism clear off the spindle as soon as you let go, but you should inspect this feature closely. On a few machines, it's possible to have the spindle lock accidentally engaged when you turn on the router, which will ruin the spindle, lock and eventually the motor. I think spindle locks are a helpful improvement, provided they're designed properly. One less wrench to lose is a nice convenience. Just be sure the spindle lock is spring-loaded on the router you buy. As a general practice, give the spindle a twist after you change a bit and before plugging the tool back in. If it turns, the spindle lock is disengaged and the tool is ready for use.

Handle Styles

Handles on fixed-base routers are generally round and shaped like knobs or balls. Plunge routers will have elongated grips, more in keeping with a shovel handle or bicycle grip. As far as material options go, handles can be made of wood, the same resin material as the motor head, a harder plastic or a core material covered with rubberlike overmolding. Which handle style works best is entirely a matter of personal preference. You'll want handles that are easy to grasp firmly, feel smooth in your palm and offer solid handling when using the tool. They shouldn't deflect when you twist them. On a plunge router, where the On/Off trigger is part of the handle, the handles should be long enough so you can both grip the tool and operate the trigger easily.

A few routers made by Milwaukee offer a unique handle style for fixed-base routers. The bases on these machines are fitted with a large plastic molding that's molded to match the contour of a medium-sized hand, which allows you to control the router by gripping the motor instead of both handles. A hook-and-loop strap keeps your hand on the grip, even if you let go. It's a unique handle style worth trying out. Some users, especially professional woodworkers and cabinet installers, prefer gripping the motor and not the handles.

The best way to evaluate handles, of course, is to try a variety of routers and see what you like best. Visit a large home center or department

Ball-style handles are common for fixed-base routers.

Straight-grip handles are the usual configuration for plunge routers, but they're also found on some large fixed-base routers.

Some users prefer a D-style or vertical-grip handle. You can buy some models with this base style or buy the base as an accessory.

One manufacturer makes a contoured grip around the router motor so you can grip the tool like a camcorder. A hook-and-loop strap keeps your hand firmly in place.

store that carries tools and put your hands on the different routers. Tool control is the main issue with handle design, but if you use a router regularly you'll sure appreciate handles that also fit your hands comfortably. Well-designed handles will make using the tool a more pleasant experience.

Dust Collection

Routing produces both chips and clouds of fine dust. Machines that come with a convenient way to vacuum dust and chips away from the bit are worth looking at more closely. Some systems work better than others, and you can't determine this at the store unless you can try out the tool. Ultimately, it's more important to buy a router that routs well, even if you have to live with the dust and chips because it doesn't have dust collection. Consider dust collection to be a nice, but not mandatory, feature. If you buy a model with dust collection, be sure the port attaches easily to a shop vacuum. Ports are usually designed to fit 1¼-in.-diameter shop vac nozzles. You may have to purchase a coupling from the manufacturer to convert from the router's port size to your shop vacuum. This is common for European-made routers.

Routers with subbases that accept guide bushings are particularly helpful whenever you need to perform template-routing tasks. Not all router bases will accept standardized guide bushing sizes, but you can retrofit any router with an aftermarket base that will fit these guides.

Subbase Standardization And Guide Collars

For template routing, other guided work and if you plan to use a dovetail jig, you'll want a subbase on your router that accepts guide collars (for more on guide collars, see Chapter Eight). Manufacturers will take two approaches to guide collar adaptability: Some will make subbases with bit openings that accept 1³/16-in.-diameter guide collars. They're the industry standard for guide collar sizing, developed by Porter-Cable. Other manufacturers take a different tack and design subbases to accept only their proprietary guide collar system. Provided you buy the proprietary guide collars and they're reasonably priced, there's no problem. However, it's more convenient if your router takes the "standardized" collars. If it doesn't, don't worry. You can replace the subbase on any router with an aftermarket base that accepts the standard guide collars (see page 197).

The other issue with subbases has to do with overall bit size limitations. Subbases are made with bit openings in different sizes. Most routers will have a subbase that's meant to be used with smaller bits (under 1 in. in diameter) and guide collars. The

A plastic vacuum port on this plunge router fits around the bit area to help collect debris. It's a typical dust collection design for plunge routers.

small hole size also provides more "footprint" for the router, which is beneficial when you're guiding the router over a small workpiece. However, the subbase may have an oversized hole instead. Here, the hole might be as large as 2½ in. in diameter, so the tool can be fitted with large panel-raising bits. The best compromise is to have interchangeable subbases with both large and small bit holes. Some routers, especially multi-base router kits, come with more than one subbase.

Router-Table Conveniences

There are numerous factors that influence which routers work best in router tables. Motor size and easy motor removal are two we've discussed already. Routers in the upper power ranges (3 or 3.25 hp are the best) and with motors that can be removed from their bases for making bit changes are better than smaller, fixed-in-place machines. Three other factors that give routers better router table manners are control placement, easy bit changing and convenient bit height adjustment.

Routers with flat-topped motor caps make it easier to stand the tool up for changing bits. It's a subtle but helpful design feature.

As far as On/Off switch and speed control placement goes, it's easier to find these controls under a router table and without looking if they line up with one another. This is especially true for fixed-base routers with twist-in helical height adjustment. On these machines, the controls move whenever you change bit height. If the controls line up with one another, once you feel one of the controls under the table, you'll know right where to find the other one — straight up or down from the first one.

Routers with flat-topped motor packs are more convenient for making bit changes than those with shaped tops. The flat top allows you to rest the motor pack on a router table or benchtop and make the bit change with both hands free. It's a subtle design advantage but one you'll appreciate if you use your router regularly.

A recent modification to some new routers is a feature called above-the-table height adjustment. For some operations, especially when cutting joinery, you may have to fine-tune bit height several times to achieve the proper cut for a tight-fitting joint. If you can tweak the bit height easily and without looking under the table each time to do it, it's a nice convenience. With this feature, the router comes with a wrench and a fitting on the base so you can adjust the motor up and down from above the router table. Or, the router may have an extension knob for the fine-adjustment knob that doesn't come up through the router table but is still easy to reach underneath.

A few routers also make bit changing easier when the tool is inverted in a router table. They're designed with bases that allow the motor spindle to pass through the base further than on other machines so you can reach the collet from above the table as well. This makes it possible to change bits without removing the motor pack or lifting the whole router out of the router table.

Some manufacturers are making depth changing easier for router table use. A tee-wrench or elongated depth change knob may come as standard accessories for this purpose.

Choosing The Right Router

Picking the right router for your needs can be a difficult decision. As this chapter points out, there are many nuances that separate fixed-base and plunge-base routers as well as other differences that make even routers of the same type different. Aside from the features a router has, there's also the intangible element of "feel" that goes along with picking the best routers for you. Here are a few general guidelines that may help when choosing a router:

- **If you're just starting out, buy a fixed-base router.** A fixed-base machine will enable you to do a wide variety of profiling work. There are numerous joints you can build that don't require plunge cuts, and fixed-base routers make great router table machines. As an all-around first router, a fixed-base machine in the mid-power range is an excellent choice.

- **For dedicated router table use, buy a big fixed-base router.** If you can dedicate one router for full-time router table use, make it a 3- or 3.25 hp fixed base. Choose one with either an extension handle or above-the-table height adjustment provisions so changing bit height is as easy as possible. With a big machine, you can rout with any bit size including the big, heavy panel-raising cutters.

- **Save a trim router for last.** Trim routers are nifty tools for small, light-duty work, but they're not essential routers to own. A mid-sized machine can accomplish most of the same tasks either used in a handheld configuration or in a router table.

- **Split the difference and buy a multi-base kit.** With all the standard features and versatility that go along with multi-base router kits, they're an ideal fit for woodworkers of all skill levels and need. If this is your first router purchase, you won't regret buying a multi-base kit over the long haul. Chances are, multi-base kits will eventually replace many of the dedicated fixed-base and plunge router models available in similar power ranges.

Routers come in a broad range of prices. These value-priced machines sell for less than $150, and they have many of the same features as more expensive "professional" grade tools. For occasional or light-duty use, a budget-priced router may be all you need.

Should You Buy A Budget-Priced Router?

Along with all the "professional" router models, there are also plenty of "consumer-grade" routers. The obvious attraction to these routers is their low price. You can buy fixed-base or plunge routers for less than $50, loaded with many of the same features as the more expensive tools. The logical question, especially if you have a limited tool budget or only need a router now and then is, why spend more? It's a good question to consider.

Depending on your needs, a consumer-grade tool may be the perfect fit. Low-cost routers that are made by reputable manufacturers can be decent tools, even for a serious woodworker. Generally speaking, the tool industry is more sensitive than ever to discerning tool buyers, and there's fierce competition between the brands for your tool dollars. So, even low-cost tools will be built with reasonably good quality, and some deliver astonishing performance and accuracy, despite the rock-bottom price. However, whenever you're shopping for consumer-grade tools, you need to shop carefully. Quality will be a much bigger variable here than if you're shopping within the spectrum of professional-grade routers where quality will be higher all around. Expect to get what you pay for, and you won't be disappointed.

As far as features go, budget-priced routers can be had with almost all the bells and whistles of their more expensive cousins: variable speed, multiple collets, micro-depth adjustment, 2 or more horsepower, spindle locks and buckle-style base locks. Consumer tools will sometimes have niceties like work lights, oversized knobs and scales or rubber overmolds that you don't find on pro tools, because manufacturers are trying to build in more obvious "curb appeal" on these entry level tools.

What's most important, regardless of cost, is that a router is accurate and sufficiently powered. Be sure the consumer model you're considering has provisions for adjusting the depth of cut carefully. On fixed-base routers, the motor should move up and down in the base smoothly and easily. The motor also needs to remain perpendicular to the workpiece when it's clamped in the base. If the motor fits sloppily or loosely in the base, accuracy will be lost. Be sure the motor also locks firmly in the base, wherever you set it, so the bit depth won't change during a cut. It's easier to control accuracy if the motor pack and base are made of metal and machined to fit together precisely. On consumer routers, the motor pack will usually be made of plastic, not metal.

For plunge routers, it's important that the plunge posts allow for smooth plunging action without binding. Try to push the router down against just one post and see what happens. If the tool racks and binds on the posts, you can be sure that this will eventually happen during a plunge cut. Don't buy a plunge router that doesn't plunge smoothly. Be sure that the plunge springs offer a firm amount of return to lift the motor up and out of the cut but not so much that the tool slams to the top of its posts when you release the plunge lock.

You won't be able to assess a router's power unless you can actually try out the tool, which usually isn't possible until you buy it. But a good indicator of power is to find the tool's amperage rating on the label. A router of 10 or more amps will be able to handle most cutting tasks and bit sizes. This is true whether you're buying a consumer router or a pro-grade tool. Budget-priced routers usually won't come with electronic feedback control or soft start, which improve performance and help extend motor life.

The bigger issue with the motors in budget-priced tools is how they're engineered, and this isn't something you can assess on the surface. Often, motors will be built with sleeve bearings instead of ball bearings. Sleeve bearings won't last as long as ball bearings, so buy a router with a ball-bearing motor if you can. However, even the bearing size can vary on ball-bearing tools. Professional routers will have oversized bearings that are better able to resist the lateral stresses applied to the tool during routing as well as higher motor speeds.

It's also a good idea to check if the tool has externally accessible motor brushes. You can tell if the tool has a pair of removable caps on the motor pack near the top. Professional routers will have this feature, which makes them easier to maintain over time. Consumer routers usually won't have this sort of accessibility to the motor brushes, which may mean the tool will need to be serviced by the manufacturer when the brushes wear out.

Professional routers will generally have heavier copper windings around the motor armature than consumer-grade tools. Heavier windings allow the motor to produce peak power with less heat, which helps the motor last longer. Again, this will be a difficult assessment to make without taking the tool apart, but it's worth knowing when choosing economy over professional performance. The biggest single cost-saving measure a manufacturer can take is in the motor, so expect that this will be where the tool may come up short over time.

Avoid buying a consumer router if the collet only accepts one bit size. Of the two sizes, collets that take 1/2-in.-shank bits are the better choice. The larger shank offers better resistance to vibration that can lead to poor cutting. Also, check to see that the collet sleeve has at least four slits for compressing around the bit. A sleeve with just one or two slits won't grip bits as firmly or as evenly as collet sleeves with more slits.

Ultimately, you want to be happy with whatever router you purchase, whether the tool costs $300 or a quarter of that amount. While low cost is satisfying initially, what you'll appreciate over the long term is how the router performs when you need it to, not how little you paid for it. While it certainly isn't a quantifiable rule, odds are you'll be more pleased with a mid-priced or professional router over time, especially as your woodworking skills and needs grow.

WHAT DOES HORSEPOWER MEAN?

Most manufacturers list a horsepower rating on mid-sized and larger routers. Although this specification can be helpful to distinguish one router from another, don't let your buying decision hinge on horsepower ratings. Routers have universal motors that are capable of developing respectable horsepower considering their light weight and small size, but what you read on the label is misleading. A router's horsepower rating is what the motor is capable of producing at the point of failure. So, a 2 1/4 hp router might be capable of reaching this power for brief periods, but only under extreme conditions before something breaks.

It's not a calculation of the router's typical output. When it comes time to buy a router, let features, comfort, your intended use and price be your guides for picking the right router for you.

Horsepower ratings are a much-debated topic in woodworking circles. Keep in mind that for routers, any specified horsepower rating represents the tool's peak — not sustained — capability. It's a somewhat dubious measure of performance.

THREE

ROUTER SAFETY
AND
MAINTENANCE

Compared with other shop and home maintenance tools, routers are among the safer power tools to use. A table saw, for instance, has a blade the size of a dinner plate — and if you saw without the blade guard in place (always a bad idea!), that blade is largely exposed. A chain saw has an exponentially larger cutting area than a router, but homeowners use chain saws all the time, often in some precarious situations. Routers have gentler manners than either of these other common tools. Most router bits are smaller than a spool of thread, and oftentimes the bit faces away from you or is completely buried in the wood. With reasonable common sense and plenty of practice with the tool, using a router shouldn't be a scary or unduly dangerous experience.

That said, routers still must be used with respect. Router motors are loud, and the cutting action creates lots of dust and debris that's potentially damaging to your senses and system. Router bits are razor-sharp, and they spin at terrific speed that makes some bits all but disappear in use. The speed of the bits and the inertia of the motor creates rotational forces capable of pulling wood or the tool violently out of your hands if you aren't careful with your setup and methods. And, complacency, distractions or just plain fatigue can lead to ruined work or physical harm.

It's not difficult to use a router safely. This chapter is meant to provide some initial guidelines to acquaint you with the safety issues you need to know. The precautions outlined here will be reinforced in subsequent chapters where you'll learn how to actually use these tools. If you're just beginning to use a router, ideally you should read this chapter before even turning the tool on. Chances are, however, you've probably already used a router some, or maybe you've been routing for a long while. It's still a good idea to refresh your memory of safety issues now and again and reflect on your own safety practices. Being too familiar with a tool can be as risky as having no experience at all. Sometimes, it's actually better to be a beginner, because you're more likely to exercise caution and restraint when you're learning to use an unfamiliar tool.

In this chapter, you'll learn about proper attire and other personal safety gear for routing. We'll review the process for installing and removing bits as well as how to feed a router properly into workpieces. Depending on your application, sometimes you'll use a router in a stationary fashion and feed the wood over the tool. There are many ways to do this without risking your fingers. Other times, you'll hold the router and make the wood stationary while moving the router over the wood. We'll cover options for anchoring the wood here, too. With routers, there's usually more than one way to carry out a technique safely, and it's helpful to know your options.

Finally, using a router safely also implies that the tool is properly maintained. Routers don't require much upkeep, but a bit of maintenace now and then will ensure that the router does what it's supposed to do effectively and prevent malfunctions from actually posing a risk to you. Routine maintenance will also add years to the life of the tool. Find out what to do and when to do it in this chapter. In regard to maintenance, be sure to read how to maintain your bits on page 112. Sharp, clean bits are safer to use than dull ones, and they produce crisp, clean cuts.

Personal Safety Gear

Routers are noisy tools, and the debris they make will definitely impact the air quality in your shop. While your first thoughts about safety probably involve getting cut by the bit, the more insidious danger actually involves hearing loss, eye injury and breathing fine, airborne wood dust. Putting on personal safety gear before you begin routing just makes sense. What you'll need to buy isn't expensive, and it's comfortable to wear. It's also the same gear you can use for other noisy, dust- and debris-producing woodworking tools. Exercise "an ounce of prevention" and invest in some personal safety equipment to make routing safer and more pleasant. Most home centers have a full selection of gear to choose from. Here are your main options:

Ear Protection

You may not mind the ringing in your ears that comes with using power tools, but over time that ringing is a telltale sign that you're losing your high-frequency hearing. Most routers create noise in excess of 85

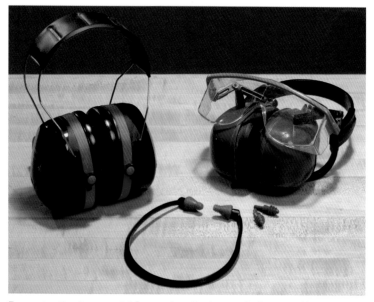

Ear protection is essential for routing. Options include earmuffs, ear plugs or headbands with ear plugs attached. You can even buy earmuffs with integral safety glasses.

decibels, which is the threshold for gradual hearing loss. The overall tool noise is unpleasant, but the high-frequency noise you don't hear is actually more damaging. Hearing loss is easy to prevent by simply putting on some protective earwear.

There are three different styles of hearing protection available, each with their own conveniences. Earmuffs are most typical, with padded, foam-lined cups that completely cover your ears. Better-quality styles are comfortable to wear for extended periods of time. Since the protective feature doesn't involve inserting anything into your ear canals, they're actually the most comfortable style to wear, and they still accommodate safety glasses and goggles. Some earmuffs even have built-in radios or filters that minimize background noise so you can carry on normal conversation even while operating tools.

Another style of ear protection to consider is ear bands or ear plugs. Ear bands have soft, pliable rubber plugs that fit in your ear canals to muffle noise. The band feature holds the plugs in place like earmuffs and keeps the small plugs from getting lost when you remove them. The bands are comfortable to wear around your neck, but the band pressure can sometimes make this style uncomfortable to keep in place for hours on end. Most ear bands are inexpensive and come with a pair of replacement plugs.

The third style of ear protection — ear plugs — fit inside your ear canals without a band. Some types are made of foam that compress by rolling in your fingers before insertion. The foam swells to fit the shape of your ear canal. These take a bit of getting used to but provide comfortable, effective noise suppression. They're also inexpensive and disposable, which is a good thing since the plugs are easy to misplace and tend to get dirty faster than the other plug style made of soft rubber. On the rubber plug type, flares keep them in place.

Routers produce loads of chips and dust that fly in all directions during routing. Protect your eyes from flying debris with safety goggles, glasses or a face shield.

Eye Protection

When freehand routing, the bit faces down and is more difficult to see. You'll find yourself crouching over and peering into the router base during the cut to see what the bit is doing. Visibility is a challenge anyway, especially with flying wood chips and dust coming off the bit. Without eye protection on, getting debris in your eyes is almost a certainty. Fine dust is annoying, but a splinter or chip is downright painful and possibly even damaging. The other potential eye hazard from routing comes from the brittle carbide on the bit. While it's unlikely, carbide can shatter from fatigue or if you accidentally hit a nail or screw. A fragment of sharp carbide in your eye will put a quick end to routing for the day.

Airborne dust also fouls prescription eyeglasses. Protective eyewear will keep your regular glasses cleaner longer. If you buy eye protection with adequate built-in vents or with lenses treated with anti-fog coating, they won't even fog up your glasses on a hot day.

Safety glasses and goggles with a head strap are the usual choices for protective eyewear. The only safe styles of protective eyewear are those designed to protect you. The glasses should provide peripheral protection and a shatterproof front lens or lenses.

Some safety glasses will fit over prescription glasses, or you can choose safety goggles or a full face shield instead. Keep your safety glasses and goggles protected when they're not in use to prevent scratching the lenses. As soon as it's hard to see out of your protective eyewear, you'll stop wearing them — so buy good quality eyewear and keep it protected.

Breathing Protection

The long-term effects of inhaling wood dust aren't entirely known, but research strongly indicates that wood dust may cause various forms of cancer. If you suffer from respiratory allergies, routing some woods like walnut, cedar and certain exotic species will probably be aggravating or even make you sick. At the very least, fine wood dust and the dust produced by composite sheet materials like medium-density fiberboard (MDF) is unpleasant when it collects in your nose and lungs and makes you cough. If you're routing for extended periods of time or working in a small, enclosed space, wear dust protection.

Since routing doesn't produce harmful vapors or fumes, any style of breathing protection will work for routing. Inexpensive dust masks, which are similar to the hospital-style masks with a paper face shield, offer decent short-term protection. Use

these masks once and then throw them away. For better protection, buy a dust respirator. Some styles look like hospital masks, but the filters trap smaller particulates, and the respirator will have a double headband instead of a single band to form a better seal around your face. Some are pleated and made of new synthetics for cooler comfort and even longer wear.

You can also buy reusable respirators that consist of a rubber half-mask with a heavy strap and a replaceable filter element. The element need only be rated for dust to be effective for routing. These are less comfortable than the lighter-duty styles, but

One way to improve airflow through your shop and draw out airborne dust is to set a box fan in a window, facing out.

the replaceable filters offer good value over the long term.

Another alternative form of breathing protection is a full face shield equipped with a built-in filtration system. These masks have a fan that draws air into the mask and filters it, then exhausts the air out. These systems are expensive but offer superior protection from wood dust. If you plan to rout large quantities of sheet materials, particularly MDF, a face shield respirator may make a sound investment.

Aside from wearing a respirator, you can purify the air by mounting a powered ambient air cleaner in your shop. These are portable units with replaceable or cleanable filter elements that cycle the air in your shop continuously. An ambient air cleaner will improve routing, sanding and sawing operations while it operates quietly and efficiently. Small units sell for around $200 through some home improvement centers and woodworking supply outlets.

Finally, you can improve the overall air quality in your shop by simply moving fresh air in and pushing fouled air out through doors and windows. A box fan placed in a window and facing out can draw away fine wood dust. If your router comes with provisions for dust collection (see page 51), certainly use them to reduce wood chips as well as dust when working indoors. Or, take your routing tasks outside in good weather to keep your shop and lungs cleaner. Indirect sunlight makes a great light source, and a cool breeze whisks the dust and chips away if it's blowing in the right direction.

Proper Attire And Atmosphere For Routing

Use the same common sense about the clothing you wear for routing as when using any other tool with spinning parts. If you're wearing a shirt with sleeves, push or roll them up, particularly when using a router table. The same can be said for long hair: pull it back. When the bit is pointed at you, it will wrap your shirt sleeve or hair into the cutter in an instant — and it only takes one brush against a spinning bit to do this. When the weather is hot, dry off sweaty hands on a towel before reaching for a router to do freehand work. A loss of grip can ruin a cut or send the router flying from the bench. Don't ever let go of the tool when it's spinning.

Wear soft-soled or athletic shoes in order to keep a solid stance in front of the router table or bench. When you're using larger bits in a router table or feeding a router around a large workpiece that stretches your reach, a firm stance prevents loss of balance. Run a broom through your shop when you're doing lots of routing to keep debris off the floor; it's a good way to tidy up, but more importantly, it prevent slips. Consider buying a rubber floor mat to place on the floor next to the bench. It will keep your feet warmer in the winter, provide some reduction in leg and hip fatigue when routing or doing other benchwork and help improve traction.

If your shop is in an unheated space and you have to work in cold temperatures, resist the urge to wear gloves when routing. Gloves can hamper your ability to flip the On/Off switch in an emergency and make it harder to grip ball-style handles firmly. There's also a chance that a glove could get caught in a spinning bit during table routing and pull your hand in with it. If your hands are too cold to hold tools without gloves, it's time to move inside, wait for warmer weather or buy a heater and warm up the shop. If it's too cold for your hands, the rest of your senses will get numb, too, as you try to stay warm.

Finally, set up an environment in the shop that's conducive to concentration. This usually costs nothing to do. If you have children or pets in the shop, send them out before you start the router. It protects their hearing and keeps them from distracting you in mid cut. Set your workspace up so you can see someone entering the shop without getting startled when

Wear comfortable rubber-soled shoes when working for extended times at the bench. Or, buy a rubber mat. Your legs will thank you at the end of the day.

operating a router or other power tools. Keep the floor around your work area uncluttered. Sometimes you'll have to change body positions around the bench or router table in order to guide the router easily, especially if you're routing large panels or odd shapes. You don't want to trip over something with a spinning router in hand. The same goes for tool and extension cords. Direct the cord off the bench so it will stay clear of your cutting path as well as your feet. You may even want to drape the cord over your shoulder to keep it elevated off the workpiece, behind you and off the bench entirely. Provide enough light over the area where you work to see what you're routing clearly. Sometimes a clamped-on articulating desk lamp can supply helpful task lighting right where you need it.

If you're using a workbench or router table mounted on wheels (a good solution for small shops), lock the casters so the table can't shift during use. Sometimes handheld or router table work involves pushing pretty firmly on the tool — enough to make the wheels roll. Use wedges, cinder blocks or a sandbag to keep the wheels from rolling if they don't lock. Push against the table before you begin routing to be sure the table doesn't move. You want to keep this platform stationary at all times.

Installing And Removing Router Bits

Installing router bits really isn't a major safety issue, unless you try to stretch the cutting capacity of a bit by pulling it too far out of the collet. The correct way to install a bit is to loosen the collet nut until the bit slides in freely and slip the bit down into the sleeve until it bottoms out. Then, pull the bit back up from the bottom about 1/16 inch. Or, if the bit has a particularly long shank, bottom it out and pull it out the same distance as other bits. This will provide some clearance at the bottom of the sleeve where it compresses, so the collet can seat properly. Sometimes this convergence of bit body and shank will increase; other times it will decrease. Either way, it won't provide the same holding power as the uniformly sized shank.

INSTALLING A ROUTER BIT

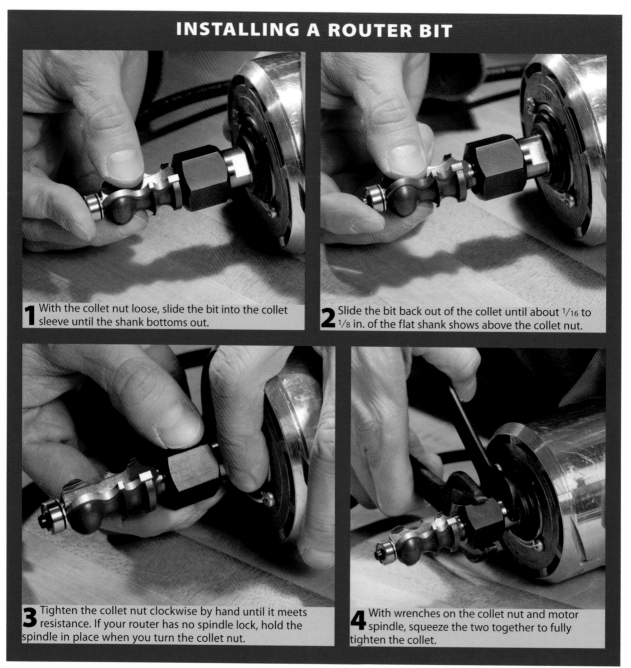

1 With the collet nut loose, slide the bit into the collet sleeve until the shank bottoms out.

2 Slide the bit back out of the collet until about 1/16 to 1/8 in. of the flat shank shows above the collet nut.

3 Tighten the collet nut clockwise by hand until it meets resistance. If your router has no spindle lock, hold the spindle in place when you turn the collet nut.

4 With wrenches on the collet nut and motor spindle, squeeze the two together to fully tighten the collet.

If the router bit you're planning to use doesn't extend far enough to reach the depth of what you need to cut, don't compromise your safety by clamping less shank in the collet. This can make some bits unbalanced so they'll cut roughly. Bits also work loose this way and ruin your cut. The better alternative to cheating the shank depth is to buy a longer router bit, no matter what the situation.

On routers with collets that require two wrenches to tighten and loosen bits, fit the wrenches on the nuts and tighten the wrenches against one another to secure the bit. About 1/4 turn past hand tight should be all that's required to hold the bit firmly. You may be able to grasp both wrenches with one hand and simply squeeze them together to tighten the nuts.

For routers with spindle locks, follow the same procedure for inserting the bit and setting the projection, then rotate the motor spindle with the collet until the lock engages, and tighten the collet nut about 1/4 turn with the wrench.

Loosening a router bit from its collet can cause bruised or skinned knuckles if you don't do it right. Here again, loosening the collet nut requires both wrenches directed toward one another, but this time, the wrench on the collet nut turns counterclockwise. The initial tension on the nut can be difficult to break free, and if you're not careful, the nut will loosen suddenly and cause you to slam both wrenches together with your fingers in between. It's a painful reminder that there's an easier way: position both wrenches on the nut and spindle flats so they're close enough together that you can grip them with one hand. Squeeze the wrenches together to loosen the nut — you'll never pinch a finger or bruise a knuckle this way. For particularly stubborn nuts that won't loosen by grip strength alone, set one wrench on the bench and press the other wrench down toward the first with an open palm.

On routers without spindle locks, tightening or loosening a bit requires two wrenches — one to hold the motor spindle and another to turn the collet nut.

Spindle locks remove one wrench from the bit-changing equation. Instead of a spindle wrench, you depress a button or engage a lever to hold the spindle stationary.

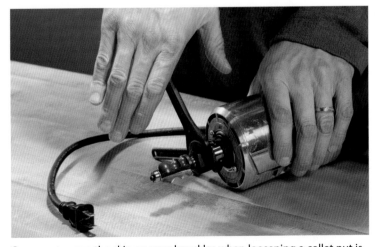

One way to save the skin on your knuckles when loosening a collet nut is to wedge the spindle wrench against the bench and press the other wrench down with an open palm.

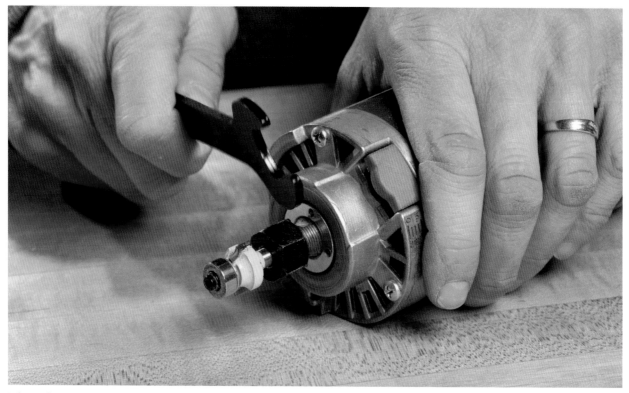

When a bit gets stuck in a collet, one last-ditch technique to break it free is to rap lightly on the flats of the collet nut. This will usually loosen the inner sleeve and release the bit.

TIP

RUBBER O-RINGS SET BIT DEPTH

One way to make bit installation faster and easier is to slip a neoprene O-ring over the shank of a router bit and roll the O-ring until it's situated at the convergence of bit body and shank. This way, you won't have to bottom out and pull up on the bit when installing it. The O-ring acts like an automatic depth stop.

Slip neoprene O-rings over your bit shanks to serve as spacers when installing them in collets. They'll keep bits from bottoming out in the collet sleeve.

On self-releasing collets, remember that the initial loosening of the nut won't necessarily loosen the grip of the inner sleeve on the bit shank. To fully release the bit, turn the collet nut by hand a turn or two more and you'll feel the nut tighten against the rim of the sleeve. Wrench the collet nut another turn counterclockwise and it will lift the sleeve out of the spindle and release the bit so you can pull it out.

Bits can be more stubborn to remove on routers without self-releasing collets. If the bit doesn't budge after you loosen the nut, give the flat faces of the nut a few gentle raps with the wrench all around the collet. This should be enough force to loosen the bit in the sleeve. Take care not to hit the cutters, or you'll probably chip the brittle carbide.

Understanding Feed Direction

Another safety issue you'll face every time you turn on a router is which direction to feed the tool over the wood or the wood over the tool. In most situations, you want to feed the router into the wood against the rotation of the bit. Doing this will present the wood to the bit's cutting surfaces so they bite into it but can't pull it along. Feeding against the bit's rotation will have the effect of pulling the router and wood tightly together and make the operation more predictable for you.

Feed Direction For Freehand Routing

When you're holding the router in hand with the bit facing downward, it will spin in a clockwise direction. To feed against the bit's rotation then, you'll move the router from left to right when feeding the router along the outside edges of a workpiece. If you're routing all the way around a board, feeding left to right creates a counterclockwise motion — exactly what you want to do. You'll feel an even and controllable resistance from the tool as the router bites into the wood.

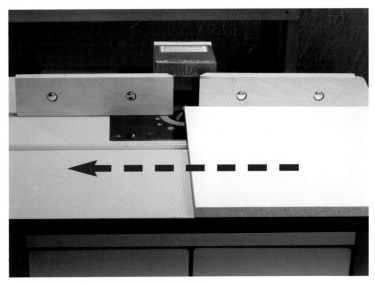

The normal feed direction on a router table for making outside cuts is to feed the workpiece from the right to left.

Sometimes when freehand routing, you'll need to rout around the inside edges of a cutaway area. Imagine routing around the inner cutout of a donut. In these situations, the feed direction changes. In order to move the router against the bit's rotation on an inside edge, you'll feed the tool clockwise — not counterclockwise. It's the mirror opposite of routing outside edges, but the guiding principle stays the same: feed against the bit's rotation for optimal control and cutting performance.

When routing by hand, the proper feed direction for inside cutouts (left) is clockwise. Feed the router counterclockwise (right) for routing the outer edges.

Inverting a router in a router table changes the feed direction from handheld routing. For inside cutouts, feed the workpiece counterclockwise.

Feed Direction For Router Tables

Working on a router table means flipping the router upside down–and this reverses the bit's spin direction. So, feed direction reverses also. On a router table, bits spin counterclockwise. For routing the outside edges of a workpiece then, you'll feed the wood from the left side of the table to the right side. Doing this forces the bit to push the wood back against you. When the router fence is attached, the router bit will also press the wood against the fence. You want to maintain this resistance against the bit to keep the cut under control. The resistance you feel from the bit also helps you determine the right amount of force to apply and how fast you can move the wood past the bit to create a clean cut.

When working around the inside edges of a cutout on a router table, feed the workpiece counterclockwise, against the bit's rotation. Again, you should feel an even amount of resistance from the forces created by pressing the wood against the bit's cutting edges and direction of spin.

Climb Cutting

Working against the bit's rotation, as outlined above, is always the safest and recommended approach to use, regardless of the routing situation. Sometimes, however, the wood you're routing will have uneven or difficult grain that doesn't rout smoothly. Working against the bit's rotation will cause the bit to tear out fibers in the wood; that leaves a rough and unacceptable surface. When this happens, one option to improve the routed surface is to set the router for a slightly deeper pass and move the router *with* the bit's rotation instead of against it. This practice is called climb cutting, because feeding with the bit's rotation will make the router want to climb out of the cut instead of digging into it. Instead of feeling the effect of resistance against the bit, the router will want to grab the wood and pull away from you when climb cutting. So, the router is harder to control and less predictable.

Climb cutting is a somewhat controversial technique for routing. It must be done cautiously, with workpieces safely clamped in place or with the router anchored in a router table. For more on how to make a climb cut, see Chapters Six and Seven.

Options For Controlling Workpieces Safely

Regardless of whether you're using a router in a handheld way and moving it over the workpiece or you're moving the wood past the router fixed in a router table, you'll always have two safety factors to consider: First, is the wood properly controlled for the cut? And second, is the router properly controlled for the cut? Unless you take both workpiece and router control into account, there's the potential for accidents — the worse-case scenario — or at the very least, the workpiece will be ruined by a poor cut.

As far as workpiece control is concerned, there are many ways to support or immobilize the wood to keep your fingers clear of the bit and to ensure that the wood won't move during cutting. Here are some of the options to help improve workpiece control:

Featherboards

Featherboards are used on router tables to press workpieces against the fence or router table, depending on the application. To do this, featherboards have a series of flexible "fingers" along one end formed at an angle. Pressing a featherboard against the wood compresses these fingers together so they act like a spring and hold the wood under tension. The angled shape of the fingered appendages also serves as kickback prevention: Wood moves easily only one way past the fingers — toward the tapered point of the featherboard. In the event the router bites too deeply and attempts to throw the wood backward, the fingers wedge against the wood and prevent kickback from occurring.

You can buy wood and plastic versions of featherboards from most home centers and woodworking

Flexible fingers on a featherboard press workpieces against the fence or router table, and the angled configuration prevents the wood from moving backward.

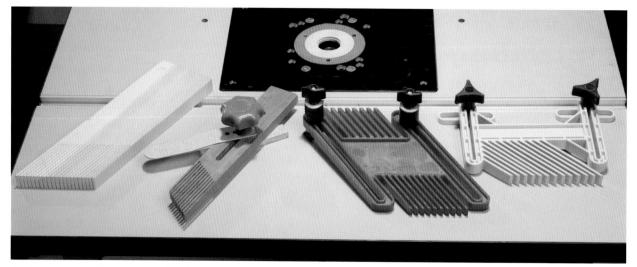

Featherboards hold workpieces firmly in place, which improves cutting performance as well as safety. They're available in a variety of forms, or you can make your own from scrap wood.

This featherboard has a runner that fits into the miter slot on a router table. It expands in the slot by tightening lock knobs, which holds the featherboard in place.

supply catalogs. Or, you can make your own featherboards from scrap (See tint box, page 69). The manufactured styles usually have provisions for clamping the featherboard into a router table miter slot (for more on miter slots, see page 120) or into a slot on the fence. Sometimes the anchoring system is a T-bolt that fits into grooves in the miter slot, or it will be a bar underneath the featherboard that expands by tightening knobs on top. When the featherboard bar expands in the miter or fence

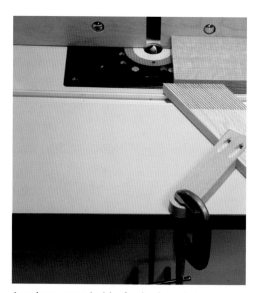

Another way to hold a featherboard stationary is to clamp it to the router table. This design has a built-in brace for mounting a second clamp.

MAKING A FEATHERBOARD

Featherboards are easy to make from virtually any regular-grained and defect-free scrap wood you have on hand. Make them from stock that's 2 to 4 inches wide and long enough to reach from the edge of your router table to the bit area. This way, you can clamp the featherboard from the table edge. Or, you can make shorter featherboards with expanding bars or T-bolts, like the manufactured varieties.

To cut the flexible "fingers," first crosscut the end of the wood to a 30-degree angle, which forms the featherboard's tapered end. Draw a reference line 2 to 3 in. in from the angled end and parallel to it. This establishes the length of the fingers. To cut the first slit, set the fence on a band saw 1/8 in. from the edge of the wood, and feed the wood along the fence to cut the first slit to the reference line you just drew. Then reset the fence each time for cutting the rest of the slits and fingers.

To make a featherboard, crosscut a piece of scrap at 30°, then cut a series of parallel slits about 1/8 in. apart along the face. Make the slits about 2 in. long.

slot, friction holds it in place. Slots in the featherboard allow you to adjust it lengthwise to suit workpieces of different widths or thicknesses, depending on the application. The same knobs that expand the bar lock the length setting.

Manufactured featherboards are inexpensive, and you'll usually get a pair of them if you buy your router table instead of building it. They're good safety devices to use, although you can also work safely on a router table without them. Be sure to try them out to see if featherboards are comfortable and helpful for your router table work.

Pushsticks And Push Pads

Keeping your hands clear of the bit is a paramount concern when using a router table. Pushsticks and push pads keep your hands up and away from the bit area while also providing good workpiece control. Pushsticks come in many shapes and sizes, but essentially they're nothing more than a handle with a notch cut into one end that fits around the edge of a workpiece. Some look more like paddles than handles, but they work the same way. Regardless of style, pushsticks are useful for feeding workpieces flat or on-edge past the bit. They're particularly effective when used in conjunction with featherboards. You can make your own pushsticks from scrap wood or buy them inexpensively wherever table saw or router supplies are sold.

Push pads are another good hand-held option for keeping your hands clear of the cutters. Push pads have a flat base lined with pliable foam rubber and a handle on top. The rubber provides good traction to hold the push pad in position. They work best for holding larger workpieces or panels facedown on the router table.

Keeping your hands clear of the bit is easier to do if you use a pushing device. Common options include push pads, pushsticks, backup boards with a handle or your router table's miter gauge.

Miter Gauges

Routing across the narrow ends of a workpiece on a router table requires that you back the workpiece up from behind. The usual accessory for doing this is a miter gauge — the same type you'll find on a table saw for making crosscuts and angle cuts. Most router tables include a miter gauge, or you may be able to use the one from your table saw if it fits your router table miter slot. If you don't have a table saw or a miter slot on your router table, another option is to attach a handle to a square of scrap wood or sheet stock about 8 to 10 in. in size. Provided the edges are square to one another, this shop-made backup board works as well as a miter gauge set for a square cut. The backup board also supports the wood from behind in the immediate bit area to keep the edges of your workpiece from splintering as they leave the bit. You'll need to make a new backup board after a few router operations have ruined its edges, but they're a quick and easy alternative to a miter gauge.

Two-Handled Hold-Down Jig

Sometimes your workpiece will be too narrow to hold safely with a push block but two wide for a pushstick. This is a common situation when making cabinet door frame components or if you're using a router table for making curved cuts without a fence in place (as you'll see later in Chapter Eight). The solution is to make a two-handled holddown jig to keep workpieces pressed against the router table but both of your hands clear. These jigs are available for purchase, or you can make one from a scrap of thick wood with a pair of dowels or other handles mounted in place. Cover the bottom of the jig with foam rubber or sandpaper to provide a high-friction surface for even more holding power.

One way to hold narrow workpieces securely while keeping both hands clear is to make a two-handled hold-down jig. Use a thick piece of wood for the base and drill two holes for dowel handles. Glue sandpaper to the base for an even better grip.

A safe way to rout narrow strips is to run them through a tunnel made from scrap wood and clamped to the router table fence.

Tunnel Jig

The ideal scenario for routing narrow workpieces is to start with stock that's wider than necessary, then cut off the routed part from the extra stock. This method keeps your hands farther away from the router bit than working with stock that's already cut to the correct but smaller size. On occasion, however, you'll find that sometimes you have to work from thin or narrow workpieces instead of oversized ones. This is particularly true when making small moldings from a limited amount of material. One way to control these workpieces safely is to feed them through a tunnel jig mounted over the bit. The jig amounts to a notch cut into a thick piece of scrap with the scrap clamped to the router table fence. Make the proportions of the notch match the stock you're routing. This way, feeding the wood through the tunnel allows the tunnel to serve as both a guide and a featherboard. Your hands stay clear of danger, and the tunnel keeps the wood from fluttering next to the bit while it's being cut. It's a simple and safe solution for manipulating narrow stock.

Hot-Melt Glue And Double-Sided Tape

Two easy and most effective options for mounting workpieces or templates to wood are hot-melt glue and double-sided tape. The glue works well for mounting small or narrow workpieces because you can dab it just where you need it, and unlike tape, there's no extra to trim away first. The glue sets quickly, holds firmly and comes off the wood easily with a sharp chisel. To release the glue bond, slip a flexible paint scraper into the glue joint and twist. Hot-melt doesn't absorb into the wood fibers like water-based glue, so its surface area is really all that holds it in place.

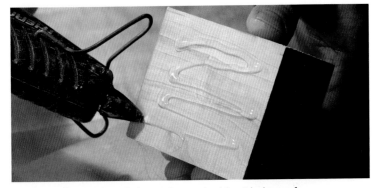

Hot-melt glue is a good alternative to double-sided tape for making temporary bonds, but you'll have to cut or scrape it off when you're through.

Double-sided carpet tape provides plenty of holding power for attaching templates to workpieces, and it's easy to remove after routing.

Double-sided or carpet tape is another good way to keep workpieces anchored firmly for handheld routing. Peel and stick one side of the tape to a base, your workbench or a template, and stick the other side to the workpiece. The thin, inexpensive varieties of double-sided tape can be hard to remove when you're finished routing, and sometimes the tape leaves adhesive residue behind. Better varieties of tape are thicker and have improved releasing qualities.

Often the safest way to rout particularly small workpieces is to do the necessary routing on an oversized piece of wood, then cut off the routed portion on a saw to obtain the actual workpiece you need. It's the safest way to make small strips of molding that couldn't otherwise be held safely with clamps, glue or tape.

Anti-Slip Mats

One option for immobilizing small work for handheld routing is to set the workpiece on a non-slip mat. Any pliable or foam-rubber mat will do, including carpet padding or the thin mats sold for kitchen sink liners for washing dishes. Whichever option you use, the mat will hold workpieces in position without the need for adhesive.

Rout narrow workpieces from wider stock when you can to keep your hands clear. Then cut the routed portion free to complete it.

You can find low-cost, anti-slip mats in the kitchen section of any department store. They make excellent holding devices for handheld routing without clamps.

A pair of common wood screws, used with other clamps, can serve as a makeshift bench vise for holding workpieces on-edge.

A starter pin, mounted in a router table, provides a firm anchor for feeding curved workpieces into the bit when you can't use the fence.

Wood Screws And Clamps

The most obvious solutions for anchoring workpieces in place are ordinary woodworking clamps, particularly when the workpiece is large or when a portion of the workpiece doesn't need to be routed and can be clamped to the bench. Any screw-type woodworking clamp will do, but spring clamps usually won't have enough holding power to keep workpieces from shifting. You'll want to have the added advantage of tightening a screw handle firmly, so avoid using spring clamps. Clamps can hold workpieces either on their faces for profiling and detailing work or on-edge for routing joints. Wood screws are particularly useful for anchoring workpieces on narrow edges, because the clamps provide a stable base.

Starter Pins

As you'll see in subsequent chapters, there are times when you'll need to rout a curved surface on the router table that involves removing the fence. The fence provides an important bearing surface for starting and guiding the cut. When you remove the fence, replace it with a starter pin mounted close to the bit.

The pin provides an anchor point for gradually tilting the wood into the bit. It prevents the bit from biting into the wood too deeply, pulling the wood out of your hands and possibly causing kickback. (Learn more about how to use a starter pin on page 178.)

Protective Guards

Another safety measure for controlling workpieces is to install a guard on your router table fence or to clamp a simple guard over the bit when the fence is removed. Some router tables come with a guard already attached to the fence as a standard accessory. Or, a guard can be as basic as a piece of scrap lumber or clear acrylic clamped over the bit area. The guard should cover the bit without restricting access to it. It also makes sense to build guards from material that router bits can cut without breaking. In the event the guard drifts slightly into the bit, you won't destroy the cutter as well as the guard.

This clamp-on guard covers the bit and provides good protection in situations where the bit can't be shrouded by a fence.

Controlling The Router Safely

Aside from anchoring the wood to rout safely, there are a number of precautions you can take to ensure safe control of the router. This is particularly important when you're using the router in a handheld fashion instead of in a router table and feeding the wood past the bit. Here are some issues to keep in mind:

Follow the bit manufacturer's recommendations for speed settings when using large door- or joint-making bits. Larger bits require slower operating speeds than smaller bits.

Selecting Safe Bit Speeds

Bits smaller than about 1 in. in diameter can be used safely at full speed in a router. In fact, small bits cut more cleanly and effectively at full speed. This isn't the case for large-diameter bits. For panel-raising and other large joint-making bits, the opposite is actually true. Often, big bits function best at around half the router's full speed, usually about 12,000 rpm. It's also unsafe to run a router at full speed with large bits. If the bit is even slightly off balance, it can cause the router to vibrate excessively and possibly damage the motor and collet. As a measure of safety, follow the manufacturer's recommendations for setting bit speed, and use a router of at least 2 hp with oversized bits.

Provide Sure Footing Under The Router

When you cut decorative profiles into the edges of a workpiece, only a portion of the router base is actually in contact with the wood. Moving the tool reduces the baseplate's footing to as little as 1/4 of its area. This can be particularly problematic for plunge routers with flat-edged bases (see page 27) or when you're using a particularly large or heavy router. With less base on the wood, it's much more difficult to control the router and keep it from tipping off the workpiece. Footing also becomes an issue when you have to guide the router around an inside cutout area where the opening is wide or the surfaces left for the router to rest on are narrow. Imagine routing the inside edges of a picture frame, for example.

One way to improve footing is simple: Install a larger baseplate on the router. Your router may come with an oversized base as a standard feature, but you can outfit any router with a larger aftermarket base. The router table insert plate you already have makes a great oversized base for freehand routing. Just use your table-mounted router without removing the baseplate for freehand cutting. Or

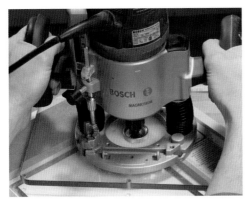

Mounting a router to an oversized baseplate increases its footing, which can help keep it from tipping off narrow workpieces and provide a stable platform for routing over open areas.

Your router table's insert plate makes a convenient oversized baseplate for handheld routing as well.

buy another baseplate — clear plates offer better visibility than solid colors — and attach it to the router you use for handheld routing. Some manufacturers also sell offset bases with a handle mounted to the base. These not only enlarge the base area but also give you more options for holding the tool during use.

For profiling particularly small workpieces, a larger base isn't the solution but footing issues are still a problem. A better option to improve footing for the router is to mount the workpiece to a base or to your workbench and surround it with pieces of scrap the same thickness as the workpiece. These supports will keep the router moving over a stable surface, even if much of area beneath the tool is actually open.

One way to improve stability for routing tiny workpieces is to stick the workpiece to a piece of scrap and surround it with scrap support pieces for the router to ride on.

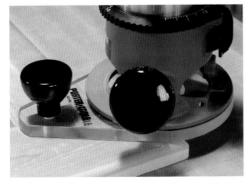

This offset router base increases the size of the router's footprint while also providing another handle for improved control. It's a helpful add-on for routing around narrow workpieces.

Use A Safe Stance For Routing

When holding the router for free-hand routing, there's a good deal of body language required to move the tool accurately and with sufficient control. Hold the router with your

For optimal control when routing freehand, keep both hands on the router at all times and your arms bent. Make sure the power cord stays clear by throwing it over your shoulder.

When feeding workpieces across a router table, keep your body clear of the path of the wood. Use your left hand as a featherboard to hold the wood against the fence and table, and feed with your right hand.

arms slightly bent — they act as shock absorbers if the bit grabs the wood unexpectedly. Pull long sleeves up to keep them clear, and drape the power cord over your shoulder to help keep the cord out of the cutting path. Your legs also serve as shock absorbers when freehand routing, so keep your knees unlocked and legs slightly bent. It helps to work at bench height that's comfortable for you. All in all, you should feel like your posture affords you good command of the tool. If you feel like your sense of balance or view of cutting operation is compromised by your stance, adjust the setup before you begin routing.

There's a correct stance for router table operations as well. Here, you'll be feeding the wood directly into the bit instead of moving the router over the wood. The correct feed direction for router table use is from the right side of the table to the left. Stand just beyond the right corner of the table so your body is clear of the bit path. This body position allows you to use your left hand as a featherboard to apply pressure against the wood while you feed it across the table with your right hand or a pushing device. In the event the bit kicks the wood back during a cut, the wood will have a clear path off the right side of the table without hitting you in the process. Rout with your legs and arms slightly bent, just as you do for freehand routing.

Comfortable Shoes And Floor Mats

If your shop has a concrete floor, or if the floor is sometimes slippery, wear rubber-soled athletic shoes that offer good traction. It's also a good idea to place a rubber mat next to the workbench or router table. The mat will improve traction and also provide some cushioning for your hips and knees for those long routing sessions. During cold months in unheated shops, a floor mat also creates an insulating layer between your feet and a cold, concrete floor, which makes routing and other benchwork more pleasant.

Be Sure Your Router Table Doesn't Move

It can be a helpful and space-saving feature to put wheels under a router table. Roll it into place when you need it, and store it out of the way when you don't. However, be sure to install locking casters when you're ready to start a routing operation to prevent the table from shifting and causing you to slip. If the wheels don't lock, back up them up with wedges of scrap wood, a few bricks or even a sandbag. Or, use wooden handscrew clamps to grip the wheels and secure them.

Avoid Overfeeding

Asking a router to remove large amounts of material quickly, especially if you set the bit depth to full profile when making the first pass, will place an inordinate strain on most machines. The safer practice is to cut the profile in a series of progressively deeper passes. Shallow passes cause less wear and tear on the router, keep the bit sharp longer and prevent overfeeding. If you bite too much wood off in one pass, the bit can actually get caught in the wood and break or even bend at the shank. Or, the momentary torque that develops with the bit

If your router table is on wheels, make sure the casters lock, or use a sandbag to hold the table stationary during use.

stopped but under power can cause you to lose control of the tool or the wood. Aside from routing in several passes, another good way to avoid overfeeding is to use bits with anti-kickback features that limit the speed at which you can feed the wood into the bit (see page 107).

Keep Hold Of A Router Whenever The Bit Is Spinning

It takes a few moments for a bit to stop spinning after you're finished with a cut and turn the tool off, but spin-down is no time to let go of a handheld router. Until the bit stops, the router still possesses some rotational forces. So, hang on until the bit comes to a complete stop. With a plunge router, you could withdraw the bit and bring the tool to the top of its plunge posts to conceal the bit, but it's still a good idea to hang on until the bit stops turning. With your hands on the router, they're out of harm's way. You eliminate the possibility of bit or tool damage as well as personal injury.

Feeding wood too rapidly past the bit, especially large bits with 1/4-in. shanks, can lead to a bent shank or broken cutter.

When you turn a router off, keep your hands on the tool until the bit stops spinning. This way, there's no chance of unexpected trouble.

Router Maintenance

A well-maintained tool tends to be a safer tool to use, so taking care of your routers is a good idea. Unlike some other woodworking machines, there isn't a great deal of preventative maintenance necessary on today's high-tech routers, but there are still a few things you can do to optimize performance and safety. Here's what to do on a periodic basis:

One way to safeguard against unexpected depth changes is to check and tighten your router's buckle lock from time to time. These will work loose with frequent use and wear.

Tighten The Router Base Buckle

Kit routers that come with multiple bases generally have buckle-style lever locks to hold the motor pack in place. If you change router bases often, the cam on the buckle mechanism will eventually begin to wear and lose grip on the motor pack. If the motor moves in the base, it will affect the router's cutting accuracy. From time to time, check the tension on the lever by locking the motor in place, then attempt to move the motor in the base. If you can shift the motor with the lock engaged, tighten the nut on the end of the lever lock slightly to increase tension on the cam. Even slightly tightening the nut should improve the grip.

Tighten Other Loose Nuts And Screws

Routers produce significant fine vibration as they operate, which is enough to loosen wing nuts and other screws on the base that are used for holding edge guides and other accessories in place. You don't want these fasteners to work loose and fall into the bit area in mid cut, and you may not notice them vibrating loose when you're using the tool. Before starting the router, give your router base a quick once-over, check-

Tighten the lock knobs and nuts on your router before each use to make sure they won't vibrate loose. Or, remove and store these until you need them.

If pounding out the collet doesn't remove all the inner debris, wipe out the inner sleeve with a clean paper towel.

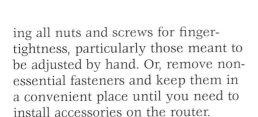

Wood dust will accumulate in a router collet after awhile, which can reduce its holding power on bits. Rap the collet nut on the bench a few times to pound out the crud.

ing all nuts and screws for finger-tightness, particularly those meant to be adjusted by hand. Or, remove non-essential fasteners and keep them in a convenient place until you need to install accessories on the router.

Collet Maintenance

After a long session of routing, the nooks and crannies of a collet fill with fine wood dust, especially if you're routing wet or resinous wood. It's important to keep the collet and inner sleeve free of build-up so it will grip bits firmly and release them easily.

Occasionally, or whenever you switch between collet sizes, rap the opening of your collet against a flat surface to loosen and pound out the dust. Take a clean, dry paper or cloth towel and clean out the sleeve, and wipe out the boring on the motor spindle where the sleeve nests in the router. Examine the sleeve for wear or signs of slipping. If it looks like the collet is losing grip on the bit (evidenced by polished, shiny rings around the inside of the spindle), replace the collet.

Clean out the inner taper of the router spindle with a pencil wrapped in a clean paper towel. This will prevent the collet's inner sleeve from sticking.

Clean and lubricate the plunge posts on a plunge router from time to time with a grease-free spray such as WD-40.

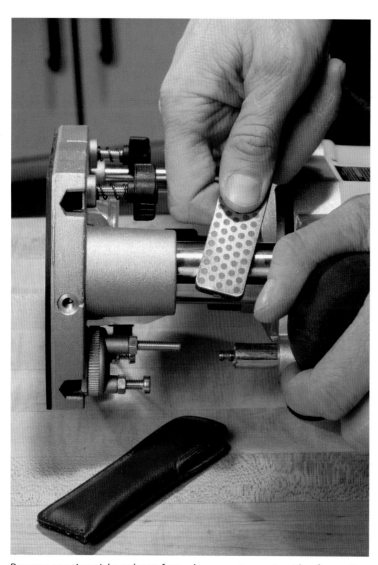

Remove any tiny nicks or burrs from plunge router posts with a fine-grit sharpening stone or emory paper.

Plunge Post Maintenance

In order for the plunge posts to slide smoothly in their sleeves, it helps to clean and lubricate them from time to time. Use a film-forming lubricant with a solvent cleaner such as WD-40 to wipe down the plunge posts first, then spray a light coating of WD-40 where the posts meet the sleeves. You can also use a "dry" spray lubricant sold for bicycle chains. Don't lubricate the posts with ordinary machine grease — it will just attract dust and form a paste that will gum up the plunge post action.

When the posts are clean, inspect them closely for nicks. Sometimes when loosening a stubborn collet nut, it's easy to accidentally hit the posts with a collet wrench. A nicked plunge post can mar the sleeve it fits into or hang up the plunging action. Use a fine sharpening stone or sandpaper backed with a block to smooth out any nicks you find on the posts.

Clean And Wax The Router Base And Motor Pack

For fixed-base and multi-base routers, occasionally wipe out the inner areas of the base and the outside of the motor pack with mineral spirits. The solvent will remove grit and residue that forms here over time. If your router bases are made of metal, give the motor pack body a

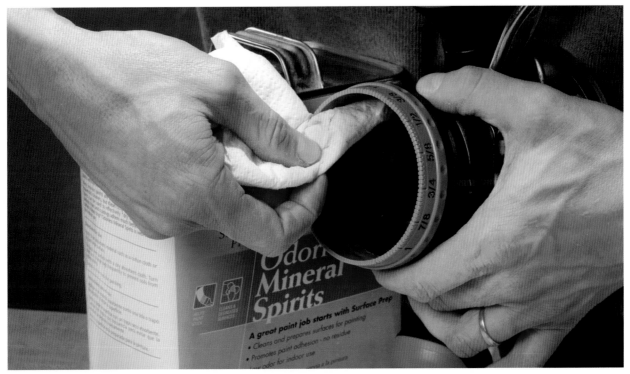

Wipe out the grime from inside your router bases to keep the motor pack from sticking and make it easier to adjust.

coating of paste wax, let it dry and wipe off the excess. Sometimes the metal-to-metal contact between the motor pack and base will form a layer of oxidation on both surfaces and make the motor harder to remove. A little wax here will slow down the oxidizing process and make the motor easier to install and adjust.

Apply a coat of paste wax to the router subbase as well. Wax will help reduce the drag between the router and the wood during use — especially after the base is covered with fine scratches from regular use.

Keep your motor pack smooth and free of corrosion with an occasional coating of paste wax.

Wax and buff your router's subbase. It will glide more smoothly over workpieces and stay cleaner longer.

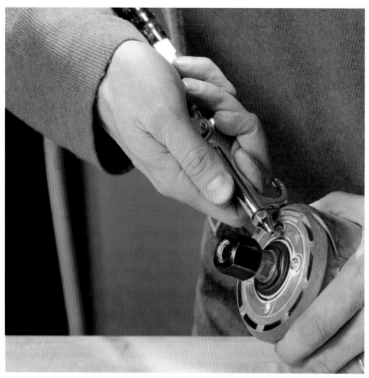

Dust will get drawn up through the router's fan and motor. Use compressed air to blow out the motor vents.

Motor Maintenance

Router motors draw large amounts of air through the housing to keep the motor from overheating. There are no filters inside, so the air that passes through is filled with wood dust. If it looks like your router motor pack is caked inside with dust, use compressed air to blow out the dust. Spray down through the top vents.

If you notice excessive sparking through the vent slits when using the router, it's a sign that the carbon brushes next to the armature are wearing out. It takes years of routine use for routers to go through a set of brushes, but the wear will happen more quickly if you use your router on a daily basis. Brushes are generally easy and inexpensive to replace. Many newer routers have a pair of removable caps on the motor housing near the top for accessing the carbon brushes. Carefully unscrew these caps (there's usually a compressed spring underneath) and pull the brushes out. If your router doesn't have motor brush caps, you may still be able to replace the brushes yourself by unscrewing the upper housing that covers the motor. Look for retaining springs on either side of the motor that hold the brushes in place. Gently pull back these springs with a needlenose pliers or small screwdriver, and slide the brushes out. If the brushes have a wire lead attached, carefully disconnect it where the lead clips to a contact on the motor.

Inspect the brushes closely for signs of crumbling or cracks. Replace the brushes if you see signs of deterioration. Look for a wear indicator line on the brushes — some brushes will show you how far they can wear before replacement is necessary. If the length of the brushes is worn to

Many professional-quality routers have externally accessible motor brushes. To change the brush, simply unscrew the outer cap and pull the brush out.

Depending on your router, the brushes may be contained inside the motor pack. You can still change them by pulling back retainer clips and sliding the brushes out.

Motor brushes eventually wear out. The brush on the left shows wear; the one on the right is new. Some brushes will have a wear-indicator line to show you when replacement is necessary.

about the same size as its width, replace the pair.

If your router motor doesn't spark but makes a buzzing or grinding sound during operation and when you turn it off, chances are the bearings are worn. Another sign of worn bearings is that the router won't cut a clean profile, even with a new bit. You can check for worn bearings by measuring the amount of runout at the router spindle with a dial indicator. Insert a smooth metal shaft into the collet and tighten it. With a dial indicator point touching the shaft and the dial set to zero, turn the shaft and watch for the pointer to deflect. If there's more than .0010 deflection, the bearings or spindle are worn, causing excessive play.

On newer routers, the bearings are permanently sealed and can't be replaced. Noisy bearings will last for awhile, but eventually they will drag and seize. If your bearings are beginning to fail, it's probably time to start shopping for a new router.

It's critical that a router spins in a true orbit. One way to check for excessive runout — which means a non-true orbit — is to use a dial indicator held against a rod mounted in the spindle.

EASY CORD WRAPS

Routers come with long cords these days, and they can be a hassle to keep organized. One way to make cords easier to store is to attach a couple strips of adhesive-backed hook-and-loop tape to the cord at the plug end. Cut two lengths of hook tape and loop tape about 9 to 10 in. long and stick them together and over the power cord near the end of the tape strips. Install the hook-and-loop wrap about 6 in. from the plug. To use the wrap, coil the cord in small loops and so the wrap ends up in the mid section of the loops. Squeeze the loops together and wrap the tape around to secure the cord.

Adhesive-backed hook-and-loop tape makes a convenient wrap for keeping power cords tidy. Stick a length of both parts of the tape to your cord, then wind the tape around the cord to bundle it together.

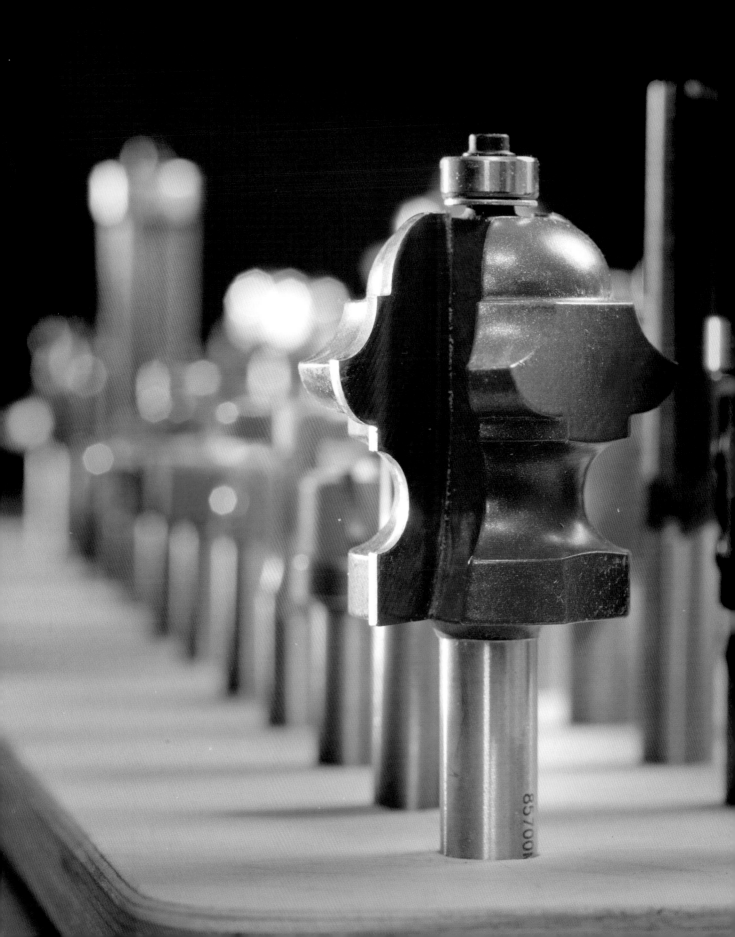

FOUR

ROUTER BITS

The fact that a router functions as both a handheld and stationary tool makes it versatile, but what really gives a router its range of applications are the bits you put in it. Bits allow your router to shape, cut, duplicate, make joints and drill holes. If you only use a router for a few of these operations, it's possible that you won't need a drawer full of different bits to meet your needs. However, over time you'll probably build quite a large collection.

As a testament to the popularity of routers, new styles of router bits are being developed all the time. It seems every new bit catalog unveils a few more unique profiles or a new innovation to make an existing bit style more foolproof or safe. You can find bits sold by blade and bit manufacturers or bits distributed through several of the leading router manufacturers. There are literally hundreds of different styles of router bits on the market, and you can even have custom bit profiles made for you if the bit you need isn't available.

The good news about bits is they offer you almost unlimited cutting and profiling flexibility. Router bits made by reputable manufacturers are also made to demanding standards, so you can be reasonably sure you'll get satisfactory results if the bits are used correctly. The bad news is, good bits aren't cheap — prices start at around $10 apiece and range upwards to $100. Most bits perform essentially a single cutting function, so you'll need a collection to really maximize the utility of your router. It doesn't take many projects for your investment in bits to reach or even exceed what you paid for your router. So, as with any other intelligent purchase, it makes sense to know the important issues about selecting and caring for your bits to buy wisely and get full value out of them.

This chapter will introduce you to the ever-expanding world of router bits. You'll learn the basics of bit anatomy, the functional differences between bits and how to identify a broad range of bit styles by shape. We'll also review the important details to look for in quality bits when you buy, and provide tips for cleaning and storing bits properly. If you buy good quality bits and take reasonable care of them, they should last for many hours of continuous use.

Bits come in all shapes and sizes. Over a lifetime of woodworking, you'll end up with a sizeable collection.

Anatomy Of A Router Bit

Router bits vary in shape and size, but there are some traits common to them all. Here is the nomenclature that describes the component parts of a router bit.

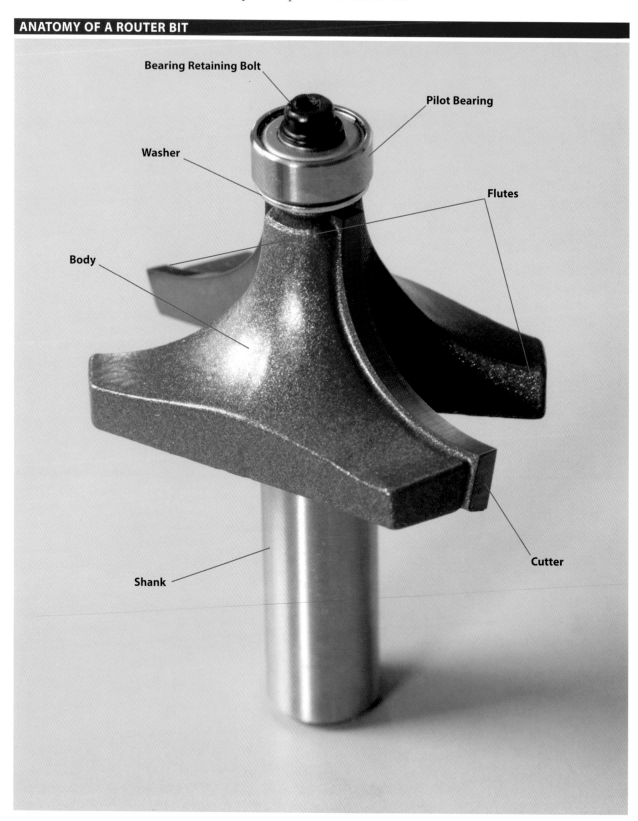

Bearing Retaining Bolt

Pilot Bearing

Washer

Flutes

Body

Cutter

Shank

Router bits are manufactured in three shank diameters: 1/4, 3/8 and 1/2 in. Most consumer routers do not come with a collet to fit 3/8-in.-dia. bits, but they are still common in industrial applications.

Shank

All bits consist of a shank that fits into a router collet and a cutting area above the shank that does the work. Shanks are generally formed either by milling a blank of high-speed or mild steel into a cylindrical shape or by a molding process that creates both the shank and the body of the bit in the same step. Either way, shanks are precision-ground in the manufacturing process to within ten-thousandths of an inch so bits will fit properly in the collet sleeve. Shank tolerances are critical for a proper fit in the collet, otherwise the sleeve won't grip the shank around its circumference. A bit that fits poorly in the sleeve could loosen during cutting or spin slightly out of balance and introduce vibration. Vibration leads to poor cutting quality, and it also makes the router harder to handle.

Router bits sold in this country come in 1/4, 3/8 and 1/2-in. shank diameters. Bits with 3/8-in. shanks are relatively uncommon, especially outside of manufacturing situations. When you shop for consumer router bits, you'll find a wide range of profiles and sizes in the other two shank diameters. Later in this chapter, we'll review the pros and cons of buying one shank size over the other.

Body

The portion of the bit above the shank, or body of the bit, forms its basic cutting profile. The bit body provides mass behind the cutters, which provides some inertia to keep the bit spinning while it helps dampen vibration. The bit body also forms a solid backing surface to help the cutting edge resist the shock that comes with pushing it into solid wood. If the cutters are made of carbide, this is particularly important, because carbide is brittle. An unsupported carbide edge will break much easier than steel under shock.

Pilot Bearing

Some bits cut decorative profiles or are designed to trim one edge flush to a template or another piece of wood. In either of these cutting operations, the bit will require a pilot to limit the cutting depth and path of the bit. Pilots can simply be an extension of the bit made of steel or a softer metal like brass. This is the old style. Today, most pilots are sealed ball bearings that fit on the bit shank, either on the tip or below the cutters.

Flutes

Flutes are the voids in front of the cutting edges. They serve as scoops

Straight bits vary in terms of the number of cutting flutes. Single-flute bits (right) cut more quickly, but double-flute bits (left) generally produce smoother surfaces.

are usually straight-cutting bits, cut rapidly but at the expense of smoothness. The chips are large and clear quickly, but the bit will leave a more ragged cut surface. Double-flute bits are common in many different profiles. Three-and four-flute bits are less common, but they make the smoothest, slowest cuts. Bits with two or more flutes will cut smaller chips than bits with a single flute, but they'll also tend to recut their own chips, which decreases cutting speed and efficiency.

Cutters

Most of today's new router bits have cutters made of small pieces of tungsten carbide brazed onto the bit body. Spiral router bits are often made entirely of carbide. Router bits that predate the wide use of carbide were made of high-speed steel. High-speed steel is a special steel alloy that withstands higher operating temperatures before the bit loses its temper. It's also hard enough to hold a sharp edge but not so hard that it can't be resharpened easily with common sharpening methods and tools. Regular carbon tool steel can't resist the heat that develops at high speeds, and the edges quickly dull. It's never been used for the cutting edges on router bits. However, it is used for the bit shanks and bodies of some bits.

High-speed steel router bits have largely gone the way of the dinosaur for modern routing. The popularity of carbide bits has driven this shift away from high-speed steel in the last 20 years or so. Despite their decline, high-speed steel router bits have a few advantages over carbide bits. The steel can be filed and ground easily if you want to modify the bit's cutting profile. You can also sharpen the cutting edges of a high-speed steel bit with ordinary sharpening stones. Steel bits are also cheaper to buy than all-carbide or carbide-tipped bits. Their big downside is that the edges don't stay sharp as long as carbide, especially when cutting sheet goods like particleboard or

to help break and clear away the chips. On spiral-shaped bits, the flutes twist up the full cutting area of the bit, but for other conventional bits, the flutes end where the bit body and cutters end. Years ago, router bits had larger flutes than they typically do today, but large flutes can become problematic on bits that cut large or deep profiles. If a bit is forced to cut faster than the flutes can clear the chips, it's easy to overload the router, which can damage both the bit and the router's motor. Overfeeding the bit can also cause the bit to grab the wood, possibly pulling the tool right from your hands. So, bits are now engineered with smaller flutes to make them safer to use but with the tradeoff of slower feed rates.

One of the ways bits are categorized is by the number of flutes they have. Flute numbers will range from one to four. Single-fluted bits, which

MDF or particularly hard or resinous woods. You'll need to sharpen or replace these bits regularly.

In terms of edge retention, carbide has become the wonder material of modern saw blade and router bit technology. It's made of a mixture of carbide granules and powdered cobalt that forms an alloy when fused together under high temperature and pressure. The ability of carbide to retain an edge has to do with its granular nature. As the bit cuts, tiny particles of carbide break away, but they expose the fresh, sharp edges of particles behind. Imagine crushed glass bound together with glue as an extrapolation of how carbide works. Generally speaking, the smaller the carbide particles, the longer the edge stays sharp. A steel edge, on the other hand, abrades into a rounded-over, smoothed shape instead of an edge.

Router bit manufacturers invest significant research and development into the formulations of the proprietary carbide they use. There are several grades of carbide used for router bits, and the grades are formulated to promote better wear resistance or shock resistance. One attribute comes at the expense of the other. The amount of cobalt in the mixture determines whether the carbide will hold an edge longer but be more brittle or have improved shock resistance but abrade more quickly. It isn't easy to know which grade of carbide you're buying. Whatever the carbide is, you can be sure it will cost more but stay sharper many times longer than a steel bit.

Router bit edges are ground to three specific angles: the hook angle, grind angle and relief angle. The three angles are easiest to see on a carbide-tipped bit when viewed from above and off the tip of the bit. The rake angle is the angle formed by an imaginary line extending from the tip of the cutter to the center of the bit. The grind angle forms the actual knife-shaped wedge along the edge of the cutter. A third angle, called the relief, also impacts cutting performance. It's the angle formed between the beveled grind angle and the bit body immediately behind the cutter. The relief angle allows the cutter to slice without dragging the back of the grind against the wood.

The three grinds form a complex geometry that enable the bit to cut efficiently, retain edge sharpness and minimize burning the wood at high speeds. Bit grinds will vary, depending on the type of cut the bit makes or the material it's intended to cut. When you're buying bits, you'll never need to know more specifics about these three cutting grinds unless you plan to do your own sharpening. But, it's instructive to at least be aware of them.

Most bits these days are manufactured with carbide cutting edges (left), but you can still find bits made from high-speed steel (right). Carbide holds a sharp edge longer, but high-speed steel is easier to resharpen and more economical.

Shear Angles

Along with cutter composition and grind, another part of a bit's geometry is how the cutters are mounted on the body, relative to the shank. Cutters can be mounted nearly parallel to the axis of the shank or at various other angles. Some bits, such as fluted straight bits, have very little shear angle. The cutter functions like a paddle against the wood and cuts in a chopping motion. Other bit styles with more shear angle cut in a slicing rather than a paddling motion. Generally, shear angle helps reduce vibration during cutting. It also contributes to a smoother cut.

Spiral bits have the greatest shear of all router bits. These bits, which are shaped more like conventional twist bits for drills, have a continuous, spiraling shear angle along the full cutter length. The spiral design means the cutters are in constant contact with the wood, which keeps vibration to a minimum while producing a knife-like slicing cut.

The shear angle of a bit, or the degree to which the cutting edge tips relative to the shank, varies among bit types. Straight shear angles (left) cut with a paddling action, while angled (center) or spiral (right) shears produce a knife-like cutting action. Angle or spiral shears tend to cut end grain and other difficult wood grains more cleanly.

Piloted And Unpiloted Bits

Routers make both guided and unguided cuts. The difference between the two types of cuts has to do with whether the router can be moved in freeform fashion, such as clearing the waste out of a large recess, or in more controlled ways, such as edge-profiling, template or joinery operations.

There are several ways to guide a router to limit its cutting path, and one of the options is to use bits equipped with a pilot. A pilot can be an extension off the tip of the bit, or it can be an enclosed ball bearing fitted to the bit's tip, mid section or shank. Pilots formed or mounted to the tip of the bit prevent the end from serving as a cutting edge. Pilots located elsewhere allow the bit to serve as an end cutter, an edge cutter or both.

The bearing on a piloted bit is actually a pair of sealed races with tiny ball bearings inside, similar to a sealed bearing on an axle. The inner sleeve of the bearing fits over a tiny shank on the end of the bit. An allen screw threads into the tip of the bit to hold the bearing and a metal washer in place.

Bits that cut similar profiles may or may not have a pilot bearing to guide the cut. Cove bits (left) and core box bits (right) both cut concave profiles, but they must be used with different router setups because of the presence or absence of a pilot bearing.

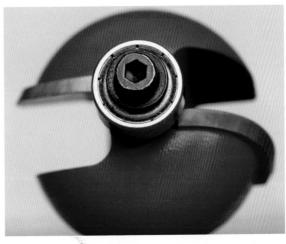

Bits intended to cut profiles along the edges or ends of a workpiece will often have a pilot bearing attached to the end. The bearing rolls along the edge of the workpiece and limits the bit's cutting path.

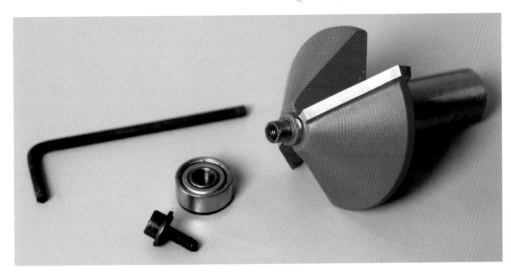

Pilot bearings resemble the same sealed bearings you'll find on larger motors and machinery. On router bits, the bearing's inner sleeve fits over a tiny shank on the bit, and an allen bolt locks the bearing in place.

Piloted flush-trim and pattern bits allow you to duplicate parts precisely using a template.

Sometimes, the outer diameter of the bearing matches the bit's cutting diameter. As you'll see in chapter eight, template routing requires this style of bit, called a pattern or flush-trim bit. Here, the bearing rides against a template mounted to wood, and a straight bit cuts an identical shape to the template. When the bearing is mounted to the bit tip, the template can be situated below the workpiece. Otherwise, the bearing can be located on the shank so it follows a template mounted above the wood. With the bearing on top, a flush-trim bit can have a sharpened tip for making plunge or clean-out cuts as well as edge cuts.

Most profiling bits have pilot bearings, but here the bearing diameter doesn't match the cutting diameter. With profiling bits, the bearing limits the bit's cutting area to the shape of the profile. By raising or lowering the router's cutting depth, you can also cut less than the full profile of the bit if you wish. Regardless of how much of the profile is engaged in the cut, the bearing still limits the cutting area to the edge or end of the workpiece.

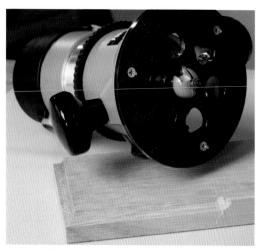

Edge-profiling bits add a decorative touch to part edges and soften sharp corners. They are available in dozens of different shapes.

Some longer profiling bits, like this crown molding cutter, make it possible to mill a decorative profile into the face of narrow stock to create custom molding.

Dovetail and other joint-making bits cut interlocking patterns into parts so they form a mechanical, sturdy connection.

A spiral or straight bit installed in a plunge router performs deep plunge cuts for making mortises or drilling holes.

Aside from template and profile bits, you can also buy joint-making, carving and lettering bits equipped with pilot bearings. These bits usually have bearings that match the overall cutter diameter, which is useful for following the templates of a dovetail, box joint or lettering jig, or for using bits to remove waste material inside a workpiece with a closed-edge template.

A few piloted bits designed for trimming plastic laminate are made of all carbide. Instead of a bearing, the pilot on these 1/4-in.-shank bits is a fixed extension off the tip. The shank can also serve as a pilot. On these bits, the actual cutting area of the bit is small because it only needs to trim through the 1/16-in. thickness of the laminate rather than serve as a longer edge cutter.

Piloted laminate-trimming bits cut plastic laminate neatly and exactly to the size of the substrate material underneath. Here, it's medium-density fiberboard.

Router Bit Styles

Despite the wide range of bit sizes, shapes, compositions and cutting geometries, router bits can be grouped loosely into six basic woodworking functions: profiling, joint-making, template routing, cutting and drilling, detailing and door-building. A few unique bits fall outside these six groupings, but most bits apply. On the next few pages, you'll see examples of each type of bit along with a sample of the shape they cut. This survey of bits isn't exhaustive — more bits exist than what you see here. However, it does give you an idea of the basic shapes of different bits that apply to the six groups described below.

In a nutshell, here's a basic description of what distinguishes the six different bit groups.

Profiling Bits

Profiling bits form the largest subgroup of router bits, given the wide range of different shapes you can apply to the ends and edges of workpieces. Profiling involves cutting all or part of an end or edge away, usually with a piloted bit. The bit can follow the perimeter of the workpiece, or it can shape the edges of an internal cutout. Some bits without pilots can also be used for profiling purposes, but in these cases the router must be used in conjunc-

Fluting bit.

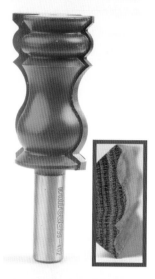

Crown molding bit.

Triple beading bit.

Bullnose bit.

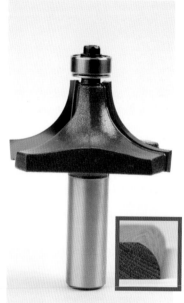

Roundover bit.

Ovolo profile bit.

tion with an edge guide to keep the bit from moving off the edge.

Profiling bits aren't limited to edges and ends. Some bits designed for making crown and other trim moldings cut wide, complex shapes into the face grain of workpieces. These bits must be used in a

Reverse curve ogee
and bead bit.

Chamfering bit.

Ogee bit.

Cove bit.

Traditional edge-bead-
ing bit.

Piloted beading bit.

Multi-profile bit.

Face frame flush-trim
and V-groove bit.

router table with a fence to be operated safely.

The typical profiling bits make chamfers, roundovers, coves, ogee curves, bullnoses, beads, flutes and other classical shapes. Some bits, called multi-profiles or multi-forms, are large, piloted bits that are milled with elaborate combinations of profiles. Depending on where you set the bit height, you can cut three or more unique profiles with the same bit. A profile can also be as simple as a stepped lip formed with a rabbeting bit, but rabbets typically fall into the next bit category.

Joint-Making Bits

Another sizable group of router bits enable you to make interlocking joint parts instead of profiled edges. Joint-making bits can be piloted or unpiloted, depending on the application and method for guiding the router against the work. The typical choices for cutting woodworking joints include dovetail and rabbeting bits, straight bits of all styles and both slot and biscuit cutters. Other more

SAMPLING OF JOINT-MAKING BITS

"V"panel bit set.

Undersized plywood mortising bit.

Biscuit joining bit.

Rabbeting bit.

Drawer lock joint bit.

Reversible glue joint bit.

recent innovations in joint-making bits include the lock miter and drawer lock joint, plus various styles of bits made for forming glue joints with increased glue surface areas. This latter variety includes the finger joint bit, which can be used successfully for joining even end grain to end grain. There are also matched sets for cutting tongue-and-groove joints and the rule joints for making drop-leaf tables.

Lock miter bit.

Slot-cutting bit.

Piloted mortising bit.

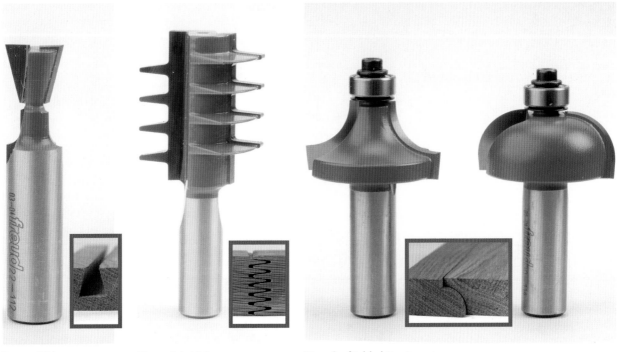

Dovetail bit.

Finger joint bit.

Drop-leaf table bit set.

Piloted flush-trim bit.

Flush-trim insert bit.

Dish-carving bit.

Template-Routing Bits

Most template routing involves guiding a bearing-piloted straight bit against a template to duplicate the template shape onto a workpiece. Recall that bits for template work are usually modified straight bits with the bearing located either on the shank or the tip. Shank-mounted template bits are typically called pattern bits, while bits with bearings on the tip are called flush-trim bits.

Other templating bits with more specialized applications include mortising and dish-carving bits. Both of these styles have cutters that extend to the end of the bit or wrap around it for end-cutting purposes. Mortising bits are sold with cutter lengths as short as 1/4 in. for making shallow hinge mortises.

Cutting And Drilling Bits

Technically, all router bits are made to cut wood, and any bit with a sharpened end can be used with some success for boring holes, provided you're using a plunge router. However, a few bits are specifically made for efficient cutting. Piloted panel bits are a prime example. The tip of these bits is ground to a drill-shaped point for plunging completely through thin plywood or other sheet material, and the area immediately above the tip is ground smooth to form a fixed pilot for guiding the bit along a surface once it cuts through. The cutters above the pilot resemble a straight bit and provide a total cutting length of up to 2 1/2 in.

Single-flute straight bits, especially those with their ends ground to a beveled point, also make excellent through-cutting bits with the added advantage of fast feed rates for lateral cutting. Since these bits have just one flute, the cut edges they produce are rougher than multiple-flute or spiral carbide bits.

Laminate-trimming bits also belong in the group of specialized cutting bits. Their intended purpose is to cut laminate smoothly and quickly, which explains why the length of the cutters on these bits is as short as it is. Laminate is very thin. Laminate-trimming bits function like a flush-trim bit with a bearing that matches the cutting width of the bit. The bit rides along the substrate material beneath the laminate, and the cutters trim the laminate flush. Some laminate-trimming bits have a beveled cutting profile to remove the sharp edge as well. Ordinarily, you'd need to file this off to prevent injuries.

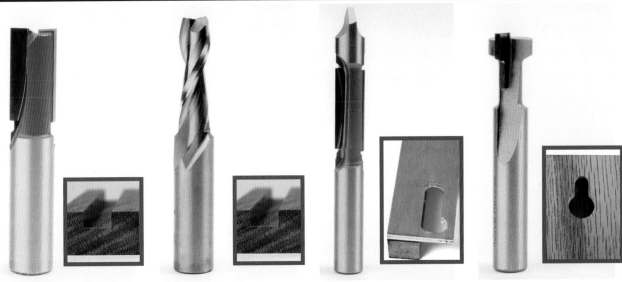

Double-fluted straight bit.   Carbide spiral bit.   Panel pilot bit.   Keyhole cutting bit.

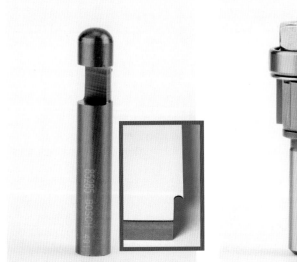

Carbide laminate flush-trimming bit.   Piloted laminate flush-trimming bit.   T-slot cutter bit.

T-slot cutters and keyhole bits also serve unique cutting functions. With a T-slot cutter, the bit must be started along the edge or end of a workpiece, and the cutters form a semi-enclosed, rectangular channel. At the same time, the bit shank is outfitted with a second cutter than opens a narrower groove through the face of the workpiece, which forms the characteristic T-shaped cut. T-slot cutters are handy for making jigs when you need to have a bolt hold a nut or lock knob fast without drilling a through-hole for the bolt.

Keyhole bits are handy for making picture frames or other wall-hung projects. The keyhole fits over a screwhead and locks underneath it to hold the wood. To make the keyhole shape, the bit must first be plunged into the workpiece to the desired depth, then directed laterally away from the entry hole to cut the narrower slot that holds a screwhead in place.

V-grooving bit.

Classical beading groove bit.

Corebox/roundnose bit.

Detailing Bits

Detailing bits form decorative relief profiles in from the edges or ends of a workpiece. The bits, of course, do not have pilot bearings on their ends. Many profiling bit shapes are also engineered into unpiloted detailing bits so you can create the look of ogees, fillets, beads and other shapes in the middle of a workpiece like you can along the edges and ends. Core box bits, that cut a half-round recess, and even straight bits that cut a flat-bottomed channel can be used as detailing bits.

Some common uses for detailing bits include veining, fluting and lettering. By cutting a shallow recess, you can then fill the area with decorative contrasting veneers to make inlays. With detailing bits, you can simulate the look of a raised panel door on a flat-faced board by forming an inner "panel" rectangle with a detailing bit instead of building separate frame and panel parts.

Door-Building Bits

This small group comprises the bits you need for making authentic raised-panel cabinet doors. The bits that make the interlocking joints for the drawer frame corners are called cope and stick sets. The most common variety of cope and stick bits are matched pairs, where one bit cuts the ends of the rails into a coped shape, while the other bit forms the female, mating shape on the inside edges of both the rails and stiles. Cope and stick bits are also sold as a single bit that cuts both the cope and stick shapes. To make the conversion from one cutting operation to the other, the cutters on the bit shank are interchangeable and bolt in place. Another option for cope and stick bits is a single tall bit with both profiles mounted permanently. Here, you raise and lower the bit in a router table to reveal just one or the other profile at a time.

The other operation for door building involves cutting the broad bevels around the inner door panel. Beveling bits for this task are called raised panel cutters. Raised panel cutters are available in a variety of profiles for cutting either flat beveled edges, gentle concaves or convex/concave ogee shapes. Panel cutters are some of the largest and heaviest router bits, and they must be used in a router table at low speeds.

There are two types of raised panel bits: horizontal style, which cut the bevels with the panel oriented face-down on the router table. Horizontal bits should only be used with full-size, variable speed routers in the 3 to 3¼ hp ranges. Some horizontal panel cutters have an extra set of cutters on top that mill a shallow recess around the back of the panel as well to help thin the tongue so it fits easily into the door frame slots. Vertical panel raisers are more compact bits with shorter cutting wings that cut panels standing on-edge or end against the router table fence. Their smaller size and weight makes it possible to raise panels with a smaller size router. Some argue that vertical panel raisers are safer to use than the horizontal style. Whether that's true or not, you're certainly exposed to a smaller cutting area with vertical bits.

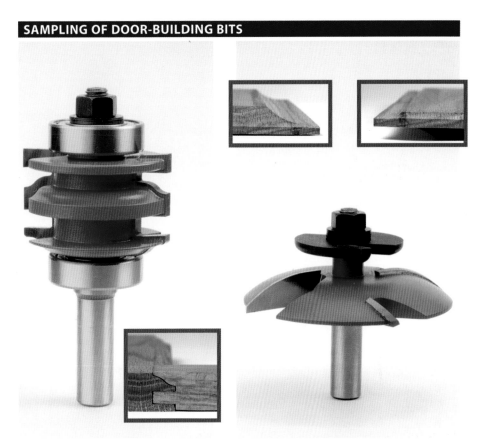

SAMPLING OF DOOR-BUILDING BITS

One-piece rail and stile bit.

Raised panel bit with backcutter.

Conventional raised panel bit.

Vertical panel raising bit.

STRAIGHT BITS

Over the course of your woodworking hobby, you'll probably end up owning more profiling bits than any other type, primary because each shape you make requires a different bit. However, for general woodworking, you'll probably reach just as often for the unassuming straight bit as you will for a more interesting edge-treatment bit. That's because straight bits perform a variety of functions when used with guide collars, an edge guide or in conjunction with a pilot bearing. A straight bit will clear waste from a hinge mortise or inlay area, cut a groove for a dado, mill a portion of a rabbet, bore holes for shelf pins and shear both edge and end grain cleanly for template work.

Double-flute straight bits come in a wide variety of diameters and cutting lengths. You can buy straight bits as small as $1/8$-in. diameter or as large as 2 in. Cutting lengths range from $1/4$ in. to $2^1/2$ in. Generally, the bit's diameter is more important than cutter length when it comes to making decisions about which straight bits to buy. Bit cutting diameter is particularly important if you use bits for making mortises, since the bit's diameter often establishes the mortise width. Occasionally, you'll have need for a particularly long straight bit, for making deep mortising or through-cuts. For most straight bit work, however, a narrow bit can make wide cuts if you make multiple passes, and a long bit can make shallow passes, provided your router has sufficient range for setting bit depths.

Given the variety of applications for which they're used, straight bits come in a wide range of cutting lengths and diameters.

Straight bits with a shear angle, and spiral bits in particular, are excellent investments — although there are fewer of these bits to choose from than the conventional, double-fluted straight bits without shear. Straight bits that make a shearing cut will cut more cleanly and smoothly than straight bits without shear. Spiral bits tend to make the cleanest cuts, and most are made of solid carbide, which makes them more expensive but last longer than high-speed steel or carbide-tipped bits. Another advantage of spiral bits over many — but not all — straight bit styles is that the tips are ground into cutting edges. You can plunge a spiral bit straight into wood like a drill and the bit will cut its way down. Some straight bits have a gap on the end between the carbide cutters that actually doesn't cut wood. The bit must be swept laterally during plunging to cut away the waste in this void area, or the bit will have to burn it away.

Spiral straight bits come in three main styles: upcut, downcut and compression. Upcut and downcut spirals are tricky to tell apart visually, but their cutting characteristics are different and important to understand. With the two bit types oriented shank-down, upcut spirals twist counterclockwise. This geometry makes upcut bits pull chips up and out of the cut like a twist drill bit, which keeps the cutting path from becoming impacted with chips. The counterclockwise twist also pulls the router base against the workpiece when freehand routing. On a router table, it will pull the workpiece against the table. Tearout happens on the top surface of the workpiece, which can be a disadvantage if the top face of what you're routing is also the "show" face.

Downcut spiral bits are milled with a clockwise twist, which forces chips down the bit toward the tip instead of upward. In situations where you're cutting completely through a workpiece, the downward chip ejection is helpful for keeping the area above the workpiece clean. However, downcut bits should be used cautiously. The vector of force created by these bits will push the bit up and out of the cut and force the wood away from the

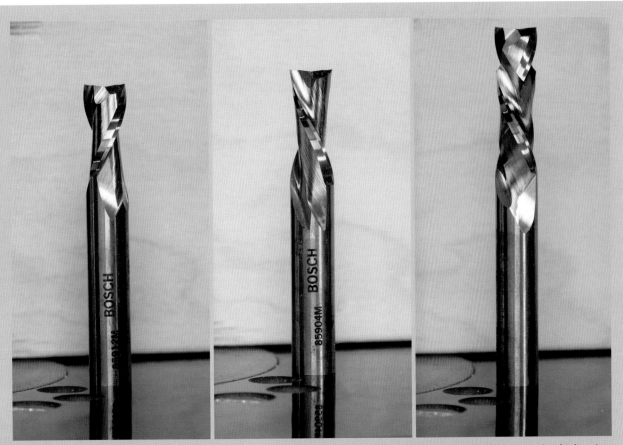

Spiral bits are manufactured in three main styles: upcut (left), which twists counterclockwise; downcut (center), which twists clockwise; and compression (right), which twists in both directions.

bit instead of draw it close. In some situations, this can literally cause the router to climb out of the cut. You'll lose control of the tool — always dangerous — and ruin the cut. Tearout with these bits happens below the cut instead of above it.

Compression bits — the third spiral style — are ground with both upcut and downcut regions along the cutting length. The tip of the bit is ground counterclockwise and upcut style, which eliminates tearout on the bottom face of a workpiece in through-cutting situations. The rest of the cutter area twists clockwise, like a downcut bit, to eliminate tearout on the top face of the workpiece.

It's helpful to have a compression bit for making through-cuts when both surfaces of the material are "show" faces and need to have little or no tearout. However, compression bits are more expensive than the other two spiral bit styles and probably not worth the extra investment to save a little tearout.

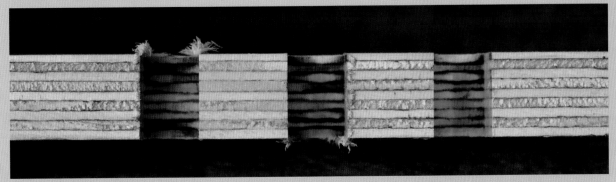

Spiral bits produce tearout in different places, depending on the twist style. Upcut bits can create tearout on top. Downcut bits tend to break fibers out below the cut. Compression bits shear both top and bottom edges cleanly.

Trapped And Untrapped Bits

Another characteristic of certain bits, particularly those that cut interlocking joints, is that once the bit starts its cut, workpieces cannot be pulled away from the cut without ruining it. The bit becomes captured inside the cut and must stay there until the cut is completed. Sometimes in these situations the bit is entirely buried in the workpiece. Dovetail bits are a good example. Or, a bit may be partially captured in the cut and partially exposed, especially in cases where the profile surrounds just part of the wood, such as beading bits.

Other bits function in uncaptured ways, particularly piloted profile bits with gradual and gentle curvatures such as roundovers, ogees, chamfers and coves. You can pull the router and bit up or away from the wood (in freehand routing) or slide the wood away from the bit (on a router table) during any point of the cut without damaging the workpiece. Rabbeting bits also make uncaptured cuts, despite the fact that they're usual use is for making interlocking joints.

Bits that make captured cuts include dovetails, cope-and-stick, lock miter, glue joint, drawer lock joint, finger, T-slot, keyhole, slot-cutting, biscuit and even straight bits when they're used for slot-cutting operations. Other bits including bullnose, bead, flute. With all these bits, it's critical to carry out the full cut without stopping and with workpieces and with the bit moving in a smooth, controlled fashion at all times. Here's where you'll want to be sure to make practice cuts first on scrap to test your setup. You won't have the luxury of changing anything about the setup once you start the actual cuts.

Some bit styles, like the three examples shown here, become imbedded and essentially "trapped" in the wood during a cut. The workpiece cannot be pulled off or away from the bit without ruining the cut.

Other bits, such as roundovers and rabbeting bits, don't trap workpieces during a cut. You can pull the wood and bit apart at any point without damaging the workpiece.

Bits With Interchangeable Parts

Some bit styles have interchangeable cutters or bearings to expand the bit's versatility. Common examples are rabbeting bits that come with several pilot bearings of different diameters. Switching bearing sizes allows you to vary the width of the rabbet shoulders you can cut by limiting the bit's cutting capacity. Multi-bearing rabbet bits are about twice the cost of single-bearing rabbeting bits, but they may come with as many as eight different bearings. With the extra bearings, it's as though you actually own eight rabbeting bits instead of one or two single-bearing bits.

Slot- and biscuit-cutting bits also are available with cutters or bearings of varying diameters. Changing the bearing or cutter diameter changes the slot depth or produces slots that match the three common wood biscuit sizes.

At one time you could buy bits consisting of a single shank and several removable bit bodies in different profiles. This way, one bit could be converted into various other bits by just removing a nut and sliding off

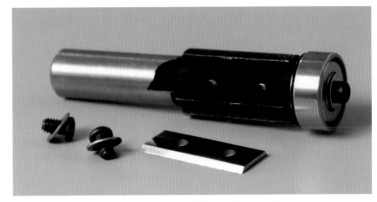

This flush-trim bit has removable carbide inserts with two sharp edges. When the bit dulls, the inserts can be flipped to the second sharp edge or replaced. These bits are more expensive than bits with fixed cutters.

the cutter. This option has all but disappeared from router bit inventories. Most bits these days are one-piece and intended to cut one profile. However, you can buy a few different router bit styles that feature replaceable cutters. The cutter inserts are made of carbide and fasten to the bit body with screws. Some inserts have more than one cutting edge. When it dulls, you flip the insert to a fresh edge. Insert bits are only available with straight edges, so their versatility is limited. They're also more expensive than conventional straight bits. But if you use straight-edged bits frequently, buying the carbide inserts is cheaper than replacing the whole bit.

Rabbeting bits with interchangeable bearings are excellent investments. The same bit can cut a range of rabbet dimensions by simply changing the bearing size and bit depth.

What To Look For When Buying Bits

Tool and bit quality has been on the rise over the past 20 years or so, in keeping with the increased interest in home woodworking. If you buy your router bits from a reputable manufacturer, it's safe to assume you'll get a bit that's been made to strict tolerances so it cuts efficiently with low vibration and leaves a smooth finish. However, there are still lemons in the vast basket of router bits, so it pays to have a closer look at the bit and the packaging details before you buy. Here are a number of factors to consider when buying bits:

Carbide Quality

Most bit manufacturers won't tell you on the packaging what grade of

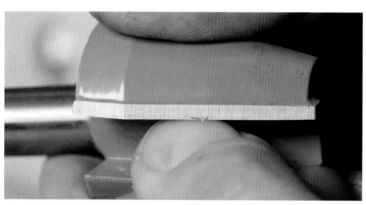

One way to inspect the sharpness of a bit is to graze the cutting edge gently against a fingernail. If the edge raises a shaving from your nail, it's sharp enough to cut wood cleanly.

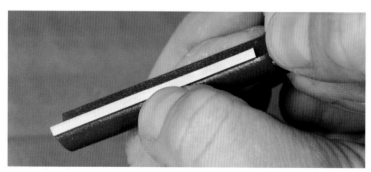

Another measure of bit quality is to run your fingernail across the broad, flat face of each cutter. A proper grind shouldn't snag your fingernail anywhere along the cutter length.

carbide you're buying, and it's not something you can distinguish by eye. One criterion that's commonly promoted on bit packaging is "micro-grain" carbide. This means the bit is made with particularly small particles of carbide. The smaller the particles, the longer the edge will last. Buy micro-grain bits when you can.

Cutters

Check the broad faces of the carbide cutters closely. The mark of a precision-ground bit is smooth, polished edges with little or no evidence of grind marks. Run your fingernail along the broad outer flat face of each cutter. It shouldn't catch anywhere along the cutting length. A good inspection of actual sharpness is to roll the sharpened edge gently against your fingernail. A properly sharpened bit should peel a tiny shaving off the nail with no extra pressure applied.

In theory, you can resharpen a carbide-tipped router bit three to five times, but most woodworkers don't go to the effort. It's still a better value in the long run to have a qualified bit sharpening service regrind your cutters than replace your bits as soon as they dull. The cost can be as little as $5 per sharpening. Look for bits with thick carbide cutters. More carbide means more sharpenings before the bit must be replaced. Thicker carbide also helps cutting edges better absorb the shock that goes along with cutting.

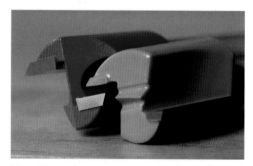

Bits will vary by manufacturer in terms of the thickness of the carbide that's brazed to the bit body. Thicker carbide (left bit) holds a more durable edge than thin carbide (right bit), and thicker carbide improves the chances that it can be resharpened when the edges dull.

Brazing

Use a magnifying glass to inspect the brazed seams along the back edge of the cutters where they bond to the bit body as well as the intersection of the cutters and flute at the deepest cutting point. The brazing should be smooth and fill these seams. Tiny pinhole voids in the brazing probably won't spell disaster if you use the bit, but high-quality bits will not have voids in the brazing.

Shank And Body Finish

Bit shanks should be ground and polished smooth, with no noticeable voids. The bottom edge of the shank should be ground to a smooth bevel. While it's critical that bit shanks be milled to precise diameters so they hold fast in the collet, you can't determine this peeking through the packaging at the store. If you end up with a bit shank that slips in the collet when other bits hold tightly, you've got a defective bit. Return it for an exchange or refund. A bit that slips in the collet can't be fixed and will ruin your collet sleeve quickly. Returning a bit shouldn't be a problem if you shop at larger home centers or at woodworking specialty stores.

As far as bit bodies go, the telltale sign of quality finishing is that the bodies will have smooth surfaces without spatters of brazing still showing. Even miniscule spatters can sometimes throw off the balance of the bit as it spins, and the lumps of brazing will give pitch a place to collect.

Some manufacturers coat their bits with various formulations of low-friction coating. The coating prevents resin and pitch from gumming up the bit surfaces and reducing cutting performance. Unless the manufacturer states that the color on the bit is actually a special coating, it could simply be paint. Buy bits with low-friction coatings when it's feasible.

Antikickback Designs

Bits with oversized bodies that reduce the size and opening of the

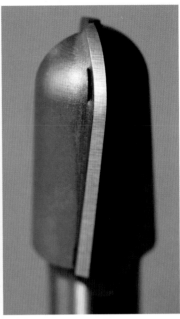

When buying new router bits, inspect the cutters carefully for manufacturing defects in the brazing. Separations between the cutter and bit body (left) or voids in the brazing (right) don't necessarily impact cutting performance or cause the bit to fail, but avoid buying or using bits with these problems.

flutes help reduce the possibility of kickback by limiting the bit's cutting aggressiveness. Some critics argue that antikickback provisions really only matter on large panel-raising or profiling bits, but an extra measure of safety can't hurt with bits of all sizes. Actually, it's getting harder to find bits without antikickback-style bodies. Eventually, all bits will probably have them — which seems a good preventative measure against injury.

It's easy to distinguish bits with antikickback features (left) from those without (right). On the left ogee bit, notice how the bit body forms a more complete circle of metal around its circumference. This is the antikickback provision. The added metal behind the cutters reduces the flutes' size, which prevents the cutters from biting in too deeply and kicking back.

A hard-working set of bits doesn't have to mean you own a hundred different styles. A flush-trim bit, several straight bits, a few joint-making bits and a handful of profiling bits may be all the bits you'll need to own for most projects.

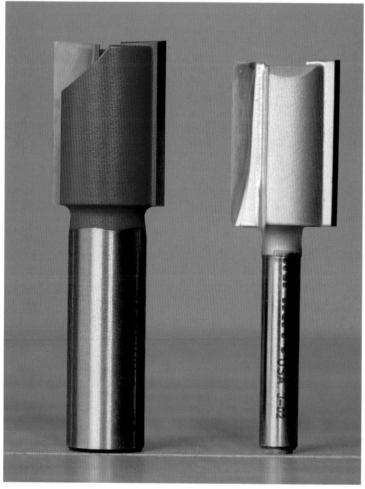

The majority of common bits are made in both ¼- and ½-in.-shank sizes. Choose the thicker shank size if you can, especially for larger or longer bits. Bits with ½-in. shanks produce less vibration and provide more support for the bit body than small-shanked bits.

Which Bits Should You Buy?

Every woodworker will have different router bit needs, so there's no one list of bits that will apply to everyone equally. In terms of performance, bits with ½-in. shanks are a better value than bits with ¼-in. shanks. The thicker shank size provides a larger circumference for the collet sleeve to grasp evenly. As bit sizes get larger, an iron-clad grip is even more important, because the collet must withstand more torque as the bit cuts. Half-inch shanks are also stiffer than ¼-in. shanks. The extra metal dampens vibration. Some smaller bits are only available in the smaller shank size, but tiny cutters are amply supported with a ¼-in. shank. It's the larger cutter styles that pose problems for small bit shanks. Generally, ½-in. shanks aren't significantly more expensive than ¼-in. shanks. Most new routers will accept this size, and aside from the slight increase in cost, there are really no disadvantages to buying the larger size. Performance and longevity make ½-in.-shank bits worth the extra investment in the long run.

If you're just beginning to build a router bit collection, some essential bits to buy include the following styles:

- **Straight bits** in ¼-, ⅜- and ½-in. cutting diameters. Bits with cutters around 1 to 1¼ in. long offer the best mix of stiffness and cutting depth. The longer the bit gets, the more likely it will be to deflect under cutting load.

- **Rabbeting bit.** Buy one with interchangeable pilot bearings for greater versatility.

- **Template bits.** Template bits with shank-mounted bearings are more useful than bottom-bearing pattern bits, but you'll appreciate having one of each style. Again, try to keep cutter lengths less than 1½ in. to minimize deflection and vibration on these finishing bits. Buy template bits in ⅜- or ½-in. diameters. They'll fit reasonably well into tight corners of templates.

- **Chamfer bit.** One piloted chamfer bit should do the trick for all but the largest chamfer cuts. Those with cutting edges between ⅞ and 1¼ in. are most useful.

- **Roundovers and coves.** Here, particularly projects will dictate the diameters you need. For general softening of sharp edges, ⅛- and ¼-in. roundover bits provide smooth relief without making project edges look overly "soft" and under-detailed. Coves in ¼-, ⅜- and ½-in. sizes will likely fill your need for this shape.

Some straight bits are better suited for creating clean-bottomed cuts than others. The middle bit in this photo has an end cutter to shear away the waste that other conventional straight bits (left) can leave behind. Spiral bits (right) are milled to cut all across the end of the bit, leaving a flat-bottomed cut.

- **Bullnose bits.** Bullnose bits form half-round, convex profiles. Two passes with a bullnose bit can even form custom doweling in any wood species you need. For rounding over the edges of ¾-in. stock in one pass, you'll need a ⅜-in.-radius bullnose bit, but smaller radii bits are also useful for making ¼-, ⅜- and ½-in.-dia. dowels. However, you can also achieve the same bullnose shape with a ⅜-in.-radius roundover bit in two passes.

Roundover bits, one of more common styles for general woodworking, come in a range of cutting diameters from ¹⁄₁₆ to 1½ in. Most have pilot bearings, so the bits can be used for handheld as well as router table use.

Other Common Profiling And Detailing Bits

Among the multitudes of other profiling and detailing bits, a few useful bits to own include roman ogee and classical shapes as well as fluting and beading bits. For half-bead shapes, you may be able to convert the roundover bits you already own into beading bits by simply installing smaller pilot bearings.

Specialized Bits

Save more specialized bits for purchasing on an "as needed" basis. Glue joint, finger joint, drawer lock and lock miter styles can be valuable purchases for woodworking projects, but many of these tasks can be accomplished more economically and just as well with other joints or woodworking techniques. It's a good idea to save door-building bits for a time when you plan to build many doors at once. The bits are expensive.

We'll show the set up processes for numerous specialized bits later in this book, but it's helpful to know up front that the process of setting them up can be exacting and time-consuming. Lock miter and horizontal panel cutting bits are also more dangerous to use than other bits, because of their size and kickback potential.

Prepackaged Starter Bit Sets

Most bit suppliers offer collections of "popular" bits that are cheaper to buy as a lot than separately. Buying a starter set of bits can be a great idea if you actually use all the bits that come with your set. Bits from a reputable manufacturer will be made to the same specifications in a set as if you bought them individually, and you'll save money while also getting a storage case. But if half of them never leave the case, you haven't saved much money over buying just the bits you really need. You'd never buy a rack full of "popular" music CDs without reviewing what albums and artists are included, and the same logic applies to bits. Look over what comes with the starter set and then consider the list of bits mentioned above before you buy. If you only have need for one or two bits in the set, or if you don't really do much routing, start with a couple bits instead of a set.

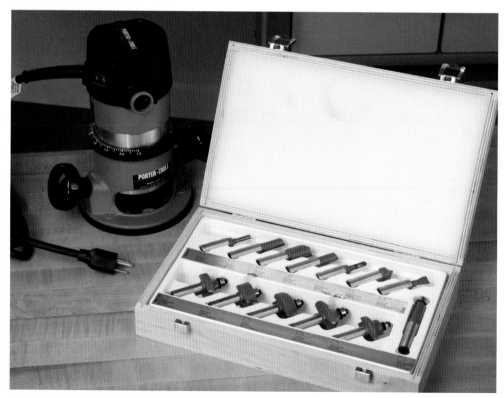

Prepackaged router bits can be a good buy if you actually use most of the bits in the case. Otherwise, it may be a better value to buy just the bits you really need and build a collection this way.

Bit Storage Options

Clean, smooth profiles and crisp, accurate joint parts are much easier to make with sharp router bits. As soon as an edge of a bit gets nicked, its cutting performance diminishes, and edge damage is particularly a problem for profile cuts that are difficult to touch up with sanding. In the case of carbide-tipped bits, which you can't realistically sharpen yourself, damaged edges require professional resharpening or even replacing the entire bit. And carbide is brittle enough that just one slip of a wrench, fall from the bench or clank against another bit can bring a quick end to a bit.

Some bits come packaged in hard-plastic, reusable cases. Hang on to these cases for permanent and convenient storage. Many bits are sold with cheap, soft-plastic packages that offer little protection. These packages won't last long, and you should store them in a more protective way. Don't store bits loosely in drawers, or they're bound to get nicked when you open and close them in search of a bit.

One easy option is to keep your bits mounted on a piece of scrap lumber or plywood with shallow holes drilled in it to hold the shanks. Space the holes far enough apart so the cutters don't make contact with one another when you're replacing or pulling bits out. For large bits, space the holes 2 in. apart. Smaller bits and most 1/4-in.-shank bits can be spaced 1 to 1 1/4 in. apart. Keep your bit board protected in a drawer or on a shelf away from other hard objects. Also keep in mind that the cutting edges on bits can cause nasty cuts in skin, so store your bits out of the reach of children.

You can also buy storage boxes with foam liners and lids for transporting bits. Or, to keep bits both visible and protected, wall-mounted storage cabinets with clear doors are also available.

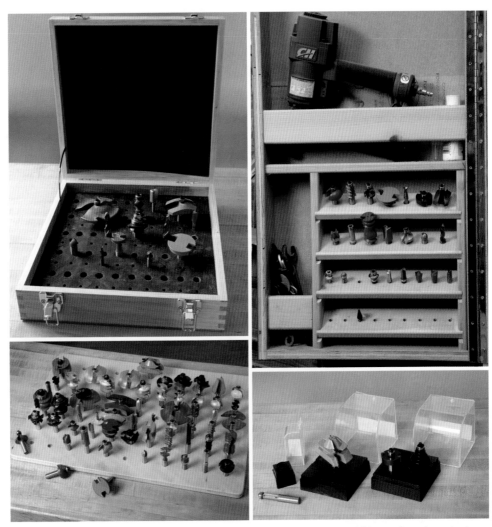

For added protection and to help preserve your investment, store router bits so the edges don't touch. Foam-lined cases, protective plastic boxes, storage trays or cabinet shelves are all good options for bit storage.

Telegraphing and burning along a routed edge are two indications of a chipped and dull or dirty bit.

If light reflects off the cutting edge of the bit, it's dull and needs to be resharpened or replaced.

Carbide holds an edge longer than steel, but it is also more brittle and prone to chipping. Carbide bits can usually be professionally resharpened, provided the damage is minimal.

Bit Cleaning And Maintenance

Sooner or later, all router bits accumulate pitch and resin with use. Accumulated crud on your bits will eventually scorch and be harder to remove. Excess pitch causes bits to overheat, and it contributes to cutting edges dulling prematurely or cutting poorly. Strong resins can actually degrade the carbide as well. To get the most from your router bits, it's a good idea to clean them from time to time. A tiny bit of build-up shouldn't impact cutting performance, but once it's really noticeable or starts to turn black, it's time for cleaning.

Woodworking suppliers sell cleaning sprays for saw blades and router bits, but you can also remove pitch and scorch marks by scrubbing with WD-40, kerosene or mineral spirits and an old toothbrush or synthetic abrasive pad. A paste of baking soda and water also works, but be sure to dry the bits thoroughly to prevent the steel shanks from rusting. Once the bits are clean, wipe them with a lightly oiled cloth.

If bits have a low-friction coating, avoid using lacquer thinner, which

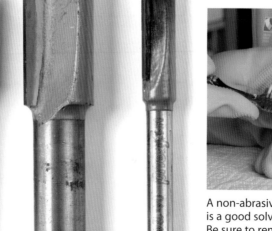

Accumulations of pitch and resin on your bits (center) will eventually lead to burned edges (right). By cleaning your bits, you can prolong the life of the carbide and keep it cutting smoothly.

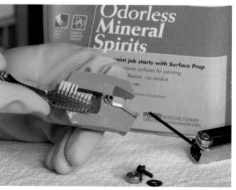

A non-abrasive cleaner, such as mineral spirits, is a good solvent for cleaning off pitch build-up. Be sure to remove the pilot bearing first, or the solvent will dissolve the bearing lubricant and ruin it.

Inspect the cutting edges and brazing on your router bits after you clean them. Use a magnifying glass to look closely for chipped edges or tiny cracks.

This bit hit an imbedded nail during routing, which severely chipped the carbide. It can't be resharpened and should be replaced.

could damage or completely remove it. Be sure to remove the pilot bearings when using any solvent cleaner to prevent the solvent from contaminating the lubricant inside the bearings.

Carbide edges not only get dull but occasionally crack as well. After you've cleaned your bits, examine them closely with a magnifying glass. Look for stress fractures along the brazing as well as the cutting edges. Be particularly concerned about bits that get dropped, rapped against a hard surface or come in contact with screws or nails during a cut. Any of these situations can crack carbide. Cracked cutters usually won't explode into tiny bits of shrapnel, but it sometimes happens. More likely, the cutter will chip off at the crack and end up imbedded in the workpiece. If you find cracks or missing portions of carbide, replace the bit. There's no way to repair the damage.

When pilot bearings seem to drag or start making noise, it's usually an indication that they're worn and need to be replaced. What you want to avoid is having a bearing seize up during use. Once it stops spinning on its own, it will accelerate to the bit speed and leave burn marks, just like

a bit with a fixed pilot. You can sometimes rejuvenate sticky bearings and extend their lives for a while by spraying them with a dry bearing lubricant. Don't use a solvent-based lubricant, or you could actually remove the rest of the original bearing lubricant and compound the problem. Even with an occasional squirt of lubricant, when bearings start to make noise or stick, they're starting to fail.

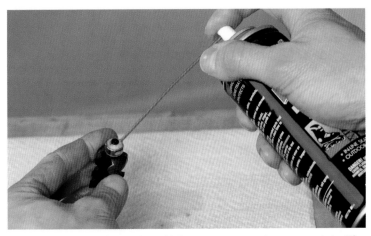

A high-grade, non-silicone based lubricant can sometimes extend the life of sticking or noisy bit bearings. But, generally, bearings that don't turn smoothly will soon need to be replaced.

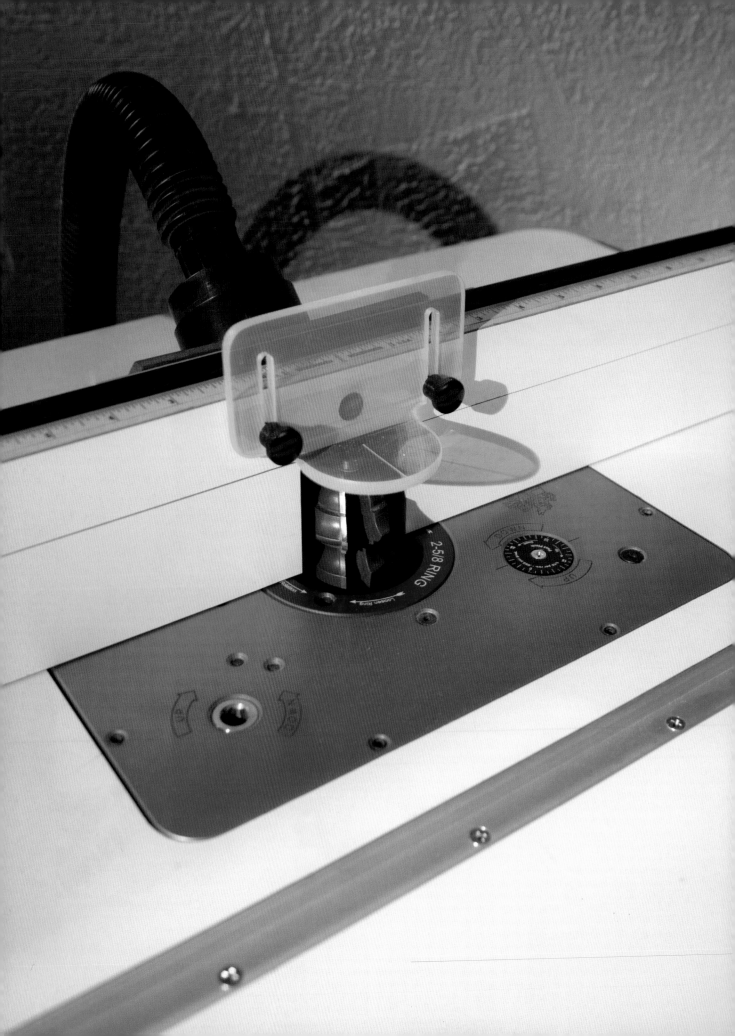

FIVE

ROUTER TABLES

There are two alternative ways to use a router: You can hold it and move it over the workpiece or flip it upside down and mount it underneath a table. Both methods of routing have their advantages in different situations. Handheld routing allows you to rout large or assembled workpieces that would be difficult or unfeasible to move over a table. Router tables, on the other hand, generally improve control and precision. With a router table, your hands are free to move the workpiece over the tool instead of the other way around, and the router stays locked in place. In effect, a router table turns a portable tool into a stationary machine.

This chapter will introduce you to the router table and show you the variety of router table styles and components available to you. There are dozens of different router tables to pick from, and manufacturers build router tables in a wide range of prices. While this chapter won't show all the router tables made, you can read about the latest trends in router tables in woodworking magazines. Router tables, like all woodworking tools, get reviewed regularly.

Another viable option is to build a router table instead of buying it. You can save money this way and make a custom table to suit your specific needs and space constraints. The final chapter of this book offers a plan for building a sturdy, basic router table. To learn more about how to use a router table, refer to chapters seven and eight.

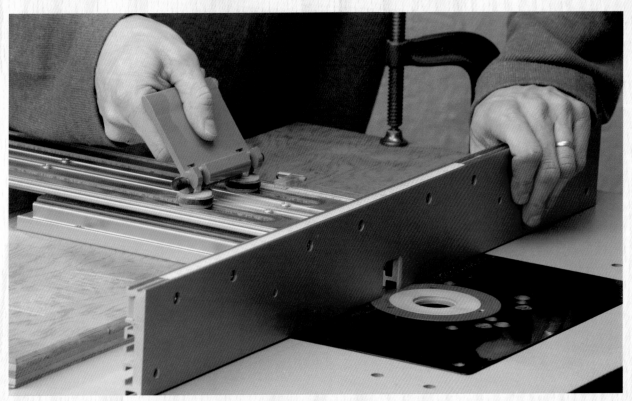

A router table effectively turns a portable tool into a stationary machine. It's a fairly expensive investment but one you'll never regret.

Why Use A Router Table?

There are five advantages to inverting a router under a table. First, a router table improves control when routing small workpieces.

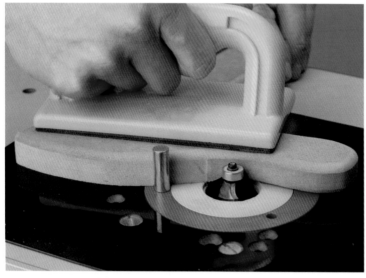

With a router table, gravity is on your side. Small workpieces are easier to rout, and the router can't accidentally tip off the wood.

With the router hanging below a table, gravity no longer works against you when you're trying to balance the tool and guide it around something small. A router table allows you to feed workpieces into the bit without any balancing required. Provided you keep your hands a safe distance from the bit, you can rout even tiny workpieces safely this way. Router tables also make it easier to rout curve-edged workpieces, especially when the workpieces are narrow.

Second, with a router table, you don't have to use an attached edge guide or run the router against a straightedge to ensure a straight cut; just mount a fence on the table to take the place of these accessories.

A third advantage to router tables is they increase the range of bits you can use for routing. It isn't safe to hold a router and use large panel raisers or other heavy shaping and joinery bits. The rotational forces developed by these bits as they spin would be difficult or impossible to

A router table fence provides a flat, adjustable straightedge for supporting workpieces from behind and through the cut.

Router tables convert a portable tool into a stationary machine. Immobilizing the router makes it possible to use larger bits that would be unsafe for handheld routing.

control by hand. A router table immobilizes the router and provides a solid platform for even the heaviest, most aggressive bits. The router can't twist out of your hands. In fact, with a full-size router in your table, a router table almost becomes a stationary shaper machine.

Router tables also expand your joint-making possibilities. Some joints like dovetails are made by holding the router and moving it along a template, but many other joints are easier to make with the router fixed in place. A router table fence enables you to register joint cuts precisely, which is critical for a proper fit. Since you don't have to balance the router over the wood, you can be sure that each cut will be square and consistent.

Finally, a router table can convert a router into a makeshift jointer as well as a cutting, shaping and joinery tool. Whatever level of woodworking you're at, doing precision work requires that boards and panels start with flat edges. If you don't own a dedicated jointer to do this work, a router table and fence makes a good substitute. You'll still need a jointer and planer for flattening board faces, but a router table makes it easy to flatten the edges.

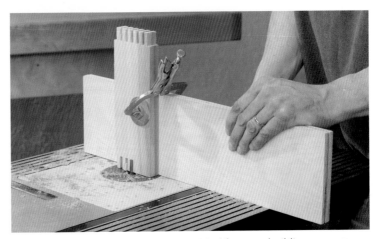

Router tables improve precision — a critical factor to building accurate, tight-fitting joinery.

If you don't own a dedicated jointer, a router table and fence can perform edge-flattening tasks easily. All you need is a straight bit.

Cabinet-style router table

Router Table Styles

Strip away all the bells and whistles, and a router table is really just a flat surface with a fence. However, manufacturers have taken this basic concept in a variety of different directions over the years to make router tables highly versatile and convenient fixtures.

Router tables are manufactured in two basic styles: floor-standing or benchtop. Those that stand on the floor will usually give you a larger worksurface, which is beneficial for routing large panels or long workpieces. The overall size of a floor-standing router table also creates a more stable platform that's less likely to move when you push against it. But, a full-size router table takes up about the same floor space as a stationary tool, and this may be inconvenient or unfeasible if you have a small basement or garage shop. A

benchtop table, on the other hand, is small enough to tuck under a workbench, set on a deep shelf or even stow in the back seat of a car if you need to take it to jobs away from the shop.

Whether it's a benchtop or full-size model, router tables are surprisingly expensive tools. Tables cost as much or more than a premium router, and a few approach the cost of a stationary table saw or shaper. Prices range from around $100 upwards to $600, depending on the model and features. The upside to buying a router table is that most are well made, sturdy and easy to use. Styles don't change dramatically over time, so one router table may be all you'll ever need to buy. Even if you change routers over time, you should be able to buy replacement insert plates that adapt your router table to suit many different routers.

Full-size router tables come in several configurations. Some have cabinets with doors and shelves under the table. The cabinet may serve as a compartment for the router, which can help reduce noise and contain dust. Or, the cabinet may provide a separate closed space beneath the router area for storing other accessories.

Other styles of floor-standing router tables have folding legs — an advantage for storing and transport — or rigid leg frameworks without extra compartments or shelving. While

Collapsible router table with folding legset

BARE-BONES ROUTER TABLE

Provided the tabletop is flat, a router table really doesn't depend on the base. If you have a lightweight router, one option is to simply mount it to a flat piece of plywood or other sheet material to form a table with a bit of bracing underneath for added stiffness. Clamp the tabletop to your workbench, to serve as a base. A flat piece of lumber or a few scraps of plywood clamped next to the bit can make a simple fence. You won't have the full range of uses with a router table like this, but it's quite functional nevertheless, and it can be a good solution for bringing a router table to jobsite situations. Best of all, you can make it from scraps at little or no cost.

In its simplest form, all a router table really needs to be is a flat surface for mounting the router underneath and a straight adjustable fence.

Router table with metal legset.

these stripped-down versions have some advantages, they aren't significantly less expensive than cabinet-style tables. If you intend to keep your router table in the shop permanently, you may appreciate the added storage space of a cabinet-style router table.

Benchtop router tables conserve precious floorspace, but the tradeoff is a smaller table and sometimes lighter-duty plastic construction. Buying a benchtop router table won't necessarily mean you'll sacrifice some of the helpful features designed into larger router tables, such as split fences, dust collection and miter slots. In fact, some of the premium benchtop router tables these days

will match a floor-standing router table feature for feature. Some models are designed for jobsite use by cabinet installers and contractors who rely on portability as well as rugged construction.

Another option is to convert one of the extension wings of your table saw into a router table. Some table saws have extension wings already set up for router table use with a hole in the middle and even bit reducer rings and a miter slot. All you need to do is mount the router to the extension wing. Or, you can replace the extension wing with a piece of flat sheet material like MDF, rout a recess for a router insert plate and create your own router table this way. Besides the space-saving advantage of having two machines in one, you can use the saw's rip fence as the router table fence.

Benchtop router table.

Instead of having a separate router table, you may be able to replace one extension wing of your table saw with a router table and have two tools in one.

Anatomy Of A Router Table

Whether you buy or build your router table or use a floor-standing or benchtop size, the parts of a router table are basically the same:

Table

The table component of a router table will vary in size from one manufacturer to another. Usually the tabletop will be at least 20 in. or more in length and 16 in. or more in depth. Unless you need a router table to be portable, a large table is better than a small one. The more bearing surface you have to work with, the easier it is to control the cuts. Large tables also make it easier to work with long boards or large panels. Tables vary in composition and thickness as well as dimension, as you'll see on pages 122 to 123. Here again, thicker is better. A thick table dampens vibration from the router that leads to smoother cuts. Thickness also contributes to stiffness. For a router table to register accurate and consistent cuts, the table needs to be dead flat — or nearly so — in all dimensions.

To help minimize friction, it helps to have a slippery surface on a tabletop. Most manufactured router tables will have a plastic laminate surface, like a countertop. A non-stick surface also helps keep wood resins from gumming up the table and making sliding more difficult.

Miter Slot

Router tables typically have a miter slot that's oriented parallel to the front edge of the table. Unless the table is made of metal, with the miter slot molded right into the casting, the miter slot will be made of a slotted aluminum extrusion and fastened to the table with screws. The slot usually fits the usual $3/8$ x $3/4$-in. bars of table saw miter gauges, so the same miter gauge can be used with both tools. A miter slot isn't an essential router table feature. Many operations don't require it, or you can use a backup board with a square edge instead of a miter gauge.

Insert Plate

Most router tables have a plate for mounting the router in the table. In this book, we'll call it an insert plate. The insert plate is generally rectangular in shape and made of a variety of materials. The purpose of the insert plate is to make the router easier to remove for making bit changes. You can even leave the plate attached to the router for certain freehand operations, because it acts like an oversize subbase.

To make the insert plate more versatile, most styles have removable rings that fit around the bit. The plate usually comes with two to four rings with varying hole sizes so you can use a range of bit diameters without creating gaping holes around the bit.

The insert plate fits into a shallow recess in the table to make the plate flush with the surrounding table. The weight of the router and the tight fit of the plate in the table are sufficient to hold the plate in place. It isn't necessary to attach the plate to the table, and the drop-in style makes it more convenient to remove the router when necessary.

Fence

Some router table operations can be done be feeding workpieces directly into the bit without other support on the table, but usually you'll use a fence to limit the cutting depth and help register the cut. Router table fences clamp or bolt to

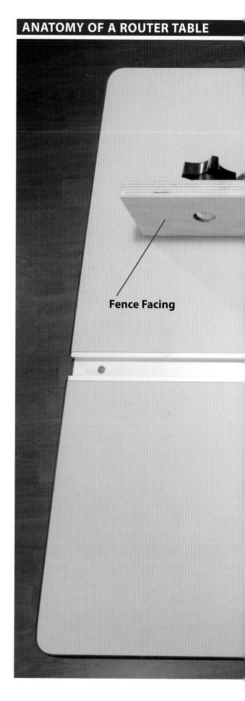

Fence Facing

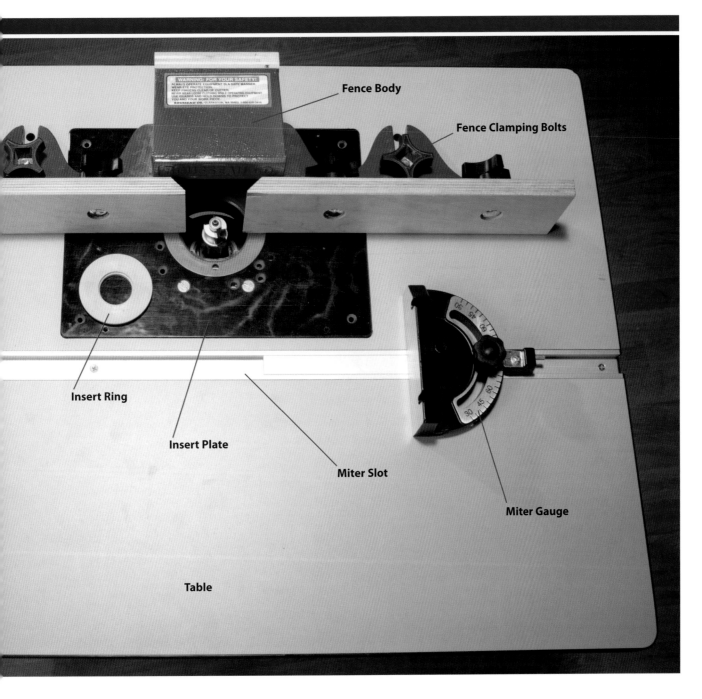

Fence Body

Fence Clamping Bolts

Insert Ring

Insert Plate

Miter Slot

Miter Gauge

Table

the table and can be adjusted forward or backward, just like a table saw rip fence. Generally, a fence will have a pair of adjustable faces that can be moved to fit around bits of any diameter. Closing the fence faces in around the bit helps to reduce tearout on workpieces. A tight bit opening in the fence also reduces the chances of the bit grabbing the workpiece and kicking it away. But the primary duty of the fence is to

index the workpiece precisely in relation to the bit. With a fence on your router table, you can set cuts an exact distance from the edges or ends of a workpiece or make stopped cuts safely. A fence can also serve as a pilot bearing for bits that don't have bearings. In fact, with the exception of straight bits and a few others, most unpiloted router bits are best used on a router table in tandem with a fence.

Tabletop Options

A router table top must be flat to produce accurate cuts, and the worksurface should be as smooth as possible to minimize friction between the table and the wood. To satisfy these requirements, manufacturers make router tabletops from a variety of materials. A thick piece of industrial-grade, medium-density fiberboard (MDF) makes a dense, flat surface, and it's a common substrate for router tables. The surface will be covered plastic laminate to seal the MDF from moisture and make the top slippery smooth. Usually the edges will be covered with plastic or rubbery molding to prevent chipping and further seal the MDF — it will swell when it gets wet.

For a low-cost tabletop, 3/4-in.-thick MDF can make a decent router table surface. The material is dense and flat, and its surface is hard enough to wear well and resist scuffing. It's a good idea to protect the surface with a penetrating oil finish or varnish to seal it from water and cover the edges with strips of solid wood.

Plywood can also make a good router tabletop if it's flat and covered with plastic laminate. It isn't the usual choice for manufactured tables, but it offers better resistance to swelling than MDF. Baltic birch plywood makes the best plywood tabletop, because it has almost double the inner plys of other common cabinet plywoods, and there are no voids between the plys. It's generally flatter than lower-quality plywoods but not as flat as MDF.

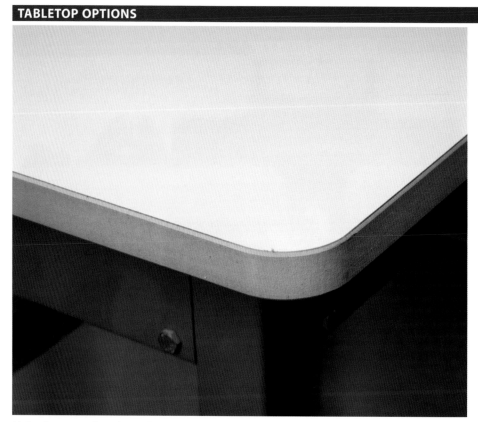

Melamine-coated medium-density fiberboard tabletop.

Another relatively new option for tabletops is an extremely dense resin called phenolic. Phenolic is impervious to water and has sufficient stiffness to stay flat even when it's thin. Phenolic tabletops will be thinner than MDF tables and usually have exposed edges that show the black resin. You'll pay more for a phenolic top than you will for MDF, but it's a good investment over time, considering it's virtually indestructible.

Metal is another option for router tabletops. Benchtop router tables usually have die-cast aluminum tables, often with a ribbed pattern molded into the surface. The ridges help to cut down on friction by reducing the overall surface area without compromising a stable bearing surface. You can also buy router tabletops made of flat sheet steel. Steel is a fine choice, but it's heavier than aluminum, and the bare metal needs to be protected from corrosion.

Bare medium-density fiberboard tabletop.

Built-up plywood tabletop covered with plastic laminate.

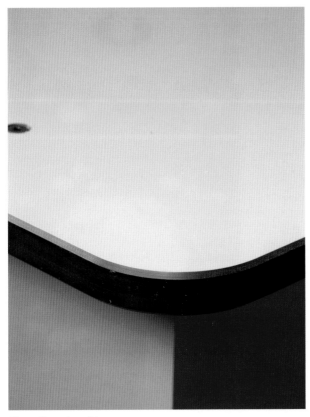

Phenolic resin tabletop.

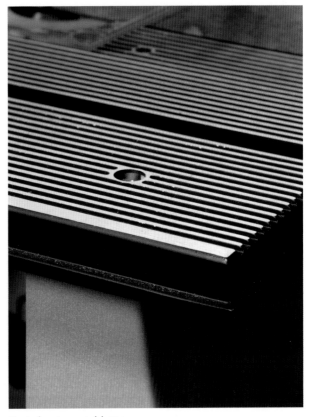

Cast aluminum tabletop.

Router table insert plates are made from a variety of materials including phenolic, glass-reinforced plastic, aluminum and acrylic. All are good options, provided the plate stays flat with a router hung beneath.

Insert Plate Styles

Router table insert plates are made from various materials. You can buy insert plates made of clear polycarbonate plastic, phenolic and aluminum. Any of these options will work, provided the plate stays flat with a router hung beneath it. The surface also needs to be smooth to keep pitch from accumulating on it and to help the wood glide easily across.

Thickness is an issue with insert plates. If you buy an acrylic or phe-nolic plate, the material should be at least 3/8 in. thick to offer adequate stiffness for larger routers. Metal is stronger than plastic, so aluminum or steel insert plates can be thinner without compromising flatness. Aluminum plates are sold in either 1/4- or 3/8-in. thicknesses. Either thickness will stay flat for even the largest routers.

Most insert plates will have one or more detachable reducer rings around the bit hole. Insert plates with rings are more versatile for a router table than plates without them. The purpose of the rings is to enable you to change the bit-opening diameter to suit bits of various sizes. The smaller the hole, the better — you reduce the chances of the workpiece dipping down into the bit hole and getting caught on the rim.

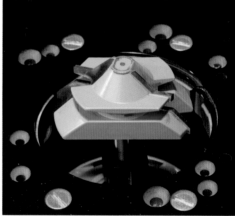

Router table insert plates are usually equipped with removable rings that fit around the bit. The rings allow you to use the same plate with both large and small bits and keep the bit opening as small as possible.

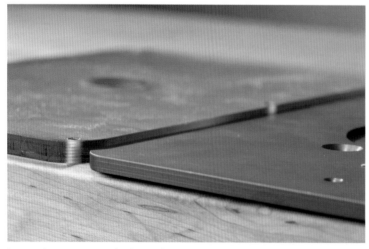

Insert plates range in thickness from 1/4 to 3/8 in. If you use a heavy router, buy a thick insert plate; it will tend to stay flatter than a thin plate.

Usually, the bit-opening rings snap into the insert plate, but some styles twist in with a wrench or fasten down with tiny screws.

The reducer rings are generally made of a stiff plastic or aluminum so they won't damage a bit if they should come in contact with it during use. Some simply sit in a recess or snap into place on the plate, or they may attach with tiny screws or twist and lock into threads around the bit hole.

Another important feature to look for on an insert plate is a starter pin for working without a fence. Starter pins are made of metal and fit into holes close to the reducer rings or sometimes drilled right into them. The purpose of a starter pin is to provide another support surface besides the bit bearing for guiding curved

workpieces during routing (see page 178). In these situations, you'll have the fence removed and nothing but the bit bearing to index the cut. Without a starter pin to hold the workpiece against, a bit may grab the workpiece when you feed it into the cutter and pull it out of your hands. Many insert plates come with a starter pin. If yours doesn't, drill a hole in the plate and fashion a starter pin from a short length of smooth metal rod. Or buy a pin instead — it's a helpful safety feature to have.

Most router tables will have some provision for leveling the insert plates with the tabletop. The usual options

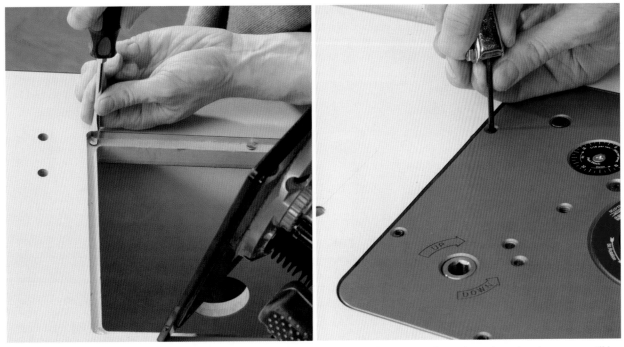

Most router tables will have provisions for leveling the insert plate in the table opening. Sometimes these leveler screws will be fitted around the recess for the plate, but they're also commonly threaded right into the plate.

are screws threaded around the insert plate recess in the table, or the plate may have leveler screws threaded into it. If your router table has metal leveler screws in the insert plate recess, consider buying a plastic insert plate instead of a metal one. What tends to happen with metal screws on a metal plate is that the plate vibrates during use, and the sound can be earsplitting. Metal-on-plastic helps muffle or eliminate the vibration noise.

Depending on the router you have, be sure to check the size of the insert plate you plan to use against the overall width of your router. Insert plates come in numerous sizes, and some are too small to fit a big router through the hole in the router tabletop. You may have to remove the

router's handles so it fits down through the insert plate opening when it's hung from the plate. If the handles don't come off, you'll have to mount the router at an angle on the plate to sneak the handles through or buy a larger router plate or smaller router.

The rounded corners of insert plates also vary in diameter from one manufacturer to another. If you switch from one manufacturer's plate to another style, be sure the new plate will match the old one in size and shape for your router table. Otherwise, you may have to enlarge the insert plate hole or change its shape to fit the new plate. Some manufacturers sell a template for this purpose so you can rout the correct shape for the plate in your table (see page 262).

When you buy a new insert plate, it may or may not come predrilled to fit the mounting holes in your router's base. Some plates are only sold as blanks so they can be fitted to any router, or the manufacturer may offer plates that are predrilled for certain popular router models. If you can buy the plate predrilled, it's a handy convenience for little or even no extra cost. But when your only option is to drill the holes yourself, it's not a difficult job if you use a simple plate marking sold by Eagle America (800-872-2511, www.eagle-america.com). See the sidebar on the next page for more information on how to mark and drill the mounting holes.

Aside from differences in thickness, insert plates also vary widely in overall proportions and corner curvature. Unless you are building a router table from scratch, be sure the plate you buy fits your router table's plate opening.

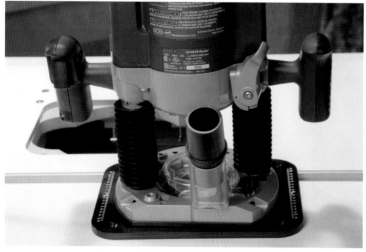

An insert plate needs to be at least as large as the span of your router's handles, especially if the router's motor pack can't be removed. In the case of this undersized plate, the router won't fit through the table opening.

Some router table insert plates are predrilled for installing various popular router models. Just locate the screw holes that match your router's base screws.

MOUNTING A ROUTER TO AN INSERT PLATE

Mounting a router to an insert plate is more than just a process of drilling the screw holes. In order for the bit reducer rings to fit evenly around various-sized bits, the router needs to be centered carefully on the plate. Using a mounting kit makes the process easier than attempting to center the router by measuring or by trial and error. The kit consists of a rod that fits in the router collet and a disk that slips over it to center it in the insert plate's smallest bit opening. A set of tiny marking screws with pointed tips thread into the base holes on the router. With the screws threaded into the router base so the pointed tips face up, set the insert plate over the rod and through the disk, align the plate and router, and tap the plate against the screws lightly with a hammer. The screw tips mark the centerpoints for drilling mounting screw holes. Remove the plate and drill countersunk holes where marked. The kit will also come with longer mounting screws for your router to accommodate thick insert plates.

1 Remove the router's subbase. It's unnecessary for installation.

2 The insert plate installation kit comes with sharpened screws that fit into the router's subbase and a centering rod for the collet. Install these on the router.

3 Snap the kit's centering disk into the insert plate's bit opening, and fit the plate over the rod to center the router on the plate.

4 Tap the plate gently so the sharpened screws mark it for drilling holes for attachment screws.

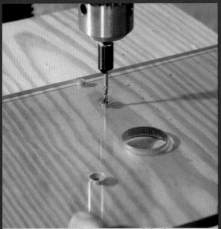

5 Carefully drill countersunk holes through the plate at the marks left by the sharpened screws.

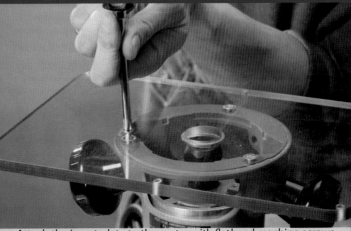

6 Attach the insert plate to the router with flathead machine screws. The screwheads must be flush with the surface of the plate. If they aren't, drill deeper holes.

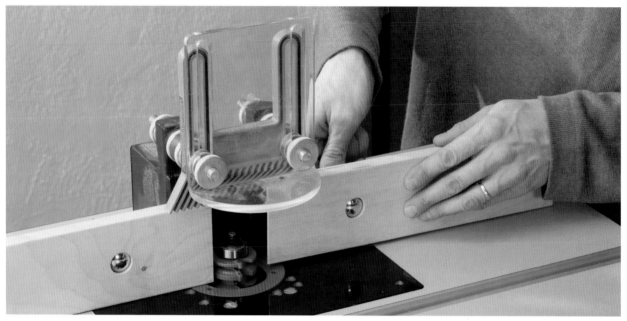

A router table fence with a split face allows you to adjust the facings close to the bit to help minimize tearout and keep workpieces from drifting into the bit opening.

Fence Options

There are two typical styles of router table fences: those with a solid, one-piece face and others with split facings on either side of the bit opening. The advantage to the split-face variety, you'll recall, is that each side of the fence can be adjusted laterally to "close up" around bits of different sizes. The fence faces can be locked in place with bolts and various styles of hand-adjusted nuts.

Some split fences have faces that also move forward and backward independently of each other, which is a convenience for using the router table as a jointer (see page 184). However, most fences have a solid body that holds the faces flush with one another — the way you'll want to keep them for the majority of router table work. Fence bodies are commonly made of aluminum extrusions, steel or an iron casting to ensure stiffness.

Fences attach to router tables in numerous ways. Some are held in place with bolts bored through the table. Elongated slots on the fence body allow you to move the fence back and forth without moving the bolts, although the range of motion is limited. Other router table styles have slotted holes in the tabletop

Router table fences usually mount to the table with a pair of through bolts and knobs, but some styles have integral clamps or require a separate pair of clamps. Regardless, the clamps should be easy to adjust and keep the fence from shifting.

A fence with a built-in dust port helps draw dust away right at the source. This fence port connects to a standard 2½-in. shop vacuum nozzle.

This fence has a wood backer plate that can be drilled to fit any size vacuum hose for dust collection.

instead of the fence to accommodate fence adjustment. Or, the fence may have clamps on the ends that wrap around the edges of the table and lock down, which eliminates the need for extra holes in the tabletop. This style of clamping gives the fence a much greater range of adjustment on the table than the through-bolt style.

Aside from the basic configuration of body, facings and clamping style, today's newer router fences are loaded with features that can be helpful to have. Most will have a dust port behind the bit area that fits a 2½-in.-diameter shop vacuum nozzle. Or, there may be a blank plate that you can drill to fit whatever diameter of shop vacuum hose you have. The dust port won't be able to draw away all the dust and accumulated wood chips during routing, but it will dramatically cut down on the amount of debris that would otherwise end up on the table, inside the router table cabinet or in the air.

Another helpful fence feature is some form of bit guard. Most styles look like a half-round piece of bent plastic that bolts directly above the bit opening. This "halo" style of bit guard offers some protection from bit contact, but basically only from above the bit and not from the side. Other guards are larger shrouds of plastic

that offer both top and side protection, similar to conventional table saw blade guards. These have hinged mounts on the fence so they can raise and lower as workpieces are fed into the bit. Bit guards obviously make sense from a safety standpoint, but they can impede some router table operations or get in the way of featherboards and pushsticks.

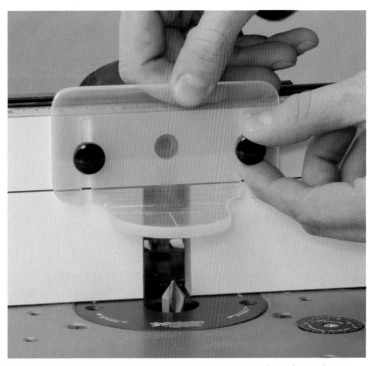

Some fence designs have a built-in bit guard that can be adjusted up or down to suit different bit heights. It's a helpful safety provision that's also easy to remove when necessary.

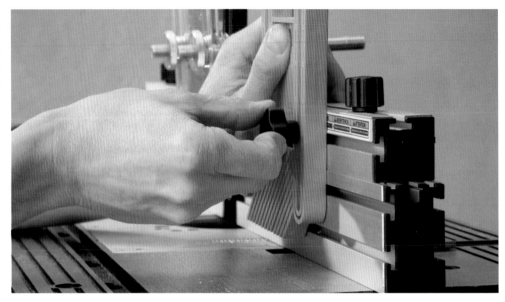

Fences with T-tracks make it easy to install featherboards, guards or other jigs without the need for separate clamps.

Fences with aluminum facings will usually have T-track slots molded into the facings for attaching featherboards or guards. Standard T-bolts generally fit these slots, so you can make and attach your own guards, jigs or a tall fence extension.

A few router table fences have micro-adjustment provisions for each of the fence facings. Micro-adjustment is primarily an advantage for setting up the fence as a jointer. You can dial the fences in or out a precise distance relative to the bit or to each other. The fine adjustment feature seems alluring, but in most cases you'll use your router fence with the faces flush with one another. So, micro-adjusters have fairly limited use. Provided you have a split fence, it's easy to slip a homemade shim behind the facing for accomplishing the same "micro" fence adjustment.

A few fence styles make it easier to create "zero-clearance" inserts around the bit. Basically, what this means is that you can all but eliminate the spacing around a bit to reduce tearout. Fences will come with blank inserts that install between the fence facings, and you'll use the bit to cut through the insert to make a mirror image insert.

Some router table operations, especially joint-building, require precise bit and fence settings. This fence has micro-adjust controls that move the fence facings in thousandths of an inch increments.

This fence has replaceable plastic inserts that can be cut to fit around different bit shapes. The inserts reduce the bit opening, which helps minimize tearout.

Other Useful Router Table Features

If you purchase your router table, different models will have an array of features that might be beneficial for you. Here are some of the more useful features:

On/Off Switch For The Router

One of the hassles of using a router table is having to feel around under the table for the router's power switch. After awhile, you'll get used to groping for it, but router tables that have a forward-mounted power switch put an end to the search for good. In most cases, the switch will be larger than the router's switch, and it usually will be a safety-style control with a removable lock-off key. Or, it may be designed as an oversized kill switch: pulling it turns the router on and bumping it shuts the router off. The switch will have a pair of power cords — one that the router's cord plugs into and another that plugs into the wall.

Some router tables are equipped with above-the-table router height controls. This feature makes it easier to adjust bit settings or change bits without removing the motor pack or insert plate.

On/Off switches are handy features on a router table. It's much easier to control the power this way as opposed to reaching underneath for the power switch.

Above-The-Table Bit Changing

Changing bits on a router table can be a chore if the process involves removing the motor pack or pulling out the insert plate and router each time. Some new routers have collets that extend all the way through the base when the tool is at full depth. This new design feature is intended to make it possible to change bits on a router table without removing the motor pack. Router tables that accept these routers will have a wrench that passes through the tabletop and connects with a fitting on the router. Turning the wrench from above the table raises and lowers the collet so you can change bits with the router in place. The height adjuster also allows for fine-tuning bit height easily — another good convenience.

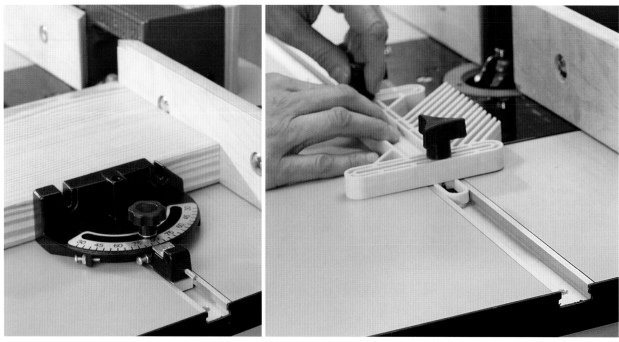

Not all router tables are fitted with miter slots, but they're useful features to have. The slot doubles as a track for the miter gauge as well as an attachment point for clamp-on featherboards.

If your shop is small, you'll appreciate having your router table mounted on wheels. Roll it into position when it's needed and out of the way when it's not. Just be sure the wheels can be locked during use.

Miter Slot

Most manufactured router tables will have a miter slot for accepting a miter gauge or for mounting featherboards. Miter gauges make it easy to rout across the grain on narrow workpieces. You'll also appreciate the slot for installing featherboards quickly and securely. There are ways to change setups or techniques if your router table doesn't have a miter slot, but the slot is definitely a helpful feature.

Wheels

If you work in a small shop or in a garage that still serves as a parking space, you may have to move your machinery in and out of position regularly. A router table that rolls can be a huge help, especially if you buy one of the larger or particularly heavy models. The wheels should swivel all around to make the table easy to position, and there should be a brake on at least two of the four casters to lock the table in place.

Enclosed Compartment For The Router

Routers are noisy tools, and any way to help reduce the noise is a benefit. Router tables with enclosed cabinets provide a means of isolating the router and muffling the noise. Enclosing a router also helps reduce some of the airborne dust. One drawback to an enclosed compartment is that you have to open and close the doors to turn the router on and off or to make bit height adjustments. It's also important to leave at least a few small openings to ensure that the router gets a fresh supply of air to keep it cool. If the compartment is sealed too tightly, the router can actually overheat and be damaged.

Enclosing a router inside a cabinet helps reduce both dust and noise, but it's important that the router has some fresh airflow to keep it from overheating.

ON-BOARD BIT STORAGE

If you use your router table regularly, some form of convenient bit storage can be beneficial, especially for larger bits like panel raisers that only get used on the router table. Most router table styles don't provide bit storage, but you may be able to retrofit your table with a tray or a drawer with dividers to store your bits. Here, several simple trays with bit shank holes slide in and out between the legs of this router table. Bits are easy to access and store safely underneath, close to where they'll be used.

Retrofitting a router table with slide-out trays is a good way to keep bits close at hand and neatly stored.

A router tabletop needs to be flat along its length, width and diagonals. Check for flatness in each of these directions with a long, reliable metal straightedge.

Readying A Router Table For Use

The two most important reference surfaces on a router table are the tabletop and the fence. It's important that the tabletop is flat and the insert plate is flush with the table. If you're setting up a new router table, check for table flatness with a long metal straightedge. Lay the straightedge lengthwise along the front and back edges as well as along the middle to check for crowning or bowing along the table surface. Then check the table for flatness widthwise and across both diagonals. Typically, a tabletop will be flat around the perimeter because it's supported by framework underneath. Sagging happens in the unsupported center of the table, especially if your router table has a large hole for the insert plate or if you're using a heavy router. If the framework is twisted, this can also introduce a twist across the tabletop that should be remedied.

The easiest way to flatten the table is to insert shims underneath where the table meets the framework. Slips of doubled-up cardboard, thin plastic or soda can aluminum make good shims. Slip a shim into low areas to help level them with higher areas, and recheck your modifications with a straightedge.

One way to correct for an out-of-flat tabletop is to insert shims underneath to raise up the low areas.

For severely sagging tables (more than about 1/16 in.), you may need to remove the tabletop and fasten crossbraces to it or to the surrounding framing. It's a hassle to have to do this, but it's worth the effort. Adding more support ensures that workpieces will meet bits squarely and accurately. You'll need this level of precision to rout joinery that fits together properly.

When the overall table is flat, it's also important that the router insert plate is flush with the table. If the insert plate is raised above the table, workpieces will catch on it as you feed them into the bit. In the same way, a sunken plate is also a problem: workpieces catch on the rim of the insert plate hole, usually in the middle of a pass.

Level your insert plate carefully using whatever provisions are designed into the router table or the insert plate. Some plates will have leveler screws threaded around the edges, or there may be leveler screws around the lip of the insert plate hole. Use a straightedge held across the table and plate to check your progress.

Flattening the tabletop is usually a corrective measure you'll only have to do once when the table is new. However, you'll probably find that you have to level the insert plate more frequently. Vibration from the router has the annoying tendency of backing the screws out of their holes, especially on metal insert plates. One way to prevent this from happening is to lock the screws in place with a drop of super glue, epoxy or automotive thread-locking compound applied at the threads.

The other critical reference surface is the router table fence. For normal routing, a fence should be flat from end to end. Check for flatness with a

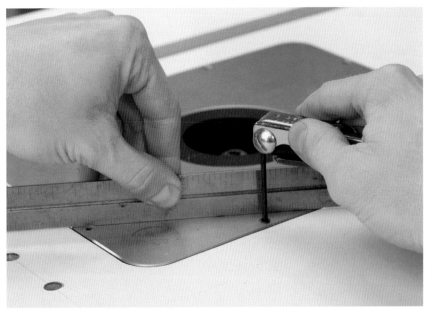

Insert plates must be adjusted level with the router tabletop to prevent workpieces from catching on the plate. Use a straightedge to inspect for flatness when adjusting the leveler screws.

Insert plate leveler screws tend to vibrate out of position. Once you've leveled the plate to your table, use a drop of thread-locking compound epoxy or super glue to set the screws permanently in place.

A router table fence must be flat along its length to work properly. Check that the facings are flush and flat with a metal straightedge.

straightedge held lengthwise along the fence. If the fence isn't flat and the fence body is made of cast material, the casting may have a defective twist. The best recourse is to return the fence to the manufacturer for an exchange. Or, you may be able to add a shim behind one of the facings to correct the defect. It's also possible that the fence may have a slight defect on the contact surfaces behind the facings. These places on the fence body should already be ground smooth by the manufacturer if the fence is made of cast iron. Check the contact surfaces closely and file off any bumps you find here.

Aside from flatness, it's also important that the fence facings meet the table surface at a right angle. Squareness is particularly critical when you're routing workpieces on-edge against the fence. Check for squareness at several points along the fence with a reliable combination or engineer's square. The best fix for an out-of-square fence, if returning it isn't an option, is to shim behind the facings. You might also be able to plane or sand the facings slightly to bring the fence into square. Shimming underneath the fence base is another alternative, but since you'll be moving and removing the fence regularly, this is an impractical location for shims.

Inspect your router table fence with a square to be sure it meets the table at 90°. If it doesn't, add shims behind the facings to bring it into square.

136

ROUTER LIFTS

In the last few years, manufacturers have developed a new option for making bit changing and height adjustments easier on router tables. The product is called a router lift, and it amounts to a specialized insert plate with a mount that raises and lowers the router. The lift replaces the router base and holds the motor pack in place. A crank handle fits into a height adjuster on top of the plate so you can raise or lower the router without reaching under the table. Lift mechanisms vary among manufacturers, but the system shown here is fairly typical. A large clamp holds the motor pack, and it moves along two large posts. A system of sprockets and a chain control the clamp movement along the posts.

Router lifts add precision and convenience to a router table, but they're expensive. Expect to pay $150 to $300 for a router lift. If you end up using your router table heavily, a router lift is probably worth the long-term investment. However, you can get the same convenience by buying a router with through-the-table height adjustment for less money.

A router lift has a built-in clamp and undercarriage for holding a router motor pack. This one uses sprockets and a chain drive to raise and lower the motor.

One advantage to a router lift is that it can raise the motor higher than is typically possible with a standard router base. The extra "reach" makes the collet accessible from above for easier bit changing.

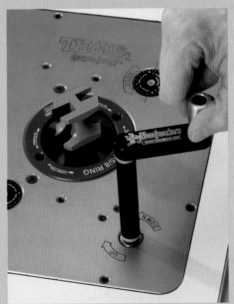

A crank that fits in the lift's plate raises and lowers the router precisely. No more stooping over to do this from under the table.

SIX

HANDHELD ROUTER TECHNIQUES

Despite the current popularity of router tables, routers are still extremely versatile tools when operated by the handles. Mounting your router under a table certainly expands the range of techniques you can perform with it, but a router table isn't a mandatory accessory. In fact, you may never need a router table to accomplish the sorts of woodworking tasks you need to do.

In this chapter, you'll learn five different handheld routing techniques: Profiling with piloted bits; using your router with an edge guide; straightedge routing; cutting circles with a jig; and flush-trimming. Four of the five techniques will require you to limit the router's cutting path in some fashion. This can be accomplished by using piloted router bits, a straightedge of one kind or another, or a jig. Because of a router's rotational cutting action, it's almost always necessary to guide the router against something fixed in place. Without a bearing or a guide of some sort to direct the router, you'll have a difficult time maintaining control of the tool and cutting accurately. The bit will drift off course and cut where you don't want

Shaping the edges of workpieces by guiding a router freehand is probably the most common router operation for woodworking.

With an edge guide attached, a router can cut both along the edges and in from the edges in a controlled fashion.

A clamped piece of scrap forms a useful straightedge and turns a router into an accurate dadoing or rabbeting machine.

Mounting your router to a pivoting fixture allows it to cut perfect circles of any size.

it to or even bite off too much at once and possibly jerk iitself out of your grip.

If you're shaping the edges of a workpiece (profiling), generally you'll use a bearing-guided bit. The pilot bearing limits the router to cutting along the edge. Edge guides provide a short fence that serves as the reference surface instead of a pilot bearing. With an edge guide, you can rout straight lines within the interior of a workpiece or make profiled edges without piloted bits. A straightedge also allows for interior, straight-line routing, but you'll use the router's subbase as the reference edge. Circle-cutting is also a restrictive cutting operation: the router is mounted to a jig and turns around a fixed center point like a drafting compass. Even flush-trimming generally involves a bearing-guided bit to keep the router tracking the edge properly and to avoid removing too much material.

Routers can also be used in hand with templates and guide collars that restrict the cutting path of the bit even more. Templates can be used to duplicate shapes or to create cutouts and mortises for hinges or joinery. Read about template routing and joint-building in the next two chapters.

Safe Bits For Handheld Routing

When you use a router in hand, your arms and upper body serve as the force that resists the rotational energy created by the router. The larger the bit, the more rotational energy it creates. When a router is fixed in a router table, this rotational energy is cancelled by the mass of the table instead of by your body, so you can use even huge panel-raising bits with reasonable safety. Not so with handheld routing. Large bits are unsafe to use in freehand situations. If you try to mill a profile with a panel-raising bit or another large cutter in a handheld router, you're tempting fate: a loss of tool control or a damaged workpiece is almost certain.

So, what bits are safe for handheld routing? In general, any bit with a 1/4-in. shank is suitable for freehand routing. The larger panel-raising and joint-making bits aren't made in the smaller shank size, so using 1/4-in.-shank bits will steer you clear of the dangerous options automatically. However, even among the 1/4-in.-shank options, there are still some fairly big bits. Use extra caution and take only shallow cuts when using these larger sizes freehand.

Among 1/2-in.-shank bits, the options for what you can put in the collet are wide open. Just about every bit style comes in a 1/2-in. shank — including, of course, the giant router table–only bits. Here, you'll

Bits with cutting diameters smaller than about a 50-cent piece (having a cutting diameter of 1¹/2 in. or less) are safe for freehand routing.

have to decide more carefully what's safe to use freehand. A good rule of thumb to follow is to only use bits with diameters smaller than about a 50-cent piece. In other words, keep bit diameters or cutting lengths smaller than about 1¹/2 in. Common sense will probably tell you that the really big bits will look intimidating to use anyway. But, if your inner sense of caution doesn't trigger a warning, use the coin guideline to avoid the unsafe, oversized bits.

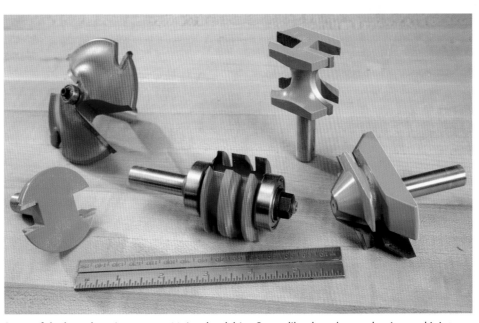

Be careful when choosing among 1/2-in.-shank bits. Some, like these heavy shaping and joint-making bits, are too large to control safely in a freehand setup.

HANDHELD PROFILING

Of all the various handheld routing techniques, you'll probably do more profiling with a router than any other operation. Basically, profiling involves molding the ends and edges of workpieces into different shapes with piloted bits. You can also shape the interior of a workpiece with decorative fluting and other detail, but edge profiling is more typical. There are several good reasons to add profiles to your projects. First, profiling breaks sharp edges and corners where they could otherwise cause injury. Tabletops, surfaces with sharp-edged laminate and furniture components like chair legs or arm leans are all good candidates for rounded edges and corners. Projects made from splinter-prone materials like oak, cedar and plywood should also have "eased" edges to help preserve the wood and make the project more skin-friendly.

A second reason to add profiles to your work is entirely aesthetic: Profiles form attractive shadow lines, create a sense of depth and turn flat, ordinary edges into surfaces that are interesting to look at and pleasant to touch. On thick parts, profiling works in a reductive way to make parts look lighter and more delicate. Adding a few judicious profiles can enhance even a basic woodworking project or give historical accuracy to a period piece. Of course, too much of a good thing can also be overkill; if every part edge is rounded over, projects tend to look overly "soft" and amateurish. Be selective about where you treat the edges. Using small profiles can also help minimize the over-rounded look.

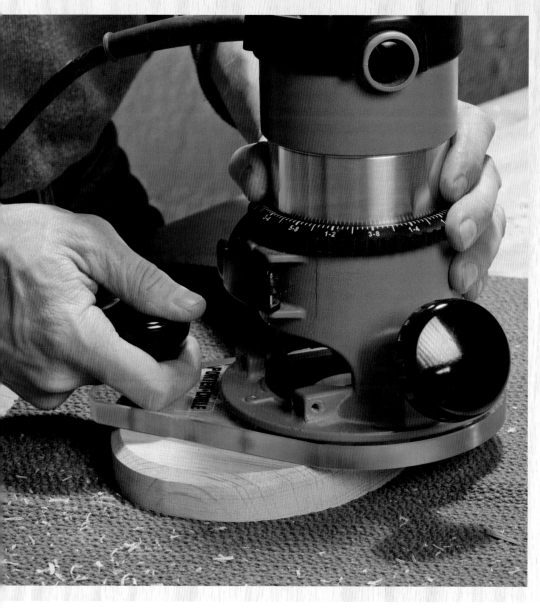

Profiling Basics

Routers are perfectly suited for profiling, whether you're routing flat or contoured edges. Other tools such as files, sanders or hand planes will also shape profiles, but routers make the task quick, easy and precise. You can use either a plunge or fixed-base router for profiling. It's even possible to cut profiles with a trim router, provided the bit is reasonably small and you make several light passes of increasing depth to cut the full shape.

How To Make A Profile Cut

First choose and install the piloted bit you plan to use. Rest the router base on the workpiece so the bit is positioned near the workpiece edge. Sight below the router base to check the bit depth, and adjust the bit up or down so the bearing rides against the workpiece. Be sure the screw that secures the bearing doesn't interfere with the worksurface below what you're routing.

Next, set the workpiece and router on an anti-slip pad or clamp the wood to your bench. You don't want the workpiece to move or tip during routing. When workpieces are smaller than the router's subbase, you may want to use hot-melt glue or double-sided tape to hold the wood in place. Fix it to a larger piece of scrap material clamped to the

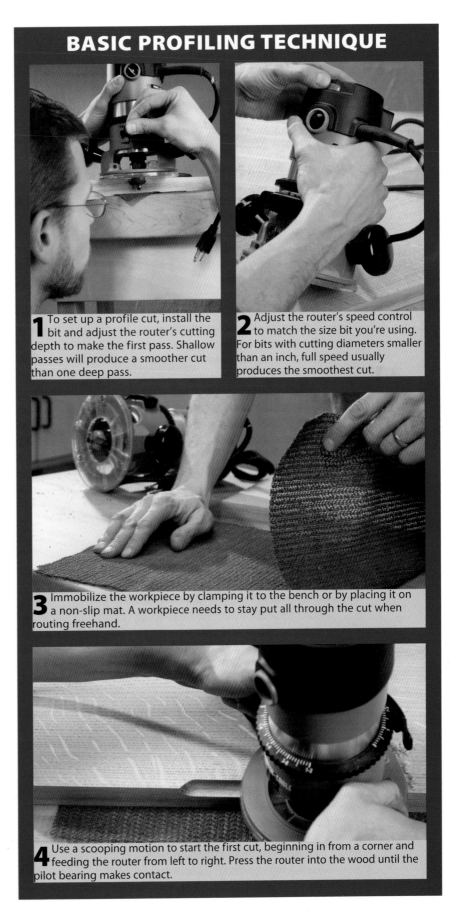

BASIC PROFILING TECHNIQUE

1 To set up a profile cut, install the bit and adjust the router's cutting depth to make the first pass. Shallow passes will produce a smoother cut than one deep pass.

2 Adjust the router's speed control to match the size bit you're using. For bits with cutting diameters smaller than an inch, full speed usually produces the smoothest cut.

3 Immobilize the workpiece by clamping it to the bench or by placing it on a non-slip mat. A workpiece needs to stay put all through the cut when routing freehand.

4 Use a scooping motion to start the first cut, beginning in from a corner and feeding the router from left to right. Press the router into the wood until the pilot bearing makes contact.

bench or stick the workpiece directly to the bench. An anti-slip mat may be all you need to hold the workpiece stationary, but if you're in doubt about stability, anchor it more firmly. For more information on profiling small workpieces, see page 150.

Without turning the router on, it can be helpful to conduct a dry run of the cut before actually carrying it out. Sometimes potential problems with the setup become apparent this way. Be sure the path of the bearing is clear all around and you're comfortable with how you'll have to move and reach to complete the cut. If you feel like you have to stretch your arms too far to guide the tool around, figure out how you can move the workpiece to gain better control.

With some bits and operations, you'll need to be selective about how fast to spin the bit. For hand-held profiling, however, set the router to its highest speed. Smaller bits will make the cleanest cuts when the router is set to full speed. To make the actual cut, start the router and feed it smoothly and firmly into the wood until the bearing makes contact with the edge. Use a scooping motion instead of stabbing the bit into the wood, and be sure to hold the router with both handles. Notice that the router motor speed will change as it adjusts to the cutting load. If the motor noise drops sharply, ease up on the pressure and engage the bit more gradually.

If you're routing all around the perimeter of the workpiece, it's better to start the cut along a long-grain edge where the wood is softer than starting in the harder end-grain surfaces. It also allows you to finish the cut along the long grain, which cleans up any tearout that happens when routing the corners of the end grain. When you're profiling just the ends, begin the cut carefully at the corner to keep the router from slipping into the adjacent long-grain edge. Or, clamp a piece of scrap material against the edge you want to leave square and start the cut in the scrap instead.

Feed the router along the workpiece from left to right, pressing the bearing firmly against the contact edge or end as you go. Turn the router so one handle is over the workpiece to give the router optimum stability. Try to maintain an even motor speed while you move the bit through the wood. That's the best way to adjust your feed rate. If the motor bogs down and you feel more resistance from the tool in the wood, it's a sign that the bit is set too deeply or you are feeding the tool faster than the motor can keep up. Slow down and let the router cut at its own speed for smoother results. Or stop the cut and reset the bit to a shallower depth.

During the cut, be sure to keep the router's subbase pressed firmly against the wood. It's easy to focus only on keeping the bearing against the wood, especially when you're just getting started with a router. Sometimes you may even lose the "feel" of when the base is firmly planted on the wood. This can happen when you are routing small or narrow workpieces where balancing the router is more difficult. If the base tips off the face of the workpiece, the profile will be uneven and the bit may gouge the wood.

Continue feeding the router along the edge or end until you reach the stopping point or pass all the way around the workpiece. Once you've finished the cut, pull the router off the wood or raise the bit (on a plunge router) and turn the motor off. For safety's sake, keep hold of the handles until the bit stops spinning. Some woodworkers lay the router on its side and let go while the bit slows down, but there's still a chance that the bit could accidentally catch on something nearby. It's better to hold on until the bit stops.

Milling Large Profiles

If you're using a bit that removes about 1/4 in. of material or less, you can usually rout the whole shape in one pass. For larger profiles, it's unsafe to cut off more than about 1/4 in. at a time. An overly deep cut can lead to the router grabbing the wood and a possible loss of tool control. It also stresses the router motor and bit, which leads to overheating, excessive vibration and possibly a broken bit. Splintery wood will break off in large pieces which can get caught in the bit or hang the router up in the cut. Avoid overly deep cuts in all router situations.

The best way to rout a large profile is to make it with a series of shallow passes, resetting the bit 1/8 to 1/4 in. deeper each time. For really

Setting a bit too deeply on the first pass can lead to broken wood fibers, called tearout. Some woods, such as oak and cedar, are more prone to tearout than others.

One way to avoid tearout is to make profile cuts in a number of shallow passes, setting the router for a deeper cut each time. Use a steady, but not rushed, feed rate.

hard woods like ebony or cocobolo, you may have to make even more passes at shallower depths. It takes longer to complete a profile this way, but your bits and router will last longer and you'll be happier with the cutting results.

When cutting a large profile, like this ogee shape, start with a shallow cutting depth to remove some of the waste material and minimize tearout. Set the bit for deeper cuts until it forms the profile you want.

The lion's share of your profiling needs can probably be met with just five different bit styles: roundovers, chamfers, beads, ogees and coves.

PROFILING'S "FAB FIVE"

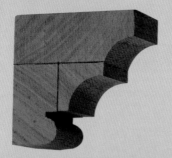

Router bit catalogs are stocked with dozens of different profiling bits, but you don't need them all to build a core set of useful shapes. Five basic bit shapes will serve you well: chamfers, coves, roundovers, ogees and beads. Chamfers, roundovers and coves are the most common options for easing edges and adding decorative detail. Chamfers convert a square corner into a 45° bevel. Roundovers create a convex quarter-circle, and coves make the mirror image of a roundover — a concave relief. A single chamfering bit is the most versatile of these three shapes, because the same bit can produce both narrow and wide chamfers by simply changing the cutting depth. Roundovers and coves are limited to cutting the size of the shape formed by their radius. You'll need a few sizes of these bits to cover the usual gamut of your project needs. An "S"-shaped ogee bit and a beading bit are two other typical and appealing profiles to add to your collection.

You can use these five bit shapes independently, or combine them to form built-up moldings with more complex shapes. The effect of building up profiles adds more visual interest. You can create build-ups that simulate crown molding or entirely unique shapes. Generally, you'll need to mill the different profiles independently, as shown in these sample build-ups, then stack the parts together. Experiment by combining the profiles in different ways until you find a shape that enhances the style of the project.

Many styles of built-up moldings are possible by combining roundovers, chamfers, beads, ogees and coves. Rout samples of each profile and stack them together in different combinations to achieve a look that's pleasing to you. In the right combination, you can achieve what appears to be custom crown molding from what's actually a stack of individual shapes.

Profiling Problems And Solutions

Cutting profiles is a fairly straight-forward operation, but it's not without its own share of correctible problems. Here are a few of the typical complications you may encounter and some easy remedies to try:

Profiling Thin Stock

Most common piloted bits are designed to rout profiles on 3/4-in.-thick wood. With the bit set to full cutting depth, there will still be room on the edge of the workpiece for the bearing to ride against the wood. When you use a particularly large bit, you may have to set the bit so low that the screw holding the bearing will actually make contact with the bench. It's important that the bearing and screw have enough room all around to operate freely. The easiest fix is to raise the workpiece off the bench on a piece of scrap or clamp the workpiece so you can rout off the edge of the bench.

If you are routing thin stock that doesn't provide a reference surface for the bearing, cut a piece of scrap wood to serve as the reference edge. Stick it to the workpiece underneath with double-sided tape or hot-melt glue. Make sure the edges line up evenly. With this setup, the bearing will roll along the scrap material instead of the workpiece.

"Telegraphing" is a condition where a bit's bearing follows irregularities along the edge of a workpiece and transfers those into the cut. Starting with smooth edges will eliminate this problem.

Telegraphing

When a pilot bearing rolls along an edge, it's actually only making contact with the wood along a thin imaginary line. Think of the bearing more as a "point-of-contact" surface than a flat edge. This means the bearing will register even tiny irregularities in the

Use a piece of scrap as a spacer underneath a thin workpiece to keep the bit's bearing screw from making contact with the worksurface. A bearing always needs an unobstructed path to move along the workpiece.

If a workpiece is too thin for the bearing to make contact with it, use a smooth-edged piece of scrap to serve as a guide surface for the bearing to roll against.

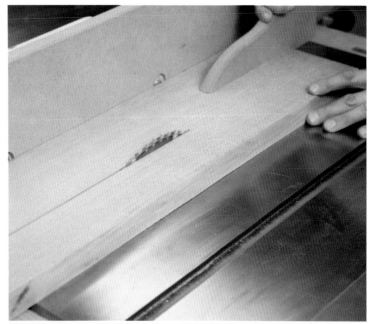

The best way to eliminate telegraphing problems is to start with smooth, blemish-free edges on your workpieces. Prepare flat edges on a table saw or with a jointer. Refine curved edges on a drum sander.

wood's surface and transfer these in the cut. In other words, imperfections along the edge will become imperfections in the profile. The larger the profile, the more this sort of telegraphing shows up in the resulting shape. The best way to avoid telegraphing is to start with well-prepared workpieces. If your reference edges need to be flattened, use a saw with a reference fence, such as a table saw or miter saw, instead of cutting the part to shape with a circular saw or jigsaw. For even better results, flatten long-grain edges on a jointer or with your router table (see page 184) to remove saw marks and improve flatness. For curved workpieces, carefully sand the curves smooth before you rout them. Remember: a profiling bit can't improve the reference edge you start with. If anything, the bit will turn a defective edge into a poor profile.

Tearout

Tearout results when a router bit chips corners or splinters the wood along a cut. Some woods are more prone to tearout than others, but you can minimize these sorts of defects easily by arranging your sequence of cuts carefully. When possible, always start your cuts in the long grain. Chipping and splintering happens most often when you're routing across the grain and reach the fragile edges of the long grain. Then follow up with the long-grain profile cuts. This way, the router will cut away any tearout present at the corners. If you are profiling all four sides of a workpiece, start the cut somewhere in the middle of the long grain and work counterclockwise around the wood. This pattern will automatically remove the tearout, because the end-grain cuts are followed by long grain cuts.

If just the end grain gets the profile and not the long-grain edges, clamp scrap wood against both ends of the cut. Rout across the scraps to preserve the long-grain corners.

It's harder to prevent tearout that happens across the face of a work-

PROFILING TO ELIMINATE TEAROUT

1 It's easy to produce splintered, chipped corners if you don't use the correct cutting sequence when routing around the ends and edges of a workpiece.

2 When possible, rout across the end grain of a workpiece first. Tearout will happen at the corners where the wood grain is weakest.

3 Once the end grain is cut, make the long-grain cuts next. The long-grain cuts will remove the tearout from the end-grain cuts and produce clean, sharp corners.

4 Option: If you only want to rout the end grain and not the long grain, clamp a piece of scrap along the edge of the workpiece to support the edge fibers, and rout across the end grain and into the scrap.

piece. Sometimes this sort of tearout is the result of a dull bit, excessive vibration or splintery wood. Try making the final profiling pass with the bit set just slightly deeper than cut before so it shears off the last bit of waste.

Burning

Scorching during a profiling cut has a number of causes. Check to make sure the bit bearing spins freely; if it sticks, the bearing might be spinning at the same speed as the bit and rubbing against the wood rather than rolling along it. It's also possible that you're taking too deep a pass or moving the bit too slowly along the wood, and the increased friction overheats the wood. Or, it may just be that the particular wood you're routing is prone to burning —

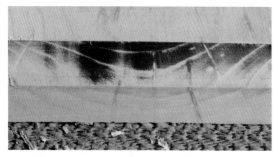

Scorching has many causes, including a dull or dirty bit, too slow a feed rate or sometimes just the particular wood you're routing. It's a common profiling problem.

One way to remove burned areas without sanding is to set the router for a light final pass and feed it right to left along the edge — a climb cut. A light climb cut will shear away the burn neatly.

cherry and maple scorch easily, even with carbide bits.

You can reduce the chances of burning by taking lighter passes, particularly on harder woods. Feed the router along the wood at a brisk pace. Keep the router moving along the cut, just below the point that the motor begins to labor.

OPTIONS FOR PROFILING SMALL WORKPIECES

One way to improve control when routing small workpieces is to use a smaller router for the job. A trim router is ideal for these situations.

An option to improve the footing is to place a piece of same-thickness scrap next to the workpiece. Use it to support the router base.

You can also stick a piece of scrap to the router's subbase, which forms a spacer of sorts for navigating around a small workpiece.

An offset base is yet another way to increase the router's bearing surface when routing around the small stuff.

Inevitably, burns will happen now and then regardless of what you try, and they're difficult to sand out. A quick way to clean them up is to set the router for a slightly deeper final pass, and feed the router from right to left to make a climb cut. A light climb cut will generally shear away most or all of the burned area. It sometimes leaves a crisp edge that needs very little sanding. Be careful here: You'll be making the pass opposite the usual feed direction, working *with* the bit's rotation instead of *against* it. Brace yourself when making a climb cut: the router will want to pull itself along the wood, and you need to counteract that force.

Profiling Small Workpieces

Profiling is easiest to do when the workpiece is larger than the router's base. There's plenty of room to move the tool around without the router tipping off. Unfortunately, you won't always have the luxury of a big workpiece, but there are several ways to handle the small ones safely. If you can, use a small router on small workpieces. A trim router can be ideal for routing parts as small as 2 to 3 in. square. But a trim router won't have enough oomph for cutting a large profile on a small piece.

If your only option is to use a full-size router, or if the profile is large, try surrounding the workpiece with support blocks of the same thickness to give the router base a broader platform. Be sure to leave enough clearance around the workpiece so the bit

Notice how a pilot bearing follows a curved inside corner as opposed to a square inside corner. As long as the bearing continues to make contact with the wood, it will cut a consistent shape. It can't follow a sharp inside corner without truncating the curve.

can move freely. Attaching the router to an offset base can also add some helpful support. Another alternative is to fix a support block to the subbase with double-sided tape. The block will function like an outrigger on one end of the router base to balance the other end supported by the workpiece. Make sure the block and workpiece thicknesses match.

Bearing Limitations

When you're planning a profiling cut, remember a couple of important issues regarding pilot bearings: First, the bearing follows a reference edge exactly. If the corner of a workpiece is sharp, the resulting profile will be sharp. Bearings will not create a smooth-radiused corner if the workpiece doesn't have a radiused corner

to start with. Bearings also require at least as much clear space as their diameters to follow an edge completely. If you need to rout into a sharp inside corner, the bearing will only track the corner if it fits completely into the corner.

Sometimes you can swap one bearing on a bit for a smaller size and achieve a slightly different profile. A roundover can be converted into an ovolo shape by using a smaller bearing to create a pair of shadow-line "steps" in the cut. But, using a smaller bearing won't let you sneak a larger profile into a smaller space without also changing the shape of the profile. If you switch to a smaller bearing, experiment on scrap to see if the change in profile is acceptable.

Remember that a bearing can't follow a cutout smaller than its diameter. In this wedge-shaped cut, the bearing stops short, and so does the bit.

Notice how changing the size of the bearing on the same bit produces two different cutting profiles. Here, this bit cuts either a roundover or an ovolo shape, depending on the bearing diameter.

151

OTHER HANDHELD ROUTING TECHNIQUES

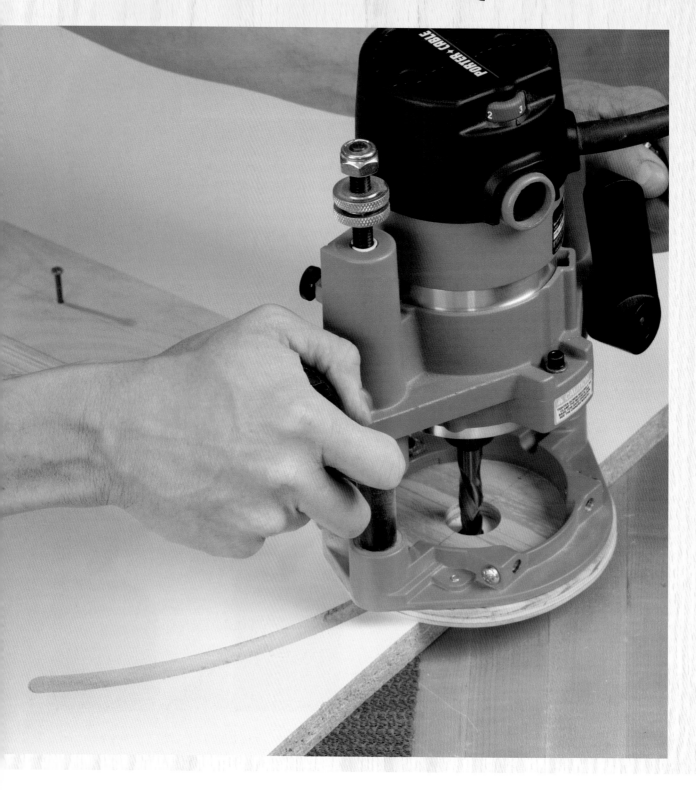

The main advantage of an edge guide is that it fixes the router at a specific distance off the edge of a workpiece. Here, it establishes the position of a dado cut.

Edge Guide Routing

Routing straight lines or profiling without a pilot bearing are both possible by attaching an edge guide to your router. Basically, an edge guide is simply a short fence that rides along the workpiece. Depending on where you place the fence, an edge guide allows the router to cut a straight path in from the edges or ends of a workpiece. Some edge guides have split fences, while others have a continuous fence. With a split fence, you can set the fence over the bit so just a portion of the profile is exposed. In this configuration, the fence acts like a pilot bearing so you can use unpiloted bits for making profiling cuts. Regardless of where you set the fence, an edge guide limits the router to cutting along a limited and controlled path.

Another use for an edge guide is to control the amount of cutter exposure on bits that don't have pilot bearings to guide them. In this setup, a roundnose bit can cut cove shapes using an edge guide.

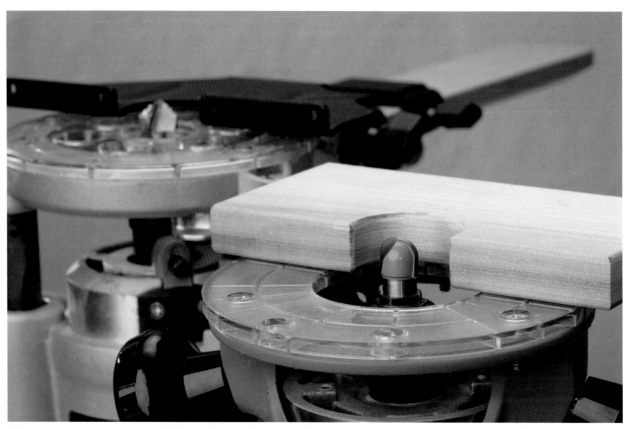

Edge guide attachments are available to fit virtually every professional router, or you can make one from scrap and attach it to the router with screws or double-sided tape.

Most router manufacturers offer edge guides to fit their routers. Usually, these guides have a pair of metal rods that fix to the router base with thumbscrews. The rods allow the straightedge to move laterally, and you can lock it wherever you need it for the cut. Some of the newer edge guides have micro-adjust features for making precise changes to the fence position.

You don't have to buy an edge guide to benefit from its functionality: Even a flat-edged piece of scrap stuck to the router base with double-sided tape can serve as an edge guide. Of course, the cutting width will be limited by the size of the router base, but for a quick-and-dirty setup, a stuck-on edge guide will sometimes suffice. Or, you can make your own adjustable edge guide by replacing the subbase with a hard-board panel, to which you can glue or clamp the fence.

Setting up an edge guide for use is simple. Follow the manufacturer's instructions for mounting the guide on the router base, then loosen the setscrews and slide the fence away from the bit the same distance you want to set the cut in from the edge or end of your workpiece. To minimize cutting errors and confusion, measure your setup from the cutting edge closest to the fence rather than the far edge — if you get confused about which edge registers the bit, you could accidentally set the cut a bit's width off from where you want it. Always check your setup by setting the router and edge guide into position on the workpiece to see where the bit will actually cut the wood.

To use an edge guide for making profile cuts, you'll need a split-fence style edge guide that can be positioned around the bit. Set and lock the fence facings close to the edges of the bit to help reduce tearout. For cutting large profiles, you can mill the shape either by making several passes and resetting the bit depth for deeper cuts, or by setting the bit to full depth and moving the fence incrementally away from the bit to expose more profile. If you choose the second option, notice that the bit's full profile will be exposed when the fences line up with the edge of the bearing.

Feed Direction With An Edge Guide

There are a few guidelines to follow when routing with an edge guide. First, feed the router counterclockwise if you're routing all around a workpiece, just as you would for profiling. If you are routing along one edge only, slide the router from left to right, just like a profiling cut. Doing so will move the router against the bit's rotation, which introduces helpful resistance in the cut. Feeding from right to left and with the bit's rotation will result in a climb cut — a less-controlled scenario. You'll know you're feeding the wrong way if the router wants to pull itself and lurch forward along the wood. When you're routing correctly, you'll feel an even amount of resistance from the bit.

The other feed direction issue is how to position your body in relation to the edge guide. For optimal control, push the router along the workpiece with the edge guide fixed on your side of the router. If the edge guide is on the other side of the router, you'll have to pull it against the wood while you slide the router along, which is harder to do. It's worth the effort to organize your setup so you're always pushing the edge guide against the wood.

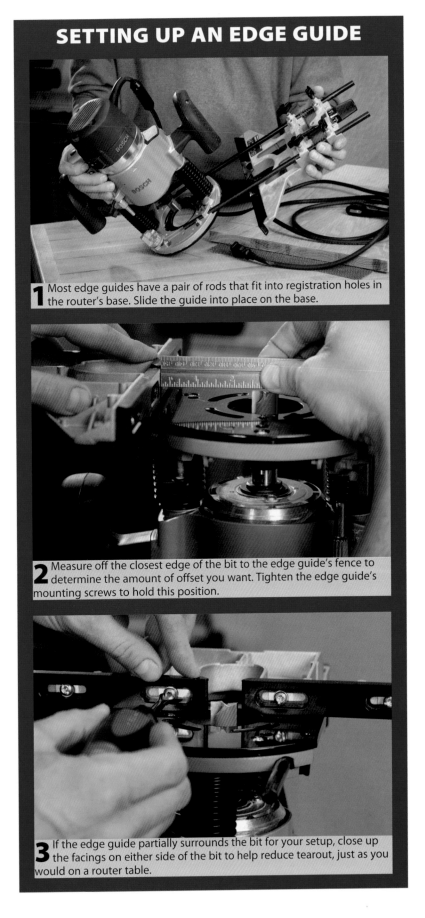

SETTING UP AN EDGE GUIDE

1 Most edge guides have a pair of rods that fit into registration holes in the router's base. Slide the guide into place on the base.

2 Measure off the closest edge of the bit to the edge guide's fence to determine the amount of offset you want. Tighten the edge guide's mounting screws to hold this position.

3 If the edge guide partially surrounds the bit for your setup, close up the facings on either side of the bit to help reduce tearout, just as you would on a router table.

A router and straight bit can be used to trim the ragged edges of a glued-up panel flush if you guide it against a clamped straightedge.

Use at least two stout clamps to keep a straightedge from shifting during use.

Routing Against A Straightedge

Another option for making straight cuts, either along the edges of a workpiece or within the interior, is to guide the router against a clamped straightedge. Any stiff, flat-edged material can serve as a straightedge. Straightedge routing is an ideal way to work with large glued-up panels or plywood and other sheet material. With a straightedge and an ordinary straight bit, you can square up the edges and ends of a panel, trim off uneven ends of a glue-up or rout dadoes and grooves wherever you want them. Moving a lightweight router against a straightedge is much easier and safer than lifting a big panel and feeding it through a table saw. If you're careful with your setup and use a reliable straightedge, you can make flat cuts on par with the best table saw fence, and the routed edge will be far smoother than a sawn edge.

You can buy straightedges designed for sawing or routing. They're made of metal with integral clamps. These are helpful because the edges are reliably flat and the metal body is thin enough to stay clear of the bottoms of the router handles when you slide the router along. A strip of flat sheet stock or lumber also makes a good straight-

A router run against a long straightedge is a safe and effective way to square up large panels of plywood or other sheet material when they are too large to feed over a table saw.

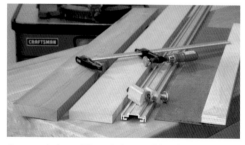

Any straight, stiff and clampable object can serve as a straightedge for routing. A piece of hardwood, sheet material, a fabricated metal straightedge or an offset guide all work equally well.

edge, provided it's wide enough to clamp in place without interfering with the router's travel. Medium-density fiberboard in half-inch thickness makes an excellent straightedge; the material is dimensionally stable and free of voids that could interfere with the router base. Plywood isn't always void-free. If you make your straightedge from a piece of lumber, choose kiln-dried hardwood. Joint and surface the edges and faces to ensure flatness. Another option is to make an offset straightedge guide for your router (see page 163).

How To Make A Straightedge Cut

Setting up a trimming cut with a straightedge involves guiding the router base against the straightedge with the straightedge indexed a precise distance from the router bit. Determine this offset by measuring from the edge of the subbase to the closest edge of the router bit. Provided you use the same straight bit and your router's subbase is perfectly centered on the base, this distance will be the same every time you set up a straightedge cut. Of

UNDERSTANDING CONCENTRICITY

Concentricity is one of those buzz words among router manufacturers that basically refers to how closely a router's collet is centered on the router base. Most good-quality routers have collets that are close to being concentric on the base, but chances are your router base isn't perfectly concentric. This is especially true for routers that have removable motor packs. Each time you remove and install the motor on the base, there's a chance of changing concentricity. A collet that's off-center on the base isn't a problem for profiling with a bearing-guided bit, but it is a concern for routing dadoes and grooves against a straightedge when using a round router base. In these situations, the actual offset between the bit and the edge of the router base can change if you inadvertently twist the router while you push it along. The deviation will cause the bit to drift off of a straight line as it cuts, resulting in wavering dado or groove cuts.

You won't be able to guarantee concentricity each time you rout, but you can account for it on a round subbase by simply marking your router base with an index. Then, make sure to hold this index mark in the same position relative to the straightedge as you make the cut. It will keep the cut fixed to a single offset distance, regardless of perfect concentricity. The other option is to use a router base with a flat edge.

A router's collet and subbase aren't always perfectly concentric, relative to one another. It's easy to see the problem if you rotate a router around while making a straight cut. Any deviation from a straight cut shows a lack of concentricity.

Subbases with a flat edge avoid concentricity issues altogether, because the router always has a fixed and consistent guide edge.

Another way to help minimize concentricity issues is to keep the same edge of the base in contact with the workpiece all through the cut. Make a reference mark, and use this as the contact point.

JOINTING WITH A STRAIGHTEDGE

It's easy to joint panels or lumber with a router and straightedge. Use a piloted flush-trim bit (bearing at the tip) or pattern bit (bearing at the shank) and run the bit's bearing against the straightedge. If you use a pattern bit, the router will ride right on top of the straightedge, so use a straightedge wide enough to provide adequate support for the router base. Or, clamp the straightedge below the workpiece so it aligns with your trim line. Make the cut with a flush-trim bit.

With either bit style, the bearing will roll along the straightedge, so there's no need to measure and mark an offset for the router base. Instead, draw a reference line where you want the cut to be, clamp the straightedge here, and feed the router bit from left to right along the straightedge. For clean, square edges, trim off not more than 1/8 in. from the edge, using gentle feed pressure and a 1/2-in.-shank bit.

course, if you use a different diameter straight bit, the offset distance will change, and you'll need to measure for the new offset.

If you're making trim cuts with a straightedge where the bit will cut all the way through the thickness of the workpiece, choose a sturdy 3/8- or 1/2-in.-diameter straight bit with a 1/2-in. shank. An even better choice is to use a 1/2-in.-shank carbide spiral bit with either an upcut or compression grind (see page 103 for more information about spiral bits). These sorts of trim cuts place significant stress on the bit, and the thicker shank will help resist flexing and extra vibration.

Mark your workpiece where you want the cut edge to be. When you can, keep the routed edge as close as possible to the rough edge of the panel. An internal through-cut places even more stress on the bit. Then mark the offset distance for your

TECHNIQUE FOR STRAIGHTEDGE ROUTING

1 Install the bit you'll use for routing, and measure from the cutting edge to the edge of the subbase to determine the amount of offset for this router and bit.

2 Mark this offset distance from a reference line that sets where you want the router to actually cut the workpiece. This will determine where to clamp the straightedge.

3 Clamp the straightedge in place to prepare for the cut. Make sure the clamps won't obstruct the path of the router from beginning to end. The straightedge thickness also needs to clear the router's handles and your fingers.

4 Make the cut by pressing the router's base firmly against the straightedge and feeding from left to right across the workpiece. The router should trim right along your reference line.

5 Option: You can also use a flush-trim bit, guided against a straightedge, for edge-trimming tasks. In this setup, there's no need to guide the router base against the straightedge.

bit and router away from the layout line. Clamp the straightedge firmly here. Set the router in place against the straightedge to be sure the bit aligns with your trim line. Make a visual check to be sure the clamps are clear of the router's handles.

To make the cut, set the bit depth slightly deeper than the panel's thickness and feed the router from left to right across the panel. Set up the cut so you can push the router against the straightedge, and stand slightly behind the router as you push it through the cut to help maintain your balance.

Cutting Dadoes And Grooves With A Straightedge

Use the same setup procedure for making dado and groove cuts with a straightedge as you do for edge trimming with a straightedge. For the sake of clarity, mark both reference lines that show the dado or groove

CUTTING DADOES AND GROOVES

1 Mark the location and width of the dado or groove on the workpiece using a square or straightedge.

2 Set the router's cutting depth accordingly. If the dado or groove is about 1/4 in. deep or less, you can probably cut it in one pass. For deeper dadoes, make a series of deeper passes.

3 Clamp a straightedge in place, using your router and bit's offset distance to determine this location. Make a short climb cut to help minimize tearout on the exit end of the dado.

4 Rout the dado from left to right across the workpiece — or by pushing the router away from your body if you are standing in line with the cut.

TIP

SHEAR VENEER FIRST

When making dado or groove cuts in veneered plywood, cutting across the grain of the face veneer can lead to splintering and tearout. You won't want this to happen on expensive sheet material, especially if the edges of the cut will show. One way to minimize the splintering is to make a shallow, shearing cut for the first pass, to slice through just the face veneer. Make the shearing cut about 1/16 in. deep. Then set the bit deeper to remove the rest of the waste. A light pass like this reduces vibration or bit flexing, which should produce crisp cut edges in the veneer.

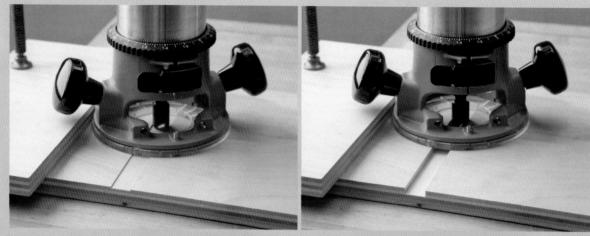

The way to make clean dado cuts on veneered plywood is to start the cut with a shallow pass to just shear the surface veneer. This will minimize splintering and tearout. Then follow up with deeper cuts as usual.

location on your workpiece. Clamp the straightedge at whatever offset distance you determine for your router base and bit diameter. If possible, choose a straight or spiral bit with a diameter that matches the width of the dado or groove. Then, instead of setting the bit to cut all the way through the workpiece, make the bit depth match the dado or groove depth. If the depth is greater than 1/4 in., make it in several passes instead of one deep pass. Feed the router from left to right along the straightedge. One way to eliminate tearout on the right (exit) end of the cut is to first make a shallow climb-cut pass *from right to left,* then carry out the full pass from left to right. Feed the router slowly when making the climb cut, and press the base firmly against the straightedge to keep the bit from grabbing.

Routing A Stopped Dado Or Groove

Not all dado or groove cuts pass completely across the workpiece. You can make these sorts of stopped cuts using a router and straightedge and limit the router's travel with stop-blocks. Here's how: First, lay out the stopped dado or groove shape on the workpiece to show the exact ends of the cut. Chuck the appropriate straight bit in the router, and clamp a straightedge made of scrap material to the workpiece. Position the straightedge the correct offset distance for your router and bit (see page 158 for determining router base offsets).

With the straightedge in position, set the router in place so the bit touches the end of the dado or groove layout marks. Screw a wood block to the straightedge so it touches the router base with the bit at the end of the cut; now you've set one end of

ROUTING STOPPED DADOES WITH A STRAIGHTEDGE

1 To set up a stopped dado cut with a straightedge, first mark the dado's proportions on your workpiece.

2 Clamp a straightedge in position on the workpiece so the router bit aligns with the dado all along its length. Use the bit and your layout lines to verify correct alignment.

3 With the bit aligned at one end of the dado, fasten a stopblock to the straightedge.
Position the stop flush against the left edge of the router's subbase. Install another block to

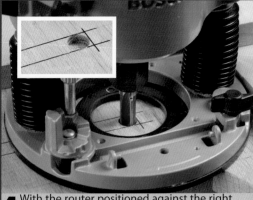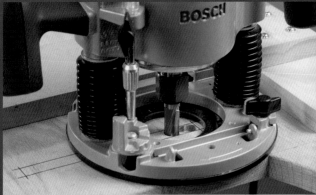

4 With the router positioned against the right stopblock, plunge the bit into the wood to begin the cut.

5 Feed the router from right to left to continue the cut. Be sure to keep the base pressed firmly against the straightedge as the cut proceeds.

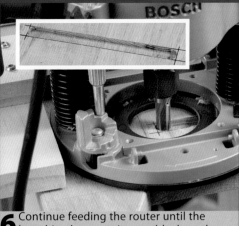

6 Continue feeding the router until the base hits the opposite stopblock on the left-hand end.

7 Make additional passes, if necessary, setting the router for deeper cuts until you achieve the full depth of cut for this workpiece.

the cut. Slide the router to the other end of the cut and install a second stopblock. Once both stopblocks are set, make the dado or groove cut in a series of increasing-depth passes, moving the router from left to right. The stopblocks should align the bit perfectly with the layout marks.

DADOING WITH A T-SQUARE OR OFFSET STRAIGHTEDGE GUIDE

Sometimes you'll need to cut a series of dadoes across a workpiece. It's a typical situation when building casework with shelving that locks into the case sides. One way to speed the setup for each cut is to use a T-square customized for your router. Fasten two strips of scrap together to form the "T," and choose the straight bit you'll use for making the dado

Another handy jig for referencing straightedge cuts is a T-square customized for your router and bit. Rout a shallow reference pass across the T-square's short leg to mark the offset distance for the jig. Align this with your layout lines on a workpiece to set the cutting path.

or groove cuts. Make a dado cut across the short "T" member of the square, running the router base against the long leg of the square. This cut automatically establishes the correct offset for the router and bit. Then, simply line up this reference cut with the dado layout lines and clamp the T-square in place. Make the cuts as usual, from left to right across the workpiece.

Another speedy option for setting up straightedge cuts is to make an offset guide for your router. This jig consists of a thin piece of base material (hardboard or thin plywood work well) with a straightedge fastened to the base. The edge of the jig base lines up with the dado reference lines to mark the cut, and the router's base follows the straightedge. Trim the thin base of the jig to establish the offset with whatever straight bit you choose to use for the jig. Then, just align the edge of the jig with your trim or dado lines to register the router correctly.

Routing Circles

Every now and then a woodworking project may require you to make a perfectly round circle. A circular tabletop or a Lazy Susan are good examples. You could duplicate a circular shape that already exists by using it as a template (see the next chapter on template routing), but usually you'll have to cut the circle from scratch. One option would be to measure and cut out the circle with a jigsaw, but it's tough to cut a perfect circle this way. A far easier method is to use a router and straight bit guided with a circle-cutting jig.

There are numerous circle-cutting jigs you can buy, but if you only need

to rout a circle now and then, it's easy to make a jig from scrap that works just as well. The principle of the jig is simple: you want to mimic the action of a drafting compass, with one point of the jig fixed in place and the router rotating around the fixed point on an arm that limits its cutting path. You can make a basic circle-cutting jig from a length of scrap plywood about 20 in. long. Any thickness plywood will do, but thinner plywood will be easier to fasten the router to. Mount the router's base to the plywood at one end using the subbase mounting screws. Before installing the router, drill a 1-in.-diameter hole where the bit will pass through the jig. (Note: For easier setups, use a plunge router with the circle-cutting jig.)

MAKING AN OFFSET STRAIGHTEDGE GUIDE

1 Measure the offset distance between the bit you plan to use with this jig and the edge of the router's subbase. You'll need to use this bit diameter and router only with this jig.

2 Cut an oversized strip of sheet stock to serve as the guide's base. Hardboard makes a sturdy and durable base for this jig.

3 Attach a flat-edged piece of scrap to the base to form a straightedge for guiding the router's subbase. Make the scrap straightedge as long as the base.

4 Cut the offset guide's base to final width by running the router along the guide's straightedge. Now the base width will match the router's offset distance.

5 To use the offset guide, align the edge of the base to your layout line, and guide the router along the straightedge from left to right. Be sure to use the correct router and bit for your guide.

Measure from the bit along the jig arm the distance you want the circle's radius to be, and drill a pilot hole through the jig to serve as its fixed centerpoint. If you use a thin piece of plywood for the jig base, attach a length of thicker scrap to the top side of the jig arm. The extra thickness will keep the nail from deflecting during use. Mark the centerpoint on the workpiece and drill a shallow hole here that matches the nail diameter. Be sure to drill into the face of the workpiece that will become the bottom, hidden face of the circle; otherwise the centerpoint hole will show.

If you're using a plunge router in the jig to cut the circle, it isn't necessary to begin from an edge of the workpiece. You have the option of plunging the bit into the wood to start the cut. For cutting circles with a fixed-base router, you'll have to begin the cut with the bit on the edge of the workpiece so it can spin freely, or gradually slide the bit into the material while moving the router around the pivot.

To cut the circle, start the router and plunge the bit into the wood or feed it in from the edge, making the initial pass at a cutting depth of about $1/8$ to $1/4$ in. A shallow pass will help minimize tearout. Guide the router counterclockwise around the workpiece, making sure the nail stays put in the centerpoint hole. Rout one full revolution. Unless the nail deflects in its hole in the jig, the result should be a perfectly round circular track.

One way to proceed from this point is to make several more, deeper passes until the router finally cuts through the workpiece. However, it's sometimes easier to control the operation if you cut away the waste with a jigsaw first. Make sure to guide the jigsaw near the center of the router track, and cut away the waste material around the periphery of the circle. Then, reinstall the router and jig, and make one final pass around the circle to clean away the jigsaw waste that's left.

ROUTING CIRCLES

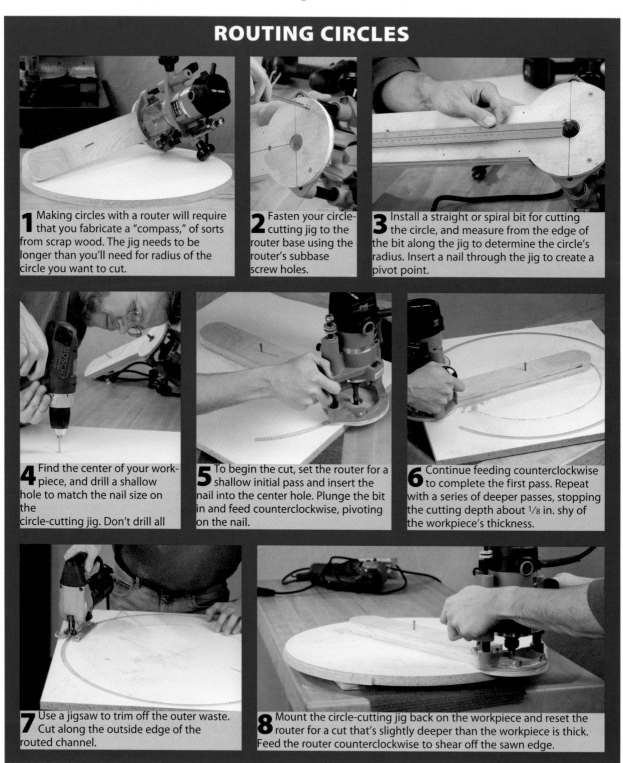

1 Making circles with a router will require that you fabricate a "compass," of sorts from scrap wood. The jig needs to be longer than you'll need for radius of the circle you want to cut.

2 Fasten your circle-cutting jig to the router base using the router's subbase screw holes.

3 Install a straight or spiral bit for cutting the circle, and measure from the edge of the bit along the jig to determine the circle's radius. Insert a nail through the jig to create a pivot point.

4 Find the center of your workpiece, and drill a shallow hole to match the nail size on the circle-cutting jig. Don't drill all

5 To begin the cut, set the router for a shallow initial pass and insert the nail into the center hole. Plunge the bit in and feed counterclockwise, pivoting on the nail.

6 Continue feeding counterclockwise to complete the first pass. Repeat with a series of deeper passes, stopping the cutting depth about 1/8 in. shy of the workpiece's thickness.

7 Use a jigsaw to trim off the outer waste. Cut along the outside edge of the routed channel.

8 Mount the circle-cutting jig back on the workpiece and reset the router for a cut that's slightly deeper than the workpiece is thick. Feed the router counterclockwise to shear off the sawn edge.

Flush-Trimming Edge Banding With A Handheld Router

When you are building finished shelving for bookshelves or cabinetry, you'll often use plywood as the shelf material. One way to cover the exposed edge plys is to apply strips of solid-wood edging. The best way to achieve a perfectly flush fit between the plywood and the edging is to start with edging that's slightly wider than the plywood is thick. Leave a bit of overhang on both faces of the plywood, and trim the overage off each face with a router and piloted flush trim bit.

The challenge of working along the narrow edge of the plywood is providing enough support under the router base to keep it from tipping off the edge. A trim router is the ideal tool choice for this application; its weight is almost insignificant to manage, and the small base is easy to control. If you're careful and have some experience with a trim router, you can guide it easily along even a 3/4-in. edge without extra base support. You can also use a full-size router to trim an edge by clamping a thick support board flush with the surface of the edging. The support block should be large enough to make the router feel stable as you push it along the edge. To trim the first overhang flush, use a piloted flush-trim bit set so the bearing rolls along the plywood under the edging. Rout from left to right along the panel. When one edge is trimmed flush, re-clamp the support board to this face and trim the other overhanging edge.

For even better router support, mount the router to an offset base (see below right) and stick a scrap under this base with double-sided tape. Install an ordinary straight bit in the router and set the bit depth so it's even with the bottom of the built-up offset/scrap base. With this jig, you can trim the edging flush without balancing the router on the edge. Just rest the router on the panel faces and sweep the bit along the overhang to trim it flush.

OPTIONS FOR TRIMMING EDGE BANDING

You can use a full-size router for trimming edge banding flush, but clamp a thick piece of scrap flush with the edge banding to enlarge the router's bearing surface.

Use a flush-trim bit to remove one side of the overhanging edge banding. Feed from left to right. Then, flip and re-clamp the scrap support board, and trim the other edge flush.

A trim router outfitted with a bottom-mounted bearing guide or a piloted flush-trim bit can also trim edge banding flush. With care, the smaller router can be guided along a narrow edge on its own.

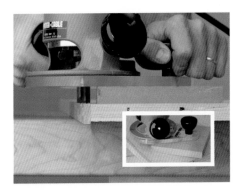
Another option for trimming edge banding is to install an offset guide on your router and tape a scrap spacer underneath. Use a straight bit set flush to the workpiece to trim the banding flush, and sweep the router along to make the cut.

SEVEN

ROUTER TABLE TECHNIQUES

Wood isn't getting any cheaper as time goes by. One way to keep more wood out of the scrap bin, as strange as this may sound, is to use a router table. A router table improves your control over the router, and that saves wood. There are several reasons why. First, inverting the router helps you see the bit clearly — something you can rarely do when the bit faces down. Better visibility allows you to set up cuts more reliably the first time, and you can monitor how the bit is cutting so you make fewer mistakes. The fence gives you a leg up on better control as well. It provides a simple and effective way to limit bit exposure, and it offers a much longer support surface than an edge guide. A router table also

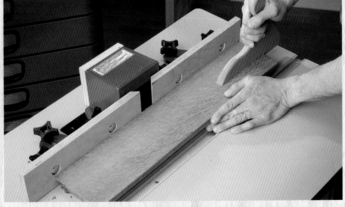

Normally, the correct method for routing straight edges or ends on a router table is to guide the wood against the fence. It provides a stable backboard throughout the cut.

The router table's fence won't help for routing curved edges. Instead, it's important to use a starter pin fitted in the insert plate to serve as a guide for starting the cut.

takes the balancing act out of routing, especially when machining small or narrow workpieces. The tabletop provides ample support, and you don't have to move the router over the wood.

With the exception of a few jig-related operations like circle cutting, most handheld router operations are possible with a router table. You can make profiles along straight or curved edges, make continuous or stopped dadoes and grooves, and rout large or small workpieces. You can even use your router table as a jointer. The procedures and setups are a bit different than handheld routing, and that's what this chapter will help you learn. Router tables are also ideal for cutting a variety of joints, as you'll see in chapter nine.

Bit, Fence And Feed Issues

Before we explore the various router table techniques you can try, it's important to understand a few setup and operational issues that make router table use different than handheld routing.

Options For Setting Bit Projection

With a handheld router, changing the bit's depth of cut typically involves raising and lowering the bit in the router base. There are more options on a router table. You can change depth of cut as you would for a handheld operation — by raising the bit to present more cutting area or lowering the bit to set a smaller

cut. However, you can also change the amount of bit projection with the fence, provided your router table has a split-style fence (see page 128) or an opening in the fence for a bit. Instead of moving the bit up or down, you can simply set the bit to full height and position the fence over the bit. In this arrangement, moving the fence forward or backward from the bit's centerpoint changes the amount of cutter exposure. This option can be helpful if you have a plunge router mounted in your router table where you have to work against the plunge spring tension to set bit height.

Minimizing Tearout And Feed Problems

Tearout is a problem for both handheld and router table operations, but there are easy ways to minimize it with a router table. If your router table has a split-style fence, set the fence faces as close as possible to the bit without making contact. This way, the fence will support workpieces right up to the bit and prevent the bit from breaking off unsupported wood fibers. In terms of tearout, minimizing the gap is mainly a concern on the infeed (right) side of the fence. The bit doesn't actually cut the wood once it passes the bit's centerpoint. The outfeed (left) fence face simply serves as a backup surface for the workpiece as it leaves the cutting area. But, minimizing the gap on the outfeed face helps

One way to change bit projection on a router table is to keep the fence where it is and simply raise the bit (as shown in these two photos). Or, you can raise the bit to full height and move the fence to increase or decrease the amount of cutter exposure.

prevent the wood from drifting into the gap and hanging up on the edge of the fence facing. Tip: It also helps to form a small bevel on the leading edge of the outfeed fence to reduce the possibility of hang-ups.

It's easy to form a close fit between the fence and bit when the bit doesn't have a highly contoured profile or if the bit is small. Larger shaped bits pose more gapping problems. One option for creating a smaller gap in these situations is to make a zero-clearance facing that fits around the bit. The process is easy: take a piece of flat, smooth scrap wood about the same length as the router table fence and set it against the fence facings. Install the bit that will be used with this fence accessory and set it to full height. Move the fence close to the bit, and draw the bit's shape onto the zero-clearance fence. Try to make the outline slightly oversized for the bit so it can spin freely. Cut out the shape with a coping or scroll saw. Then clamp the zero-clearance facing to the fence or stick it in place with double-sided tape. Depending on the shape of the bit's cutting profile, you may need to move the fence instead of raising and lowering the bit for changing the amount of cutter projection.

Another preventive measure to keep wood moving smoothly past the

One preventive measure for minimizing tearout is to move the fence facings as close as possible to the bit without touching it. This also helps keep workpieces from drifting into the bit opening.

bit is to close up the bit hole in the table as much as possible. If your router table's insert plate comes with reducer rings, choose the ring with the smallest diameter opening that fits around the bit. Reducer rings don't reduce tearout, but they do prevent workpieces from accidentally tipping down into the bit opening on the outfeed side. When this happens, you'll probably ruin the cut. If your insert plate doesn't come with reducer rings, you can also cover the table with a piece of hardboard with a

MAKING A ZERO-CLEARANCE FENCE FACE

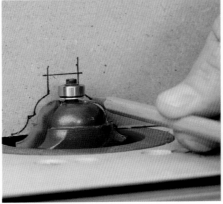

Large profiling bits with deep profiles require a large opening in the fence, which creates big gaps around the cutting area. To close up this gap, you can make a zero-clearance fence face. Draw the shape of the bit onto a piece of scrap and cut it out, then clamp this to the router table fence.

To keep workpieces on track as they move past the bit, it's also advisable to close up the bit opening in the insert plate with a smaller reducing ring.

Body Position And Feed Direction

You may recall from chapter three that the feed direction for router tables is opposite that of handheld routing. For ordinary profiling along the edges and ends of workpieces, you'll feed from the right (infeed) side of the table to the left (outfeed) side. Feeding from right to left presents workpieces to the bit against its counterclockwise rotation. This way, the bit will force the workpiece against the fence and provide helpful resistance as you push workpieces past. Feeding from left to right, on the other hand, usually creates a climb-cutting situation. Here, you present the wood in the same direction that the bit is spinning, so it can grab and pull the workpiece along instead of pushing against it. If the cut is light, you may not feel the pull, and sometimes you can rout without incident.

cutout for the bit to pass through. It's not an ideal fix, but this option is a better alternative than leaving a gaping hole around the bit.

DOES THE FENCE NEED TO BE PARALLEL TO THE BIT?

When setting up a cut, you may wonder whether the fence needs to be positioned parallel, in some fashion, to the bit. Actually, there's no way to make the two parallel. To clarify this, think of the relationship between a router bit and the fence like that of a point (the bit) and a line (the fence). It takes two lines to form parallelism. Since the bit and fence don't form parallel lines, parallelism is a non-issue. Regardless of where you clamp the fence on the table, the point-and-line relationship stays the same. This is a different geometric arrangement than say, a table saw fence and saw blade, which form a pair of parallel lines. Parallel lines can be set skewed to one another, in which case the distance between them varies. On a table saw, if the fence is set skewed to the blade, the resulting misalignment produces poor cuts and trapped wood. Router tables don't present that potential problem. So, just set the fence to account for bit projection or spacing from the bit, and you're all set. Whether the fence is parallel to the edges of the table or completely crooked doesn't matter in the least.

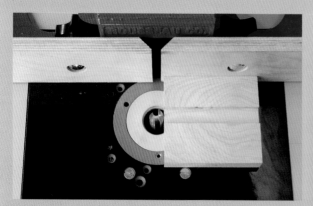

Don't worry about keeping the fence parallel with the bit on a router table. The only thing that matters is the distance between the fence and bit, whether the fence is clamped in line with the tabletop or skewed to it. Parallelism is a non-issue.

But, a deeper cut can lead to a hazardous loss of control if the bit jerks the wood out of your hands.

Here's how to position yourself for a safe right-to-left feed: Stand near the right corner of the table, facing the fence. Balance your weight evenly on both feet — it's always important when feeding the workpieces to maintain your balance and avoid over-reaching. Start the router. Set the workpiece against the fence on the right (infeed side) and near the bit area. Place your left hand along the outside edge of the workpiece. Keep your left hand clear of the cutting area by positioning it at least 6 in. to the right of the bit. You'll use your left hand as a featherboard of sorts to press the workpiece against the fence and down on the table simultaneously.

Grab the back edge of the workpiece with your right hand; it will provide the feed pressure to move the wood past the bit. Without moving your left hand, feed the workpiece slowly and steadily into the bit with your right hand. When your right hand (and the end of the workpiece) reaches the right edge of the router table, shift your right hand to the outer right corner of the workpiece so it stays clear of the bit. As a general rule of thumb (and in order to keep your right thumb!), use a pushstick or push pad to guide the cut the rest of the way if the workpiece is narrower than about 6 to 8 in.

Continue feeding the wood across the table. Near the completion of the pass, your right hand should meet your stationary left hand. Keep the wood moving, but lift and reposition your left hand along the edge of the workpiece on the outfeed side of the table. For a moment, your right hand becomes both a feeder and a featherboard. Shifting your left hand will ensure that the workpiece stays pressed against the fence as it leaves the bit, and it gives you more room to move your right hand the rest of the way through the cut.

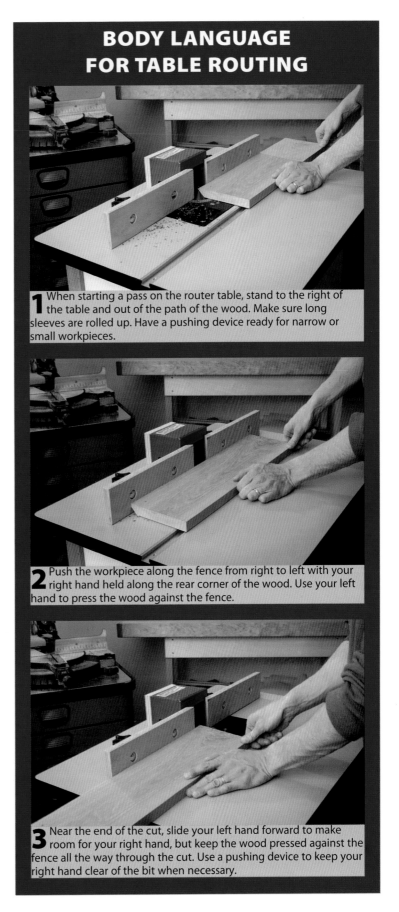

BODY LANGUAGE FOR TABLE ROUTING

1 When starting a pass on the router table, stand to the right of the table and out of the path of the wood. Make sure long sleeves are rolled up. Have a pushing device ready for narrow or small workpieces.

2 Push the workpiece along the fence from right to left with your right hand held along the rear corner of the wood. Use your left hand to press the wood against the fence.

3 Near the end of the cut, slide your left hand forward to make room for your right hand, but keep the wood pressed against the fence all the way through the cut. Use a pushing device to keep your right hand clear of the bit when necessary.

Profiling On A Router Table

Router tables are ideal for profiling operations. You can shape the outside edges and ends of a workpiece or an inside cutout, and either curved or flat edges are fair game. In fact, for ordinary profiling tasks you may find that a router table is preferable to handheld routing. With the router mounted to the table, you can focus entirely on guiding the wood. Gravity works with, rather than against you as it sometimes does with handheld profiling. The smaller the workpiece, the more you'll appreciate having the router held stationary under the table.

There are a couple scenarios where router tables are less convenient than handheld routers. If you're profiling a large board or panel that's difficult to maneuver by hand, do the profiling with a handheld router instead of on the table. In this situation, a handheld router offers better control. Another case for handheld profiling is when you need to shape the edges of a partially assembled project. If there isn't a smooth, flat surface to move over the table, the only feasible option may be to rout by hand. Here's where a trim router can be a miracle tool.

When To Use The Fence

A router table fence offers solid backing for routing flat surfaces, so take advantage of it. You may be tempted to use a piloted bit without a fence to rout a flat edge, and just feed the wood in, as you typically do for handheld profiling. The danger comes with starting the cut on the corner or at the end of the workpiece. Without a fence to guide and limit the cut, it's possible for the bit to catch the wood and climb cut along the leading edge of the workpiece. Using the fence is definitely the safer approach, and the setup doesn't take much time.

Setting The Fence And Bit

Recall that you have two options for setting bit projection: raising and lowering the bit or moving the fence with the bit locked at full height. The fence setup will depend on which option you choose, and different bits will present their own setup issues.

If you plan to raise the bit incrementally to cut a profile, set the fence so the bit will cut its full profile when fully raised. To do this with a pilot-bearing bit, install and raise the bit so the bearing is above the table. Hold a straightedge against the side of the bearing, and move the fence until the faces line up with the bearing. Lock the fence and drop the bit to begin your sequence of cuts. Sometimes the bit won't have a pilot bearing to use as a reference for lining up the fence. In these situations, the centerpoint of the bit becomes what would be the edge of the bearing. Line up the fence with the bit's centerpoint by eye, and lock the fence here.

BIT SETTING OPTIONS

Use the head of a combination square to establish the cutting height for bits without pilot bearings. Raise the router until the bit just touches the head of the square.

For bits with pilot bearings, use a rule to align the fence with the rim of the bearing. This will present the bit's full cutting profile when it's raised to full height.

For unpiloted profiling bits, aligning the fence with the centerpoint of the bit is the same as making the rim of the bearing flush with the fence on piloted bits.

On this bullnose bit, the deepest part of the concave cutting edge represents the bit's full cutting depth. Set the fence here to cut the full roundover shape.

If you'd rather move the fence back each time to make the profile instead of moving the bit up and down, just raise the bit to full cutting height. Pull the fence forward and lock it down to expose just a portion of the cutters for the first pass. Then shift the fence back with each successive pass to cut more of the bit's shape. Make these fence shifts about 1/8 in. at a time to avoid overloading the router or the bit. When the fence reaches the rim of the bearing, you'll be cutting the bit's full profile. Or, if the bit has no bearing, the portion of the profile closest to the center of the bit marks its cutting limit. You can cut even farther across the bit if you are using a straight bit rather than a shaped bit.

Sometimes you may only want to cut a partial profile into the edge of a workpiece, and the bit height needs to mark the transition or limit of the cut. Use a combination square held against the bit to index the cutting height. You can set the head of the square on top of the bit with the rule locked to the bit height you need and measure this way. Or, line the head up with the end of the rule first and stand the head on the table next to the bit. Raise the bit until it aligns with the correct cutting height on the rule.

However you set up the bit and fence for cutting profiles, it's always

Cut the profiles of large bits in several passes, raising the bit about 1/8 to 1/4 in. each time. This reduces the chances for kickback and produces a smoother routed edge.

advisable to make the profile cuts in several passes rather than one, deep pass. The larger the bit or the harder the wood, the more important this becomes. Granted, it takes a little longer to complete the profile this way, but you'll prolong the life of your bits and router as well as leave fewer burn marks or tearout on the wood.

Working With End Grain

Handle splintery, and tearout-prone end grain the same way you do when profiling with a handheld router. Use a piece of scrap as a backer board behind the workpiece when you're cutting just the end grain and not the long grain. The backer board will support the fragile corner fibers that might otherwise break away. If you need to cut the end grain on matching workpieces, just set them together and rout across all the ends at the same time. In cases where you're routing a profile all around the workpiece, start with a long-grain edge, preferably in the middle so the last pass is on long grain.

When routing all four edges of a workpiece, be sure the final pass happens on a long-grain edge. If you finish on an end, the bit could produce tearout at the corner.

If you are routing the end grain of a workpiece only, use a backup board to support the rear corner of the workpiece to keep the fragile corner grain from tearing out.

Making Stopped Cuts

Cutting slots or mortises that start or stop midway across a workpiece is easy to do with a router table fence and straight bit. The cutting procedure is "blind" in the sense that the bit will be imbedded in the wood, but you'll mark its whereabouts right on the fence or table so you can set your cutting limits for precise cuts. Here's a case where the setup will involve raising the bit incrementally but leaving the fence locked in the same place for the whole operation.

The first step in setting up a stopped cut is to make reference marks that indicate where the leading and trailing edges of the bit are. Depending on the proportions of the workpiece, you may be able to make these marks near the top of the router fence faces, but the visibility is usually better if you mark the bit's parameters in front of the bit on the insert plate. Draw the marks on a piece of bright masking tape so you can see them easily and remove it when you're through. Hold a combination square against the infeed and outfeed cutting edge to index each of the two marks on the tape.

With the bit's location marked, lay out the stopped cut on the workpiece, and extend hash marks onto the side of the workpiece you'll see during the cut. The hash marks set the length of the cut so you can start and stop the cut accurately with the bit hidden. Make a second set of hash marks on the end of the workpiece to indicate how far the cut is inset off the fence. Sometimes these marks will be centered on the thickness of the wood and other times not, depending on where the stopped cut needs to be. Line the bit up with these marks and lock the fence with the workpiece held against it. Then lower the bit to about 1/8 in. for a light first pass to shear the surface fibers.

There are two schools of thought on how to actually make the incre-mental cuts. The procedure involves setting the workpiece against the fence with the back corner of the wood planted firmly on the router table, and tipping the workpiece down into the spinning bit. For optimal control, you may want to clamp a stopblock to the fence behind the workpiece. This will help anchor the back corner of the workpiece for starting the plunge cut. Or, you can simply hold the wood firmly at the back corner instead of using a stopblock, provided you keep your hands clear of the bit area and set the bit low to take a reasonable first pass. Either way, line up the workpiece so the "outfeed" (left) edge of the bit will just hit the first layout mark on the workpiece when you tip the wood down. You may even want to clamp a second stopblock to the fence to stop the wood where the cut needs to end (at the right hash mark). Or, you can stop the cut by eye and without a stopblock.

Make the first cut by starting the router, lining up the cut and slowly pressing the wood down into the bit without moving it forward. Keep the hand that presses the wood downward clear of the bit area, even though the bit is shrouded by the wood.

To complete the pass, slide the wood slowly from right to left until the other index mark on the wood meets the "infeed" (right) bit mark you made on the router table or fence. Hold the wood in place, and turn off the router before lifting the workpiece up and off the bit. Check your accuracy. If the cut lines up properly, raise the bit 1/8 to 1/4 in., and make the second and subsequent passes the same way until you reach the full depth of cut. Depending on the bit you use, you may need to dig out the chips that accumulate in the slot after each pass or run the part across the bit a second time to clear the impacted chips. One way to keep the slot clear is to use an upcut spiral bit, which will pull chips down and out of the slot while you rout it.

MAKING A STOPPED CUT

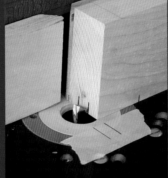

1 Apply a piece of masking tape in front of the bit and use a square to mark the bit's cutting width on the tape. The tape will be your reference for where the bit is located when it's inside the wood.

2 Lay out the stopped cut on the workpiece. In this example, it's a mortise.

3 Extend the layout lines around to the face of the workpiece, then mark the length of the cut. These will establish your starting and stopping points during routing.

4 Extend the width and position of the stopped cut around to the end of the workpiece, and use these marks to set the fence so the bit aligns properly with the cut.

5 For the first pass, set the bit low, and pivot the workpiece down over the bit so the left workpiece and bit layout marks line up. Keep the workpiece pressed against the fence, and use extreme caution when plunging the bit into the wood.

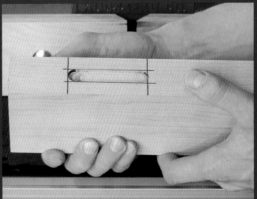

6 Complete the first routing pass by sliding the workpiece along the fence until the right pair of layout marks line up. Turn off the router and wait for it to stop before lifting the wood up and off the bit.

7 If you start and stop your cuts carefully, the bit should cut right to your layout lines. Raise the bit with each additional pass to cut to the desired depth.

Making Dado Or Groove Cuts

Cutting dadoes or grooves on a router table is as easy as making profile cuts. Recall that dado cuts cross the wood grain, while groove cuts follow it. Choose a straight or spiral bit to cut dadoes and grooves. For these operations, you'll use the bit height to set the dado (or groove) depth and the fence to reference how far the cut insets from the edge or end of the workpiece. Mark a pair of hash marks on the end of the workpiece to indicate where the bit should enter the wood, and lock the fence so the marks line up with the bit.

For the first pass, lower the bit to about 1/8 in. to shear the wood's surface fibers. Start the router and push the wood past the bit, feeding from right to left as usual. If the workpiece is wide enough to keep your hands a safe distance from the bit area, you can feed the wood without a pushstick or push pad, but be extremely careful to keep your feeding hand clear of the bit path along the back edge of the workpiece. In mid cut, the bit will be hidden inside the wood. If the cut passes all the way from one end of the workpiece to the other, you won't know exactly where the bit will pop out of the wood until it does — and you don't want your hand to discover this spot first! For narrow workpieces, always use a pushing device to help feed the wood.

The easiest way to cut dadoes and grooves to the correct width is to use a straight bit with a diameter that matches the dado width. When you don't have a bit that's wide enough, you can use a narrow bit and widen the cut by moving the fence. First, make the normal series of incremental-depth cuts to create a slot to the correct depth. This will remove most of the waste and bring the bit to the right depth. Line up these first cuts so the bit cuts the wall of the dado *on the fence side* of the bit. Now, widen the dado by shifting the fence *back from the bit* and feeding the workpiece from right to left to cut away more

1 Use a pair of reference marks on your workpiece to mark the exact position of the inset cut on the workpiece. Move the fence until the bit's cutting edges and layout marks line up.

4 To widen a cut without creating a climb-cut situation, rout the "inside" edge of the cut, closest to the fence, first. Then, move the fence away from the bit to cut away the remaining waste. Feed from right to left as usual.

waste. This will remove the waste *on your side* of the bit, while still allowing you to feed safely against the bit's rotation. If you were to widen the cut by cutting away material *on the fence side* of the bit (and moving the fence forward instead of away from the bit), feeding right to left would create a climb-cut situation and a possible loss of feed control. In this scenario, you'd need to feed from left to right instead, so the "waste" side of the dado would meet the bit against its rotation.

When you need to cut a dado across the grain of a narrow work-piece, back up the cut with either a miter gauge or a backup board. A good way to minimize tearout when using a miter gauge is to attach an auxiliary scrap fence to the miter fence. For optimal accuracy, clamp the workpiece to this fence before making the cut. Otherwise, the bit can pull the wood out of alignment during the cut and ruin accuracy. If you use a backup board instead of a miter gauge, screw a handle of some sort to the board to give your feed hand good purchase and avoid holding the backup board along the back edge.

MAKING INSET CUTS

2 Guide the workpiece from right to left across the table, just as you would for making a profiling cut. Use a push pad or other pushing device if it helps keep your hands clear of the bit.

5 To make an inset cut across the grain of a narrow workpiece, use a miter gauge rather than the fence to support the wood from behind. Add a longer scrap fence to the miter gauge if it helps improve support.

3 Once the cut is started, the bit disappears inside the wood on an inset cut. Be sure to keep your hands clear of the back edge of the wood — you don't know where the bit will exit until it cuts through.

Routing Curved Edges

Routing profiles into curved edges on a router table involves using piloted bits, just like handheld routing. Obviously, the fence won't help support a curved cut, but it's also unsafe to make curved cuts by simply pushing wood into the bit. Depending on your angle of approach, the bit can grab the wood and pull it out of your hands in an instant. The solution for starting curved cuts safely is to install a starter pin near the bit and use it as a fulcrum to pivot the wood into the bit. Most router table insert plates come with a starter pin that presses or screws into holes already drilled in the plate. If your router table's insert plate doesn't come with these provisions, you can drill a hole and install a piece of dowel or short length of steel rod to serve the same purpose.

To start a curved cut, insert the starter pin in a hole on your side of the bit. Set the workpiece against the starter pin with the wood clear of the bit. Now, pivot the wood against the starter pin and slowly into the spinning bit.

It's imperative that the bit and pin are in contact with the same edge of the workpiece. Never allow the workpiece to pass between the pin and the bit, or the bit will grab the wood and jerk it from your hands. When the wood reaches the bit's pilot bearing and stops, begin to feed the workpiece from right to left as usual, so the bit follows the curve. As long as you keep the wood against the pilot bearing, it no longer needs to ride against the starter pin. You'll probably find that feeding the wood along the curve will naturally cause you to swing the wood away from the starter pin anyway. The starter pin simply serves as a bearing surface only when engaging the bit in the wood.

ROUTING CURVES WITH A STARTER PIN

1 Most router table insert plates have several holes near the bit opening for using a starter pin. Press the pin into any of these holes. Or, drill a hole for a pin if your plate doesn't have one.

2 A starter pin serves as a fulcrum and a point of support for beginning a curved cut. Without it, it's easy to overfeed the wood into the bit and create a kickback situa-

3 Press the workpiece against the starter pin and pivot it into the bit to begin the cut. Introduce the wood to the bit slowly and steadily until the bit's pilot bearing makes contact with the wood.

4 Feed the wood along the bit with the workpiece always pressed against the pilot bearing. It can also make contact with the starter pin.

5 Once the pilot bearing makes contact with the workpiece, the starter pin is no longer necessary. Don't be afraid to let the cut drift away from the starter pin.

Controlling Trapped Cuts

Some styles of bits "trap" the wood during a cut, so pulling the wood out or away from the bit is impossible without ruining the workpiece. Angled lock miter bits, T-slot bits, keyhole bits, dovetail bits and some profiling bits are other examples of bits that make trapped cuts.

The way to cut successfully with these bits is to make sure the cutting path of the bit is controlled all the way along. Use a table-mounted featherboard or two to press workpieces firmly against the fence on either side of the bit area. If your router table fence is tall enough, you may also want to install a featherboard over the bit to keep workpieces from creeping up as they pass through. This would also ruin the cut.

Another trapping situation to avoid is feeding narrow workpieces between the bit and fence to remove material. When a fence is positioned over a bit, normal feed direction is from right to left. However, if a fence is set back from the bit, feeding wood between the bit and fence from right to left actually becomes a climb cut, because the wood is meeting the bit on the opposite side of its rotation. Instead of pushing against the wood as it should, the bit will pull the

The style and cutting manner of some bits makes a trapped cut unavoidable. Use featherboards to keep workpieces anchored securely against the table and fence. If necessary, change your feed direction so the bit presses the wood against the fence.

wood through the cut, usually when you least expect it and faster than you can control.

The best way to avoid this form of trapping danger is to remove material with the bit partially shrouded by the fence. If your only setup option is to back the fence up behind the bit so the two are clear of one another, you'll need to reverse your feed direction and feed the workpiece from left to right. Avoid this potentially confusing situation whenever you can.

It's never a good idea to feed workpieces between the bit and fence, as shown in the left photo above. This traps the wood and allows the bit to grab the wood and pull it through unexpectedly. The safe way to make this cut is to set the bit partially in the fence instead. With this setup, the wood is no longer trapped in the cut.

Other Common Workpiece And Setup Issues

Table routing is easiest when workpieces are large enough to handle comfortably and keep your hands out of harm's way. Sometimes luck will be on your side and your workpieces will be ideally sized. But, in the real world of woodworking, you'll have just as many occasions when the proportions of the wood are less than ideal. You'll end up with some that are huge, tiny, thin or that otherwise place your hands close enough to the bit to trim your nails. In cases like these, you'll need to know how to work safely. Here are some guidelines and setup helps to try.

Routing Small Workpieces

One of the big benefits of a router table is that the bulk and weight of your router aren't an issue with the tool under the table. It's the perfect setup for routing smaller workpieces, because visibility is vastly improved and gravity is working with you. However, you'll still need to be mindful of how to keep your hands out of harm's way. If the workpiece is smaller than about 8 to 10 in. square, use pushsticks and backup boards to feed the wood through. Let common sense guide you here — if your hands feel too close to the bit, use a pushing device or two to protect yourself. In situations where the wood is particularly small, you can even stick the workpiece to a larger scrap with hot-melt glue or tape to make it safer to handle. It's always worth the extra effort to keep your hands clear of danger.

Be particularly cautious when routing small pieces against a starter pin. Even though a starter pin offers essential support for starting curved cuts, there's a whole lot more bit exposed to your hands.

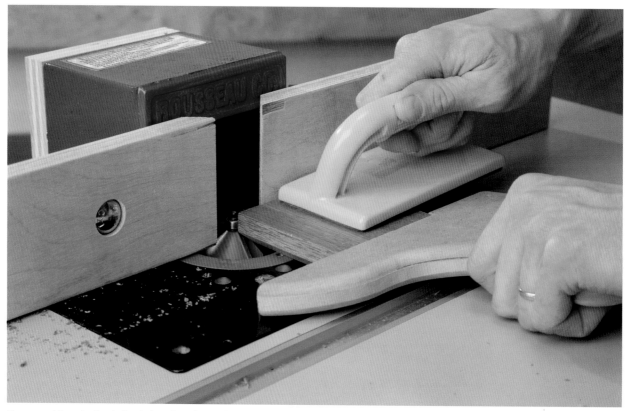

Use a pushing device in both hands to keep them safe for routing a small workpiece. Better yet, start from a larger workpiece and cut off the routed portion, if possible.

Routing Thin Strips

Router tables are perfect for making custom molding strips, but here again, the proportions of the workpiece can place your hands too close to the bit to feed safely by hand. Thin strips of wood are also flexible, and during heavy profiling they can begin to flutter against the bit, which produces a ragged cut. Install featherboards to the side and above the workpiece to improve stability and keep the wood traveling in a controlled path through the bit. If you have many strips to rout, feed them one after the next so they double as pushsticks for one another. Or, use a scrap of the same proportion to push the strip through if you just have one short piece to rout.

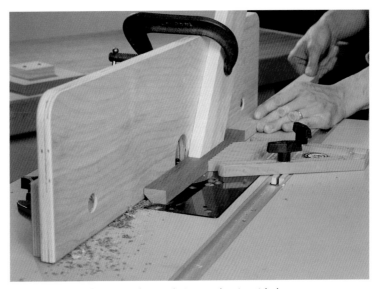

If you can't rout from a wider workpiece to begin with, be sure to use featherboards to keep narrow workpieces under control. Use a piece of scrap to feed the workpiece through so your hands stay clear.

Routing Long Workpieces

There's really no limit to the length of a workpiece you can feed across a router table, provided you support the wood adequately when it extends off the table. Use featherboards to keep a long workpiece firmly planted near the bit. They can serve as a second set of hands if you need to push the wood across the table from several feet away. For really long strips of lumber, use some form of workstand, feed rollers or a sawhorse on either side of the table to keep the wood even with the tabletop.

Provided the wood is held firmly in place by featherboards, you can also feed it in safely from one end, let go and pull it through from the outfeed side. This can sometimes be helpful if you are working alone or without the aid of sawhorses or other support devices next to the router table. Test your featherboard setup first before routing to be sure there's enough pressure to keep the wood immobile when you let go. It shouldn't lift off the table or move backward with the featherboards in place.

When routing long workpieces, start the cut as usual, supporting the wood from behind. Use featherboards to control the cutting path at the table.

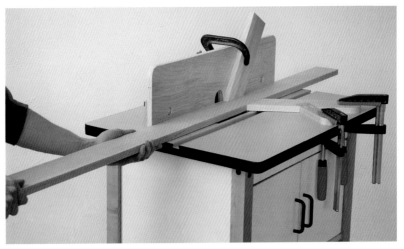

Provided the featherboards are installed securely, you can pull the wood through the cut from the left side if this helps keep it from tipping off the table.

Routing Narrow Workpieces On-End

Sometimes your only option for routing narrow workpieces is to stand them on-end and feed them against the fence. The big risk here is that a narrow-ended workpiece will tend to tip forward or backward or rock away from the fence when you slide it along its end. A particular problem with narrow workpieces is that the workpiece is more likely to tip down into the hole around the bit, leading to a kickback or ruined cut. When routing workpieces like this, close up the bit hole as much as possible with a small-holed reducer ring.

One easy way to add helpful support for on-end routing is to back up the workpiece with a wide piece of scrap cut square. A backer board like this adds stability to the tippy end of the workpiece and keeps it moving squarely along the table while also preventing tearout at the back edge of the wood. Another option to prevent rocking is to install a tall auxiliary fence on your router table's fence. With a tall fence, there's no second-guessing whether or not the wood is firmly pressed against the fence and square to the bit — you'll know it easily. A tall fence really helps when profiling the edges and ends of large panels with vertical panel-raising bits.

Narrow workpieces present problems if you have to rout them on-end. Install a tall fence and back up the workpiece with a wide scrap backup board.

When it's necessary to stand a tall workpiece on-end for routing, fasten a taller auxiliary fence to your router table fence to improve support. Use a thick featherboard to control the bottom end.

Routing Large Panel Material

Usually, it's easier to rout large panels with a handheld router setup instead of on the router table. At some point across the range of workpiece sizes, it becomes easier to move the router over the wood than to maneuver a large panel over the table. Still, if you decide to use the router table for routing a large panel, try to set up the operation with the panel oriented facedown on the table rather than on-edge. With a big panel, you'll want to use as much of the table as you can to improve the support. Remember that the fence can be positioned any way you need it to be on the table. Clamp it crosswise, diagonally or opposite the usual direction if it helps increase the amount of table surface you have to work on. Feed direction stays the same, provided you position yourself in front of the fence as usual. Many router tables actually offer more workspace on the back side of the table instead of the front side. Make use of it.

Profiling That Cuts Away Bearing Surface

If you use multi-profile or other deeply shaped profiling bits, be careful that your cuts won't remove all the flat-bottomed bearing surface on the workpiece. Be particularly careful about this if you are using a bit design that's new to you. If the bit cuts the entire bottom away from the wood, you're headed for trouble. At some point along the cut, the workpiece will tip down against the table and the cut will be ruined. You also want to avoid binding the bit when the wood tips, which could lead to a kickback.

The way around these problems is to forecast how much material the bit will remove before you start the cut. Sight down from the end of the fence with the wood

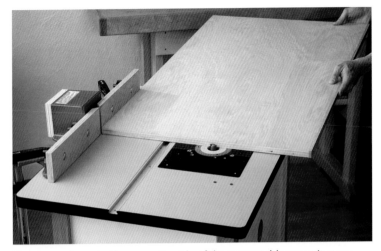

Move your fence to the opposite side of the router table or set it crosswise if it helps add bearing surface for supporting large workpieces.

held against it to visualize what the bit will do. If the bearing surface on the workpiece will be entirely or nearly cut away, use double-sided tape or hot-melt glue to attach a piece of scrap alongside the wood to add more support. Or, switch to thicker or wider stock so you can't cut all of the bottom material away. Then saw off what you don't need after routing the profile.

Some profiling bits will cut away all the workpiece material that touches the table, particularly when the wood is narrower than the bit's profile. When this happens, the wood tips down and the bit ruins the cut. To prevent this situation, start from a wider workpiece or mount the wood to a piece of scrap that can serve as extra support during the cut.

Jointing With A Router Table

With a straight bit and some minor fence modification, you can turn your router table into a fine jointer. A router's higher operating speed and smaller-diameter cutter will deliver more cuts per inch than a stationary jointer, which can actually make it superior to a jointer. The only real limitation here is that router tables don't offer as much workpiece support as a long-bed jointer. Wider router tables with long fences make better jointers than smaller, benchtop router tables.

Here's how jointing works on a router table: Your straight bit will shave the wood on the infeed (right) side of the fence, and you'll set the outfeed side of the fence so it "catches" the wood flush with the bit. With the left fence set flush, the workpiece can't tip back into the bit as its edge is cut away. If it did, the jointed edge would have a step at some point along its length instead of being flat from one end to the other.

In theory, any straight bit can function as a jointing bit. Even a flush-trim bit will work, provided the bearing doesn't interfere with the wood. For best results, use a 1/2-in.-shank bit with a diameter that's at least 1/2 in. A 1/4-in.-shank bit doesn't offer enough stiffness to keep the bit from flexing and vibrating during jointing, so use the larger shank size if you can. Obviously, the cutting length of the bit will need to be at least as long or longer than your stock is thick, but an overly long bit isn't necessarily better than one just long enough. Excessive cutter length invites more vibration. If you're working with 3/4-in.-thick material, a 1-in. cutter length, double-fluted straight bit in a 1/2- or 3/4-in. diameter is ideal for jointing.

Setting Up A One-Piece Fence For Jointing

If your fence has a single facing, or if the two facings are always flush when they slide apart, you'll need to create an offset so the infeed and outfeed sides aren't flush. The way to do this is to apply a piece of plastic countertop laminate to the left (outfeed) side of the fence. The thickness of the laminate (around 1/16 in.) creates the necessary offset between the infeed and outfeed sides of the fence, and it also establishes how much material the bit cuts away. Laminate is ideal for this application: it has a

Any bit that cuts a straight edge can be used for jointing, including a conventional straight bit, a flush cutter or a spiral bit. Longer cutting length bits will allow you to joint thicker lumber.

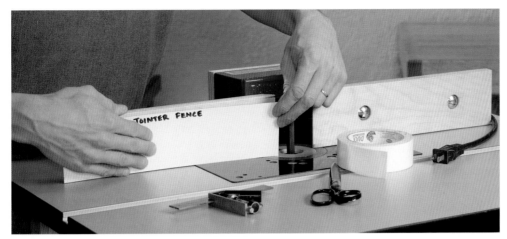

If your router table has a split fence with a single spine, set it up for jointing by applying a piece of plastic countertop laminate to the left fence facing with double-sided tape.

slippery surface that makes feeding easier, and it limits the bit to making a light, smooth cut. If you use thicker material like hardboard instead of laminate to create the offset, the bit will have to cut more deeply, and it could leave a rougher cut.

Stick the strip of laminate to your fence with double-sided tape. Use a metal rule to align only the laminate side of the fence with the bit's cutting edge. Lock the fence, and you're ready to begin jointing. Feed workpieces from right to left, as usual.

Adjust the fence so the left fence facing is flush with the bit's cutting edge. This will create a narrow offset on the right facing and establish how much material will be removed when you joint an edge.

Setting Up A Two-Piece Fence For Jointing

Some router table fence styles have two halves to the base that slide independently. With this fence type, you won't need the laminate to establish an offset between the infeed and outfeed fences. Instead, mark a test workpiece to trim off about 1/16 in. from one edge, and set the infeed (right) fence so the bit will cut to this mark. Slide the outfeed (left) fence back and clear, and rout about 6 in. off the edge of the test piece using only the infeed fence. Stop the cut and keep the test piece in place against the infeed fence. To create the offset, slide the outfeed fence forward so it is flush with the routed edge of the test piece, and lock down this half of the fence. It's now ready to go. Feed workpieces from right to left.

Some router table fences are made of two separate parts. On this fence style, there's no need for plastic laminate to set up jointing operations. Simply adjust the left fence facing even with the bit and set the right fence in slightly from the left so the bit makes a shallow cut.

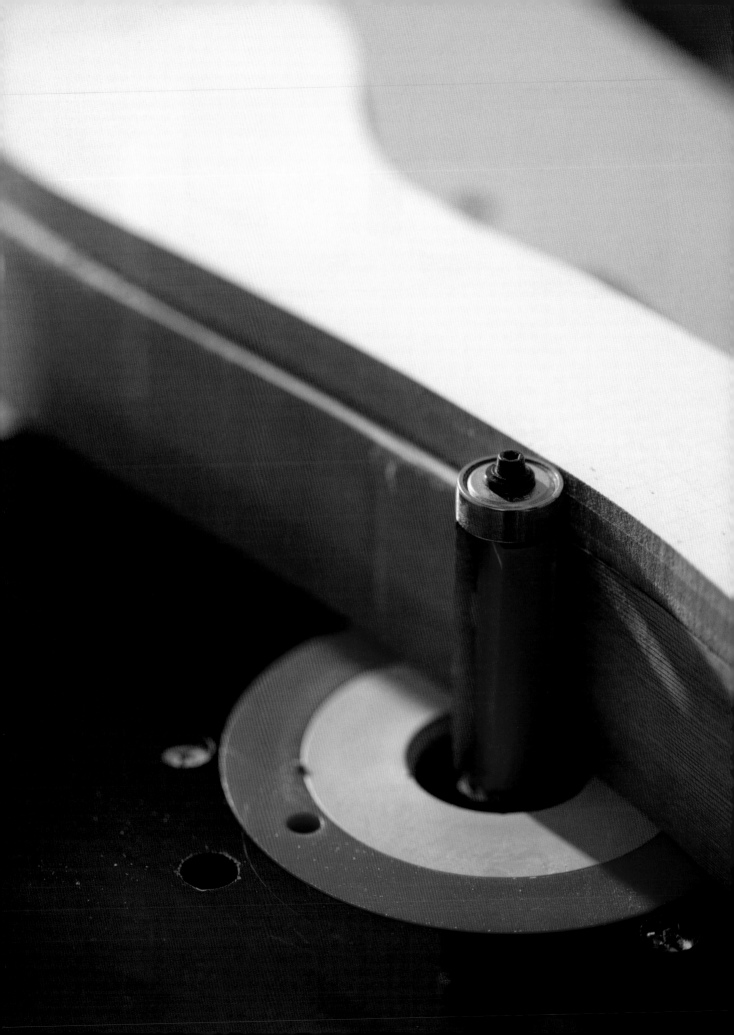

EIGHT

TEMPLATE ROUTING

In previous chapters we've seen how a router can be guided against its subbase, an edge guide, a straightedge or other jigs to cut in a variety of controlled ways. Another highly precise option for guiding a router is to use a template. Templates are simply rigid patterns cut and sanded to shape. By adhering the template to a workpiece, you can use your router and a straight bit with a pilot bearing or a guide collar and straight bit to duplicate the template shape onto the wood. Essentially, templates turn routers into woodworking's version of cookie cutters.

Templates provide helpful and reusable patterns for cutting multiple parts to the same size and shape. If you make your template carefully, part duplication is quick and easy.

Generally, templates are used for replicating a part that would be more time-consuming or difficult to do one at a time. For instance, say you were making a garden bench with curved back slats or a series of Christmas tree shapes for a run of table decorations. You could cut each slat or tree by hand with a jigsaw or on

the band saw. Trouble is, no two shapes would match precisely, despite the time and effort you'd spend trying to make them the same. A template takes much of the work out of the process. Once the template is carefully made, all you need to do is cut the workpiece roughly to shape and slightly larger than the template. Running the router against the template cleans up the edges of the workpiece to create a perfect copy. This way, you can make one, ten or a thousand Christmas trees that have exactly the same shape.

Using templates for duplicating the outside shape of an object is only one of several templating applications. You can also use templates for making internal cutouts, such as inlays or hinge mortises. Templates are even a good way to cut dadoes or stopped slots for mortise-and-tenon joints, as we'll see in chapter nine.

Another use for templates is to limit the router's cutting path to a specific length or direction. Here, a template allows the router to cut a series of straight slots for installing shelving.

Depending on the application, you can use templates to form shapes by cutting around the outer edges or, in the case of this template, an inside cutout.

Making Templates

You can make router templates from a variety of materials. There are a few important criteria to keep in mind when choosing template material. First, a template should have two smooth faces. A smooth top surface will ensure that the router slides easily all around and doesn't bind on the template, which could affect the cut. A smooth bottom makes for a more secure contact surface between the template and the workpiece. If the bottom surface is uneven or bumpy, it will reduce the holding power of whatever you use to stick the template down. When a template breaks loose during routing, you'll lose your accuracy and probably ruin the workpiece.

Templates should also be made of material with consistent and solid thickness. This is especially important if you use a piloted bit for making the cut. Voids or weak areas inside the template material can catch the bearing and interrupt the cut. A few of the best material options for templates include hardboard, medium-density fiberboard, thick plastic and plywood — provided the plywood is high quality and free of open pockets inside. All these options are relatively inexpensive, and you can find them at any home center. They're also easy to machine with common woodworking saws and sanders and hold up well for repeated use. Wood scraps also make good templates, but be sure the wood is flat and planed or sanded smooth on both faces.

There are several good material options for making templates, including medium-density fiberboard, void-free plywood, hardboard or sheet plastic.

Drawing Templates

The first stage of creating templates involves sketching the shape onto the template material. You can use any method that works for you. Generally, you'll probably want to draw and refine the template shape on a piece of cardboard or paper first, then cut this out and use it as a pattern for tracing onto the template blank. It's easier to erase and make changes on paper than trying to do this on the template stock. In the event you wear your template out with repeated use (or accidentally ruin the template with a router bit!), it's a good idea to save this paper or cardboard pattern so you can re-create the template easily at a future date. If a template shape is symmetrical, sometimes all you need to do is draw half the pattern shape and flip it over to trace the full profile.

Grid paper makes handy pattern material for sketching those highly

If a part shape is symmetrical, make a cardboard pattern of half the shape, then flip it over on your template blank to draw the full shape.

precise templates or for making workpieces with parallel edges and square corners. Since grid paper is thin and hard to trace around, draw the pattern on a full sheet of paper and mount it on your template stock with spray adhesive. Then cut out the template following the pattern you drew on the grid.

Grid paper makes excellent pattern material for drawing templates. Stick your gridded shape to the template stock with spray adhesive, then cut along your outline.

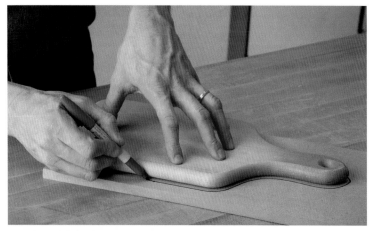

Another way to make a template is to simply trace an existing shape onto your template material. This is a good approach to avoid damaging the original object by using it as the template instead.

With care, you can use the actual object you want to replicate as the template itself, although the risk here is that you could damage the original in the routing process.

Another option for creating a template is to use an existing shape you want to match and simply trace around it onto your template stock. Or, you may be able to use the object for creating a matching template by sticking it to the template stock and actually routing around it. This works best with objects that have thick, smooth edges. It may be tempting to use your finished object as the template instead of going to the trouble of making a separate template, but it's a good idea to prevent damaging the object with a router bit.

Once you've traced the pattern outline onto your template stock, the next step is to cut the template out and shape it carefully. The template's accuracy really hinges on doing a careful job at this stage. For highly contoured templates, a scroll saw is an excellent choice for cutting the template to shape. Use a table saw or band saw with a fence to cut flat edges and ends of the shape in order to produce reliably flat surfaces. Refine the cut edges with a file or by sanding carefully so the router bit can follow the shape without introducing telegraphing problems. Making the template can seem like time-consuming work, but if you do a careful job, the time spent now will be rewarded by accurate part duplication later.

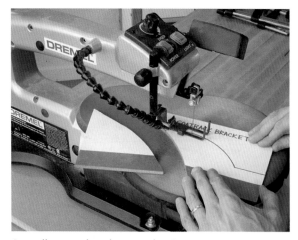

A scroll saw or band saw makes it easy to cut out templates with complex or curved shapes. Use a fine-tooth blade to minimize the blade marks, and cut just outside your layout lines.

A template will only be as accurate as its reference edges, because your router will copy the exact shape, errors and all. Sand up to your layout lines to perfect a template's shape and to remove all traces of blade marks.

On an "outside" template, you'll use a router and bearing-guided straight bit to follow just the outer edges to duplicate the shape.

Another way to create a shape is by cutting around the inside edges of an "inside" template. For duplicating smaller parts, inside templates can offer better support for the router.

Types of Templates

There are really only a few types of templates you can make. In the case of our Christmas tree and bench slat example, these are "outside" templates. Here, the template's purpose is to replicate the outside profile of the tree shape. Sometimes you'll want to use a template for creating an inside cutout instead of an outside shape. These "inside" templates allow you to cut out an exact shape from a larger workpiece you want to preserve — inlays are good examples — or to rout away an interior waste area quickly and easily. An inside template and a router will cut hinge mortises much faster than a hammer and chisel.

In this inside template application, the router is used to remove all the inner waste and create an hourglass relief area in the workpiece.

The best way to save extra wear and tear on your router bits and create the smoothest edges is to saw about 1/16 in. outside your layout lines, then reattach the template and rout away the extra material.

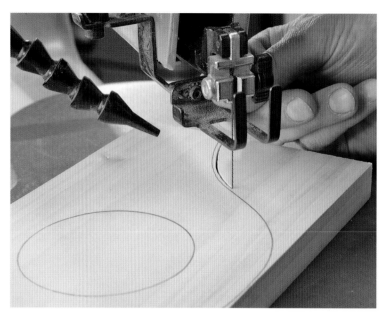

Workpiece Preparation And Mounting A Template

Once your template is prepared for use, there's a bit of prep work to prepare the workpiece for routing. Make sure to joint and plane or sand your workpiece smooth on both faces. When template routing, you want the template to attach securely to a flat, smooth workpiece face. It doesn't take much distortion in the wood for the template to work loose during routing.

Trace around the template onto the workpiece with a heavy line that's easy to see, and cut out the shape about 1/16 in. outside your layout lines. In the case of an inside template where the internal piece will be routed completely away, draw the cutting line 1/16 in. inside the penciled layout lines. Cutting the object to rough shape with a saw before routing with the template is mainly a good way to preserve your router bits. You could simply stick the template to the workpiece and do all the cutting work with the router, but it will involve making repeated passes to cut through the workpiece, and this puts more wear and tear on the bit edges and router motor. It also creates more debris. When there's only 1/16 in. or so of material to rout away, the final edges also tend to be smoother and more precise.

With the workpiece rough-cut to size, attach the template so it aligns with your initial tracing again. The most forgiving options for attaching a template are double-sided carpet tape or hot-melt glue, with tape being the easiest to remove. You can also tack a template down with short brads. Choose a length that's short enough so just the points of the brads enter the workpiece. Short screws also work, but use them when you can mount the template and rout into the back side of the workpiece. This way, it won't matter if you leave screw holes behind.

How you mount a template to your workpiece depends on whether fastener holes are acceptable or not on the finished shape. The best non-marring options are hot-melt glue and double-sided tape.

Template Routing With Piloted Bits

One technique for routing against a template is to have the bit's bearing follow the shape. You can use either a pattern bit, with the bearing mounted on the shank, or a flush-trim bit with the bearing mounted below the cutters. Either way, the bearing follows the edge of the template, and the bit cuts even with the bearing's rim. Which bit style you choose depends on whether the template is on top or underneath the workpiece as well as whether you're using a handheld router or routing at the router table.

As far at bit specifics go, choose a pattern or flush-trim bit with cutters somewhat longer than the workpiece is thick but not overly long. Excessively long bits just transfer more vibration into the cut. A particularly long flush-trim bit may even make it impossible to template-rout a thin workpiece with a handheld router; there's a limit to how far you can retract the bit before the router's motor pack doesn't engage the base properly. The stiffness of 1/2-in.-shank flush-trim bits is preferable to that of 1/4-in. shanks. Most pattern bits are available only in 1/4-in.-shank sizes.

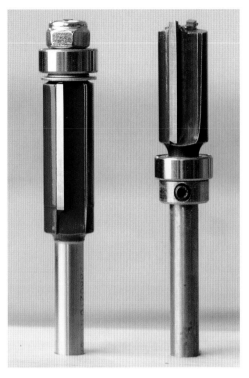

The two bearing-guided bits you'll use for template-routing include flush-trim bits (left), where the bearing is located at the tip of the bit, or pattern bits (right), with the bearing mounted on the bit's shank.

underneath the workpiece. In this case, switch to a flush-trim bit so the bearing is below the workpiece. Either way, set the bit depth so the bearing makes full contact with the template and the cutter meets the workpiece as deeply as you want the finished edge to be. In most situations, you'll be making a trim cut across the full thickness of the workpiece. If you've trimmed the workpiece within 1/16 in. of the template, the bit should be able to cut away all the waste in one pass with good results.

Template Routing With A Handheld Router

Choosing the correct bit for your template arrangement and router setup is easy. If the template is on top and you're routing with a handheld router, use a pattern bit so the bearing meets the top-mounted template. Occasionally you may need to mount the template

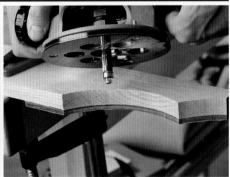

TEMPLATE SETUPS FOR FREEHAND ROUTING

One configuration for setting up a template cut is to mount the template on top of the workpiece and use a pattern bit to follow the template edge (left). To accomplish the same cut with a flush-trim bit, mount the template below the workpiece instead of above it (right).

With a handheld router, the feed direction for making these cleanup cuts is counterclockwise around an outside template or clockwise for an inside cutout. This holds true regardless of where the bearing happens to be, so use the same approach with flush-trim or pattern bits. These feed directions present the cutters to the wood against the bit's rotation, which helps pull the bit tightly against the template. Feeding the other way would result in a climb cut. Sometimes a climb cut can be helpful if the wood has uneven grain or if you're routing around a shape with coarse end grain. If routing conventionally seems to produce excessive tearout, try a climb cut in the rough areas instead, but do this cautiously. Climb cutting can lead to a loss of router control.

Template Routing On The Router Table

Template routing on a router table involves reverse setups and feed direction from handheld routing. If the template is on top of the workpiece, you'll have to use a flush-trim bit instead of a pattern bit so the bearing meets the template above the workpiece. If the template is mounted below the workpiece, use a pattern bit.

Feed direction reverses as well; remember, the bit spins the opposite way when you invert the router. So, to rout around an outside template, feed the workpiece clockwise against the bit to avoid climb cutting. For making internal cutouts, the correct feed direction is counterclockwise. It seems confusing initially and hard to remember, but after awhile the correct feed direction becomes intuitive. If you start the pass the wrong direction, you won't feel the familiar resistance offered by the bit when it's cutting against its rotation — and a climb cut will want to pull the wood along erratically. Go with the direction that feels most controlled, and you'll surely be cutting against bit rotation.

TEMPLATE SETUPS FOR A ROUTER TABLE

Bit and template configurations are reversed from freehand setups when using templates on a router table. Mount the template on top when using a flush-trim bit (top) or under the workpiece with a pattern bit (bottom).

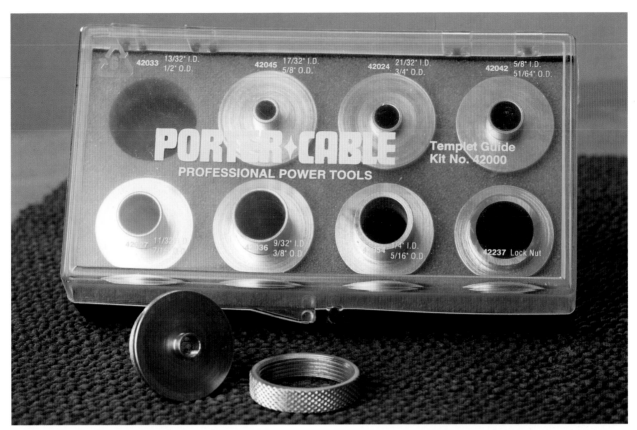

Guide collars are sold as kits to fit a variety of bits. The inside and outside diameters of the bushings vary, so you can set up different offsets depending on the collar and bit you choose.

Template Routing With Guide Collars

Another option for routing with templates is to use guide collars and a straight or spiral bit instead of a piloted bit. Guide collars, which are also called rub collars or guide bushings, are simply short bushings cast into a flange that fits into a hole in the router's subbase. Guide collars are made in a variety of inside and outside diameters to fit around straight bits of different sizes. In a template-routing setup, the bushing portion of the collar follows the template rather than a pilot bearing.

There are several advantages to using guide collars instead of piloted straight bits. For one, the guide collar absorbs most of the lateral stress as you press the router against the tem-plate. With a piloted bit, the bit has to absorb this stress instead, which accel-erates wear and tear on the bearing. Guide collars also lead to fewer mis-takes; you have the option of present-ing only the amount of cutter to the wood that's required to make the cut. In this regard, a guide collar allows a single straight bit to serve as a vari-able-depth cutter. Pattern and flush-trim bits are more limiting — you may need to own several bits with different cutter lengths, depending on the thickness of your template and work-piece. You may discover that a set of guide collars and a few straight bits can entirely take the place of flush-trim or pattern bits, which saves you money — and the straight bits work for either template routing or other straight bit tasks. If you use your guide collars properly, the bit's cutters should never come in contact with the bushing, so a set of guide collars could easily last the lifetime of your routers.

Installing a typical guide collar involves threading the knurled ring onto the guide collar's flange from inside the router base.

Guide collar styles vary somewhat by manufacturer. The standard style (right) has a threaded outer flange that fits in the router's subbase hole and is held in place with a threaded lock ring. Bosch guide collars (left) have notches that fit into a locking insert in the router base.

Types Of Guide Collars

The popularity of Porter-Cable's guide collar system has made it almost the industry standard for guide collar sizing. Porter-Cable sizes the flange portion of the collar to 1³/16 in. diameter, regardless of the bushing size. Consequently, the standard subbase for a Porter-Cable router has a 1³/16-in.-dia. bit hole which fits all the guide collar sizes. The flange is threaded, and the knurled ring threads on from inside the router base to hold the collar in place.

KEEPING GUIDE COLLARS TIGHT

Threaded guide collars can occasionally vibrate loose unless you tighten them securely. If you need to use a guide collar for several hours at a time, give the lock ring an extra twist with a pair of pliers or a slip-jaw wrench to ensure it won't come loose. Or, wrap the threads on the guide collar flange with a few layers of plumber's Teflon pipe tape. Wind the tape around clockwise so it won't unravel when you screw the locking ring in place. The tape forms an effective, temporary thread locker.

Guide collars must be tightened securely on the router base or they can vibrate loose during routing. One way to keep the bushing tight is to wrap the threads with plumber's Teflon pipe tape.

Not all router manufacturers follow the Porter-Cable guide collar system. Bosch, for instance, uses a proprietary flange with notches cut around it. Bosch guide collars fit into a recess in the subbase, and a sliding lock holds the guide in place. But even Bosch now makes a 1³/₁₆-in. conversion fitting that adapts Bosch's subbase opening to accept standard guide collars.

If your router doesn't have a subbase that accepts 1³/₁₆-in. guide bushings, one option is to replace the stock subbase with an aftermarket base that fits the guide collars. Many woodworking and router bit supply companies offer these bases to fit any router. You may need to drill mounting holes to fit the screw hole pattern for your particular router (see page 127), but it standardizes any router to accept guide collars.

Some router subbases don't have a standard guide collar opening, but you can retrofit any router with an aftermarket subbase for this purpose.

The length of a guide collar's bushing will influence how it works with your template. Long bushings will require thicker templates. Short bushings are often more convenient.

always be shorter than the template thickness to work properly. This predicament presents two possible solutions: You can switch to thicker template material and leave the guide bushing length as is. However, you may need to use a longer straight bit to make up for a thicker template. Another solution is to change the bushing length by grinding or sawing the bushing to shorten it. Don't hesitate to cut your guide collars down to size — about 1/4 in. of bushing length is all you'll need for most operations. The shorter bushing size works equally well with both thin and thick templates.

Guide Collar Length

One issue you'll face when template-routing with guide collars is that the length of the guide collar's bushing can impact your choice of template material. Depending on which collars you buy, the length of the bushing is sometimes too long to use with thin hardboard or plastic templates. The bushing length must

Understanding Guide Collar Offset

No matter which guide collar or straight bit combination you use, there will always be an offset between the edge of the bit and the outside edge of the guide collar. The bit needs room to revolve inside the collar, which creates a gap. The thickness of the bushing that rubs against the template adds to the offset. If the bit fills the collar opening and the bushing is thin-walled, you'll end up with a relatively small offset. When

If a guide collar's bushing is too long for your templates, you can shorten it by sawing off the excess with a hacksaw. Fasten the guide collar to a piece of scrap hardboard with its lock ring to hold it steady during cutting. Then file the cut edge smooth.

The amount of offset created between the template and the workpiece depends on the outside diameter of the collar's bushing and the diameter of the router bit. In these two examples, changing the guide collar size creates two different offsets with the same router bit.

the bit is considerably undersized for the collar, you'll get a bigger offset. One way or the other, the offset will affect the size of the workpiece. On an outside template, the guide bushing offset will result in the workpiece being larger than the template, because the bit meets the wood farther away than the guide collar meets the template. When you're cutting around an inside template, the offset will make the cutout area smaller than the opening in the template for the same reason.

If it doesn't matter that a workpiece ends up larger or smaller than the template you're using, offset may not be a concern. Generally, however, you'll probably want your templates to create workpieces of a specific size and shape, which means you'll have to account for offset when you lay out the template. Here's one method for doing it: In the cactus inlay shown here, the goal is to get the dark cactus shape to fit precisely inside another board. The process for creating a template that will make a matching recess for the cactus requires factoring in the size of a guide collar-and-bit offset. Since the template will make a cutout shape for the cactus, it's an inset-style template. The template opening will have to be larger than the actual cactus shape, due to the offset. You can use a pilot bearing from a router bit as a spacer to trace an oversized copy of the cactus on the template material. The bearing serves as an easy way to draw a consistently oversized shape. Any bearing size will do.

Once the oversized tracing is complete, use a dial calipers to measure the bearing width from inside to outside rim. You don't have to calculate what the exact measurement is — just lock the calipers to the bearing width. Now, select a straight bit and guide collar from your guide collar set that creates an offset matching the caliper distance. You'll have to try a few different bit and collar groupings to find the right offset, mounting both parts in your router and checking the offset

Routing around an outside template with a guide collar will make the workpiece larger than the template, due to the offset between the guide collar and bit.

against the calipers. If you've got a full set of guide collars and a few straight bits with different diameters, you're bound to find a match.

Cut out the oversized cactus tracing from the template, and sand or file the opening to just hit your penciled tracing line. Now, mount the template to the wood and use the guide collar and bit you chose to rout out the recessed area for the cactus. If you've measured and cut carefully, the cactus should fit almost seamlessly into its opening.

For simpler shapes, you may be able to pick a bit and guide collar first, measure the offset and skip the tracing step. Just make the template larger or smaller by the size of the offset, plotting the template shape carefully.

Offset works in reverse when routing around an inside template. Because of offset, the guide collar will make an inside cutout smaller than the template's opening.

ACCOUNTING FOR OFFSET WHEN FITTING AN INLAY

1 To make a relief area that matches this inlay shape, use a guide collar and an inside template. To do this, you'll have to account for guide-collar offset. Create the offset by tracing around the inlay using a router bit bearing as a spacer.

2 Measure the "offset" you've just created on the template by measuring the bearing from its inside to outside rim with a dial calipers. Lock this distance on the caliper.

3 Use the dial caliper distance to find a matching offset between your straight bits and guide collars. You may have to try several bit and collar arrangements to get the correct match-up.

4 Cut the inside template to shape by following the offset layout lines you drew using the bearing spacer. Cut and sand the shape carefully to final size.

5 Rout the relief area for the inlay using the appropriate bit and guide collar you found with the dial calipers.

6 If you measured the offset distance accurately and cut the inside template carefully to shape, the inlay shape should fit precisely into its relief area.

Other Template Routing Operations

Routing Thick Workpieces With A Template

On occasion you may need to make parts from lumber that's thicker than your bits are long. The way to tackle these situations is to pair up both a flush-trim and pattern bit and use each bit to rout about halfway or

TEMPLATE-ROUTING THICK WORKPIECES

1 When you don't have a pattern or flush-trim bit long enough to template-rout a thick workpiece, you tackle it by making a pair of cuts with each bit type. The cutting length of each bit must be more than half the thickness of the workpiece and template combined.

2 Start the shaping work with the pattern bit mounted in your router table. Set it to full cutting height with the template mounted below the workpiece. Rout the template shape all around.

3 Flip the workpiece over so the template is now on top, and switch to a flush-trim bit. Raise the bit so the bearing will follow the edge made by the pattern bit. Rout the remaining rough edge away to bring the workpiece to final shape.

ROUTING HINGE MORTISES WITH A PATTERN BIT

1 Hinge mortises are easy to rout with a pattern bit. If the hinge has radiused corners, make sure to use a pattern bit with a matching cutting diameter.

2 Routing the mortise will require a simple template. Make it by first tracing the hinge leaf on your template material. Trace the full leaf or just the portion that will actually mortise into the door edge.

3 To cut out the mortise with the pattern bit, build up reference surfaces around the tracing with pieces of scrap and double-sided tape. Make sure the scraps line up exactly with the layout lines.

4 Use the pattern bit for the mortise to rout away the waste area. Set the bit so the bearing rolls along the scrap, and make several sweeping passes to remove all the waste. Then pull off the taped-on scrap.

5 Fasten the template to another piece of scrap to serve as an edge guide. Be sure to set these parts so the template accounts for the hinge leaf overhang on the door.

6 Clamp the hinge template in place on the door, and rout the hinge leaf mortise to shape. You may need to switch to a pattern bit with a short cutter length to make this shallow cut.

7 If you made your template carefully and chose the correct bit diameter for the hinge, the hinge leaf should fit neatly into its mortise.

more through the thickness of the wood. Start with the pattern bit and the template mounted either above or below the workpiece, depending on whether you're using a handheld router or router table. Rout around the template to trim about halfway across the workpiece. Then, remove the template and switch to a flush-trim bit. Flip the workpiece over so the surface routed by the pattern bit now becomes the reference surface for the flush-trim bit to follow. Rout away the rest of the waste. The combination of two bits should form a flat, smooth and even surface on oversized stock.

Routing Hinge Mortises With A Pattern Bit

You can cut hinge mortises quickly and precisely with a template and pattern bit. Woodworking and builder's supply houses sell pre-made templates for this purpose, but they're just as easy to make yourself. If you're installing hinges with radiused corners, you'll need a pattern bit with a radius that matches the hinge radius. The specific radius will be noted on the hinge carton. This template method will also work with square-cornered hinge leaves, but you'll have to square up the corners of the door mortises with a chisel after routing them.

To make the template, start by tracing the hinge leaf shape along one edge of the template material. You can trace the full hinge leaf or just the portion that will actually mortise into the door. Tape extra scraps of template material along the hinge outline; these will create the reference surface for the bit bearing to follow. Provided the radii of the hinge and the bit match, the bit will cut a perfect copy of the hinge shape. Make sure these scraps are wide enough to create a stable platform for the router base.

Rout away the waste material inside the built-up area of the template, using the pattern bit. Make sweeping, left-to-right passes to remove this waste with a handheld router. Then remove the scrap material and fasten a piece of scrap underneath the template to serve as a fence for aligning the template on the door edge. It will help to rest the template on the door and align it properly first. Draw a reference line on the template where the door meets the template back, and attach the fence along this line to complete the template.

Clamp the template to the door edge, and set the bit depth for a shallow cut that matches the thickness of the hinge leaf. You may need to switch to a pattern bit with a shorter cutter length in order to do this, but make sure the bit's radius matches the one used to make the template. Experiment with bit depth as well as with the template on scrap wood before committing to the actual door. When all the settings are correct, rout away the waste area inside the template to form the hinge leaf mortise on the door. If the hinge has square corners, just square up and chisel away the rounded corners.

Routing Hinge Mortises With A Guide Collar

Another option for routing door hinge mortises is to use a guide collar and straight bit instead of a pattern bit. The advantage to this method is that you can rout any hinge radius without having to use a bit with a matching radius.

The setup for this operation will require an inside template, and the shape of the hinge leaf cutout will be oversized for the hinge to account for the offset between the guide collar and the router bit. Use a router bit bearing as a spacer to trace an enlarged hinge leaf shape on the template stock. The bearing provides an even and oversized offset. It isn't crucial to use a specific bearing size or diameter, but it can be helpful if the bearing's inside-to-outside rim measurement is $1/8$ in. It will be easier to choose an appropriate guide collar

ROUTING HINGE MORTISES
WITH A GUIDE COLLAR

1 To rout a hinge mortise with a guide collar, you'll need to establish an offset around the hinge to match your collar and bit. A router bit pilot bearing makes a handy tracing guide for this purpose.

2 Measure the offset distance on your layout or by measuring from the bearing's inside-to-outside rim with a dial calipers.

3 Find a guide collar and straight bit that match the offset of the hinge you found in Step One. It may take several tries to find the correct pairing.

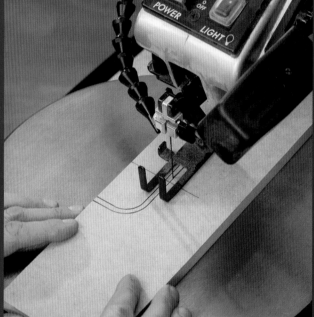

4 Use a scroll saw or band saw to cut just inside the offset layout line on your template, then sand the cut edge smooth. The accuracy of your hinge mortise depends on this step.

5 Fasten a scrap to your template to serve as a clamping surface for holding the hinge template in the correct position on the door edge. Rout away the mortise waste with a shallow cut.

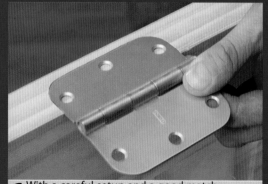

6 With a careful setup and a good match between template and offset, your hinge should fit the door mortise accurately.

and bit diameter this way. Whichever bearing you use for tracing, measure its width with a dial calipers.

Use the dial caliper measurement to check the offset between the guide collar and bit you'll use for cutting the final hinge mortise. The caliper and offset measurements need to match, or the hinge mortise will be too large or small for the hinge.

Next, cut out the template, following the oversized bearing shape you drew. Cut carefully and just inside your layout lines with a scroll saw, then refine the final shape with a file. The accuracy of the template's mortise shape and final fit of the hinge in the mortise depend on careful cutting and shaping at this stage.

Set the template in place on the door and adjust the mortise opening to achieve the correct overhang of the hinge knuckle. Mark the door's position on the bottom of the template, and attach a piece of scrap to the template along this reference line. The fence will provide a way to clamp the template in place on the door for routing, and it will automatically index the mortise properly for all the hinge mortises you need to cut.

Adjust the straight bit depth so it will cut the hinge leaf thickness but no deeper. Experiment with bit depth by using the template on scrap wood before committing to the actual door. When you're satisfied with how the hinge fits into a mortise on scrap, clamp the template to the door and cut the mortises by making sweeping left-to-right passes.

Routing Butterfly Keys

Butterfly keys can serve either functional or decorative purposes on a woodworking project. Making keys from contrasting wood adds a decorative touch, and the shape forms a locking connection between two boards, which gives this sort of inlay a structural benefit as well.

The easiest way to make butterfly keys is with a router inlay kit. The usual kit provides a specially sized guide collar, a carbide spiral bit and a second bushing that fits over the guide collar to create an offset that is exactly the diameter of the bit. You use the kit components to make the butterfly key as well as a matching mortise shape that fits the key.

Start the process by creating the key. Draw the key shape onto a piece of tagboard or heavy paper. It looks best if both "wings" of the butterfly match. Trace your shape onto template stock — 1/4-in.-thick material will typically do for this template. Use a scroll saw to carefully cut out the key from the template. Refine the internal cutout shape with a file or sandpaper to complete the template.

To rout the actual key shape, install the kit's guide collar on your router without adding the bushing. Attach the template to the workpiece you'll use for the key and rout out the shape with the tiny spiral bit. If the key stock is the correct thickness for your application, just cut completely through to release the key. You can also rout the key in thicker material. Make the cut in a series of increasing-depth passes until the bit depth matches the thickness of the key you want to use. Release the key from the blank by slicing it free on a band saw.

Routing the matching butterfly mortise is easy: Use the same key template you made, but this time slip the bushing over the guide collar to reduce the mortise shape to the correct proportion. Attach the template to the workpiece and set your bit depth to match the key thickness, or just slightly shallower. Do this with a plunge router, and remove the waste with a series of plunging passes to the final bit depth. Trim the corners of the butterfly mortise with a chisel so they match the key.

If you worked accurately when making the template and routing the male and female parts of the inlay, the key should fit nicely in the mortise. Glue it in place and sand the key flush with the surrounding wood.

ROUTING BUTTERFLY KEYS

1 In order to rout butterfly keys or other decorative inlays accurately, it helps to use an inlay kit with specially sized spiral bit, guide collar and oversized bushing. The kit automatically registers the correct offset.

2 The first step in creating a keyed inlay is to draw a pattern of the butterfly shape and trace it onto your template material. You can make the key any size you like.

3 Cut the key template to shape and use it with the guide collar and bit to rout the inlay piece that will fit in a matching recess. Rout carefully around the inside template cutout or you'll damage the inlay piece.

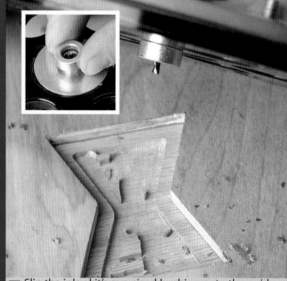

4 Release the inlay piece from its blank by slicing through the blank with a band saw. Set up this cut so the inlay piece will be slightly thicker than the recess you'll make.

5 Slip the inlay kit's oversized bushing onto the guide collar bushing to inset the bit further. Now rout the recess in the matching workpiece using the key template.

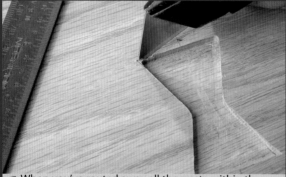

6 When you've routed away all the waste within the recess area, trim the rounded corners of the butterfly to a point with a sharp utility knife or chisel.

7 It may take a bit of fine sanding to refine the shape of the inlay piece, but the parts should fit together seamlessly with little effort.

Cutting Straight Lines With A Jig And Guide Collar

Aside from duplicating parts or creating accurate mortises and inlays, guide collars also work well for limiting a router to a straight cutting path. All it takes is a straight-slotted jig where the slot size matches a guide collar bushing. In this setup, the router's path is completely controllable, and you can achieve accuracy on par with or even better than using a dado blade on a table saw.

Here's a simple slotted jig you can build that uses this principle for cutting dadoes and short grooves. In the next chapter, you'll see that the same jig can be employed whenever you need to make dead-straight cuts. Depending on your cutting situation, you can make lap joints, mortises and other joinery by simply limiting the slot length or shifting and re-clamping the jig to cut a wider area.

Essentially, the jig amounts to a slotted board wide enough to provide sufficient bearing surface for the router base. A straightedge mounted on one end of the slotted board ensures that the slot is always perpendicular to the edge of the workpiece. You'll need to make the jig fit a specific guide collar and straight bit, so choose a large collar and a straight bit that will cut a practical dado size. A 3/4-in. O.D. guide collar used with a 1/2-in. straight bit is a good combination here. For this style of jig, it's also a good idea to choose a guide collar size that you can cut with a typical straight bit. Here, a 3/4-in. straight bit is what you'll need to make the slot, but it's a fairly common bit size you may already own.

To build the jig, start by cutting a 3/4-in. slot along the jig's crosspiece. Cut the slot starting from one end of the workpiece and stopping the cut several inches from the other end.

Choose a blank for this crosspiece that's wide enough to support your router base and long enough to cross a standard piece of lumber with a few extra inches to spare. A 16- to 18-in.-long workpiece is long enough to make dadoes across a standard 1 x 10. Center the 3/4-in. slot on the workpiece, and cut it at the router table using the fence as a reference. Make the slot cut in several passes, raising the bit each time until it comes through the top.

Next, screw the slotted crosspiece to a straightedge that's longer than the crosspiece is wide. Mount the straightedge to the open end of the slotted piece. Use your 3/4-in. O.D. guide collar as a spacer when you attach the parts to hold the slot open correctly. Otherwise, the slot could close slightly and cause the guide collar to bind during use.

Fasten a pair of scrap blocks to the overhanging ends of the straightedge. These will serve as clamping surfaces for holding the jig in place against a workpiece. Make sure these clamping blocks are the same thickness as the crosspiece and not thicker, or they could interfere with the router base.

The final step in readying the jig for use involves cutting across the straightedge using the 1/2-in. straight bit you'll use each time in this jig. Mount the 3/4-in. O.D. guide collar to your router, chuck the bit and set its depth to cut partially into the straightedge but not all the way through. Slip the guide collar's bushing into the jig slot and cut across the straightedge. Now you have an exact reference for where the bit will intersect the workpiece. Use the edges of the bit "track" on the straightedge to line up your dado cuts. Label the jig to indicate which guide collar and straight bit to use as a quick reference later.

You can modify this jig design for use with even larger straight bits and guide collars. If it would be more useful to have the jig cut 3/4-in. dadoes, use a 3/4-in. bit and a 1-in. O.D. guide collar instead. Rather than cutting a slot to make the crosspiece (a 1-in.-dia. straight bit is difficult to find), make it from two strips of stock instead of one. Use the guide collar and a piece of 1-in.-wide scrap to control the slot width when attaching the crosspiece to the straightedge. You'll also need a "bridge" piece on the other end of the crosspiece parts to close and fix the far end of the gap.

CUTTING DADOES WITH A GUIDE COLLAR JIG

1 This guide collar jig enables you to rout straight dadoes with a guide collar and straight bit. The guide collar follows a slot in the jig that matches its outside diameter.

2 To make the jig, first choose a guide collar that you'll use specifically with the jig. It should be a collar that matches the cutting diameter of a large straight bit — you'll need this bit to cut the jig's slot.

3 Make a series of passes and raising the bit each time to cut a slot along the top board of your jig. Start the cuts in from one end and rout all the way through the other end to form an open-ended slot.

4 Fasten a scrap straightedge along the open end of the slotted board. Use the guide collar as a spacer to hold the slot open correctly.

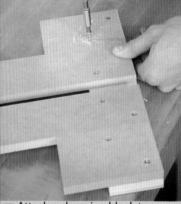

5 Attach a clamping block to the jig's straightedge, one on each side of the slotted board. These will hold the jig in place on your workpieces.

6 To prepare the jig for use, install the straight bit you'll use with this jig and cut a shallow pass across the straightedge. This will establish the exact cutting zone of the bit.

7 Use the shallow dado in the jig to register the bit with layout lines on your workpieces. Provided you always use the proper bit, the jig will cut exactly where you line it up.

8 Option: You can build this slot-cutting jig for use with oversized guide collars, even if you don't have a straight bit large enough to cut the initial slot. Just use a pair of strips to make the top, slotted portion and hold them apart with a spacer. Here, this jig will be used with a 1-in. guide collar and a 3/4-in. straight bit.

TEMPLATES FOR SIGN-MAKING

Another popular template application is to use a guide collar and letter templates to make signs. The letter kits are reasonably priced and the technique is simple. Basically, the process involves installing plastic letter templates in a framework that holds them in position. The frame clamps to your workpiece, and a guide collar directs the router to trace the template shapes. For a basic overview of the procedure, follow the photo series shown here. You can use straight bits, veining bits with pointed tips or roundnose bits to form the letter recesses. Each bit creates a different letter style, which adds visual interest to your signage.

ROUTING LETTERS AND SIGNAGE

1 A guide collar and sign-making jig are all you need to "carve" decorative letters. The letter templates come in several sizes and font options.

2 Lay out a pair of reference lines on your blank sign to register the letter templates and jig framework accurately.

3 Slide the letter templates into the routing frame, and tighten the stops on the frame to hold the letters securely. Then install the appropriate guide collar and bit for use with these templates.

4 Rout the letters by making a plunge cut to start each letter and feeding the router along the template opening.

5 It helps to make these letter cuts in a series of deepening passes, especially if you are routing letters into hard lumber. This helps reduce burn marks as well as stress on the plastic templates.

NINE

BUILDING JOINERY WITH A ROUTER

Much of the success or failure of your woodworking projects over the long term really boils down to how well you make the joints. If you choose your joints carefully and build them precisely, that table, chair or drawer could very well outlast you. Build the joints poorly, and your project might not make it a year. The difference between a few hundredths of an inch, in some cases, can make a joint slip together like a hand in a glove or not fit at all. Although glue and nails add permanent strength, most joints that interlock should almost hold themselves together without extra help. It takes precise machining and careful setups to build accurate joints. Your router and router table are perfect tools for the task.

There are more than a dozen different joints you can build with a router, but some of the options require specialized bits that are expensive or difficult to use successfully. Lock miter joints, for instance, require an expensive bit and many exacting setups to achieve a satisfactory joint. There are much easier options. In this chapter, we'll take a simpler approach. You'll learn how to build a core group of eleven common woodworking joints that should satisfy the needs of almost every project you build. You probably own most of the bits you'll need already, and the joint-making procedures will be both safe and easy to carry out, even if you're just getting started as a woodworker. As your skills and bit collection grow, you can always add the trickier or more fanciful joints to this core group.

No other woodworking machine can cut as many styles of joinery as a router. It's the perfect tool for the task.

Double rabbet joint.

Overlap rabbet joint.

Rabbet Joints

Description And Usage

Rabbets are simply offset tongues formed on the edges or ends of a workpiece. You can make the tongue long enough to cover over the end of the mating part, forming an overlap rabbet joint. This is a common joint style for making simple box corners or for hiding the edges of the back panel on cabinetry and other case-work. By shortening the tongue, you can make a pair of rabbets fit together to form two different interlocking joints. The shiplap joint combines two matching rabbets into a flat joint for making panels. Or, you can arrange the rabbets so they meet at 90° and form a double rabbet joint.

The side of the rabbet tongue that establishes the tongue's thickness is called the cheek, and the flat ledge at the base of the tongue is called the shoulder. Regardless of which machining option you use, the setup will involve cutting a portion of both the cheek and shoulder at the same time with each pass.

Bit Options

Piloted rabbeting bit, wide straight bit, spiral bit.

Bit options for routing rabbets include piloted rabbeting bits, carbide spiral or fluted straight bits.

Shiplap rabbet joint.

Rabbets can be cut on a router table either facedown or on-edge with an ordinary straight bit. Support narrow workpieces from behind with a backup board.

Machining Options

Cutting rabbets on the router table: A router table offers the best control for cutting rabbets, particularly if workpieces are narrow and you are cutting rabbets on the short ends. You'll use a combination of the fence and the bit height to limit the cut and establish the rabbet proportions. Either a wide straight or spiral bit will work for cutting rabbets this way, or you can use a piloted rabbeting bit with its bearing flush, or behind in the router table fence. If you use a straight or spiral bit, choose a bit diameter that's wider than the cheek and shoulder dimensions, if you can. This way, you can set the bit partially inside the fence and use the width of the bit to cut most or all of the rabbet tongue or cheek in one setup.

The decision you'll need to make when cutting rabbets this way is whether to orient the workpieces facedown on the table or stand them on-end, vertically. For long, narrow workpieces, the facedown approach is safer than trying to guide the workpiece standing up. Back up the workpiece with your miter gauge or a push block. For wider workpieces with dimensions more square than rectangular, you can rout rabbets safely either facedown or standing on-end. If the panel is particularly long, install a tall auxiliary fence to your router table fence so there's plenty of vertical support behind the panel to keep it from tipping.

If you're just getting started with woodworking, it helps to mark the actual proportions of the rabbet on your workpiece and use it to help set the bit height and fence position. After you get used to the process of cutting rabbets (and other joinery), you'll probably stop marking workpieces this way and create the proportions by simply measuring off the bit or fence.

One way to ensure an accurate cut, especially if you are just beginning to build rabbet joints, is to draw the rabbet's proportions on the workpiece.

Use the rabbet layout lines on the workpiece as guides for setting up the bit and fence to cut it to shape. Aim to just remove the layout lines.

One way to cut rabbets is to set the bit so it cuts all the way to the cheek or shoulder line, then shift the router table fence back a little with each pass to remove all the waste area.

Whether you decide to feed workpieces vertically against the fence or facedown, you'll also need to choose how to cut the waste material away most efficiently. There are two options here: You can move the fence away from the bit with each pass but keep the bit height the same. Generally, this method works best for cutting long rabbet tongues with the workpiece facedown on the router table. Set the bit height to cut to the rabbet's cheek, and shift the fence back with each pass until the bit reaches the rabbet's shoulder. Feed the workpiece from right to left as usual. You can also use this method for routing workpieces vertically against the fence, but here you'll set the bit height to cut to the shoulder. Each time you shift the fence back, the bit will cut closer to the cheek.

The other setup option is to fix the fence in place and raise the bit. If the workpiece is facedown, set the fence so the bit will cut to the shoulder line with the first pass. Raising the bit some with each additional pass even-

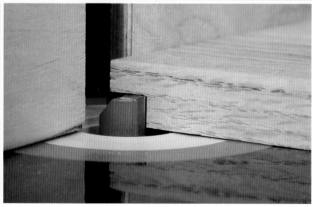

Another setup option for cutting rabbets is to set and lock the router table fence in place so the bit cuts to the cheek or shoulder, then raise the bit a little with each pass to remove the waste.

The easiest way to cut rabbets freehand is by using a piloted rabbeting bit. The bit's depth and bearing diameter are the two variables that establish the rabbet's cheek and shoulder proportions.

tually forms the cheek. When the workpiece is positioned vertically against the fence, set the fence so the bit cuts to the cheek on the first pass. Raise the bit to work your way to the final shoulder height.

If you use a piloted rabbeting bit in the router table instead of a straight bit, install one of the smaller bearings that usually come with the bit so you can use as much of the cutter width as you need. Sneak up on the cut just as you would with a straight bit, either by moving the fence or raising the bit. For rabbets with dimensions less than about 1/2 in., use the bearing that will enable the bit to cut both the cheek and shoulder in a single pass. In these cases, set the fence even with the rim of the bearing and adjust the height to cut right to your layout lines.

You can also use a piloted rabbeting bit in a handheld router to cut rabbets. It's better to reserve this option for when you're cutting wide workpieces or panels that can provide plenty of support for the router base. For a moderately sized rabbet, you can usually make the full cut in one pass. Just choose the bearing that allows the bit to trim to the shoulder, and set the bit depth to cut the cheek. Feed the router from left to right, as you would for any other handheld router operation.

Cutting rabbets with an edge guide: Another option for cutting rabbets is to use an edge guide mounted on a handheld router. Use a wide straight bit to make the cut. Set up the cut so the bit is partially imbedded in the edge guide's fence opening. Measure off the edge guide fence to set the amount of bit projection. Usually, the bit depth will set the cheek portion of the rabbet, and the projection from the edge guide will form the rabbet's shoulder.

It's possible to cut rabbets freehand with a straight bit using an edge guide attached to the router. Set the bit and fence on the edge guide just as you would with a fence on the router table.

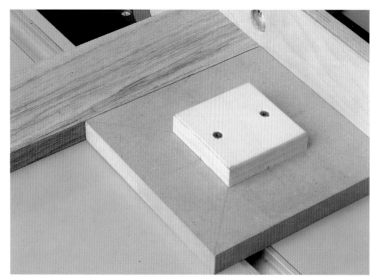

Use a scrap backup board to support narrow workpieces from behind when rabbeting short ends.

you take some precautions to prevent this from happening. It's the same situation you face when making profiling cuts. If you are cutting rabbets with workpieces facedown on the router table, support the wood from behind with a scrap backup board. Otherwise, the tearout will occur where the bit exits the wood at the rear corner.

To avoid tearout when routing end-grain rabbets with a handheld router, there are two options. You can clamp a piece of scrap to the exit side of the workpiece and rout into the scrap to finish the cut. Make this cut from left to right. The scrap will support the fragile corner grain. Or, you can skip the scrap and start the rabbet cut on the *exit* side of the workpiece instead of the left side. Make a short climb cut to remove the corner grain. Use care when doing this to keep the router from pulling itself along. Then perform the rest of the cut as usual, routing from left to right to meet the climb cut.

Avoiding tearout when cutting rabbets: When you are cutting rabbets or other styles of joinery, keep in mind that routing across the corner of the end grain fibers will produce splintering and tearout unless

OPTIONS FOR AVOIDING TEAROUT WHEN CUTTING RABBETS

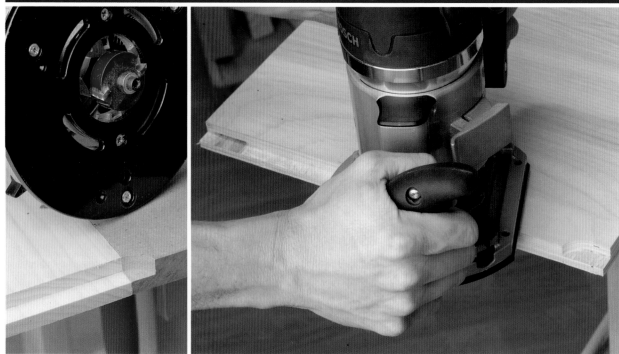

Cutting across the end grain when routing rabbets or other joints can lead to splintering at the corners where the grain is weak. One way to prevent tearout is to clamp a piece of scrap next to the workpiece to support the corner fibers and rout right into scrap to finish the cut (left photo). Or, make a short climb cut from right to left to remove the corner grain, then rout normally from left to right (right photo).

Housed dado joint.

Stopped dado joint.

Dado Joints

Description And Usage

Dadoes are simply three-sided slots cut across the grain of a workpiece. When the slot runs along the grain instead of across it, technically the slot becomes a groove instead of a dado, but the term dado is often used synonymously for both styles of slot cut. There are two basic types of dado joints you can cut with a router. A housed dado joint runs completely across the workpiece, and the mating part that fits the dado shows through on both ends of the joint. The other option, called a stopped or "blind" dado joint, involves cutting the dado only partway across the workpiece, stopping short of the "show" edge. The mating joint part has a notched front corner that fits around and into the stopped portion of the dado. When the joint is assembled, it looks like a conventional butt joint, and the dado is completely hidden from view. Either dado joint style makes strong connections for installing dividers or shelving in cabinetry or casework.

Bit Options

Any straight bit will work for cutting dadoes. Carbide spiral upcut bits are also good choices for cutting dadoes with a handheld router; use a spiral downcut bit for making dado cuts on a router table. If you are joining plywood together with dadoes that match the plywood thickness, be aware that most plywood these days isn't a full 3/4 in. thick. To make a tight-fitting dado, you'll need an undersized plywood cutting bit, which generally measures about 23/32 in. Or, you'll need to use a bit narrower than 3/4 in. and make more than one pass to sneak up on a proper fit.

Bit options for routing dado joints include undersized plywood bits, carbide spiral or fluted straight bits.

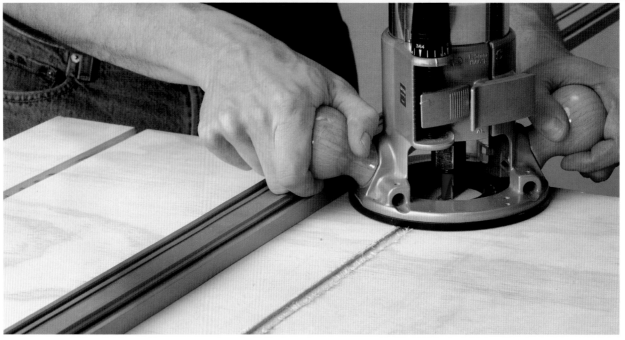

A clamped straightedge is often the most convenient option for cutting dadoes across a wide panel. Feed the router against the straightedge from left to right.

Machining Options

The easiest method for routing dadoes, particularly when the board is wide, is to clamp a straightedge in place and run the router's subbase against it. In order to line up the cut properly, you'll need to measure from the cutting edge of the bit to the edge of the subbase to determine the offset. Then clamp the straightedge the "offset distance" away from your dado layout lines so the bit lines up exactly. Feed the router from left to right across the workpiece to make the cut. If it's a deep dado, make the cut in a series of passes that increase in depth to prevent overloading the bit or router.

When you're milling dadoes across a narrow workpiece, use the router table instead of making the cut handheld-fashion. You'll get better control of the cut if you don't have to balance the router on a narrow surface. Set the fence so the bit aligns with your dado layout lines, and support the cut from behind with a backup board to prevent

tearout along the back edge. Or, back up the cut with a miter gauge fitted with a scrap fence to control tearout. Either way, backing up the cut also keeps the workpiece square to the fence.

A third way to make accurate dado cuts is to use a slotted dadoing jig with a guide collar fitted around the bit. (Learn more about building a slotted dadoing jig in chapter eight.) Essentially, the jig's slot fits precisely around the outside diameter of the guide collar bushing, which limits the bit to cutting a perfectly straight line. The jig is simple to align with your dado layout lines, because the slot you cut in the jig's crosspiece matches the bit's diameter. Just align the bit slot with your dado layout lines and clamp the jig in place. Make the cut by feeding the router from left to right across the workpiece. If you need a slightly wider dado than the jig will make in one pass, shift and re-clamp the jig as needed and make any additional passes to widen the dado.

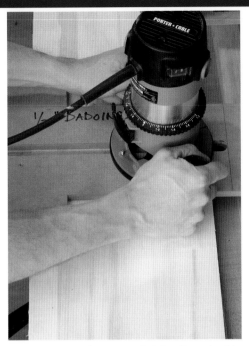

For narrower workpieces, a dadoing jig and guide collar provide excellent control and accuracy for cutting dadoes. To build this jig, see page 208.

A router table fence and straight bit are also a good combination for cutting dadoes. When cutting across narrow workpieces, be sure to support the cut from behind with a backup board or miter gauge.

Making Stopped Dado Joints: You can cut the dado slot for a stopped dado joint in several ways. One option is to run the router against a straightedge with a stopblock clamped or screwed to the straightedge to index where the bit stops (see page 161). The challenge with this approach is there's always a possibility that the router will drift away from the straightedge during the cut and ruin your accuracy. A more reliable method is to use a slotted dadoing jig and guide collar.

To use the jig method, start by laying out the dado proportions and stopped end. Install a straight bit that matches the dado width you need and the guide collar that fits the jig. Measure from the edge of the bit to the edge of the router's subbase with a combination square, and lock the square to this distance.

Clamp the slotted jig to the workpiece so it aligns with your dado layout lines, and use the combination square you just determined on the router to index the stopped end of

the dado cut. Clamp a stopblock here. The stopblock will ensure that the bit stops cutting precisely with your layout mark.

Set the router in the jig slot and make the cut from right to left across the workpiece, working toward the stop block. If the dado is deeper than about 1/4 in., you may need to make two or three more shallow passes, extending the bit farther into the cut with each pass to reach the final depth of cut.

The bit will leave the stopped end of the dado round, so square up the cut with a sharp chisel. Mark the mating joint part with a notch at the front corner that matches the proportions of the dado's stopped end. Cut out this notch with a jigsaw or band saw.

Test the fit of the parts. If the notched workpiece stands proud of the front of the joint, cut the notch a little deeper to improve the fit. It's easier to do this than re-clamping and adjusting the stopblock to rout a slightly longer dado slot — but that also works.

ROUTING A STOPPED DADO JOINT WITH A JIG

1 To make a stopped dado, begin by laying out the proportions and stop location for the dado on your workpiece. We'll use a slotted dadoing jig (see page 161) for making this cut.

2 To set the jig accurately for stopping the cut, measure the distance from the edge of the bit to the edge of the router's subbase. A combination square makes this easy if you lock the head over the subbase edge.

3 Use a snug-fitting scrap in the jig's slot to serve as a stop for the router. Use the combination square setting you just established to set the stop away from the stopping point of the dado. Clamp the stopblock to the jig.

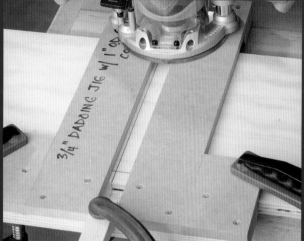

4 Install the appropriate guide collar in the router for your jig, and set the proper bit depth for the dado. If it's deeper than 1/4 in., make the cut in several passes of increasing depth.

5 Feed the router across the jig until the base meets the stopblock. Make a light first pass so you can check the stopblock's setting and accuracy against the actual cut.

6 When you've cut the dado to full depth, remove the jig and use a sharp chisel to square up the stopped end to complete the cut.

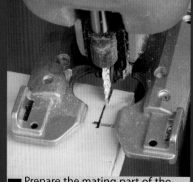

7 Prepare the mating part of the joint (usually a shelf) by notching the corner to fit around the stopped end of the dado. Use a jigsaw or hand saw to remove this notch.

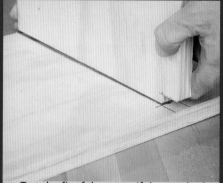

8 Test the fit of the parts. If the notched member of the joint doesn't meet flush with the edge of the dadoed workpiece, trim the notch as needed to adjust the alignment.

Dado-rabbet joint.

Dado-Rabbet Joints

Description And Usage

A dado-rabbet joint is a good option for joining plywood when you don't have an undersized straight bit that matches the plywood's thickness. The dado doesn't have to match the workpiece thickness to make an effective and strong joint — here, it's much narrower than the thickness of the mating part, which must be cut into a rabbet. Dado-rabbet joints make good connections for drawer corners, because the joint forms a mechanical connection that resists coming apart. Usually, the dado extends about halfway or slightly less into the thickness of the workpiece. The rabbet tongue thickness is typically $1/4$, $5/16$ or $3/8$ in. depending on which bit you use for cutting the dado.

Bit Options

Straight or spiral bit for cutting the dado; straight, spiral or rabbeting bit for cutting the rabbet.

Machining Method

Build this joint following the same methods you'd use for cutting a rabbet or a dado individually. Start by laying out the joint on both workpieces. The joint will be easier to adjust to fit if you make the dado first, then the rabbet. Tweak the rabbet's tongue dimensions to fit the dado.

Make the dado cut on the router table by lining up the fence to meet your dado layout lines and clamping it in place. Use a backup board or a miter gauge outfitted with a scrap fence to support the cut from behind and keep it square. Rout the dado across the workpiece.

Set up for the rabbet cut, either milling the shoulder or the cheek with the first pass. Notice in the photos that the cut is being made with the workpiece facedown against the fence with the bit aligned to cut the shoulder. Make a series of passes to cut to the cheek layout line, raising the bit a little each time. It's a good idea to test your rabbet setup and sizing on a test piece and check its fit in the dado. Adjust the cheek and shoulder position as needed until the rabbet fits snugly into the dado without forcing it into place.

ROUTING A DADO-RABBET JOINT

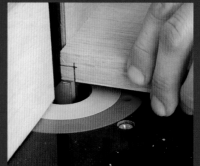

1 The best procedure for cutting a dado rabbet joint is to cut the dado portion first. Set up your dado cut indexing the bit off of your layout lines.

2 Rout the dado in a series of shallow passes until the bit reaches full depth. Back up the cuts with a piece of scrap, a miter gauge or a backup board to minimize tearout and provide workpiece support.

3 With the dado completed, set up the rabbet cut by imbedding a straight bit partially in the router table fence. Here, the straight bit will cut to the shoulder line of the rabbet.

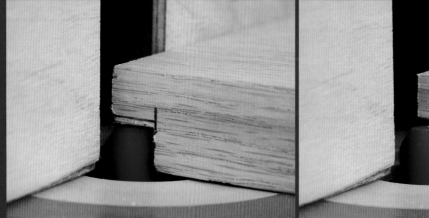

4 Cut the rabbet in a series of passes, either moving the fence or raising the bit to remove the waste. Here, raising the bit each time eventually cuts the rabbet's cheek.

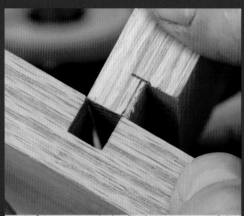

5 Before you reach the final proportions of the rabbet, test the fit of the joint parts. Use your final pass or two of the rabbet cuts to "sneak up" and refine the fit of the joint.

6 You'll know you've reached a good fit when the rabbet's tongue seats fully in the dado and the parts slide together easily. If the joint doesn't fit together well, adjust your rabbet setup on the router table slightly and make another pass to improve the fit.

Tongue-and-groove joint.

Tongue-And-Groove Joint

Description And Usage

You've probably seen tongue-and-groove joints used for flooring or board paneling, but they're also a good choice for joining solid-wood edging to the front of a shelf or for building simple door joints in rails and stiles. The joint is configured with a short, centered tongue on one part that fits into a matching slot cut into the other part.

Bit Options

Size the joint so the tongue is about 1/3 the thickness of the workpiece and 1/2 or 3/4 in. long. This way, you can use a standard 1/4-in. straight, spiral or slot-cutting bit to make the groove easily.

Bit options for routing tongue-and-groove joints include fluted straight bits or carbide spiral bits and slot-cutting bits.

CUTTING TONGUE-AND-GROOVE JOINTS WITH A STRAIGHT BIT

1 Mark the workpiece that will receive the groove cut, and adjust your router table fence and straight bit to align with the groove's layout marks on the workpiece. Try to center the bit on the workpiece as closely as possible.

2 Slide the workpiece along the fence to cut the groove. One way to ensure a centered groove is to flip the workpiece from one face to the other and make another pass. Any misalignment on the first pass will now be eliminated with the second pass.

3 Switch to a wider straight bit for cutting the tongue portion of the joint. Raise the bit to the same height as the groove depth, and use the groove workpiece to align the bit for cutting the cheeks of the tongue.

4 Feed the tongue workpiece along the fence to cut one cheek and shoulder of the tongue to shape. Support the cut from behind with a backup board.

5 After the first cheek and shoulder are cut, flip the workpiece to the other face and make a second pass to cut the other cheek and shoulder of the tongue.

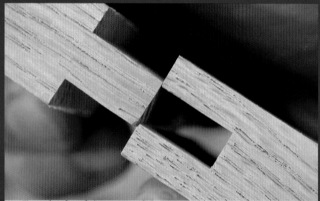

6 Test the fit of the parts. If the tongue is too wide, as shown here, shift the router fence slightly back from the bit and make two more passes to trim a thinner tongue. If the tongue is already too thin for the groove, adjust the router fence and cut a new workpiece.

7 A correctly fitted tongue-and-groove joint should slip together with just a bit of friction between the parts but without extra force. Forcing together a tight-fitting tongue can break the groove walls.

Milling Options

Making tongue-and-groove joints with a straight bit: Lay out the joint proportions on both mating parts, and begin the machining process by cutting the groove first. Install your straight or spiral bit and center it on the groove layout lines. You'll need to make the groove with the workpiece standing on-end, so install a taller auxiliary fence to your router table fence if the workpiece is long.

Use a backup board to support the workpiece from behind, and cut the slot by feeding the workpiece across the router table from right to left. Chances are, your slot won't end up perfectly centered after the initial pass. One helpful trick is to flip the workpiece around and make a second pass to center the slot exactly. It will produce a slightly wider groove, but this usually doesn't matter in the final joint.

You can mill the matching tongue with the workpiece positioned vertically against the fence or facedown on the table. One advantage to making the tongue on-end is that you've already established the proper tongue length with the straight bit setting that cut the groove. To complete the setup, keep the straight bit set at the groove height and shift the fence closer to the bit. Hold the grooved workpiece against the fence and use the thickness of the groove wall on the first workpiece to align the bit's projection out from the fence.

Cut one side of the tongue's cheek and shoulder by feeding the workpiece from right to left past the bit. Flip the workpiece to cut the other cheek and tongue. Test the fit of the parts after cutting both sides of the tongue. Usually the tongue won't fit perfectly in the groove on the first try. If it's too thick, move the fence slightly away from the bit and make two more passes on the tongue workpiece to shave the tongue thinner. Be extremely conser-vative when making this fence change — the amount you shift the fence will double the amount you'll actually remove from the tongue. If the tongue is too thin to begin with, you'll have to start over on a new workpiece. Shift the fence slightly *toward* the bit to cut a thicker tongue. As a general rule, cut the tongue on scrap material first to refine your settings before committing the actual project parts.

When fitting a tongue-and-groove joint, the goal is to mill the parts so they slip together with just a bit of friction but without extra play. If you plan to glue the joint, you may want to drop the bit height slightly when making the tongue so it doesn't quite bottom out in the groove. The gap will provide some extra room for the glue to fill.

Making tongue-and-groove joints with a slot cutter: Another option for making tongue and groove joints in 3/4-in. material is to use a slot cutter. With this bit, you'll cut the groove and tongue with workpieces facedown on the router table. Set the bit so its height aligns the cutters with the groove location. Move the fence so the slot cutter will cut to the full groove depth. Make a centered groove by passing the workpiece on one face past the bit, feeding right to left, then flip the workpiece to the other face and make a second pass to center the cut.

With the groove cut, making the tongue is easy: Simply lower the bit so the upper edge of the cutter aligns with the groove wall. Cut the tongue in two passes, flipping the workpiece from one face to the other. If the tongue turns out too thick, raise the cutter slightly and make two more passes. If it's too thin, make a new workpiece and lower the bit a tad. Again, cutting the tongue on a test piece first will economize material and help you refine your setup before making your final workpiece cuts.

CUTTING A TONGUE-AND-GROOVE
JOINT WITH A SLOT CUTTER

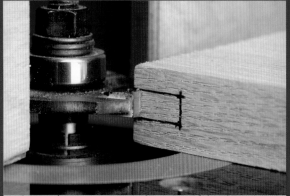

1 Set up the groove cut so the cutter of the slot-cutting bit aligns with your layout lines on the workpiece. Align the router table fence so the bit will reach to the base of the groove.

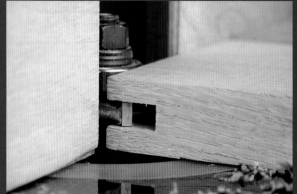

2 Cut the slot by feeding the workpiece from right to left, as usual. To center the slot, flip the workpiece to the other face and make a second pass, just as you would when cutting the slot with a straight bit.

3 You can cut the tongue side of the joint with the same slot-cutting bit and fence setting. To set up the cheek cuts of the tongue, lower the bit until the cutter aligns with the wall of the groove.

4 Cut one cheek and shoulder of the tongue by feeding the workpiece past the bit from right to left. Keep the workpiece pressed firmly against the table and fence.

5 Flip the workpiece to the other face to cut the tongue's other cheek and shoulder. Make a visual check to see that the shoulders of these two cuts line up across the tongue. If they don't, it means the workpiece shifted off the fence slightly for one of the two cuts.

Lap Joints

Description And Usage

If you're familiar with the process of building rabbets and dadoes, lap joints are easy. You'll cut lap joints using similar machining methods. This is because lap joints are essentially wide rabbets joined with wide dadoes. Half-lap joints combine two rabbets; T-laps are unions of a rabbet and dado, and cross laps are made by fitting two wide dadoes together. You can use lap joints for making cabinet face frame joints or for making picnic table and other outdoor project framework. Usually, the mating parts of these joints are made by cutting halfway through each workpiece. T-lap and cross-lap joints are particularly sturdy; the joints form interlocking connections that don't depend entirely on glue bonds for their strength. Half laps are also strong options, but they require glue and usually another form of reinforcement, such as screws, nails or dowels driven across the joint.

Bit Options

Wide straight or spiral bits are good options for cutting either the rabbet or dado portions of lap joints. You can also use a long or short pattern bit with a shank-mounted bearing.

Cross-lap joint.

Half-lap joint.

Bit options for routing lap joints include pattern bits, carbide spiral or fluted straight bits or piloted mortising bits.

T-lap joint.

ENHANCED BACKUP BOARD FOR CUTTING LAPS

Cutting lap joints involves making a series of repetitive passes. If you make these cuts on the router table, holding the joint parts by hand against a backup board can get tiring. Depending on how you cut the joints, hand-holding can also reduce accuracy if the bit pulls the workpiece out of alignment. One way to improve holding power and comfort is to make a modified backup board. Form a thick tab along the outside edge of the block to provide an extension for installing a clamp. Insert a dowel in the middle of the block to make a simple handle.

This simple push block with a dowel handle provides ample support for routing narrow joint parts. The tab along the front edge creates a handy attachment point for a clamp.

When laying out a lap joint, it can be helpful and more accurate to use the joint parts for setting the layout lines rather than measuring.

Machining Options

Layout tips: Before choosing a method for cutting the parts, you'll need to lay out the joint. On lap joints, an accurate way to do this is to lay one joint part on the other and mark the part width this way. It helps to minimize measuring errors. Since the mating parts will be cut halfway through their thickness, you can also set accurate bit height by routing partway across a piece of scrap, flipping the wood and routing

Many lap joints are made by cutting halfway through the thickness of both joint parts. One way to ensure your router bit is set to correct height is to cut partway across both faces of a test piece. Adjust the bit height until the cuts split the thickness of the test piece, as shown here.

to meet the first cut. The scrap thickness must match your workpiece thickness. If the cuts meet but do not overlap, you'll know the bit is set correctly for routing both halves of the joint.

Making lap joints on the router table: Using a router table for lap joints works best when milling half laps on the ends of shorter parts. Your router table may not be large enough to reach cross or T-lap joints along the length of long workpieces, and you may not want to use a router table even for end laps if the parts exceed a couple feet in length. But if the table size allows it and the part sizes are moderate, any lap joint style can be cut on a router table.

It helps to use a wide straight bit in the router table to reduce the number of repetitive passes you'll need to make. Lay out the thickness of the lap tongue (or dado depth, depending on the lap joint style you're making). Or set bit height using the double-cutting method described in the layout section above.

Set the fence position so the bit aligns with the shoulder layout line, and lock the fence in place. This will automatically index the final cut so you don't have to do it visually when routing the joint.

To mill the wide rabbet, clamp the workpiece to a backup board so the first cut removes wood at the end of the workpiece. Feed from right to left across the table to make the first cut. Then shift and re-clamp the workpiece on the backup board for the next pass, to cut more of the waste away. Repeat the process until you reach the final shoulder position and the workpiece touches the fence.

If you are making cross- or T-laps, cut the two walls of the dado with the first cuts, then remove the waste in between with a series of repetitive passes. Clamp the workpiece to a miter gauge with a long, scrap fence installed, to keep these cuts square to the workpiece.

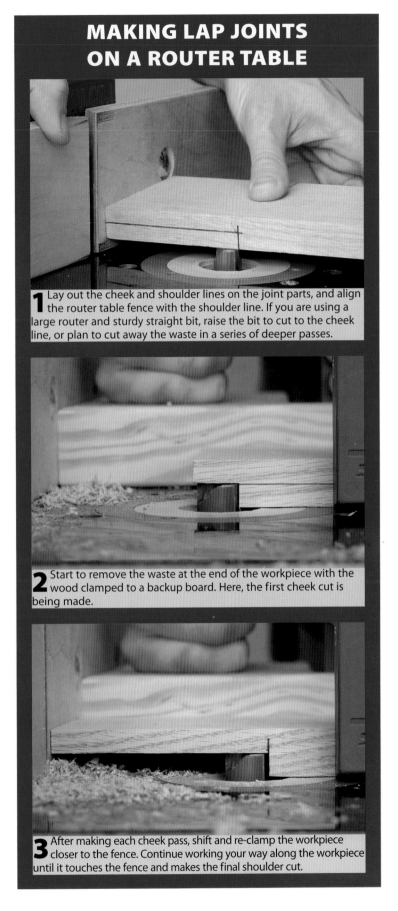

MAKING LAP JOINTS ON A ROUTER TABLE

1 Lay out the cheek and shoulder lines on the joint parts, and align the router table fence with the shoulder line. If you are using a large router and sturdy straight bit, raise the bit to cut to the cheek line, or plan to cut away the waste in a series of deeper passes.

2 Start to remove the waste at the end of the workpiece with the wood clamped to a backup board. Here, the first cheek cut is being made.

3 After making each cheek pass, shift and re-clamp the workpiece closer to the fence. Continue working your way along the workpiece until it touches the fence and makes the final shoulder cut.

CUTTING LAP JOINTS WITH A SLOTTED DADOING JIG

1 You can use a slotted dadoing jig, guide collar and straight bit to cut lap joints without a router table. Essentially, it's the same process as cutting an extremely wide dado.

2 Lay out the cheek and shoulder cuts for the joint as usual, extending the layout lines along the edge of the workpiece so they're easy to see during routing.

3 Establish the bit depth for your plunge router by inverting the router and setting the dadoing jig and workpiece on top. You'll want to remove this waste in a series of deepening passes, but here's where to set the maximum cutting depth on the router's depth stop.

4 Align the dadoing jig with the shoulder line on the workpiece and clamp a scrap backup board behind the workpiece to minimize tearout. Install the correct guide collar and straight bit for this jig.

5 Make the shoulder cut by feeding the router across the jig's slot. Rout partially into the backup board, and stop the cut.

6 Once the shoulder cut is made, shift and re-clamp the jig on the workpiece to cut away the rest of the waste in a series of side-by-side passes. Notice how the backup board has prevented tearout along the back edge of the workpiece.

Making lap joints with a slotted dadoing jig: One reliable option for making lap joints on long workpieces is to use a handheld router and slotted dadoing jig (see facing page). Install the appropriate guide collar and straight bit in the router for your jig. Use the workpiece marked with the lap joint layout to set bit depth. Hold the workpiece against the jig to do this easily.

Set up your series of repetitive cuts on the workpiece, starting with the lap's shoulder cut. Clamp the jig so the bit aligns with the shoulder layout line. To minimize tearout, clamp a piece of scrap behind the workpiece as well. Rout the shoulder, feeding the router away from you, or from left to right. Then shift and re-clamp the jig to make more passes across the workpiece to remove the remaining waste.

Making lap joints with a pattern bit and straightedge: If you haven't made a slotted dadoing jig, another alternative for cutting end laps is to use a pattern bit guided against a straightedge. Pattern bits with shorter cutters are more versatile in this situation, because the cutting depth usually isn't more than 3/4 inch and the bit's bearing needs to make contact with the straightedge. If your pattern bit has a long cutter, you'll need to use a thicker straightedge to make this work.

To make the lap cuts, set the bit depth to reach the cheek, and clamp the straightedge to remove the waste from the end of the lap first. It's a good idea to clamp a piece of scrap behind the cutting area to help reduce tearout, or start each cut on the far end with a short climb cut, pulling the router toward you (or, right to left). For the climb cut to be effective, you only need to remove a bit of the edge material.

Continue removing the waste by re-clamping the straightedge and cutting away more waste until you reach the shoulder layout line. For deep lap cuts, you may need to make one series of cuts at a shallow depth all the way to the shoulder, then cut a second or even third series of cuts with the bit set lower each time to reach the final lap depth.

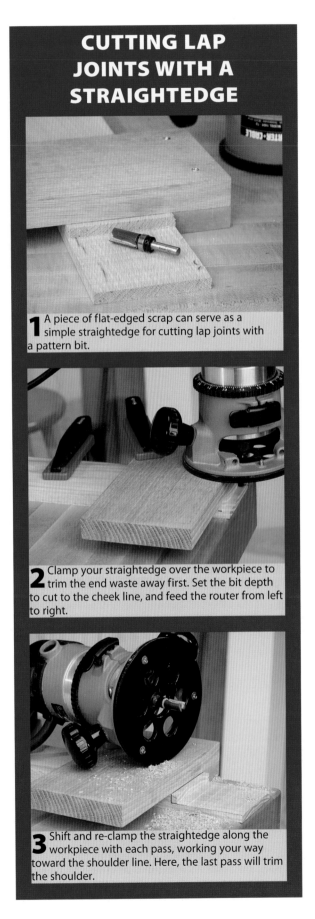

CUTTING LAP JOINTS WITH A STRAIGHTEDGE

1 A piece of flat-edged scrap can serve as a simple straightedge for cutting lap joints with a pattern bit.

2 Clamp your straightedge over the workpiece to trim the end waste away first. Set the bit depth to cut to the cheek line, and feed the router from left to right.

3 Shift and re-clamp the straightedge along the workpiece with each pass, working your way toward the shoulder line. Here, the last pass will trim the shoulder.

TIP

One way to improve the straightedge here is to attach a crosspiece underneath one end. The advantage to the crosspiece is that it automatically squares the straightedge to the workpiece wherever you position it.

Mortise-and-tenon joint.

Loose tenon-and-mortise joint.

Bit options for routing mortise-and-tenon joints include short or long pattern bits, fluted straight bits or spiral carbide bits. You can also cut short tenons with a piloted rabbeting bit (not shown).

Mortise-And-Tenon Joints

Description And Usage

If you're familiar with Arts-and-Crafts furniture, you've no doubt seen the rectangular ends of tenons poking through leg joints. Other furniture styles use mortise-and-tenon joints also, but generally the tenons are hidden. Mortises and tenons make excellent connections between legs and aprons or stringers on tables and chairs, and they're arguably some of the best joints for doors. The joint can be machined using several different woodworking tools, including a router table.

A mortise-and-tenon joint gets its strength primarily from the interlocking nature of the parts. The tenon is basically an elongated and centered tongue, usually with four shoulders formed around the edges where it transitions back to the workpiece's faces and edges. These shoulders add strength and keep the tenon from racking. The more common tenon style is cut into the end of the workpiece, but a second evolution of this joint — called a "floating" or "loose" tenon — involves making the tenon from a separate piece of material. As far as proportions go, tenons are generally 1/3 the thickness of the workpiece, and their length varies from as little as 3/8 in. to several inches, depending on the application.

The mortise consists of a matching, rectangular hole cut in the mating workpiece. The short ends of the mortise are usually chiseled square, but they can also be left round when cut with a router. Round-ended mortises are then fitted with rounded conventional-style or loose tenons.

Bit Options

Both parts of a mortise-and-tenon joint can be cut with straight or spiral bits. The diameter of bit used to cut the mortise should match the final mortise width, in order to make the mortise efficiently and accurately. The mortise depth depends on bit length. The tenon can also be cut with various straight or spiral bits. Wider bits cut tenons more quickly than narrow bits. You can also cut tenons with a pattern bit, similar to lap joints.

The conventional way to make mortise-and-tenon joints is to start with the mortise, then cut the tenon. If the fit of the joint needs to be refined — and it usually does — you'll adjust the tenon a little at a time until it fits the mortise. When cutting either the mortise or tenon, it's always a good idea to make test cuts on scrap first. You can adjust your machine setups this way without ruining the important project parts.

Machining Options For Cutting Mortises

Making mortises on the router table: Cutting mortises on the router table is a "blind" operation, because you'll cut the mortise by plunging the wood down onto the bit where the cutting action is entirely concealed. The first step in the milling process involves laying out the mortise shape. Extend the lines that define the ends of the mortise around to a face of the workpiece so you can see from the side where the mortise begins and ends.

Next, install the straight or spiral bit you'll use to cut the mortise, and set the fence back from the bit the same distance as the mortise is inset from the face or edge of the workpiece. Set

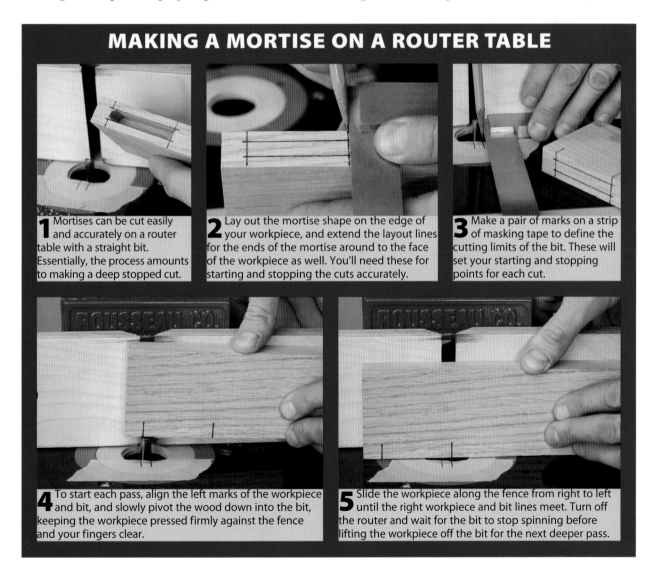

MAKING A MORTISE ON A ROUTER TABLE

1 Mortises can be cut easily and accurately on a router table with a straight bit. Essentially, the process amounts to making a deep stopped cut.

2 Lay out the mortise shape on the edge of your workpiece, and extend the layout lines for the ends of the mortise around to the face of the workpiece as well. You'll need these for starting and stopping the cuts accurately.

3 Make a pair of marks on a strip of masking tape to define the cutting limits of the bit. These will set your starting and stopping points for each cut.

4 To start each pass, align the left marks of the workpiece and bit, and slowly pivot the wood down into the bit, keeping the workpiece pressed firmly against the fence and your fingers clear.

5 Slide the workpiece along the fence from right to left until the right workpiece and bit lines meet. Turn off the router and wait for the bit to stop spinning before lifting the workpiece off the bit for the next deeper pass.

ROUTING MORTISES WITH AN EDGE GUIDE

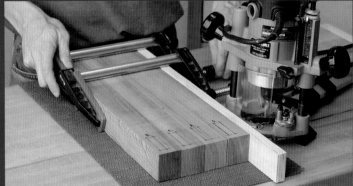

1 You can use an edge guide mounted on a handheld router to cut mortises, but be sure to provide plenty of support for the router base. Clamping similar workpieces together, such as these table legs, creates a broad worksurface for the router. A longer scrap keeps the edge guide's fence from tipping off the ends of the workpieces.

2 Set the edge guide so the router aligns correctly with one of the mortises. It doesn't matter which one you rout first — the edge guide's position won't change.

3 Make a series of shallow plunge cuts to rout the first mortise. You'll need to start and stop these cuts by eye, so work carefully. Feed the router from left to right for each cut.

4 Once the first mortise is cut, rearrange the order of the workpieces to move another workpiece to the "A" position, as shown here. Continue routing and re-shuffling the workpieces until all four mortises are milled. This way, the bit and fence positions don't need to change — only the workpiece arrangement.

the fence carefully; it will establish the exact position of the mortise. Now stick a piece of masking tape in front of the bit on the router table. Put the tape far enough forward so it won't interfere with the workpiece when you slide the wood along. Use a square to mark the bit's diameter on the tape.

The process of cutting the mortise is simple: Set the bit to a height of about 1/4 in. for the first pass, and lower the wood down onto the spinning bit so the left mortise layout line aligns with the left bit line on the tape. When you do this, it should be a pivoting motion with the rear corner of the wood held against the router table. A stopblock clamped to the table or fence can help anchor this corner for even better stability. Press the wood down slowly into the bit, keeping the workpiece firmly against the fence.

Once you've made the first plunge cut and the first set of marks align, slide the wood slowly from right to left along the fence until the second set of marks line up. Again, you can clamp a stopblock to the fence on the left side to stop this cut, to improve accuracy.

Repeat this process, raising the bit with each pass until you reach your final mortise depth. You'll probably need to blow or dig out impacted wood chips periodically; the mortise slot tends to fill quickly. Or, make a second pass without changing the bit height to clear out the mortise.

Making mortises with an edge guide and plunge router: A plunge router and edge guide also work for cutting mortises, but the challenge here is providing enough support for the router base. This tool setup is best used when you have several similar workpieces to rout with matching mortises. By clamping them together, you can create a broad base to stabilize the router.

Set up the cut by aligning the parts so the ends are even and all the mortises line up. If the mortises are near the ends of the workpieces, you may also need to clamp a longer piece of scrap next to the parts to create a surface for the edge guide to slide against.

Install the edge guide and straight or spiral bit in your plunge router, and set the edge guide so the bit lines up with one of the mortises. It doesn't matter which one. Lock the edge guide in place.

You'll cut each mortise in a series of deeper passes to achieve the final depth. Use the turret depth stop on your router to set the first cut to 1/8 or 1/4 in. Make the first pass by plunging the bit into the wood on the far end of the mortise (if you are standing facing the ends of the workpieces) or on the right end (if you are facing the sides of the workpieces). Then pull the router toward you or push it to the left to cut the full mortise length. Watch the cut closely to prevent cutting past your layout lines. Repeat with deeper passes until the first mortise is cut to full depth.

With the first mortise cut, there's no need to reset the edge guide position. Just unclamp the workpieces and rearrange the finished part to another position in the stack. Reclamp and you're all set with a new, uncut workpiece. The bit will line up perfectly if you've drawn the mortise shapes carefully.

Making mortises with a mortising template: Another accurate way to cut mortises with a plunge router is to use a modified slot-cutting template jig. The jig has a pair of concentric, straight slots — one is sized to fit the bushing of a guide collar, and a narrower inner slot matches the bit you'll use to cut the mortise. The jig has a fence fastened beneath the slotted base for clamping to the workpiece.

To make the jig, start by extending the mortise layout lines from your workpiece to a piece of scrap materi-al you'll use for the jig base. Wrap these end-mortise lines around the edge of the scrap so you can cut the workpiece "blind" on the router table, just as you would for cutting a mortise on the router table.

Install the bit you'll use for cutting the mortise in your router table, and set the fence so the bit will be centered on the jig base piece. Mark the bit limits on the router table with tape. Then make a series of increasing-depth passes, feeding right to left, to cut all the way through the jig base. Stop these cuts carefully; they'll determine the final mortise length on the jig.

Without changing the fence position, switch to a larger-diameter straight bit in the router table, and make a new set of bit marks on the tape. The bit's diameter should match the bushing size for the guide collar you'll use in the jig. Make one or two passes with this bit to cut an oversized slot around the bit slot in the jig base. Remember, this larger slot should form a "step" with the smaller bit slot; it only needs to be deep enough to accommodate the length of your guide collar's bushing. The larger slot will be automatically centered on the smaller slot if you line up the larger bit marks with the original layout marks on the jig when cutting the oversized slot.

To complete the jig, fasten a fence to the jig base with screws. The easy way to find the correct fence position is to first lay the jig base on top of your marked workpiece and match up the inner bit slot with the mortise layout lines. Hold these two parts together and tuck the fence into place. Attach the jig base to the fence with countersunk screws.

To cut the mortise, clamp the workpiece and jig to your bench, and install the correct guide collar and bit in your plunge router. Make the mortise in a series of increasing-depth passes, sliding the router along the jig slot. Be careful to keep the guide collar's bushing seated in the jig slot.

ROUTING MORTISES WITH A TEMPLATE

1 Mortises are easy to rout with a handheld router if you limit the plunge cuts with a guide collar that fits in a slotted template.

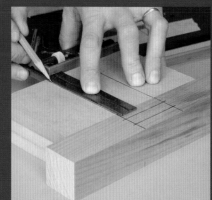

2 To build the template, start by transferring the mortise layout lines from the workpiece to the baseplate of the template. Choose a baseplate wide enough to provide plenty of support for the router base.

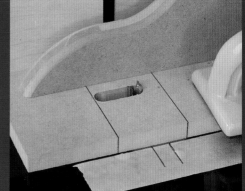

3 Install a straight bit in your router table that matches the mortise width. Make a series of deepening cuts to rout a slot through the jig that stops at the mortise layout lines. Use masking tape to mark the bit's position on the table for registering these cuts.

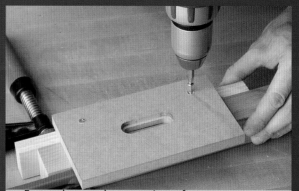

4 Install a wider straight bit that matches the guide collar bushing you'll use with the template, and cut an oversized slot around the mortise slot. Keep the router table's fence in the same position to rout this slot.

5 Fasten the template to a piece of scrap to serve as a straightedge. Register the two parts of the jig directly off of your workpiece and mortise layout lines when attaching these parts.

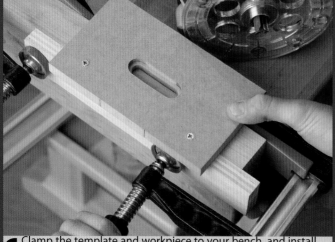

6 Clamp the template and workpiece to your bench, and install the correct guide collar and straight bit in the router for cutting the mortise.

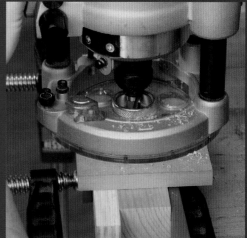

7 Rout the mortise in a series of deepening plunge cuts with the guide collar following the template slot.

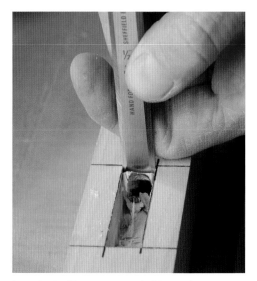

In order to fit a square-ended tenon in a mortise, you'll have to chisel the ends of a routed mortise square. Keep the chisel square against the ends and walls as you drive it into the mortise with a mallet.

Squaring Up Mortises With A Chisel

If you're making a square-cornered tenon, you'll need to square up the rounded ends of the mortise to match. Use a sharp chisel for this task. Keep the chisel's beveled edge facing inward, and carefully tap the chisel down the walls and ends of the mortise using a hammer or mallet. Chisel this waste away a little at a time, changing the chisel's position from the end of the mortise to the walls of the mortise, chipping away the waste in layers.

Machining Options For Cutting Tenons

Cutting tenons facedown on the router table: You have two options for cutting tenons on the router table: either facedown, which generally provides better control, or standing on-end against the fence. For the first approach, start by setting the bit height. If the mortise happens to be centered on the thickness of the mating workpiece, use this piece as a reference aid for setting the bit height for cutting the tenon. Set it next to the bit and raise the bit until it aligns with the lower wall of the

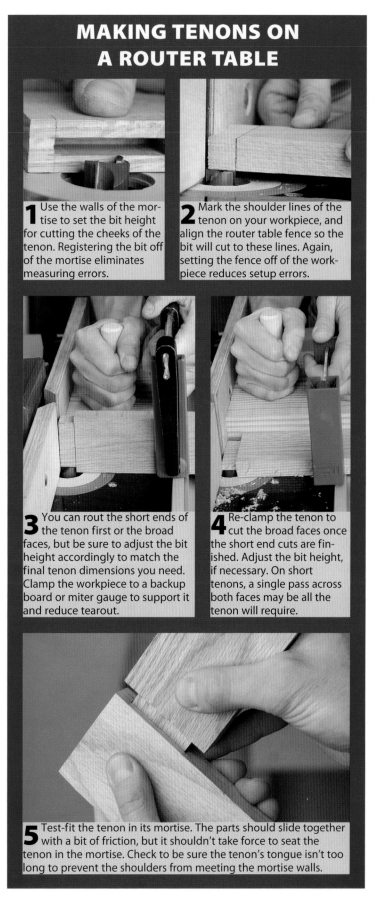

MAKING TENONS ON A ROUTER TABLE

1 Use the walls of the mortise to set the bit height for cutting the cheeks of the tenon. Registering the bit off of the mortise eliminates measuring errors.

2 Mark the shoulder lines of the tenon on your workpiece, and align the router table fence so the bit will cut to these lines. Again, setting the fence off of the workpiece reduces setup errors.

3 You can rout the short ends of the tenon first or the broad faces, but be sure to adjust the bit height accordingly to match the final tenon dimensions you need. Clamp the workpiece to a backup board or miter gauge to support it and reduce tearout.

4 Re-clamp the tenon to cut the broad faces once the short end cuts are finished. Adjust the bit height, if necessary. On short tenons, a single pass across both faces may be all the tenon will require.

5 Test-fit the tenon in its mortise. The parts should slide together with a bit of friction, but it shouldn't take force to seat the tenon in the mortise. Check to be sure the tenon's tongue isn't too long to prevent the shoulders from meeting the mortise walls.

mortise. This will establish the tenon cheek locations as well as set the tenon thickness.

With the bit height set, mark the tenon shoulder lines on the workpiece, and adjust the fence so the bit will project far enough out to cut to the tenon shoulders. If the tenon is short, a wide bit may be able to cut all the way to the shoulder in one setup.

If the tenon has short end shoulders, cut these first to help eliminate tearout. Stand the workpiece on-edge, and clamp it to a suitable backup board. The backup board shown on page 228, used for lap joints, provides excellent support here as well. Cut one short shoulder, flip the workpiece to the other edge, re-clamp and cut the second shoulder.

Once the end shoulders are cut, flip the workpiece to each face and cut the broad shoulders. Clamp the workpiece to your backup board for these cuts as well.

In situations where the tenon has wider end shoulders than face shoulders, you may need to finish up with more end-shoulder cuts. Raise the bit to rout these shoulders to their final proportions.

Once the tenon is routed, try to fit it in its mortise. You'll know you'll have a correctly-fitting mortise-and-

tenon joint if the tenon slides with just a bit of resistance into the mortise. You shouldn't have to pound or force the parts together. If the tenon is slightly too thick, use a file or shoulder plane to take a little off the tenon's broad cheeks for a better fit. File or plane both sides of the tenon equally in order to keep it centered on the workpiece. If your router setups were accurate, a few strokes with a plane or file should be all that's required.

If the tenon fits too loosely in the mortise to begin with, you may be able to glue a thin shim to each broad cheek of the tenon to build it up to a thickness that you can then refine with a plane or file. But generally, it's faster and easier to start over with a new workpiece. In this situation, you'll realize why making test cuts on scrap can be a real time and material saver!

Cutting long tenons on the router table: The method just shown for cutting tenons facedown on the router table also works for making long tenons. In these situations, set the fence so the bit lines up with the tenon's shoulder line. Rout the tenon to shape, starting from the end of the workpiece and working toward the shoulders in a series of side-by-side passes. Clamp the workpiece to a

CUTTING LONG TENONS ON A ROUTER TABLE

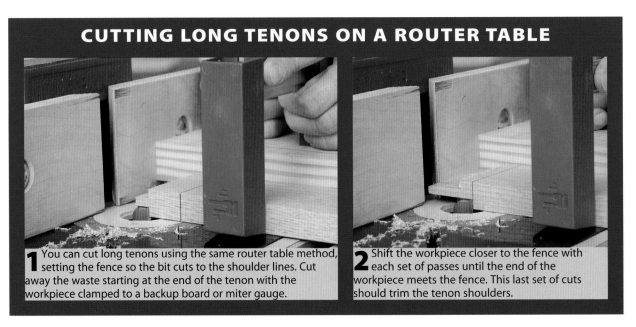

1 You can cut long tenons using the same router table method, setting the fence so the bit cuts to the shoulder lines. Cut away the waste starting at the end of the tenon with the workpiece clamped to a backup board or miter gauge.

2 Shift the workpiece closer to the fence with each set of passes until the end of the workpiece meets the fence. This last set of cuts should trim the tenon shoulders.

suitable backup board to keep the cuts square and the workpiece firmly supported.

Cutting tenons on-end on the router table: For shorter workpieces, you can also cut tenons standing the workpiece on-end against the router table fence. The main concern here is that there's adequate fence and backup support to keep the workpiece from tipping either away from the fence or down into the bit hole. That's why this method will be impractical for cutting tenons on workpieces longer than about 2 ft.

If the tenon is short, you may be able to cut both the cheeks and shoulders in a single setup of bit and fence. For long tenons, cut the shoulders in a series of passes, raising the bit each time until you reach the final shoulder lines.

Cutting tenons with a pattern bit and handheld router: Using a router table to cut tenons is an excellent choice when you can use the fence to improve accuracy and control. However, a particularly long or large workpiece can make it difficult to use

Tenons can also be cut on the router table on-end rather than facedown. Use the bit's projection from the fence to establish the width and height of the tenon shoulders. Back up these cuts to keep the workpiece from tipping as you slide it past the bit.

Another option for cutting tenons is to clamp a wide straightedge along the shoulder layout lines and use a piloted pattern bit to cut the cheeks and shoulders. A trim router works well for making tenons this way on narrow workpieces.

the router table for cutting tenons. Another good option for tenoning is to run a pattern bit in a handheld router against a straightedge. Clamp the straightedge on top of the workpiece so it lines up with the tenon's shoulder layout lines. Set the bit depth to reach just to the tenon cheeks, and cut away the waste in several sweeping passes. To help reduce tearout, it helps to make the first pass a short climb cut on the right side of the tenon to shear off the fragile edge-grain, then proceed with left-to-right passes to remove the rest of the waste. Cut one side of the tenon, then flip and re-clamp carefully to cut the other side: with this method, if you don't line up the straightedge accurately, you'll end up with a tenon that has uneven shoulders. It will be difficult to rout the short end shoulders with this method, but they're easy to trim to shape on a band saw or by hand with a backsaw.

Cutting loose tenons: Loose-tenon mortise-and-tenon joints start with a pair of conventional mortises cut in both mating parts. It can be advantageous to use this joint style when workpieces are too long to cut easily on the router table. Make the mortise depths match, so the loose tenon is split evenly across both halves of the joint.

Make the tenon by first planing down a blank of stock that fits the width of the mortises. Size this material so the tenon stock slips into the mortise with just a bit of friction but not loosely.

Next, rip the tenon to width on a table saw or band saw. Make sure the width of this strip matches the mortise length exactly — it's difficult to refine the final tenon width once the edges are rounded over, and the tenons should fit the full length of the mortises. Use a roundover bit to convert the tenon to its oval shape. Choose a bit with a radius that's half the diameter of the bit you used to cut the mortises. A convenient scenario is to make 1/2-in.-wide mortises so you can use a 1/4-in.-radius roundover bit. Ease all four edges of the tenon stock on the router table.

To determine the correct length of the tenon, add the depths of the mortises together and subtract 1/16 in. from this measurement to give the tenon a bit of "play." Crosscut the tenon to length. Check the final fit of the joint with the parts dry before gluing the tenon into both mortises.

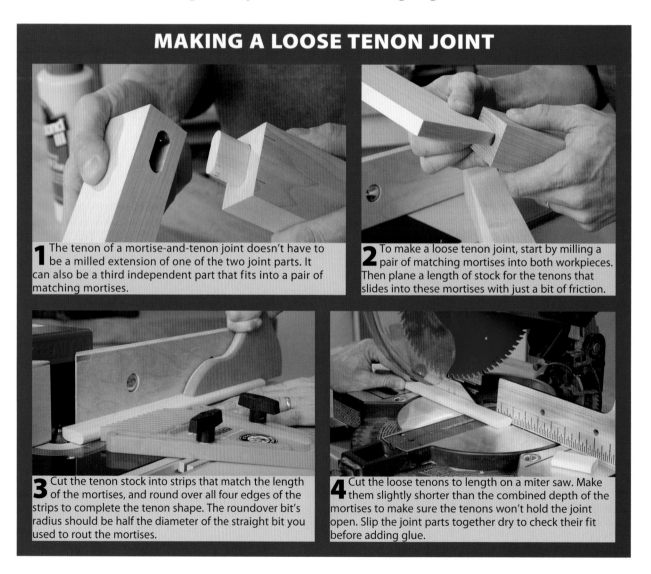

MAKING A LOOSE TENON JOINT

1 The tenon of a mortise-and-tenon joint doesn't have to be a milled extension of one of the two joint parts. It can also be a third independent part that fits into a pair of matching mortises.

2 To make a loose tenon joint, start by milling a pair of matching mortises into both workpieces. Then plane a length of stock for the tenons that slides into these mortises with just a bit of friction.

3 Cut the tenon stock into strips that match the length of the mortises, and round over all four edges of the strips to complete the tenon shape. The roundover bit's radius should be half the diameter of the straight bit you used to rout the mortises.

4 Cut the loose tenons to length on a miter saw. Make them slightly shorter than the combined depth of the mortises to make sure the tenons won't hold the joint open. Slip the joint parts together dry to check their fit before adding glue.

Box Joints

Description And Usage

Box joints provide a beautiful symmetry of straight pins and slots that interlock. These are great joints to use for box-building of all sorts, including bookshelves, chests and drawers. They were often used for joining crates and boxes before the advent of cardboard. All the surface area formed between the pins and slots provides a broad area for glue, which makes these joints both sturdy and attractive.

Bit Options

Either a fluted or spiral straight bit can be used to cut box joints. The same bit cuts both the slots and pins. Because of the setup and machining methods for this joint, use a router that's at least 1½ hp so you can cut the slots within one pass without overwhelming the router motor.

Box Joint Jig Design

The secret to cutting a repetitive series of pins and slots is to use a simple jig on your router table. Styles of box joint jigs vary, to some degree. The type you see here is most typical: it consists of a sled with a runner attached that slides in the router table's miter slot. The sled holds workpieces on-end and keeps them

Box joint.

square in relation to the bit. A second facing with a small protruding pin clamps to the sled. The thickness of this pin needs to match your router bit diameter perfectly. It will be used to index one pin or slot from the next as you cut them. Make your jig about 12 to 14 in. wide and about 6 in. tall to provide ample vertical backup support for workpieces. Use a strip of dimensionally stable hardwood, such as hard maple, to make the jig runner and the indexing pin. Size the runner carefully so it slips into the miter slot with just the slightest amount of play; it should slide but not move from side to side in the slot. A sloppy fit of the runner in the slot will lead to joints that don't mesh together.

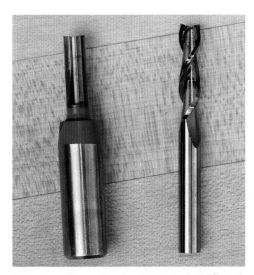

Bit options for routing box joints include fluted straight or carbide spiral bits.

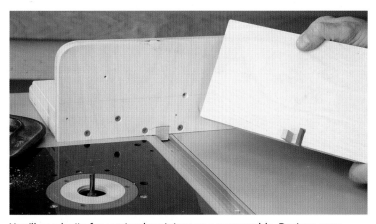

You'll need a jig for cutting box joints on a router table. Designs vary slightly, but most amount to a sled with a runner than fits in the miter slot. A pin and slot on the sled or on a separate facing index the cuts against the straight bit.

Setting Up The Jig

To prepare the jig for use, install the straight bit in your router table that matches the pin thickness on the jig facing, and raise the bit. The bit height at this point isn't crucial — you're just using the bit to index the pin facing. With the facing loosely held against the jig and the jig installed in the miter slot, slip a matching spacer between the bit and the pin. If possible, use a piece of scrap left over from when you initially made the pin for the facing. Hold the facing so the pin, spacer and bit are pressed together, and clamp the facing to the jig.

If you are borrowing a used box joint jig from another woodworker, there may already be a slot cut next to the pin on the jig facing. In this case, if the slot is oversized, it can lead to tearout on your workpieces when you cut the pins and slots. Install a hardboard facing over the pin so you can cut a fresh slot that will match your setup. If you are using a new jig with an uncut slot in the facing, there's no need to add this extra backer material.

Routing The Pins And Slots

With the jig prepared for your router table and bit, the first step in milling the parts is to lay out the joint and set an accurate bit height. Ideally, your workpieces should be cut to a width that's evenly divisible by the bit diameter you'll use for the joint. It's also a good idea to design the joint so the outer edges of one workpiece have pins on them. A joint that begins with a pin on one end and ends with a slot looks out of balance, so plan accordingly on your project.

If both workpieces are the same thickness, raise the bit to match this thickness. Sometimes, however, you may want to make box joints on parts with two different thicknesses, such as drawers with 3/4-in. faces and 1/2-in. sides. In this case, set the bit height to match the workpiece that will have pins on both outside edges. We'll rout these first.

Begin the slot-cutting process by butting a pin-ended workpiece against the jig's pin and holding or clamping it in place against the jig fence. Rout the first slot, which also creates the first pin. Feed the workpiece and jig slowly across the table and through the bit.

Once the first slot is cut, slip the slot over the jig's pin to index the next pin and slot cut. Cut this slot, then proceed across the rest of the workpiece in the same fashion to cut all the slots and pins to shape. If the opposite end of the workpiece will receive the same configuration of pins and slots, rout these now by flipping the board end-for-end.

Once the pin-ended board is milled, use it to index the first cut on the slot-ended board. Be sure to change the bit height now, if the joint parts aren't the same thickness. To cut the first slot, slip the outermost slot of the pin-ended board (the workpiece you've already routed) over the jig's pin, and butt the mating board against the first. Rout the first slot along the edge of this board with both workpieces held firmly against the jig fence.

Continue routing slots across the face of this board until you've cut the other end slot. If your workpieces are accurately sized to width, the outermost slots should end up being the same width.

Test-fit the joint. The parts should slide together with a bit of friction, but you shouldn't have to force them. If the fit is too tight or loose, you'll need to unclamp and shift the pin facing slightly and re-cut new parts. Just the slightest shift of the facing will change how the parts go together, so be careful when making any changes. Another common problem is that the endmost slots or pins aren't the same size. The solution here is to recalculate your part widths and make sure they're evenly divisible by the bit diameter. Box joints are definitely worth trying on test material first to dial in an exact fit. Don't get discouraged if you have to try test joints several times before arriving at the proper fit — it's worth the extra effort.

ROUTING A BOX JOINT

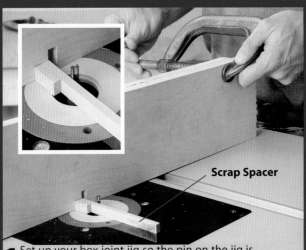

Scrap Spacer

1 Set up your box joint jig so the pin on the jig is exactly one pin's width away from the bit. A scrap spacer that matches the pin thickness makes this alignment step easier.

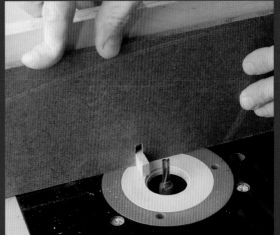

2 Slip a piece of scrap hardboard over the jig pin so the bit will cut a clean slot. This will prevent tearout on the workpieces. If the box joint jig is new, you can skip this facing.

3 It's crucial that your straight bit is set to the correct height to make snug-fitting box joints. Use the mating workpiece of the part of the joint you'll cut first to set bit height.

4 Set the workpiece against the jig fence and pin to cut the first pin and slot on the workpiece. Hold the workpiece firmly, or clamp it to the jig, and slide the jig slowly over the bit to make the slot cut.

5 Mill the rest of the pins and slots across the workpiece by slipping each new slot over the jig pin to cut the next pin and slot.

6 To cut the mating joint part, the configuration of pins and slots is the mirror opposite of the first workpiece. Fit the outermost slot of the first workpiece over the jig pin, and hold the mating workpiece against the first to cut a slot along the edge of this workpiece.

7 Cut the rest of the pins and slots to shape on this workpiece, working your way across to the other edge. If you laid out the joint accurately, the last cut should create a slot along the edge.

8 Dry-fit the joint parts together. They should slip together without requiring much force but not loosely. If the parts fit poorly, you'll need to adjust the distance between the jig pin and bit slightly. If the pins are too long or short, adjust the bit height up or down. It may take several attempts on fresh workpieces to get an acceptable fit, so make your setup cuts on scrap first.

Sliding dovetail joint.

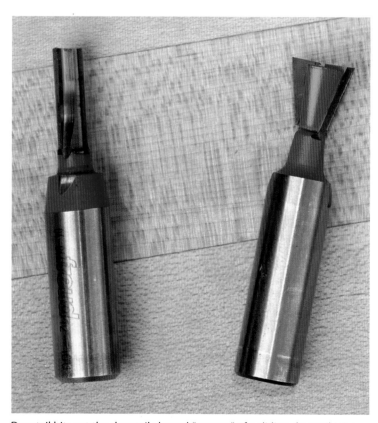

Dovetail bits cut the dovetail-shaped "tongue" of a sliding dovetail joint, but a straight bit is helpful for first removing the majority of the waste from the slotted half of the joint.

Sliding Dovetails

Description And Usage

Sliding dovetail joints look like a modified tongue-and-groove joint, with a dovetail-shaped tongue fitting into a matching groove. Unlike the usual repeating dovetail pattern of other joints, this one consists of a single, long dovetail. Sliding dovetails are interlocking, visually appealing and easy to build on the router table. They're also versatile: you can attach breadboard ends to tabletops, join drawer box parts or install shelving and dividers in bookcases or cabinets, all with sliding dovetails.

Bit Options

On 3/4-in. stock, 1/4-, 5/16- or 3/8-in. dovetail bits are several options for making this joint. One way to spare some wear and tear on the dovetail bit is to remove most of the waste with a straight bit first.

ROUTING SLIDING DOVETAILS

1 Lay out your sliding dovetail joint with a line that indicates where you want to center the joint. Extend the line onto both joint parts. It will help you register the router table fence and bit settings.

2 Start the milling process by removing most of the waste for the dovetail "tongue" with a straight bit. Use a bit with a diameter that matches or is slightly smaller than the narrowest part of the dovetail bit you'll use for cutting the joint. Center this cut on your layout line.

3 Replace the straight bit with a dovetail bit and make another pass to convert this slot to a dovetail shape. Leave the router table fence locked in place so the dovetail cut remains centered.

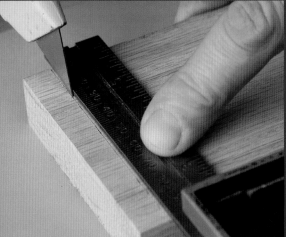

4 To make the dovetail tongue on the mating workpiece, first score the wood fibers at the dovetail shoulders with a utility knife. This will help prevent tearout when you rout the dovetail to shape.

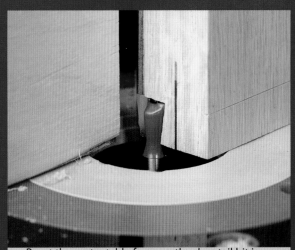

5 Reset the router table fence so the dovetail bit is partially shrouded, and slide the workpiece past the bit vertically to cut one side of the dovetail tongue. Do not change the bit height from the previous machining step.

6 Flip the workpiece to the other face and rout the second side of the dovetail tongue. Notice how the bit removes the waste right to the score lines, leaving clean shoulders for the joint.

7 Slide the joint parts together. They should slide together without gaps. If the dovetail tongue fits tightly in its slot, shift the fence slightly further away from the bit and make two more passes. If the tongue fits loosely, shift the fence toward the bit and rout a fresh workpiece to make a thicker tongue.

Making A Sliding Dovetail

The first helpful step in creating a sliding dovetail joint is to mark a centerline across both joint parts where you want the dovetail shape to be positioned.

The correct cutting sequence for making a sliding dovetail is to cut the groove side of the joint first, then rout the dovetail tongue to fit this groove. Choose the dovetail bit you'll use for making the slot, and decide how deep you'll want to make the tongue extend into the matching groove. Generally, the base of the tongue should be about 1/3 as wide as the thickness of the workpiece, to keep the walls of the joint thick enough to be sturdy. Choose a straight bit the same diameter as the base of the tongue or slightly narrower to "hog out" most of the waste from the dovetail groove; it can prevent the relatively fragile dovetail bit from breaking under the stress of such a heavy cut. Set the straight bit height so it will cut all the way to the bottom of the groove, and adjust the router table fence so the straight bit is centered on your original centered layout line. Use a backup board to support the workpiece from behind as you rout the groove to rough shape.

Without switching the fence position, replace the straight bit with the dovetail bit. Adjust the bit height to match the top end of the straight bit cut. Make another pass to convert the straight groove to a dovetail shape.

With the dovetail groove completed, you need to create a matching, dovetail "tongue" to fit the cutout. Use a utility knife to mark the shoulder lines of the dovetail; doing this also helps eliminate tearout on splintery woods when you rout away the waste. Mark and scribe both long shoulders of the tongue. Use the slotted workpiece as a reference for finding the correct shoulder locations.

Reset the router table fence so it partially covers the dovetail bit, but leave the bit height as is from the previous machining step. You want to project just a portion of the bit past the fence facings: the goal here is to cut one half of the dovetail tongue to shape by sliding the workpiece vertically along the fence. It's a good idea to start with a shallower cut than necessary, so you can "sneak up" on a final fit. Back up this first cut with scrap from behind.

Now, flip the workpiece to the other face, and cut the other half of the dovetail shape. Test the fit of the dovetail tongue in the groove. If the tongue is too thick, back the fence slightly away from the bit to shear more material off the sides of the tongue. Consider this to be a fine fence adjustment, because the amount you move the fence will actually double the amount you remove from the tongue when you make the pair of trimming passes. Always take a pass from both faces of the workpiece to keep the dovetail centered on the workpiece.

Slip the parts together to check the final fit. A correctly made dovetail tongue should nest completely into its groove, and the parts should slide together with only a slight amount of friction. This goal can be a tough one to achieve at times. What's tricky about this joint is that if the tongue is just slightly thicker in one area, it will be difficult to slide into the groove. On the other hand, if you trim off slightly too much material, the tongue will fit loosely in the groove, which sacrifices joint strength and looks sloppy. Take your time and make thorough, careful router passes to refine the joint fit.

When you achieve a satisfactory dry fit and are ready to glue up the joint, be prepared to work quickly. Once you apply the glue, the tongue will swell as it absorbs the glue. The swelling can make it hard to slide the parts together. Spread a sparing amount of glue on the tongue and slide the parts together immediately. Have a rubber mallet or dead-blow mallet ready to tap the parts along if the going gets tough.

Splined miter joint.

Splined Miter Joints

Description And Usage

Typical miter joints are inherently weak. The contact surfaces create an end grain-to-end grain connection, which has little strength. Glue soaks up into the wood pores and further compromises the adhesive bond. There are a number of ways to strengthen miter joints, including adding a long-grain spline between the mitered parts. The spline provides more surface area for glue while also making the joint lock together mechanically. Routing the joint involves cutting a centered slot along each mitered end of the joint parts. You can rout these slots with the workpieces facedown on the router table or standing on-end, but either option requires making a simple angled jig to hold the workpieces steady. Once the slots are cut, the spline slips into place with glue to lock the joint.

If you are joining 3/4-in. material, make the splines 1/8 to 1/4 in. thick. The width of the splines is up to you — 1/2 to 1 in. will provide plenty of joint strength. You can use contrasting wood for the splines to add visual appeal or the same wood as the mitered parts to help hide the spline. For stronger splines, use thin plywood instead of solid wood. When designing your joints, keep in mind that thicker, narrower splines are stronger than thin, wide ones. On the other hand, an overly thick spline weakens the walls of the mating parts that sandwich it. You want a happy medium between these two extremes.

Bit Options

Either a slot cutter or a straight bit can be used for cutting splined miter joints.

Bit options for routing splined miter joints include narrow straight bits or slot-cutting bits.

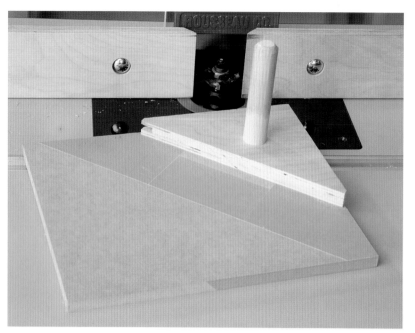

Making splined miter joints is easy if you use a simple jig that slides along the fence to support the mitered workpieces. Attach a mitered backup block to the jig's base to hold workpieces at 45° when you move the jig along the fence. A few strips of sandpaper glued to the jig base also help anchor the angled joint parts firmly on the jig.

Splined Miter Jig Design

There are various styles of spline-cutting jigs, but this one is simple and effective. Essentially, it amounts to a base of sheet material (plywood, hardboard or MDF will work equally well) with an angled backup block fixed on top. With the jig, you don't have to slide the mitered workpieces along the router table, where they could creep out of position. You'll slide the jig instead. A strip of sandpaper glued to the top of the base makes it even easier to hold workpieces in the jig. Install a thick section of dowel in the jig to make a handle. Make the jig base about 10 x 10 in. so it's large enough to hold a variety of mitered part lengths securely.

Making A Splined Miter Joint

The first step in making this joint is to mark the spline location on the thickness of one of the joint parts. Install a 1/8 or 1/4-in. slot cutter in the router table, and raise the bit so the cutters intersect your marked lines with the workpiece resting on

the jig. It's important that you set the bit precisely midway across the thickness of the workpieces, because cutting each half of the slot will require flipping one of the joint parts to the opposite face. If the slots aren't centered, the joint parts won't have flush faces when they're assembled.

Set the router fence so the rim of the bit's bearing lines up with the fence faces. Or, if you prefer a narrower spline, set the fence further over the bit to expose less of the cutters.

With the bit height and projection established, hold the workpiece in the jig and slide the jig past the bit to cut one half of the spline slot. Switch to the other workpiece to cut the other half of the slot.

Plane your spline stock down to the correct thickness for the slots. The splines should slide into the slots with just a bit of friction. Glue will cause them to swell when the joint is assembled, so a little extra play here is okay. Rip the spline material into strips that match the width of the combined slot, then crosscut them a little longer than necessary so the spline overhangs the ends of the joint.

If the spline and slots fit correctly, spread a thin coat of glue on the spline and slide the parts together. Clamp the joint until the glue cures, then use a dovetail or Japanese saw to trim the spline flush with the mitered parts. Sand the spline smooth to complete the joint.

Option for cutting spline slots: It's possible to use the same spline-cutting jig to make the slot cuts vertically and with a straight bit instead of a slot cutter. Set the fence so the bit is centered on the workpiece when it's held against the jig. Raise the bit to cut half the spline slot, and make the cut by sliding the jig and workpiece along the fence and through the bit. Cut the mating half of the joint the same way.

ROUTING A SPLINED MITER JOINT

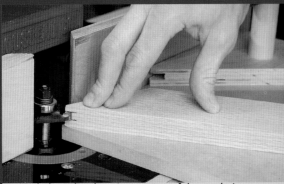

1 Mark the spline location on one of the workpieces. Generally, it's best to center the spline on the workpiece thickness. Raise the slot-cutting bit to meet these lines with the workpiece resting on the jig.

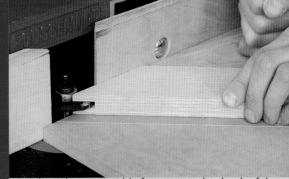

2 Adjust the router table fence to set the depth of the spline cut. Then hold the workpiece firmly against the jig's backup block and slide the jig along the fence to make each spline cut.

3 With the spline cuts made, plane a length of stock to match the spline slot width, and rip this stock to match the combined length of the spline slot depths. Crosscut the splines longer than necessary.

4 Dry-fit the joint together to check for an easy friction fit, and then glue the spline in its slots. If the spline fits tightly or loosely, remake the spline stock thicker or thinner rather than adjusting the slots you've routed in the workpieces.

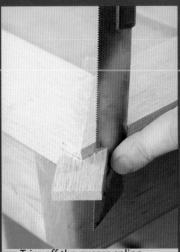

5 Trim off the excess spline material with a fine-toothed saw, and sand or plane the spline flush to complete the joint.

6 Option: If you don't have a slot-cutting router bit, you can use the same jig vertically against the router table fence with a straight bit to cut the spline slots. Line up and rout the spline cuts in the same fashion as you would with the slot cutter.

Biscuit joint.

Biscuit Joints

Description And Usage

Biscuits are football-shaped wafers of compressed hardwood. They expand when covered with glue to form a tight fit inside a joint. Biscuits bridge wood joints like a spline, either for alignment purposes or to create a mechanical connection between the joint parts. They fit into curved slots you can cut with your router table and biscuit-cutting bit. You can use biscuits in many applications: to reinforce face frame corners, assemble boards into larger panels or assemble casework components.

Bit Options

Biscuit-cutting bit.

Making A Biscuit Joint

In this example, we'll use biscuits to help align the parts of a glued-up panel. Biscuits help keep all the boards flush when installing and tightening the clamps. To build these joints, first mark the biscuit locations along each of the mating board edges. Use a biscuit as an indexing aid for marking the length of the slots you'll need to make.

Cutting the biscuit slots is a similar procedure to other slot cuts shown throughout this book. Install the biscuit cutter and set the bit height so it will cut slots about halfway across the thickness of the workpieces. Exact centering isn't really necessary here — you'll cut all the workpieces in the same faceup orientation, so all the slots will align with one another even if they aren't perfectly centered in the wood. Adjust the cutter out from the fence so it will make a slot half the width of the biscuits you're using — there are three different sizes of biscuits.

With the height and projection set, stick a piece of masking tape to the router table fence, high enough so it won't interfere with the wood when you make the slot cuts. Use a square to make a pair of marks that show the limits of the bit's cutters on the fence.

To make the slot cuts, first plunge the workpiece slowly into the bit so the left mark on the wood aligns with the left bit mark. Then slide the workpiece along the fence until the right marks align.

If you need to cut a slot on the end of a narrower workpiece, such as the stile or rail of a face frame, clamp a pair of large stopblocks on either side of the bit opening to help start and stop the cut. Slide the workpiece

Biscuit joints are made with a narrow slot-cutting bit machined specifically to mill the narrow biscuit slots. The cutter can be adjusted vertically on the bit shank by adding or removing washers.

straight into the bit with the wood against the right stopblock first, then press it against the left stopblock and plunge it into the bit to complete the slot.

Spread glue along the mating edges of the boards and into the bis- cuit slots, insert the biscuits and clamp the parts together to complete the joint. Even though biscuits will help keep the faces of the parts flush, check for flush as you are tightening the clamps; some biscuits fit more tightly than others.

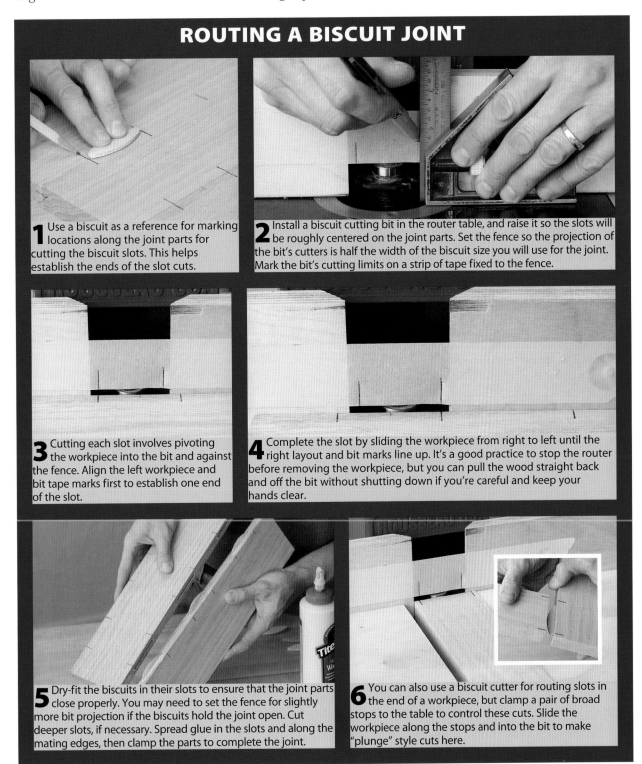

ROUTING A BISCUIT JOINT

1 Use a biscuit as a reference for marking locations along the joint parts for cutting the biscuit slots. This helps establish the ends of the slot cuts.

2 Install a biscuit cutting bit in the router table, and raise it so the slots will be roughly centered on the joint parts. Set the fence so the projection of the bit's cutters is half the width of the biscuit size you will use for the joint. Mark the bit's cutting limits on a strip of tape fixed to the fence.

3 Cutting each slot involves pivoting the workpiece into the bit and against the fence. Align the left workpiece and bit tape marks first to establish one end of the slot.

4 Complete the slot by sliding the workpiece from right to left until the right layout and bit marks line up. It's a good practice to stop the router before removing the workpiece, but you can pull the wood straight back and off the bit without shutting down if you're careful and keep your hands clear.

5 Dry-fit the biscuits in their slots to ensure that the joint parts close properly. You may need to set the fence for slightly more bit projection if the biscuits hold the joint open. Cut deeper slots, if necessary. Spread glue in the slots and along the mating edges, then clamp the parts to complete the joint.

6 You can also use a biscuit cutter for routing slots in the end of a workpiece, but clamp a pair of broad stops to the table to control these cuts. Slide the workpiece along the stops and into the bit to make "plunge" style cuts here.

Half-blind dovetail joint.

Dovetail bits in a variety of widths can be used with a dovetailing jig to rout dovetail joints. Be sure to use the specific bit required for each template of your dovetail jig.

Half-Blind Dovetail Joints

Dovetails are monikers of quality craftsmanship, whether you are the woodworker making them or the bystander checking for them on every drawer. We love these dovetail joints, and for good reason. The angular, repeating symmetry is pleasant to look at, and all those interlocking surfaces create a huge gluing area that makes a rock-solid joint. Half-blind dovetails are the most popular style for drawer joinery. The sides of the drawer are outfitted with the tails of the joint, and these fit into mirror-image pin slots in the ends of the drawer face. With a dovetail jig and handheld router, half-blind dovetails are relatively easy to make — and the joint will take your projects to a new level of detail and skill.

Bit Options

Dovetail bit required by the dovetail jig you use.

Dovetail Jigs

There are at least a dozen different models of dovetailing jigs available, with each manufacturer attempting to make an easier, foolproof design. The fact of the matter is, every jig will challenge you with its own unique learning curve. The most common style of dovetail jig consists of a heavy base with a pair of clamps on top and in front to hold both halves of a joint at once. Usually, a metal or plastic template fits on the jig to establish the exact spacing of the pin and tail pattern. Dovetail jigs are really just modified templates. Most jigs can be outfitted with different templates to cut several sizes of half-blind dovetail joints as well as through dovetails or box joints. You'll use a guide collar that fits into the template slots, and the bit will cut both the pins and tails at once.

Making A Half-Blind Dovetail

Be sure to carefully read and follow the setup instructions that come with your dovetail jig. Typically, there are numerous adjustments to be made before the jig is ready for use. The manual will probably outline in detail the step-by-step process for making a half-blind dovetail joint

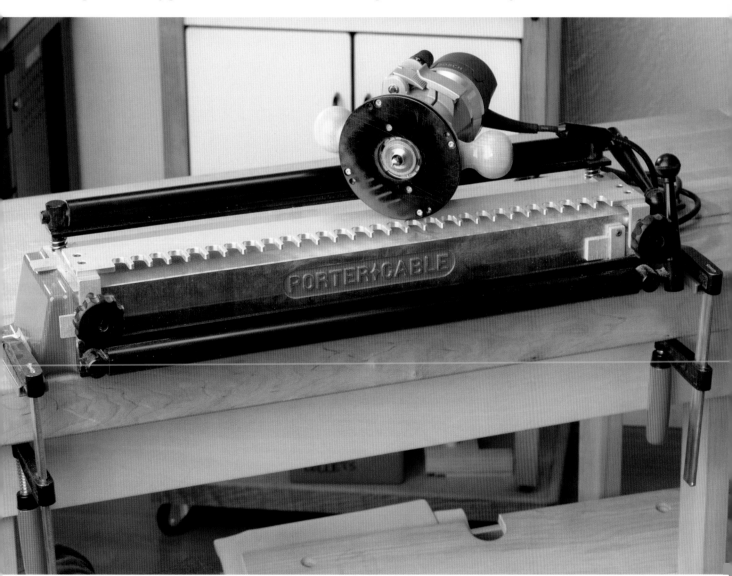

Cutting dovetail joints is essentially a template-routing operation with a dovetailing jig. The router, equipped with a guide collar and dovetail bit, follows a "fingered" template to cut both halves of the joint at once.

using the starter template supplied with the jig. Mount this template on your jig.

Next, install the appropriate guide collar and dovetail bit in your router, and adjust the bit depth to the manual's specifications. Be aware that precision is critical with each step of this process. If the manual says $^{19}/_{32}$ in. for a depth setting, do your best to set this accurately. Each variable in the setup will affect how well the joint fits together in the end.

The best way to ensure an accurate setup is to make test cuts on scrap material that matches both the width and thickness of your final workpieces. Slip these test parts into the jig. Generally, the drawer front installs on top of the jig, and the drawer side fits vertically in the front clamp, with the board facing the floor. There will be an offset required between these two parts when you fit them in the clamps, so follow the manual carefully. Again, this offset will be a precise distance that must be set carefully.

It's important that the workpieces are absolutely flat, square on the ends and uniformly thick. You should also find out whether your jig requires parts made to a specific width; some jigs won't cut an even pattern on the ends of the joint unless the part width is evenly divisible by a set measurement. Learning this will save you frustration in the end.

Make final adjustments to the jig before cutting the test parts. Some jigs, like the one shown here, will have adjustable stops that need to be set. Once these are accurately positioned, you can cut joint after joint of the same size without calibrating the jig again.

For the jig shown here, the first cut to make is a climb cut that shears away the face grain on the back of the drawer side. Slide the router from right to left to make this cut.

To shape the matching pins and tails, feed the router in and out of the template "fingers" from one end of the joint to the other, working left to right as usual. Make this cut gently to prevent tearout and to help minimize excessive strain on the bit. Before removing the parts from the clamps, be sure you've cut every finger slot carefully; as a preventive measure, go back across the joint a second time with the router to clean up any remaining waste. Even the smallest bit of extra waste can keep the parts from fitting together.

Unclamp and remove the workpieces and inspect the finished joint. Notice how the slotted tails have curved bottoms that fit the curved backs of the pins. It's a clever bit of engineering and a brain-teaser to understand until you see both halves of the joint side by side. If luck is on your side, both ends of the tail board (drawer front) should be evenly sized so the pattern looks balanced from one end to the other.

Now is when you can hear that drum rolling for the big moment of truth: fitting the parts together. Again, if Lady Luck is smiling on you, the pins and slots will mesh together with a slight amount of friction and no significant gaps. Don't be surprised if they don't, however. You'll probably need to adjust the bit depth or workpiece positions in the jig slightly to create a tighter or looser-fitting joint. You may also have to make adjustments to create a pattern that begins and ends evenly on the edges of the parts. If it's back to the drawing board for another round of cuts, slice this attempt off the ends of your test pieces, and make a few more adjustments to your set-up. Try to work systematically with each test cut, changing one variable at a time to see how that change affects the outcome. Do your best to keep from getting frustrated. Eventually you'll arrive at the right combination of settings to achieve the perfect joint. Take notes as you go so you can refer to them the next time you need to set up the jig.

ROUTING A HALF-BLIND DOVETAIL JOINT

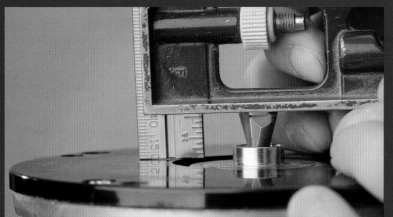

1 Install the correct dovetail bit and guide collar in your router, as specified in the manual that comes with your dovetail jig. Set the bit depth carefully — it will determine how tightly the joint parts fit together. And, once the parts are cut, you can't refine the fit without re-cutting a fresh set of workpieces.

2 Mount the dovetailing template in your jig after carefully following the setup instructions for other components of the jig.

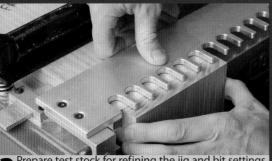

3 Prepare test stock for refining the jig and bit settings, and clamp the mating parts in the jig. With most jig designs, one workpiece clamps horizontally under the template, and its mate butts vertically in another clamp. This way, both halves of the joint are routed in one step, and the parts register directly off of one another.

4 Aside from bit depth, you'll probably also have to set other stops carefully on the jig to register the joint and any necessary offset correctly. Follow the manual to make these adjustments.

5 On this jig, the first cut shears off the fragile face-grain fibers to prevent tearout on the back, inside face of the joint.

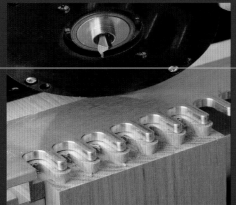

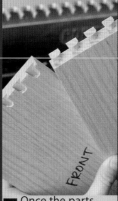

6 You'll see the joint take shape when you feed the router in and out of the template fingers, which cut both the pins and tails in one operation. Work from left to right along both workpieces, then make a second pass through the template to make sure all of the waste is removed.

7 Once the parts are routed to final shape, removing them from the jig reveals the clever interlocking pattern of a half-blind dovetail.

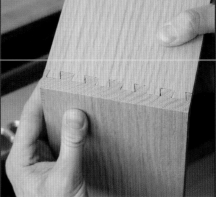

8 Given the complexity of setting bit depth and making jig adjustments, chances are your first set of test parts won't fit accurately. Don't lose patience. Follow the manual and cut more test pieces until your joint fits together without gaps or excessive force.

TEN

ROUTER PROJECTS

The last chapter of this router book is devoted to projects. There's no better way to get acquainted with your router than to pick a good router project, roll up your sleeves and start using this versatile and hard-working tool.

The chapter kicks off with a must-have router accessory: a portable, yet full-service router table. Use your router to trim the plastic laminate top, then rout the cutout for the polycarbonate insert plate. It's a good exercise in template routing (see chapter eight). Remember to read page 127 for more information on installing your router on an insert plate.

Our second project, the substantial garden gate on page 264, will challenge your router joint-making skills. Don't worry — chapter nine will teach you how to make all the joints you'll need for this project, including mortise and tenons, half-laps, tongue and groove joints and rabbets.

A Stacked Mirror Frame (see page 272) comes next, and it lends an opportunity to rout some custom cove and chamfered molding, plus fluted corner plaques. It's a smaller project in this grouping, which makes it both affordable and fun to build with a router and other basic woodworking tools. So is the White Oak Adirondack Chair on page 277. If you like the design, why not build a few chairs

With the first nine chapters of this book under your belt, it's time to turn your router loose on great projects.

using some hardboard patterns and template routing techniques?

The remaining projects in this chapter offer their own individual router challenges. Want to spend some time cutting rabbets? Try the modular end table and bookcase on page 283. The Wall Desk on page 289 features a molded top, elongated spline joints in the door and stopped grooves throughout — all straightforward router fare here. If you build the expanding Gateleg Table on page 295, it could be a good excuse to invest in a biscuit-joining router bit and matched bit set for making the drop leaves (see these bits in chapter four). The unique open dovetail joints on the legs of the Robust Workbench (page 301) are only practical to make with a router, and there are plenty of biscuit joints to make here as well. Finally, you can mill all the architectural moldings for the Top-Shelf Bookcase (see page 307) on a router table, including baseboard, base shoe and top cap. You could even drill the shelf pin holes with a plunge router, straight bit and guide collar.

After building a few of these projects, you'll realize how invaluable a router, router table and a few bits are to full-fledged woodworking. We hope this book will continue to be a resource you'll return to again and again for these and all the projects you design and build.

ROUTER TABLE
Simply Best

A router table should be a simple, efficient tool. Simple, however, doesn't mean crude. This router table, for instance, has precision features such as a flat, rigid top; a versatile table insert plate; efficient dust collection and an accurate, easy-to-use fence. The Porter-Cable plunge router mounted in the table has features that suit it particularly well.

This router table is a refinement of previous tables. Long ago, we found that overly large and complex router tables (shaper wannabes) defeat efficiency rather than contribute to it. In most instances, you use a router table to mill pieces that are too small or awkward to shape with a handheld router. Router tables are benchtop tools. Floor-standing, shaper-size router tables may look impressive, but they take up valuable shop space and don't improve performance. The ability to store this router table on a shelf leaves room for tools with a legitimate claim to floor space (table saw, band saw, etc.).

Our router table is simple yet versatile. It employs a 2-hp plunge router that's ideal for this application. The table plate has interchangeable inserts for safety and efficient dust collection. Routing narrow pieces is easy with a push block, and the plate is equipped with a starting pin for routing irregular workpieces.

Router Table

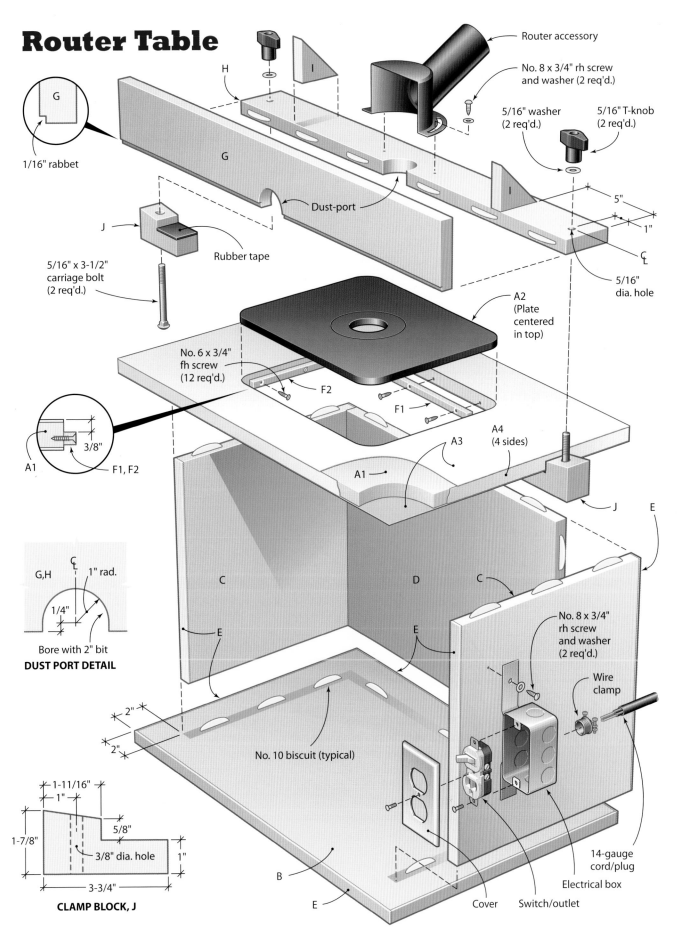

G

1/16" rabbet

H

I

Router accessory

No. 8 x 3/4" rh screw and washer (2 req'd.)

5/16" washer (2 req'd.)

5/16" T-knob (2 req'd.)

G

Dust-port

I

5"

1"

℄

5/16" dia. hole

J

Rubber tape

5/16" x 3-1/2" carriage bolt (2 req'd.)

A2 (Plate centered in top)

No. 6 x 3/4" fh screw (12 req'd.)

F2

F1

A4 (4 sides)

A3

3/8"

A1

F1, F2

A1

J

E

G,H

℄

1" rad.

1/4"

Bore with 2" bit

DUST PORT DETAIL

C

D

C

E

No. 8 x 3/4" rh screw and washer (2 req'd.)

Wire clamp

E

E

2"

2"

No. 10 biscuit (typical)

1-11/16"

1"

5/8"

1-7/8"

3/8" dia. hole

1"

3-3/4"

CLAMP BLOCK, J

B

E

Cover

Switch/outlet

14-gauge cord/plug

Electrical box

MATERIALS AND CUTTING LIST

KEY	NO.	DESCRIPTION	SIZE
TABLE			
A1	1	Top, MDF	$3/4$ x 16 x 24 in.
A2	1	Table plate*	$3/8$ x $9 1/4$ x $11 3/4$ in.
A3	2	Laminate top/bottom	$16 1/2$ x $24 1/2$ in.**
A4	4	Laminate edges	1 x $24 1/2$ in.**
B	1	Base, birch plywood	$3/4$ x $15 3/4$ x $23 3/4$ in.
C	2	Sides, birch plywood	$3/4$ x $11 3/4$ x $13 1/2$ in.
D	1	Back, birch plywood	$3/4$ x $13 1/2$ x $18 1/2$ in.
E	1	Edge banding, birch	$1/8$ x 1 x 136 in.***
F1	2	Plate cleats, hardwood	$3/8$ x $3/8$ x 10 in.
F2	2	Plate cleats, hardwood	$3/8$ x $3/8$ x 7 in.
FENCE			
G	1	Face, hardwood	$3/4$ x $3 1/2$ x $27 1/2$ in.
H	1	Bottom, hardwood	$7/8$ x $2 3/4$ x $27 1/2$ in.
I	2	Gussets, hardwood	$3/4$ x $2 3/8$ x $2 3/8$ in.
J	2	Clamping blocks, hardwood	$1 1/2$ x $1 7/8$ x $3 3/4$ in.

*See text, SHOPPING LIST

**Cut oversize, trim to fit

***Cut lengths to cover exposed plywood edges

SHOPPING LIST

MATERIALS
$3/4$ x 48 x 48-in. birch plywood (1)
24 x 48-in. medium-density fiberboard
24 x 48-in. plastic laminate (1)
$7/8$ x 6 x 26-in. hardwood (for edge banding)
1 qt. contact cement
No. 8 x $3/4$-in. roundhead screws and washers (4)
No. 6 x $3/4$-in. flathead wood screws (12)
$3/4$-in. brads
No. 10 plate-joining biscuits
Yellow glue
Self-adhesive rubber tape (see text)

HARDWARE
$5/16$ x $3 1/2$-in. carriage bolts and washers (2)
$5/16$-in. T-knobs (2 req'd.; Rockler catalog No. 71514)
Table plate (Woodhaven catalog No. 147)
Dust-collection ports for Porter-Cable router, model 7529 (see text)
Electrical box with mounting strap
15A single-pole switch with receptacle
Box cover
Wire clamp
10 ft. 14-gauge wire with ground
Three-prong plug

Design Considerations

Choosing a router is the first step in designing a router table. The Porter-Cable model 7529 plunge router is ideal for this use. It has integral dust collection, which is incorporated into the table design. You can set the plunge-lock lever open to allow micro depth adjustment. Its $2 1/4$-in. plunge depth provides lots of cutting capacity. Other features such as a 2-hp soft-start motor and variable speeds further enhance the tool's suitability for router table use.

Although the Porter-Cable has a second power switch on the top of the motor housing that's meant to be used when it's mounted in a router table, we opted to use a separate switched outlet (see photos, drawing) because it's easier to find and use quickly. Wire the switch using the directions on the box.

Cabinet size was determined based on these factors: the size and plunge travel of the router, the size of the top and plate, the height of the top when mounted on a workbench and efficient use of materials (you'll need half a sheet of birch plywood). We designed a 2-in. lip on both the top and the base on all sides of the cabinet. The lip allows you to clamp the base to a bench or to clamp jigs to the top in any position. The fence also clamps onto the lip.

We didn't include a miter slot in the top because you can use a push block off of the fence's face or the top's front edge to do the same work as a miter gauge. Miter slots also have the unfortunate trait of collecting sawdust and debris that can interfere with a cut.

Rather than making my own table plate, we used a phenolic plate manufactured by Woodhaven because it offers superior performance and versatility (Woodhaven also sells less expensive acrylic plates). The 3/8-in.-thick phenolic plate is extremely rigid, and it's less likely to deflect from the weight of a heavy router than an acrylic plate. This plate comes with three snap-in inserts: two with bored holes (1 3/16 and 2 in.) and one blank. A starting pin for routing irregular-shaped work is also included. To drill the mounting holes for your router, simply use the router's baseplate as a template.

The fence has several features that make it functional and easy to use. Rather than cutting slots in the top for the fence's clamping bolts, we used L-shaped clamping blocks that grip the table from the sides. Not only is the table stronger without slots, but it's also much easier to remove the fence when it's not needed.

We cut the top of the clamping blocks at an angle so the top outside edge acts as a fulcrum against the fence bottom. This allows the clamping block jaws to get a firm grip on the top (see drawing, photo) with the help of some self-adhesive rubber weatherstripping. Note that the through hole for the 5/16-in. carriage bolt is 3/8 in. This allows the wiggle room necessary for the pivoting action.

We also cut a 1/16 x 1/16-in. (nominal) rabbet in the bottom of the fence's front face to prevent dust buildup from holding the stock away from the fence.

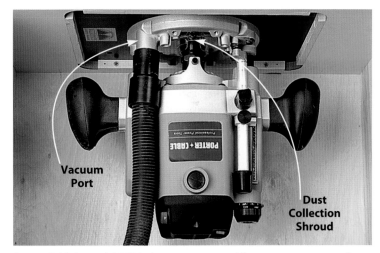

Porter-Cable's model 7529 plunge router provides a vacuum port and a plastic shroud for bottom dust collection.

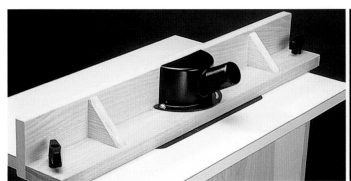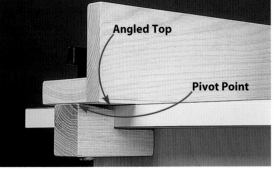

Dust collection from the top is handled with the router's dust collection cup mounted to the reinforced fence (above). The angled top of the fence's clamping block allows it to pivot behind the bolt to achieve a firm grip on the top.

Making The Top

The top is the heart of the router table, so it's important that you make it as precisely as possible. Medium-density fiberboard (MDF) works particularly well for the top substrate because it's hard, rigid and stable. We covered all six of the top's surfaces with plastic laminate. The laminate not only provides a smooth, durable surface, it also prevents warping and further stiffens the top, much like a stress-skin panel.

Laminate the edges of the top before the top and bottom. Because the cut edges of MDF are very porous, apply two coats of contact cement to them. The combination of dust and contact cement often leaves rubbery "flags" on the substrate after you rout off the excess laminate. It's important to file, sand or scrape off these flags when you level the edges to the top and bottom (see photo 2). Leaving them can cause the laminate to lift.

Keep the work area perfectly clean. Even a tiny bit of debris trapped between the substrate and the laminate will create a noticeable bulge. Apply pressure with a J-roller or a rubber mallet and board to ensure good adhesion. With the laminate in place, file all of the edges so they're smooth and free from catches.

Once you've finished laminating the top, you'll need to make an accurate template to rout the table plate opening. (Woodhaven sells a hardboard template if you prefer to bypass this step.) Trace the shape of the table plate onto a piece of 1/4-in. hardboard. Carefully cut on or just inside the line with a scroll saw

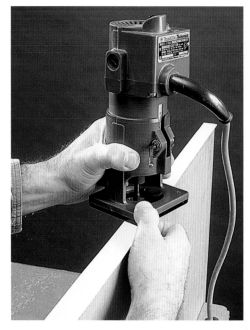

1 Apply laminate to the edges of the top first and trim with a laminate trimmer (shown) or a small router.

2 File or scrape the laminate edges flush with the top and bottom surfaces before applying the face laminate.

3 Make a hardboard template for flush-routing the plate opening. The opening must be the same size as the plate.

4 Center the template on the top and trace the opening. Then scribe the line with a utility knife to prevent chipping.

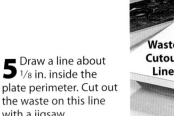

5 Draw a line about 1/8 in. inside the plate perimeter. Cut out the waste on this line with a jigsaw.

Waste → Cutout Line

← Plate Perimeter

6 Position the template on the plate perimeter line and rout using a flush-trim bit with a top-mounted bearing.

7 Place the top and plate facedown on a flat surface, then glue and nail the plate cleats (see text).

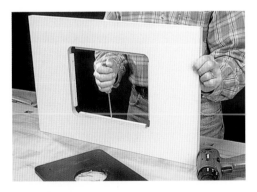

8 Reinforce the plate cleats with No. 6 x 3/4-in. flathead wood screws. Don't overtighten or the screw holes will strip.

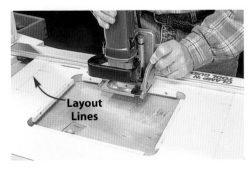

9 Draw layout lines for the table cabinet and joining biscuits. Use a fence to guide the plate joiner.

Layout Lines

or jigsaw. Fine-tune the edges with a sanding block or file (see photo 5) until the plate fits perfectly in the template.

Center the template opening on the top and trace around the inside with a pencil. Then score the line with a sharp utility knife to prevent chipping. Now draw a line 1/8 to 1/16 in. inside the table plate perimeter line as a guideline for your jigsaw. Bore a starter hole for the blade, then cut out the waste. To finish the opening, clamp the template on the top and use a flush-trim bit with a top-mounted pilot bearing to remove the remainder of the waste. The plate should fit with little or no play.

To install the plate cleats, turn the top and plate upside down against a flat surface such as your table saw top. Press the top and plate flat, then glue and nail the cleats (see photo 7). Follow up with wood screws to ensure that the cleats stay put.

10 Assemble the back and sides first, then the bottom and top. Clamp the assembled parts for a tight fit.

GATEWAY TO A GARDEN
Refined Joinery For Rugged Duty

Gates and fences are built by carpenters, conventional wisdom says, while woodworkers craft highboys and grandfather clocks. But in truth, some of the most appealing woodworking projects cross over into the carpentry field. This mahogany gateway combines solid carpentry with furniture-quality craftsmanship, stepping boldly from the woodshop to stand guard at the entry to a charming garden.

If you look closely at the photo, you'll notice that something is missing from this gate project: a fence. Instead, the gateway includes small wings to provide stability, context and a sense of visual flow. You can certainly build the gate and install it in an existing fence opening. Or you can design a full fence that incorporates the basic wing design in each panel. However you choose to surround it, you'll see that a gate can be more than simply an outdoor door — it can add beauty and character to your yard, while helping define your outdoor living space.

Stylistically, this gateway incorporates features of both Japanese and Arts-and-Crafts design. The profile on the top rail of the gate, known as a "cloud lift," is used in Japanese architecture to create a sense of uplifting spirit. The lattice infill in the open sections of the gate and wings is a common Arts-and-Crafts motif but also imparts an Oriental flavor. The solid-wood frame parts and the heavy-duty mortise-and-tenon joinery are hallmarks of Arts-and-Crafts design.

The two most suitable wood options for the gateway are white oak and mahogany. Both are excellent exterior materials; we chose mahogany because it is lighter and more workable. If you'd rather not pay $500 to $700 for the wood, you could save money by building it out of cedar. You could use teak or redwood as well, but they'll likely cost as much as mahogany. If your budget is tight, make the gateway from pine, ash or poplar and paint it.

We spent several days building the gateway. We drew on extensive woodworking experience to fashion some of the best-fitting mortise-and-tenon joints ever seen. Unlike metal fasteners or other types of reinforced butt joints, the joints on this gate won't deteriorate in a few years.

Although the gateway requires the same precision and attention to detail as a piece of fine furniture, it offers one time-saving advantage over interior woodworking: no sanding. Clear finish is all this outdoor project needs.

Garden Gate

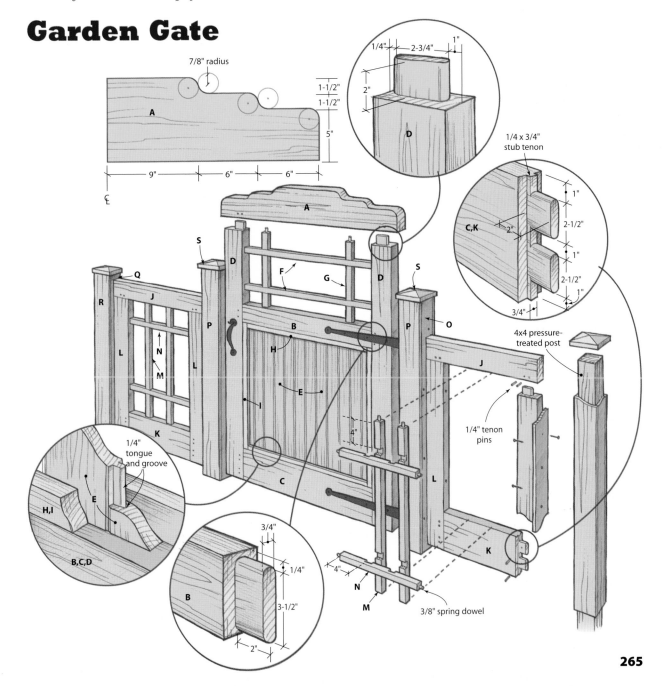

MATERIALS AND CUTTING LIST

(ALL HONDURAN MAHOGANY)

KEY	NO.	DESCRIPTION	SIZE
A	1	Top rail (gate)	$2^7/_8$ x 8 x 42 in.
B	1	Middle rail (gate)	$2^1/_4$ x 4 x 36 in.
C	1	Bottom rail (gate)	$2^1/_4$ x 8 x 36 in.
D	2	Gate stiles	$2^1/_4$ x 4 x 60 in.
E	12	Gate slats	$3/_4$ x $3^1/_8$ x $31^1/_2$ in.
F	2	Horizontal lattice	$1^1/_4$ x $1^1/_4$ x 34 in.
G	2	Vertical lattice	$1^1/_4$ x $1^1/_4$ x 18 in.
H	2	Horizontal retainers	$3/_8$ x $3/_4$ x $33^1/_2$ in.
I	2	Vertical retainers	$3/_8$ x $3/_4$ x 27 in.
J	2	Top rail (wings)	$2^1/_4$ x 4 x 24 in.
K	2	Bottom rail (wings)	$2^1/_4$ x 8 x 20 in.
L	4	Wing stiles	$2^1/_4$ x 4 x 40 in.
M	4	Wing lattice (vert.)	$1^1/_4$ x $1^1/_4$ x 32 in.
N	4	Wing lattice (horiz.)	$1^1/_4$ x $1^1/_4$ x 26 in.
O	4	Post cladding	$5/_8$ x $3^3/_4$ x 48 in.
P	4	Post cladding	$5/_8$ x 5 x 48 in.
Q	4	Post cladding	$5/_8$ x $3^3/_4$ x 43 in.
R	4	Post cladding	$5/_8$ x 5 x 43 in.
S	4	Post caps	1 x $5^1/_2$ x $5^1/_2$ in.

Posts are treated 4x4s set in concrete below the frost line. Tall posts project 48 in. above ground; short posts project 43 in. above ground.

Preparing The Stock

To build the gateway, we bought slightly more than 100 bf of Honduran mahogany. We used 10/4 stock to make the rails and stiles for the gate and wings, 4/4 stock for the gate slats and post cladding, and a laminated double layer of 6/4 stock for the top gate rail (final thickness was $2^7/_8$ in.). Squaring, planing and preparing the stock is a time-consuming task, but careful work yields the perfectly square parts that are essential to mortise-and-tenon joints.

Here's a tip: Always cut the parts to rough length (a couple of inches longer than final size) before you joint and plane them. If you've ever tried to wrestle a 10-ft. board through a jointer, you'll understand the benefit.

SPRING DOWELS

If you understand how a toilet paper holder works, you'll know how to install the lattice in the gate and wings. The dowels are set into guide holes that are fitted with small springs in the ends of the lattice sections. When the lattice panel is aligned in the frame opening, the springs cause the dowels to pop into the mating holes. You can buy springs at any hardware store. To accommodate the springs, the holes in the lattice are about 50 percent deeper than the dowel length. Experiment with scrap pieces before you drill into the workpiece. To

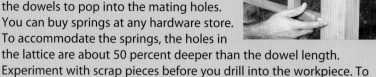

help the dowels move easily, use a drill bit that's $1/_{64}$ in. larger than the dowels. For example, use a $25/_{64}$-in.-dia. bit for $3/_8$-in. dowels. Only six dowels are needed to secure the lattice. Don't drill holes in the bottom frame rails because water will collect in them and promote rot.

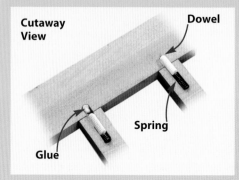

Cutaway View

Dowel

Spring

Glue

1 To create the cloud-lift pattern on the top rail, first form the inside radii with a 1³/₄-in.-dia. Forstner bit. Clamp the workpiece securely to prevent skating.

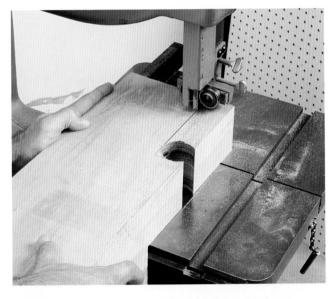

2 Cut away the waste with a band saw. Cut just outside the layout line and use a fence to keep the cut straight. Then remove the outside-radii waste with a saw and a block plane.

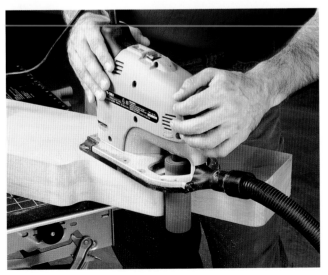

3 Sand the cut smooth with a portable oscillating spindle sander or a sanding block and 80-grit paper. Use the layout lines as a guide.

The Cloud-Lift Rail

The cloud-lift profile on the top gate rail depends on symmetry and proportion. All shoulders and roundovers should be the same radius (⁷/₈ in. in our gate); and the straight run along the top should be at least twice as long as the straight runs on the lower stepped sections. You can make the top rail the same thickness as the rest of the rails and stiles, but we chose to beef it up for emphasis and to create an attractive shadow line between parts.

We laid out the top-rail profile on the workpiece using a compass set to a ⁷/₈-in. radius. If you have a good grasp of geometry, making the S-curves and roundovers is relatively easy. Otherwise, draw a grid on a piece of hardboard or cardboard and copy the drawing onto the grid; then cut it out to make a template.

Once you've laid out the profile, chuck a 1³/₄-in. Forstner bit into a drill press and carefully drill out as many of the S-curves as you can (see photo 1). Then make the straight cuts at the tops of the shoulders to connect the holes — we used a band saw (see photo 2). Trim or file the sharp edges to the curved layout lines, or use a portable oscillating spindle sander (see photo 3). This is precisely the kind of job for which this tool was created.

Mortise-And-Tenon Joints

Except for the lattice strips, all of the wood joints in the gateway are mortise-and-tenon. The bottom rails are joined to the stiles with double mortise-and-tenon joints that combine forces with 1/4-in. stub tenons to keep the joints from racking or twisting. Tenons near the edges of the parts are offset slightly to create a thicker mortise wall that won't blow out during cutting. All mortise-and-tenon joints are pinned for strength and appearance.

Carefully lay out all of the joints at once (see photo 4). Cut the mortises first, using a plunge router and 2-in.-long straight bit (see photo 5). With big joints like these, it's easier to round over the tenons than to square-off the corners of the mortises. Once the mortises are finished, cut the tenons (see photos 6 and 7). Use production-style setups to cut the tenons slightly large; then pare each one to fit the mating mortise. We used a micro plane rasp for the job (see photo 8).

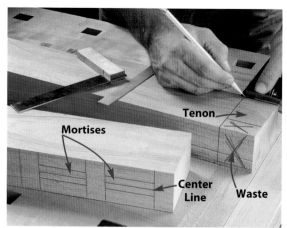

4 Lay out all joinery in pencil before you cut. This helps to prevent mistakes and allows you to orient the workpieces for the best grain and color match. Identify the waste areas with a large X.

5 First bore out the mortises with a drill press and 1/2-in. brad-point bit. Then rout the mortise with a 3/4-in. bit. Center the cut using the router's edge guide, and make successive passes to the finished depth of slightly more than 2 in.

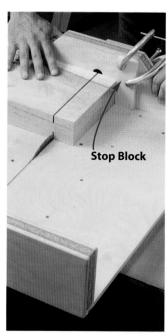

6 Cut the tenon shoulders using a table saw crosscut sled. Clamp a stopblock to the sled to ensure consistent cuts.

7 You can use a band saw or table saw to cut tenon cheeks, but with either tool, leave the tenons slightly thick. Many saws aren't tuned (or made) well enough to cut perfectly consistent tenons, so it's best to fit them by hand.

8 Pare the tenon cheeks with a low-angle block plane and a chisel. Remove small amounts of stock, and check the tenon fit in each mortise. Once the tenon's thickness is perfect, round the corners with a micro plane rasp.

9 Dry-fit the gate and wings and mark all corresponding joints with numbers or letters on tape. Then lay out and mark the rabbets for the gate slats.

10 You'll need to make stopped cuts in the stiles for the gate-slat rabbets. Establish the corresponding position for the starting and stopping points on the router fence and workpiece and mark with tape or pencil. Pivot the workpiece slowly into the router bit.

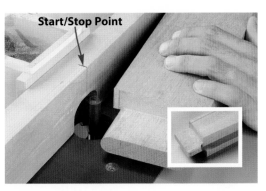

Start/Stop Point

11 Once you've glued and clamped the gate, fit and cut the slats to size. Lay out slats so the colors and grain patterns are harmonious; then number them sequentially.

Number Labels

12 Drive pins through the tenons to reinforce the joint. To ease installation, pare the square edges where they transition into a cylinder.

Frame Assembly

Individually test the fit of each joint; then dry-assemble the frames on a flat surface. Make sure everything is square (although if it's not, there's little you can do to fix it at this point). Lay out a $3/4$-in. rabbet around the perimeter of the lower open section of the gate (see photo 9). This rabbet, which needs to be $1 1/4$ in. deep, provides bearing surface for the gate slats. If you can find a piloted rabbet bit that's long enough to make a $1 1/4$-in.-deep cut, use it. Otherwise, cut the rabbets in each piece on a router table (take apart the dry assembly first) as we did. The process gets a bit tricky at the top of the opening, where you'll need to make stopped cuts to minimize the amount of tenon removed from the ends of the middle gate rail (see photo 10).

Glue and clamp the frames for the gate and wings, using an exterior-rated glue such as polyurethane glue. We clamped the bottom and middle joints on the gate but pinned the top rail to the stiles to secure the joint while the glue set. The pins are made from $1/4$ x $1/4$-in. strips of mahogany that are rounded off halfway down the shaft to fit a $3/16$-in.-dia. guide hole (see photo 12). Once you've glued the frames, you can fasten the gate slats in the lower gate opening. You'll need to mill tongue-and-groove joints in the slats. Dry-fit the slats first (see photo 11). You may need to trim a few of them to get a perfect fit with just enough play.

Attach the slat with pin nails; then conceal the nail heads with retainer strips. To attach the retainers, use wood screws long enough to penetrate the gate rails and stiles.

After the glue dries, pin all of the mortise-and-tenon joints and flush-cut them so the tops are even with the surrounding wood.

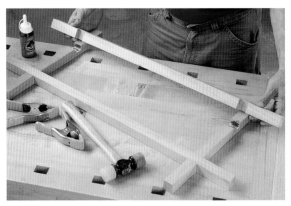

13 Cut half-lap joints in all the lattice pieces; then assemble them with polyurethane glue and spring clamps.

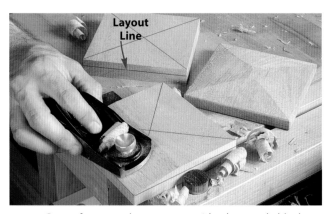

Layout Line

14 Create facets on the post caps with a low-angle block plane. Note the layout line on the caps' edge to limit the facet depth.

Finishing Touches

The strips for the lattice in the top gate opening and the wings are made from 1¼-in.-square stock. We reserved some cutoff scraps to make the lattice. Assemble the pieces with glued half-lap joints (see photo 13). To install the lattice assemblies, use a spring-activated dowel technique (see "Spring Dowels," p. 272). Make the lattice in the shop, but wait to install it until you've transported the frames to the site.

The posts for the gateway are made from pressure-treated pine 4x4s set in concrete. The 4x4s are clad with ⅝-in.-thick mahogany strips. Mill all the cladding you'll need and cut it to width. The post tops are capped with 1-in.-thick x 5½-in.-square post caps. To promote rain runoff, plane facets into the top surface of each cap (see photo 14). The facets are triangular and meet in a peak at the center of the cap.

Installation

Even lightweight gates place a lot of stress on a gatepost, but a 5½-ft.-tall, solid-mahogany gate requires an extremely well anchored post for support. For starters, set the hinge post deep and in concrete. Dig the hole about 12 in. in diameter at the top and widen it to 24 in. at the bottom, below the frost line for your area. Attach several pairs of 8-in.-long treated 2x4s to the below-grade end of the

post to stabilize it in the concrete (see photo 15). The latch post and the wing posts won't undergo nearly as much stress as the hinge post, so you don't need to dig them as deep.

15 Attach pairs of treated 2x4 cross-braces to the bottom of the hinge post to stabilize it in the concrete. The cross-braces should be shorter than the top diameter of the hole. The top pair should be 8 in. below grade when the post is set into the posthole. Orient the post so the top and bottom pairs are parallel to the implied fence line.

16 Attach one of the narrow cladding strips to the edges of each wing that will fit against a post. The bottom edge of the cladding is 1 in. below the bottom of the wing. Center the cladding edge-to-edge and attach it with 3-in. deck screws.

17 Clamp each wing between a post pair, level and plumb the posts and then attach a brace to a post to hold everything in position. Attach the wings to the posts by driving 3-in. deck screws through the cladding edges and into the posts.

18 Add the remaining cladding strips to wrap the posts. Trim them at the top when you cut the posts to height.

To guarantee that your posts will be level, plumb and spaced correctly, attach the wings to the posts and square everything before pouring the concrete. Brace the posts; then attach one of the narrow cladding strips to each wing face that will fit against a post (see photo 16). Use 3-in. deck screws driven through the cladding and into the wing to attach them. Then clamp the wings between the posts on each side of the gate opening. Adjust the post positions as needed until they're plumb and the right distance apart. (Our clad gateposts

are 45¼ in. apart.) Attach the wings to the posts by driving 3-in. deck screws through the exposed edges of the cladding strips and into the posts (see photo 17). Once you've installed the wings, you can attach the lattice in the wing and gate frame opening.

Check your post and wing alignment and spacing; then pour concrete into the postholes. Crown the concrete tops an inch or two above ground level so water will run off.

Attach the rest of the post cladding strips after the concrete has set (see photo 18). Wait a day; then remove the bracing, trim the posts to height and attach the post caps.

Finally, hang the gate and install the latch hardware (see photo 19). A coat or two of clear wood sealer will deepen the tones and even out color variations in the mahogany. But even with sealer, the wood eventually will fade to a soft silver tone.

19 Hang the gate and install the latch hardware. We used heavy-duty strap hinges with thumb-screw-style hangers so the gate can be removed easily

STACKED MIRROR FRAME
Outstanding Stacked-Frame Construction

Unlike a picture frame, which should complement the work it holds, a mirror frame must be attractive enough to stand on its own. At the same time, a mirror frame works best when it harmonizes or blends with its surroundings. This frame has a classic architectural look, rather than a decorative style.

One of the most versatile approaches to frame making is to use nesting moldings. By combining a variety of molding patterns, you can create different styles. The more moldings you nest together, the deeper the frame appears. Conversely, if you stack moldings from the outside to the inside, the center of the frame projects rather than recedes.

You can also combine different woods and molding sizes to create a frame with more depth and visual appeal. We used cherry for this frame's larger outside molding and maple for the inside cove molding and corner plaques. The contrast and color differences between cherry and maple are slight at first but intensify as the cherry darkens with age. Other attractive wood combinations are oak with ash and mahogany with walnut.

Before you start on this project, keep in mind that you can modify the size of your frame to suit its function. For instance, we made this entryway mirror just large enough to reflect a visitor's head and shoulders.

Contrasting woods and nesting moldings provide visual appeal for this simple mirror frame.

Stacked Mirror Frame

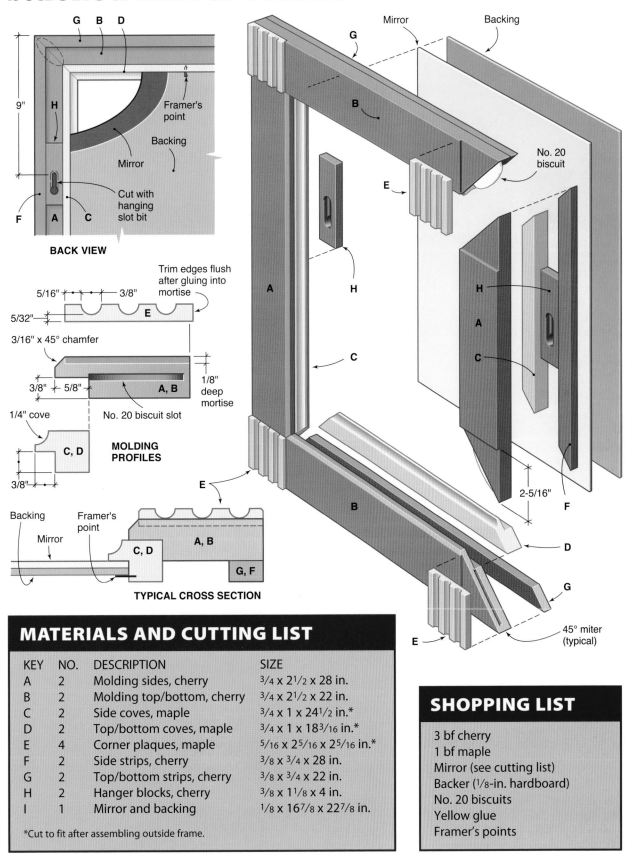

BACK VIEW

Framer's point

Backing

Mirror

Cut with hanging slot bit

9"

G B D

H

F A C

MOLDING PROFILES

Trim edges flush after gluing into mortise

5/16"   3/8"

5/32"   E

3/16" x 45° chamfer

3/8"   5/8"   A, B

1/8" deep mortise

No. 20 biscuit slot

1/4" cove

C, D

3/8"

TYPICAL CROSS SECTION

Backing

Framer's point

Mirror

C, D   A, B

G, F

Mirror   Backing

G

B

E

H

No. 20 biscuit

A

C

H

A

C

F

2-5/16"

D

G

E

45° miter (typical)

MATERIALS AND CUTTING LIST

KEY	NO.	DESCRIPTION	SIZE
A	2	Molding sides, cherry	$3/4$ x $2^1/2$ x 28 in.
B	2	Molding top/bottom, cherry	$3/4$ x $2^1/2$ x 22 in.
C	2	Side coves, maple	$3/4$ x 1 x $24^1/2$ in.*
D	2	Top/bottom coves, maple	$3/4$ x 1 x $18^3/16$ in.*
E	4	Corner plaques, maple	$5/16$ x $2^5/16$ x $2^5/16$ in.*
F	2	Side strips, cherry	$3/8$ x $3/4$ x 28 in.
G	2	Top/bottom strips, cherry	$3/8$ x $3/4$ x 22 in.
H	2	Hanger blocks, cherry	$3/8$ x $1^1/8$ x 4 in.
I	1	Mirror and backing	$1/8$ x $16^7/8$ x $22^7/8$ in.

*Cut to fit after assembling outside frame.

SHOPPING LIST

3 bf cherry
1 bf maple
Mirror (see cutting list)
Backer ($1/8$-in. hardboard)
No. 20 biscuits
Yellow glue
Framer's points

Make Molding

Using the proper sequence when milling frame stock can be the difference between success and failure. Cutting out of order can prevent you from safely completing the molding or leave a ragged edge. Setting up your tools properly also contributes to precision — but more important, it ensures safety. For the best results, follow the steps shown in the photos and outlined below.

This project is made out of 3/4-in.-thick stock that's available at any home center. To get the 1 1/8-in. finished thickness for the molding, we glued 3/8-in.-thick strips to the back of the frame. These strips were simply the waste from trimming the molding to width. To have enough waste, you'll need to buy boards that are at least an inch wider than the finished molding.

Frames don't require much stock, so matching wood is a luxury you can easily afford. Cut all the frame's stock out of a single board so the color and grain will match perfectly. If you rip a board in half, orient the ripped edges to face each other when you assemble the frame so the grain appears balanced.

Once you've ripped the molding to the proper width, cut the rabbets (see photo) in both the cherry and maple (cove) moldings. Use featherboards and hold-downs as needed, particularly with smaller stock that can chatter or rise off the blade. We prefer to cut rabbets on the table saw rather than on a router table because router bits can splinter the edge of the stock. The table saw fitted with a good combination blade (such as a 50-tooth ATB with raker) always produces a clean edge.

Use a router table to cut the chamfer, cove and channels in the moldings (see drawing and photos). We used three common router bits for these cuts: a 45-degree chamfer bit, a 1/4-in. cove bit (both with ball-bearing pilots) and a 3/16-in.-radius core box bit. You probably have these bits in your collection, but if you don't, you can substitute bits with similar profiles.

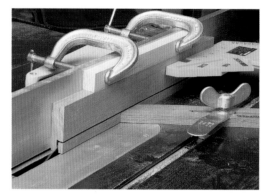

1 First cut the rabbet in the molding stock. Be sure to use featherboards and a hold-down to prevent kickback.

2 Next, chamfer the molding edge on a router table. Use featherboards to ensure a smooth cut.

3 Miter the ends of the molding and then cut centered biscuit slots. Be sure the stock is clamped securely to the bench.

4 Make the plaque-mortise shoulder cuts with a sliding table on your table saw. Use a stopblock for consistent cuts.

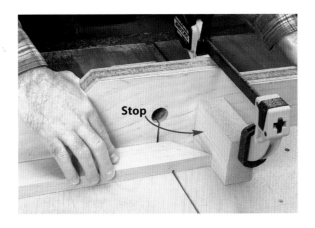

Stop

5 To remove the mortise waste, cut slowly with the band saw or make repeated passes on the table saw.

6 Cut the channels in the plaque stock with a 3/16-in.-radius core box bit. Rout the center channel last.

7 Resaw the plaque stock in half; then plane or sand the back flat to bring it to the correct thickness.

Details And Joinery

To make the corner plaques, start with a 3/4 x 2⁵/₁₆-in. piece that's about 12 in. long. The thicker stock makes it safer to rout the channels (see photo). Once you've routed the channels, resaw and then sand or plane the stock to the final 5/16-in. thickness. Then you can cut the plaques to size.

Before you cut miters on your finished cherry stock, make test cuts on a scrap piece of the same thickness and width. Unless your saw is making true 45-degree cuts, either the inside or outside corner of the miters will be open when the frame is assembled. To test, make a 45-degree cut in the center of the scrap piece; then turn one half over and make a second cut. (This creates a V-shaped waste piece.) Abut the mitered ends of the two halves to form a straight edge. If the edge isn't straight, you'll need to adjust your saw. Don't cut the miters on the maple cove stock until you've assembled the cherry molding.

We used No. 20 biscuits to join the miters. Biscuits make strong joints and align parts precisely. If you don't have a plate joiner, you'll need to fasten the miters with dowels, wood splines or even plugged screws. Glue alone won't hold on the miter's end grain.

You can cut the mortises for the corner plaques as we did, by first making a shoulder cut on the table saw and then removing the waste on the band saw. Or you can remove the waste by making repeated passes on the table saw. The mortise bottom must be flat and smooth to glue on the corner plaques.

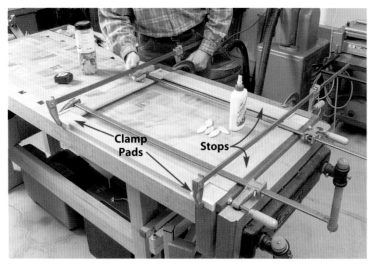

8 Before assembling the frame, set up two perpendicular stops on your bench to keep the stock square when clamping.

9 Glue and brad-nail the strips F, G to the back of the frame. The strips give the frame a thicker profile.

Assemble And Finish

Sand all the cherry parts with 120-grit paper before assembly. Be sure the parts fit together properly before gluing, and check that the assembly is square by measuring diagonally from corner to corner.

Once the glue has dried, cut the maple (nesting) moldings to fit; then glue them in place. If you plan on staining the cherry parts to increase the contrast between woods, you should do this before gluing the cove moldings.

To ensure the mirror would always hang straight and rest flat against the wall, we routed keyhole slots in the back with a hanging-slot bit. Glue the hanger blocks between the side coves and the side strips, centered about 9 in. from the top. Set up a fence and stopblock (see photo) and cut the slot with a plunge router.

Keep your finishing simple. Good finishing options are Danish oil, wipe-on varnish or aerosol clear lacquer. Back the mirror with 1/8-in. hardboard before hanging.

10 Cut each nesting cove molding individually to ensure a tight fit; then glue the moldings into the rabbet.

11 Bevel the edges of the corner plaques and glue them in position with the channels running vertically.

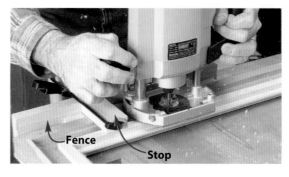

12 Rout a keyhole slot in the hanging block that ends about 9 in. from the top of the frame.

WHITE OAK ADIRONDACK
A Durable Outdoor Classic

Next to baseball, nothing says summer fun and relaxation more than an Adirondack chair. It's not surprising — both of these classics are products of the same nostalgic era. But what makes this icon of outdoor furniture eternally popular among woodworkers is its ease of construction and supreme comfort.

The Adirondack chair's basic A-frame design lends itself to countless modifications to the size, decorative shapes, back angle and curve. You can craft one of these chairs with the care you'd use to make fine furniture (some people do use them indoors) or you can nail one together in a few hours using construction lumber — it's your choice. You'll find our chair to be a nice compromise between highly finished and rustic. There's no complex joinery, only glue, screws and mostly butt joints. You should have no problem completing this project in a weekend.

We designed this chair with a back that's slightly reclined and curved for comfort. We made it out of white oak for its beauty, strength and excellent weather resistance. The oak is from a local hardwood supplier and was already planed to 3/4 in. Other woods that work well are Honduras mahogany, teak, cedar, redwood and kiln-dried pressure-treated pine (KDAT). Don't use red oak (it will rot) or undried pressure-treated wood (it will shrink and warp).

The Adirondack chair gets its name from the mountain range in New York state where this simple chair has been a fixture at resorts for well over 100 years. Long popular throughout the country, this easy-to-build project is a perennial woodworking favorite.

White Oak Adirondack

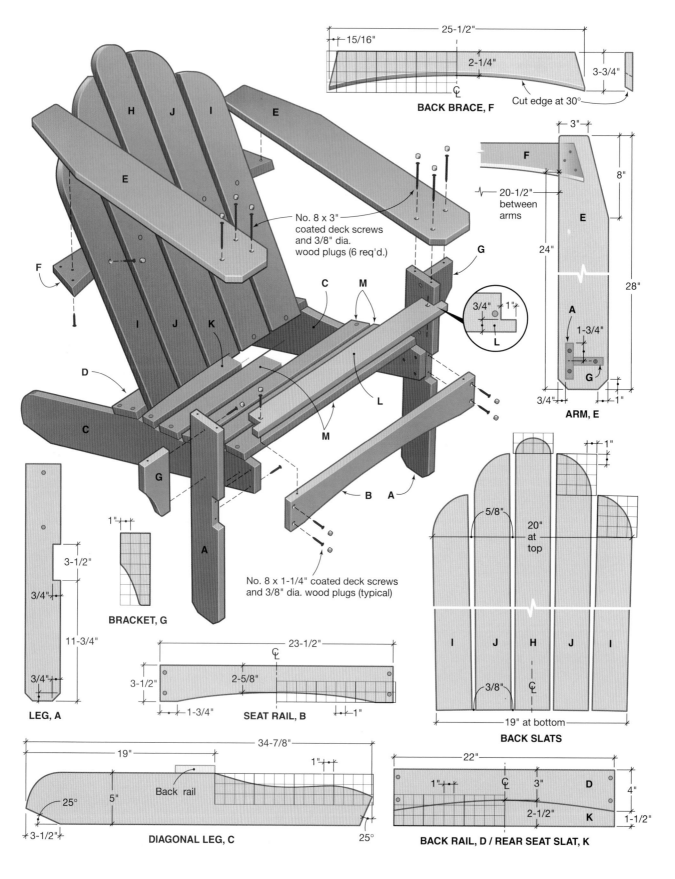

BACK BRACE, F

25-1/2"
15/16"
2-1/4"
3-3/4"
Cut edge at 30°

No. 8 x 3" coated deck screws and 3/8" dia. wood plugs (6 req'd.)

ARM, E

3"
20-1/2" between arms
8"
24"
28"
1-3/4"
3/4"
1"
A
E
G
F

3/4" 1"
L

No. 8 x 1-1/4" coated deck screws and 3/8" dia. wood plugs (typical)

LEG, A

3-1/2"
3/4"
11-3/4"
3/4"

BRACKET, G

1"

SEAT RAIL, B

23-1/2"
3-1/2"
2-5/8"
1-3/4"
1"

BACK SLATS

1"
5/8"
20" at top
I J H J I
3/8"
19" at bottom

DIAGONAL LEG, C

34-7/8"
19"
Back rail
1"
25°
5"
3-1/2"
25°

BACK RAIL, D / REAR SEAT SLAT, K

22"
1"
3"
D
2-1/2"
K
4"
1-1/2"

MATERIALS AND CUTTING LIST

KEY	NO.	DESCRIPTION	SIZE
A	2	Front legs	3/4 x 31/2 x 23 in.
B	1	Seat rail	3/4 x 31/2 x 231/2 in.
C	2	Diagonal legs	3/4 x 5 x 347/8 in.
D	1	Back rail*	3/4 x 4 x 22 in.
E	2	Arms	3/4 x 5 x 28 in.
F	1	Back brace	3/4 x 33/4 x 251/2 in.
G	2	Arm brackets	3/4 x 3 x 7 in.
H	1	Center back slat	3/4 x 31/2 x 31 in.
I	2	Short back slats	3/4 x 31/2 x 251/2 in.
J	2	Long back slats	3/4 x 31/2 x 291/2 in.
K	1	Rear seat slat*	3/4 x 21/2 x 22 in.
L	1	Front seat slat	3/4 x 21/2 x 24 in.
M	4	Seat slats	3/4 x 21/2 x 22 in.
N	40	Plugs	3/8 in. dia.

All parts white oak

* Cut the back rail and rear seat slat from the same piece of stock; see text and drawing.

SHOPPING LIST

20 bf 3/4-in. white oak
No. 8 x 11/4-in. coated deck screws
No. 8 x 3-in. coated deck screws
Polyurethane glue
Water-repellent finish

Preparing Stock

It takes about 15 bf of lumber to make one chair, but get 20 bf to be on the safe side. (In construction lumber terms, 20 bf would be about four 1x8

1 Make a hardboard half-pattern for the seat-rail and the back-brace curves; then trace on the stock with a pencil.

x 8-ft. boards.) The extra stock ensures that waste and mistakes won't leave you short. We prefer to make chairs in pairs, so we usually double the amount of stock. Be sure to pick boards of a size that keeps waste to a minimum. It's important to have straight edges for the chair to fit together properly, so saw the stock edges straight if necessary.

This is outdoor furniture, so you don't need to sand the wood unless it's particularly rough or you just want it to look better. If you must, a quick going-over with 80-grit paper on a random-orbit sander will do the trick.

The seat rail (B), back rail (D) and back brace (F) have curved edges (see drawing). You'll need to make two hardboard half-patterns: one for the seat rail and one for the back rail and back brace (which have the same curve, but are cut at different angles) using the grids in the drawing. You can also draw the curves directly onto the stock using the grids, but you'll be able to make smoother, more uniform curves with a half-pattern (see photo 1).

Use a photocopier to enlarge the grids to full scale or draw out the grids and copy the line position in each grid square. Either way, you'll probably need to refine the curves by eye. Don't worry about being too precise; all that matters is that the curves are smooth and look good to you.

The back brace is the trickiest part to make because you'll need to cut the curve at a 30-degree angle (see drawing) so the back slats lie flat. The easiest way to cut the angle is to use a band saw and tilt its table. If your jigsaw has a tilting base, that will also work. But if your jigsaw's base is fixed, you'll have to make an angle block (see photo 2). Use a piece of 2x4 stock to make the block and cut the angle with a circular saw or a table saw. Cut a slot for the blade, then attach the block temporarily to the base with screws or hot-melt glue.

You could also cut the back rail's curve at a 5-degree angle, but the slight difference in its angle and the angle of the back slats isn't critical. However, you should cut the back rail and the rear seat slat (K) out of one piece of stock (see drawing) so their curves will match.

The diagonal legs (C) are also curved where the seat slats are attached. But unlike the back rail and seat rail, you don't need a separate pattern — the workpiece is your pattern. Just draw the curve on one leg and cut it out; then use the first leg as a pattern for the second one. Be sure to cut the 25-degree angles on the leg ends accurately.

The only joints you'll need to cut are the seat rail notches in the front legs. Make the cuts with a jigsaw and clean up the joints with a chisel. The face of the rail should be flush with the edges of the legs.

Complete the detail cuts on the parts, such as clipping the leg and arm corners and cutting the curves on the top of the back slats. (Use the same technique of cutting one piece and using it as a pattern.) Then sand the sawn edges to remove roughness. We routed almost all of the edges with a ¼-in. roundover bit (see photo 3). It gives the chair a more finished look and you can sit without fear of picking up splinters.

2 Cut the back-rail curve with a 30-degree angle block (see text) attached to the base of the jigsaw.

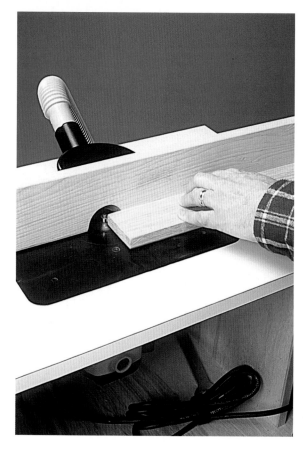

3 To reduce the possibility of splinters and to get a smoother look, ease all the edges with a ¼-in. roundover bit.

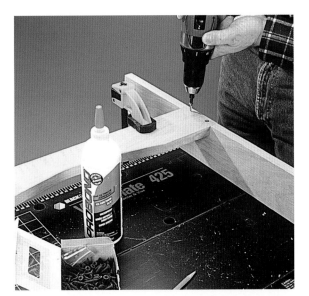

4 Drill counterbored screw holes to join the seat rail and front legs. Assemble with waterproof glue and deck screws.

5 Join the front leg assembly and the diagonal leg assembly on a flat surface, being sure the front legs are plumb.

6 Glue and screw the back brace to the arms from the bottom. The assembly must be square (see text).

Assembly Sequence

Assembling the chair won't take much time, but you must put all the parts together square and plumb so the chair sits flat and doesn't rock. First you'll make sub-assemblies; then you'll join these together and finally add the back and seat slats. To ensure that the chair holds up outdoors, use only waterproof glue such as polyurethane or waterproof yellow glue. Galvanized screws will stain oak, so use coated or stainless deck screws.

Begin by assembling the front legs and the seat rail (see photo 5). Lay out the screw holes 3/8 in. from the rail edge; then drill counterbored holes in the seat rail (you'll plug these later). Next, clamp the diagonal legs to the front and use a framing square to check that the front legs are perpendicular to the ground. The diagonal legs' feet should be resting flat and their front corners should be even with the top of the seat rail notches. Mark the leg positions with a pencil. Then disassemble, apply glue to the joints, align the legs and screw them together. Countersink but don't counterbore these screw holes or the screws will exit on the other side. Now attach the back rail.

Lay out the back brace and arms on a flat surface. Be sure the parts are square and that the top edge of the back brace is exactly 24 in. from the front of the arm as shown in the drawing. Changing this dimension will alter the seat angle. Glue and screw these parts together just as you did the legs.

Attach the brackets (G) to the arms with glue and screws. (Counterbore these screw holes for plugs.) Prop the arm/brace assembly on the legs (see photo 7) using a clamp or a piece of scrap. Make sure the arms are level and positioned correctly over the legs (see drawing); then mark the screw hole locations. Use 3-in. deck screws to fasten the arms and leave the brace propped until you attach the first back slat.

To achieve even spacing, screw the center back slat (H) in place first, then the short slats and finally the long ones. Note that the slats are slightly fanned so the spacing is wider at the top than at the bottom. Once you've installed the back slats, screw the seat slats to the legs starting with the rear and front ones; then space the remaining slats evenly.

Make enough plugs (N) to fill the counterbores using a plug cutter (available at any home center or hardware store). Glue the plugs with their grain oriented in the same direction as the surrounding wood. Trim the plugs with a chisel or flush-trim saw.

White oak will hold up well for many years without any care. But applying a water-repellent or clear deck finish every few years will help preserve the wood's integrity and natural beauty.

7 Attach the arm assembly to the front legs. Support the back brace with a clamp and level the arms.

8 Install the back slats, then the seat slats. Place wood strips between them to achieve uniform spacing.

9 Fill all the exposed screw holes with horizontal-grain wood plugs (see text), then pare them flush with a chisel.

PERFECT PAIR

Exploit The Efficiency Of Modular Construction

With the benefits of modular construction in mind (using similar-size components to make different pieces), we designed this bookcase and end table, which even a beginning woodworker can build. The pieces use the same stock and joinery, so you can complete both in about the same time as it takes to make just one.

All of the materials can be found at a home center. If you already have a basic shop setup (table saw, router, drill/driver, etc.), the only specialty tools you'll need are a self-centering dowel jig and a 35mm Forstner bit.

Because the doors add a little more complexity, the following steps focus on how to build the end table. Any additional steps specific to the bookcase are addressed in "Build the Bookcase," page 291.

This end table and bookcase are built with the same construction methods and materials, resulting in two pieces in the time it takes to make one.

End Table

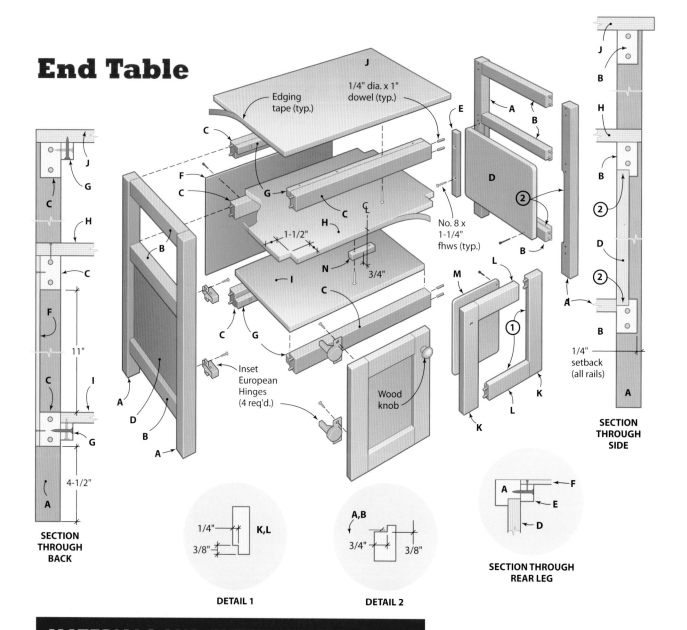

Edging tape (typ.)

1/4" dia. x 1" dowel (typ.)

No. 8 x 1-1/4" fhws (typ.)

Inset European Hinges (4 req'd.)

Wood knob

1-1/2"

3/4"

SECTION THROUGH BACK

11"

4-1/2"

1/4" setback (all rails)

SECTION THROUGH SIDE

1/4"

3/8"

K,L

DETAIL 1

A,B

3/4"

3/8"

DETAIL 2

SECTION THROUGH REAR LEG

MATERIALS AND CUTTING LIST

KEY	NO.	DESCRIPTION	SIZE
A	4	Legs, poplar	$1^{1}/_{2}$ x $1^{1}/_{2}$ x $27^{1}/_{4}$ in.
B	6	Side rails, poplar	$1^{1}/_{4}$ x 2 x $12^{1}/_{4}$ in.
C	5	Front/back rails, poplar	$1^{1}/_{4}$ x 2 x $20^{1}/_{4}$ in.
D	2	Side panels, birch plywood	$3/_{4}$ x $11^{3}/_{4}$ x 13 in.
E	2	Back panel ledgers, poplar	$3/_{4}$ x 1 x 11 in.
F	1	Back panel, birch plywood	$1/_{4}$ x 15 x $20^{1}/_{4}$ in.
G	4	Top and bottom ledgers, poplar	$3/_{4}$ x 1 x $20^{1}/_{4}$ in.
H	1	Shelf, birch plywood	$3/_{4}$ x $15^{1}/_{8}$ x $23^{1}/_{8}$ in.
I	1	Bottom, birch plywood	$3/_{4}$ x $12^{1}/_{4}$ x $20^{1}/_{4}$ in.
J	1	Top, birch plywood	$3/_{4}$ x 16 x $24^{3}/_{4}$ in.
K	4	Door stiles, poplar	$3/_{4}$ x 2 x 13 in.
L	4	Door rails, poplar	$3/_{4}$ x 2 x 6 in.
M	2	Door panels, birch plywood	$1/_{4}$ x $6^{5}/_{8}$ x $9^{1}/_{2}$ in.
N	1	Doorstop, poplar	$3/_{4}$ x 1 x 3 in.

SHOPPING LIST

1x4 x 8-ft. poplar boards (2)
1x6 x 8-ft. poplar boards (3)
$1/_{4}$-in. x 2 x 4-ft. birch plywood
$3/_{4}$-in. x 4 x 4-ft. birch plywood
$1^{3}/_{16}$-in.-dia. wood knobs (2)
Inset (Euro-style) cup hinges
Birch plywood edging tape
$1/_{4}$ x 1-in. dowels
No. 8 x $1^{1}/_{4}$-in. wood screws
$5/_{8}$-in. brad nails
$1^{1}/_{4}$-in. finish nails

Bookcase

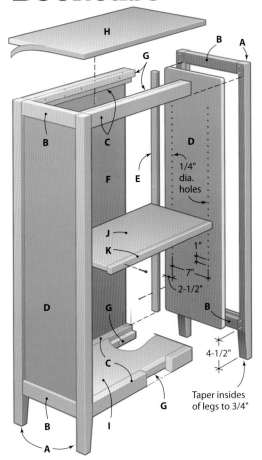

MATERIALS AND CUTTING LIST

KEY	NO.	DESCRIPTION	SIZE
A	4	Legs, poplar	$1\frac{1}{2}$ x $1\frac{1}{2}$ x $47\frac{1}{4}$ in.
B	4	Side rails, poplar	$1\frac{1}{4}$ x 2 x $10\frac{1}{4}$ in.
C	4	Front/back rails, poplar	$1\frac{1}{4}$ x 2 x $22\frac{1}{4}$ in.
D	2	Side panels, birch plywood	$\frac{3}{4}$ x $10\frac{7}{8}$ x $38\frac{7}{8}$ in.
E	2	Back panel ledgers, poplar	$\frac{3}{4}$ x 1 x $38\frac{1}{2}$ in.
F	1	Back panel, birch plywood	$\frac{1}{4}$ x $22\frac{1}{4}$ x $42\frac{1}{4}$ in.
G	4	Top and bottom ledgers, poplar	$\frac{3}{4}$ x 1 x $22\frac{1}{4}$ in.
H	1	Top, birch plywood	$\frac{3}{4}$ x 14 x 27 in.
I	1	Bottom, birch plywood	$\frac{3}{4}$ x $10\frac{1}{4}$ x $22\frac{1}{4}$ in.
J	3	Shelves, birch plywood	$\frac{3}{4}$ x $11\frac{1}{4}$ x $22\frac{1}{4}$ in.
K	3	Shelf edging, poplar	$\frac{3}{4}$ x 1 x $22\frac{1}{4}$ in.

SHOPPING LIST

2x4 x 8-ft. pine (3)
$\frac{3}{4}$-in. x 4 x 8-ft. Honduras mahogany plywood (5)
$\frac{3}{4}$ x 3-in. x 8-ft. Honduras mahogany (7)
$\frac{3}{4}$ x 6-in. x 8-ft. Honduras mahogany (1)

Scrap $\frac{3}{4}$-in. plywood or lumber
Shelf pins (72)
Flathead wood screws (3, $2\frac{1}{2}$, $1\frac{3}{4}$, $1\frac{5}{8}$, $1\frac{1}{2}$, $1\frac{1}{4}$ in.)
$\frac{3}{8}$-dia. x 2-in. dowels (24)
Wood glue
Finishing materials

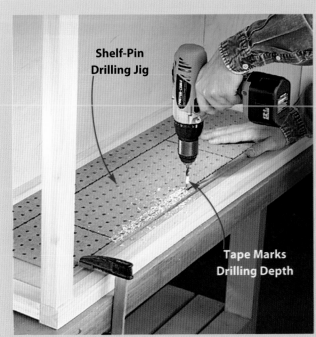

Shelf-Pin Drilling Jig

Tape Marks Drilling Depth

BUILD THE BOOKCASE

The following additional steps are necessary to build the bookcase:

• Taper the bottom $4\frac{1}{2}$ in. of the inside face of each leg. You can use a tapering jig and table saw, but because the leg posts are so long, It is easier to cut with a jigsaw following a straightedge.

• Drill shelf-pin holes in the sides using a scrap of $\frac{1}{4}$-in. perforated hardboard as a template. Attach a stop or a piece of tape to the drill bit to mark the drilling depth and prevent drilling through the sides (photo, left).

• Make adjustable shelves by attaching solid-wood edging to the front of each shelf board with glue and $1\frac{1}{2}$-in. finish nails. Finish the shelves to match the bookcase.

Mill The Legs And Rails

The legs and rails for the end table and bookcase are made from 1x poplar that is face-glued to create 1½-in.-thick stock. Cut 1x4 poplar into four 28-in.-long pieces for the end table legs, and cut the 1x6 into six 35-in.-long pieces for the end table rails. Face glue the pieces in pairs (see photo 1).

When the glue has cured, rip the 1x4 leg stock to 1½ in. wide and the 1x6 rail stock to 2 in. wide; then rip the thickness to 1¼ in. Cut the legs and rails to final length. Each 35-in. rail blank will yield one side rail and one front or back rail.

Using a self-centering dowel jig, drill ¼-in.-dia. x 1⅛-in.-deep dowel holes at all of the leg/rail connections. Center the dowels on the rails, and offset the dowel positions on the legs to keep the rails and posts flush on the inside of the case (see photo 2).

Make The Top And Shelves

We used ¾-in. birch plywood for the top and shelves. The top shelf and bottom shelf are notched to fit around the legs.

Heat-activated wood edge banding conceals the edges that will be exposed, including all four edges of the top and the outside edges of the top shelf. Cut the banding 2 in. longer than the edge to be covered. Activate the banding with a household iron (see photo 3). After the edge banding has cooled, trim the excess with a sharp chisel. (You can purchase a special trimmer designed for this purpose.) Lightly sand to ease any sharp edges.

A plywood top is easy to make, but it has drawbacks. The texture of the plywood core can telegraph through the surface veneer, especially if you apply a glossy finish. In addition, the veneer is very thin, making future repairs virtually impossible.

If you want to enhance the strength and appearance of the top, make it out of solid wood. Lumberyards may carry some varieties of preglued panel

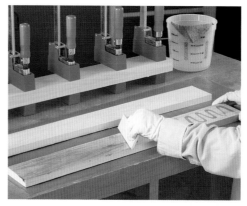

1 Apply polyurethane glue to one surface only. Spread the glue evenly over the part (legs are shown here), and use several clamps to ensure tight contact.

Spacer

2 Place a ¼-in.-thick spacer between the jig and the inside face of the leg to offset the dowel locations on the legs. The offset positions the rail flush with the inside of the leg.

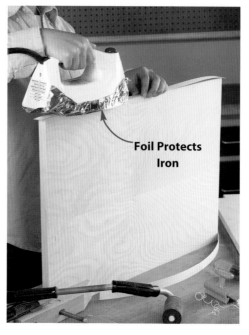

Foil Protects Iron

3 Press the edge banding down along each edge of the top and shelves, using an iron set on low heat. To ensure a good bond, follow the iron with a small roller while the edging is still warm.

stock, but you will most likely have to edge-glue your own panel. You must attach any solid top with tabletop fasteners or corner blocks with slotted screw holes. Both are designed to allow the wood to expand and contract as humidity changes.

Assemble The Case

Whether you're building the end table or the bookcase, the case-assembly technique is the same: Start with the sides and build inward.

Apply glue to the dowels and assemble the sides, making sure they are square (see photo 4). After the glue has cured, rout the 3/8-in.-wide x 3/4-in.-deep rabbets for the side panels using a 3/8-in.-dia. bearing-guided rabbeting bit (see photo 5).

Cut the side panels to size, and trim the corners to fit inside the 3/8-in.-radius corners of the rabbets. Apply glue in the rabbets and fasten the side panels with 1 1/4-in. brad nails. Solid panels must be able to expand and contract, but you can glue plywood panels in place. In fact, gluing provides reinforcement and prevents racking.

Next, connect the two side assemblies. Working with the case on its side, first glue the front and back rails into one side. Then fit the shelf in position and secure the other side assembly to the rails. The shelf must be installed at this stage because it will not fit into place later. After assembly you'll clamp the top shelf to the rails with glue and finishing nails.

Clamp the case parts together and then place the assembly upright on a flat surface. Adjust the clamps as necessary to square the case. Glue and fasten the back panel ledgers and back panel while the case-frame assembly is still clamped (see photo 6).

Fasten the ledgers to the rails with 1 1/4-in. screws, and attach the bottom to the bottom ledgers with 1 1/4-in. screws. Do not attach the top until after you've applied the finish.

Make And Hang The Doors

Measure the opening and cut the door stiles and rails to fit. Like the side panels, the door panels fit into a rabbet.

4 Clamp the side frame with soft-face jaws or clamping pads to prevent marring. Check that the frame is square by measuring the diagonals.

5 Position the side frame on the workbench with the inside faceup. Use a bearing-piloted rabbeting bit to cut the 3/8 x 3/4-in. rabbet in multiple passes.

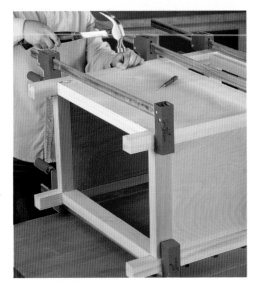

6 Connect the two side frames and remaining rails with the top shelf in place. Glue and fasten the back panel with 1 1/4-in. finishing nails while the case is still clamped to keep it square.

Assemble the door stiles and rails with dowels, making sure the frames are square. After the glue has cured, rout a 3/8-in.-wide x 1/4-in.-deep rabbet around the inside edge of each door frame. Glue and fasten the panels in the rabbets with 5/8-in. brad nails.

We used flush-hanging cup hinges (Euro-style) to hang the door. These hinges are easy to adjust and remove. Use a 35mm bit and drill press to bore the hinge cup mortises in the doors (see photo 7). Screw the hinges to the door, and attach the mounting clips to the cabinet. Snap the doors into place, and center them using the built-in hinge-adjustment screws (see photo 8).

Center and fasten the doorstop to the bottom of the top shelf with 1 1/4-in. screws. Drill 3/16-in.-dia. holes at each doorknob location.

Finish The Parts

You can use paint or stain and polyurethane to finish the table. We decided to leave the top natural and paint the case and shelves.

Sand the top with increasingly finer grades of sandpaper (ending with 220-grit). We applied a first coat of oil-base polyurethane diluted 50/50 with mineral spirits. After the first coat dried, we lightly sanded with 320-grit paper. Then we applied two additional coats of undiluted polyurethane, sanding lightly between coats.

The quality of the paint job can make or break a furniture project. We chose water-base enamel designed for furniture, but you can use oil or latex interior trim paint instead. To achieve the best finish, follow these tips:

- Hold a light at a low angle to look for major scratches or dents. Fill deep blemishes with wood putty, and sand the entire piece with 150-grit sandpaper. The paint will cover any swirl marks.

- Apply primer to block stains and seal the wood so it will evenly receive a topcoat. If you are using a dark-color paint, ask the paint supplier to tint the primer for easier coverage.

- When using latex paint, mix it with Flood Floetrol, an additive that extends the open time and makes the paint flow more like oil-base enamel.

- Brush the corners and seams first and then use a 1/4-in.-nap or foam roller to cover the large areas. Start with the inside faces and move to the outside, covering one side entirely before moving on to the next.

- Give your project an extra day to dry before attaching the top and placing it on carpet. Even when latex paint appears to be dry, it may still be sticky.

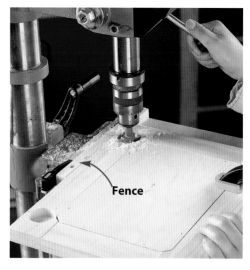

7 Drill a 35mm (or 1 3/8-in.-dia.) mortise for the cup hinges. Clamp a fence to position the center of the bit at the specified distance from the edge of the door. Mark a bit centerline on the top of the fence and a hole centerline on the door.

8 Fasten the hinge to the door and the mounting bracket to the cabinet (inset photo). Slide the hinge arm onto the mounting bracket, and center the door in the cabinet opening using the adjustment screws.

WALL DESK
A Great Way To Organize That's Off The Wall

A wall desk provides compact storage for stationery and bill-paying supplies. It works best in a kitchen or hallway where floor space is scarce.

Modern life seems to be marked by piles of paper — junk mail, bills, fliers, newspapers, books, magazines and to-do lists. Of course, most of these items are important, and we need to keep them organized.

This wall desk provides a place for you to begin that task. Constructed out of solid mahogany, this desk has a drop-down door that also functions as a writing surface. The actual writing surface is plastic laminate, which is smooth and easy to maintain and provides an interesting color contrast with the mahogany frame.

Gathering Materials

We used 4/4 and 5/4 mahogany for the desk. Because mahogany is readily available in wide boards, you should not need to glue up panels for the wider case parts. If you choose another hardwood, you may have to assemble the panels for the top, bottom and sides from narrow stock.

The case back and door panels are 1/2-in. mahogany veneer on a medium-density fiberboard (MDF) core. We chose this core stock because it tends to be flatter and more stable than a veneer core. These panels are generally available from hardwood suppliers and some home centers. Because the project calls for only two small pieces, you might try to purchase a 4 x 4-ft. panel instead of the normal 4 x 8-ft. sheet.

If you don't own a jointer and planer, have your lumber supplier plane the 4/4 stock to 13/16 in. thick and the 5/4 stock to 1 in. thick. You should insist that the stock be flat, without any cupping or warping in the boards, because it is almost impossible to build a high-quality piece of furniture with material that's not flat. You will also need a small amount of 3/4-in.-thick maple stock for the wall cleats and splines.

Wall Desk

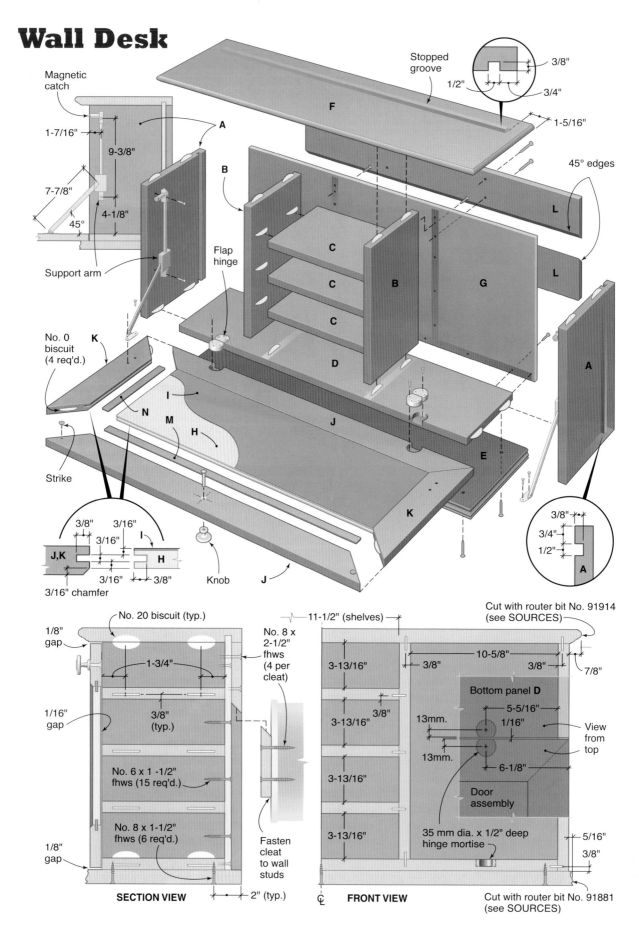

Magnetic catch

Stopped groove

3/8"

1/2"

3/4"

1-5/16"

F

1-7/16"

9-3/8"

A

45° edges

7-7/8"

B

L

4-1/8"

45°

L

Support arm

Flap hinge

C

C

B

G

C

D

No. 0 biscuit (4 req'd.)

K

A

I

N

M

J

3/8"

3/4"

1/2"

A

H

E

Strike

3/8"   3/16"

3/16"

J,K

I

H

Knob

K

3/16"   3/8"

J

3/16" chamfer

No. 20 biscuit (typ.)

11-1/2" (shelves)

Cut with router bit No. 91914 (see SOURCES)

1/8" gap

No. 8 x 2-1/2" fhws (4 per cleat)

10-5/8"

3/8"

3/8"

7/8"

1-3/4"

3-13/16"

3/8"

1/16" gap

3/8" (typ.)

3/8"

Bottom panel D

5-5/16"

13mm.

1/16"

View from top

3-13/16"

13mm.

No. 6 x 1-1/2" fhws (15 req'd.)

6-1/8"

3-13/16"

No. 8 x 1-1/2" fhws (6 req'd.)

Fasten cleat to wall studs

Door assembly

1/8" gap

35 mm dia. x 1/2" deep hinge mortise

3-13/16"

5/16"

3/8"

SECTION VIEW

2" (typ.)

FRONT VIEW

Cut with router bit No. 91881 (see SOURCES)

MATERIALS AND CUTTING LIST

KEY	NO.	DESCRIPTION	SIZE
A	2	Sides	$13/16 \times 10^{1}/_2 \times 16$ in.
B	2	Inner partitions	$13/16 \times 9 \times 15^{3}/_{16}$ in.
C	3	Shelves	$13/16 \times 9 \times 11^{1}/_2$ in.
D	1	Inside bottom panel	$13/16 \times 9 \times 34^{3}/_8$ in.
E	1	Bottom panel	$1 \times 11^{7}/_{16} \times 36^{5}/_8$ in.
F	1	Top	$1 \times 12 \times 37^{3}/_4$ in.
G	1	Back, plywood	$1/2 \times 16^{3}/_8 \times 35^{1}/_8$ in.
H	1	Door panel, plywood	$1/2 \times 9^{3}/_4 \times 30$ in.
I	1	Plastic-laminate panel	$1/16 \times 10^{3}/_4 \times 31$ in.**
J	2	Door rails	$13/16 \times 3 \times 36$ in.
K	2	Door stiles	$13/16 \times 3 \times 15^{3}/_4$ in.
L	2	Wall cleats, maple	$3/4 \times 5 \times 34^{3}/_8$ in.
M	2	Spline	$3/16 \times 3/4 \times 29$ in.
N	2	Spline	$3/16 \times 3/4 \times 8^{3}/_4$ in.

*All parts mahogany except as noted

**Trim to finished size after laminating

SHOPPING LIST

1/2-in. mahogany plywood (1/4 sheet)
8 bf 5/4 mahogany (surfaced to 1 in.)
12 bf 4/4 mahogany (surfaced to
   13/16 in.)
3 bf 4/4 maple (surfaced to 3/4 in.)
3 sf plastic laminate
Fall-flap support arms; Rockler No.
   30741 (2)
Fall-flap hinges; Rockler No. 29447
   (1 pair)
Router bits: Rockler catalog No.
   91914 and No. 91881
Knob; Rockler No. 42852 (1)
No. 6 x 11/2-in. flathead wood screws
No. 8 x 21/2-in. flathead wood screws
No. 8 x 11/2-in. flathead wood screws
No. 20 plate-joining biscuits
No. 0 plate-joining biscuits
Yellow glue
Contact cement
Transparent finish
Brown mahogany wood stain

1 Shape the ends and front edge of the case top with a molding bit. Clamp a fence to the router table to help guide the workpiece.

2 When cutting biscuit slots in the center of a panel, clamp a straightedge to the piece and position the plate joiner.

Case Work

Begin by cutting all case parts to finished dimension. All joinery is done with plate-joining biscuits, so no allowances are needed for tenons.

Install the molding bit in the router table for shaping the case top profile. Although the bit has a ball-bearing pilot, clamp a fence to the table for safety's sake. Keep the leading edge of the fence flush with the bearing. Cut the profile on the panel ends first; then shape the front edge (see photo 1). Change bits to shape the bottom panel.

Next, mark the biscuit slot locations in the case top, sides, shelves, partitions and inside bottom panel (see drawing). Use the plate joiner to cut the slots. When you need to cut slots in the face of a panel, clamp a straightedge to the workpiece to help position the plate joiner.

The case back rests in a groove cut in the case top and sides. Use a router with a spiral up-cutting bit and edge guide to make these cuts. Notice that the groove in the case top stops short of the panel ends. Square the ends with a sharp chisel.

We used special fall-flap hinges for mounting the desk door. These hinges fit in a 35mm-dia. mortise cut in both the desk bottom and door. Clamp a fence to the drill press table to properly locate the holes. You'll need a 35mm bit to bore the mortises. (This size bit is commonly used to mount Euro-style hinges for cabinet construction, so if you need to purchase one, it will be a handy addition to your tool kit.) Lay out and bore the mortises in the case bottom; then leave the drill press set up to bore the door mortises later.

Sand all interior surfaces of the case parts before you start assembling the case. This eliminates the need for awkward sanding in narrow spaces after assembly. Use 120-, 150-, and 220-grit sandpaper, dusting off thoroughly each time you change grits.

Once you've completed sanding, spread glue in the biscuit slots and on the biscuits for the partition-shelf joints. Join the shelves to the partitions and clamp them to draw the joints tight. Compare opposite diagonal measurements to check that the assembly is square (see photo 6). If necessary, adjust the clamps until the measurements are identical; then let the glue set before removing the clamps.

Next, join the partitions to the inside bottom panel; then add the case sides. When you clamp the sides, make sure that they stay square to the bottom. When the glue sets, remove the clamps and add the case top.

Slide the case back into position in the side and top grooves. Drill and countersink pilot holes and screw the back to the partitions, shelves and bottom. Drill and countersink pilot holes in the bottom panel; then fasten it to the case.

Rip and crosscut ³/4-in.-thick maple stock to size for the wall cleats. Use

3 Rout the grooves in the case back, top and sides using a spiral up-cutting bit. Mount an accessory edge guide on the router.

4 Clamp the fence to the drill press table; then bore the 35mm hinge recesses in the inside bottom panel.

5 Begin case assembly by joining the shelves to the inner partitions. You can save time by sanding the parts before assembly.

6 Measure diagonally to be sure that the assembly is square. Adjust clamping pressure to square the assembly.

the table saw to rip a 45-degree bevel along one long edge of each piece. Drill and countersink pilot holes in one of the strips for mounting it to the case back. Position the holes so the screws run into the edges of the partitions. Attach the cleat to the case. Note that the long point of the bevel should be positioned away from the back panel.

7 Join the partition/shelf assembly to the inside bottom; then add the case sides. Be sure that the sides remain square to the bottom while the glue sets.

8 Slide the back panel into position. Drill and countersink pilot holes; then fasten the back to the shelves, bottom and partitions with flathead screws.

9 Spread contact cement on the door panel and plastic laminate. When the cement is dry to the touch, place dowels on the panel and position the laminate.

10 Cut splines about 1 in. shorter than panel dimensions; then carefully cut the door frame parts to size with 45-degree mitered ends.

Door Parts

After you've attached the cleat, begin making the door. Cut the door panel to size; then cut the plastic laminate about 1 in. longer and wider than the panel. You can use a jigsaw or band saw with a metal-cutting blade to cut the laminate. Next, coat the back of both the panel and laminate with water-based contact cement. Use a brush or roller to spread the cement, taking care to coat all surfaces evenly and completely. Allow the cement to dry until it doesn't feel sticky when you touch it.

To attach the laminate, first place a row of dowels across the door panel; then position the laminate over the dowels. The laminate should overhang the panel evenly on all edges. Start at one end and remove the dowels one at a time until the laminate rests on the panel. Note that the cement grabs immediately, so adjusting the laminate is impossible. Use a small roller to press the laminate onto the panel. This works out any bubbles and ensures a good bond. Once the laminate is bonded to the panel, rout the overhang with a flush-trimming bit.

Next, place a $3/16$-in. slotting cutter in the router table and clamp a fence to the table to yield a $3/8$-in.-deep cut. With the laminate side down on the table, cut a slot in all edges of the door panel. To make the door frame, rip the stock for the door rails and stiles to width; then cut it to rough length. Readjust the height of the slotting cutter in the router table to cut a slot in the edges of the frame parts. Then install a chamfer bit in the router table to shape the molded edge of the frame parts. Cut 45-degree miters on the ends of the frame at the finished length. Lay out and cut biscuit slots in each mitered face.

Finally, cut splines to size for the door frame and panel and dry-assemble the parts to check the fit (see photo 6). If everything looks good, apply glue to the spline and biscuit joints and assemble the door. Use clamps to pull all joints tight; then let the glue set fully.

Hardware And Finishing

Once you've assembled the door, bore the door-hinge mortises; then attach the hinges to the case and the door. Engage the door hinges with those in the case (see photo 11) and tighten the large screws that hold the parts together. Use the small adjustment screws to level the door with the inside bottom panel. Attach the fall-flap supports to the case sides; then hold the door level to mark the pilot holes for the screws that attach the support arms. Mount the strikes for the magnetic catches. Drill 1/16-in.-dia. pilot holes for the strikes; then tap them in with a hammer. Finally, bore and counterbore a pilot hole for the knob, but don't mount it yet.

Finishing the case is easiest if you can break it down into component parts. To that end, remove the door and all hardware; then remove the bottom, wall cleat and case back. Sand all parts with 220-grit paper, and ease all edges as required.

I decided to stain the exterior of this case and leave the interior a natural mahogany color. Before staining, apply masking tape to the interior surfaces that abut the areas to be stained. Press the tape firmly onto the wood surface so the stain cannot bleed underneath. You should also mask the edges of the plastic-laminate writing surface so the finish won't stain the surface.

I used a water-soluble brown mahogany stain, but use any stain that suits your design scheme. Water-soluble stains tend to raise the wood grain. To eliminate this problem, first lightly wipe the areas to be stained with a damp sponge. Then, when dry, lightly wipe the surface with 320-grit sandpaper to remove the raised grain. Do not sand too aggressively. Finally, apply the stain according to the manufacturer's directions.

When the stain is dry, you can apply the first coat of finish. Use a brush or rag to coat the wood surface, allowing the finish to soak in for 20 to 30 minutes; then wipe off any excess. After overnight drying, lightly scuff the surface with 320-grit sandpaper and dust off. Apply two or three more coats, using the same technique. When the last coat is dry, you can buff the finish with 0000 steel wool and polish with a soft cloth.

Installation

Once the finishing is complete, assemble the case parts, including all hardware. To hang the desk on the wall, first locate the wall studs with an electronic stud finder. Transfer the stud location onto the wall cleat; then drill and countersink pilot holes for No. 8 x 2½-in. flathead screws. For a writing surface height of 29 in., mount the cleat to the wall with its bottom edge at a height of 35 in. The long point of the bevel should be held away from the wall surface. Make sure that the cleat is installed level. Finally, hang the desk on the wall, engaging the two beveled wall cleat edges.

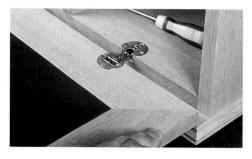

11 Install the fall-flap hinges in both the case bottom and door. Engage the two parts of the hinge and lock them together with the large screw.

12 Attach the fall-flap supports to the case sides; then hold the lid in a horizontal position to mark the location of pilot holes for the support arm.

13 If you're staining only the outside of the case, apply masking tape to protect the areas adjacent to the stained surfaces. Also mask the plastic laminate.

GATELEG TABLE
Tradition Meets Practicality

Traditionally, gateleg tables share two general design elements: They are small (tea-table or occasional-table size) and have round or oval tops. When we decided to resurrect the gateleg approach, we deliberately disregarded tradition, choosing instead to make a large, rectangular-top kitchen table with a drop leaf at each end.

The resulting table has a top that's generously proportioned to make it useful even when the leaves are down, but it's compact enough to fit into a small alcove or up against a wall. With the leaves extended, the table can seat six diners comfortably. Because each end has not one but two gatelegs, you can slide chairs under the table on all sides. The gateleg pairs also provide more stability and support than a single gateleg or a pull-out drop-leaf support.

We used hard maple for the table base and maple-veneered medium density fiberboard (MDF) for the tabletop and leaves. MDF-core sheet stock is denser than veneer-core plywood, which makes it more stable and less prone to deflection or warping and gives it a heavier feel. We chose sheet stock with plain-sawn hard maple veneer that looks more like solid wood than the more typical (but considerably cheaper) rotary-cut veneer.

In redesigning the classic gateleg table, we came up with this variation that is both practical and elegant, with room for six diners, yet small enough for almost any space.

Gateleg Table

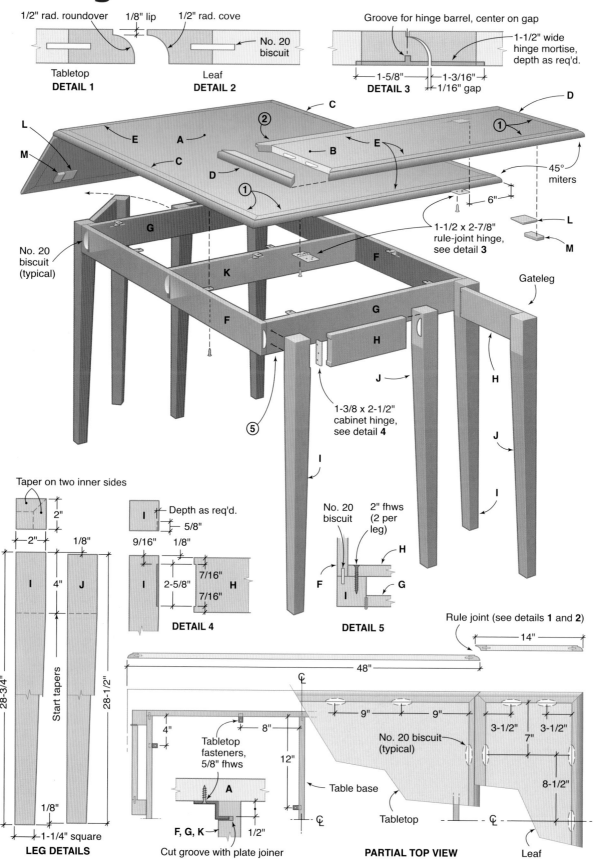

DETAIL 1
1/2" rad. roundover
1/8" lip
Tabletop

DETAIL 2
1/2" rad. cove
No. 20 biscuit
Leaf

DETAIL 3
Groove for hinge barrel, center on gap
1-1/2" wide hinge mortise, depth as req'd.
1-5/8"
1-3/16"
1/16" gap

C
D
L
M
E
A
B
E
C
D
45° miters
6"
L
M
1-1/2 x 2-7/8" rule-joint hinge, see detail 3
No. 20 biscuit (typical)
G
K
F
F
G
H
Gateleg
J
H
J
I
1-3/8 x 2-1/2" cabinet hinge, see detail 4
I

Taper on two inner sides
2"
2"
1/8"
I
J
4"
Start tapers
28-3/4"
28-1/2"
1/8"
1-1/4" square
LEG DETAILS

Depth as req'd.
I
5/8"
9/16"
1/8"
I
2-5/8"
7/16"
7/16"
H
DETAIL 4

No. 20 biscuit
2" fhws (2 per leg)
H
F
G
I
DETAIL 5

Rule joint (see details 1 and 2)
14"
48"
9"
9"
3-1/2"
3-1/2"
7"
No. 20 biscuit (typical)
8-1/2"
4"
8"
12"
Tabletop fasteners, 5/8" fhws
A
F, G, K
1/2"
Cut groove with plate joiner
Table base
Tabletop
PARTIAL TOP VIEW
Leaf

MATERIALS AND CUTTING LIST

A	1	Tabletop, veneered MDF	3/4 x 31 x 45 in.
B	2	Leaves, veneered MDF	3/4 x 11 x 31 in.
C	2	Banding	3/4 x 1½ x 48 in.**
D	4	Banding	3/4 x 1½ x 14 in.**
E	6	Banding	3/4 x 1½ x 34 in.**
F	2	Front/back rails	3/4 x 3½ x 42½ in.
G	2	End rails	3/4 x 3½ x 27 in.
H	4	Swing rails	3/4 x 3⅜ x 10 in.
I	4	Legs	2 x 2 x 28¾ in.
J	4	Gatelegs	2 x 2 x 28½ in.
K	1	Spreader	3/4 x 3½ x 27 in.
L	4	Leveling wedges	1/4 x 2 x 2 in.
M	4	Stopblocks	3/8 x 1 x 2 in.

*All parts solid maple except as noted   **Finished size, see text

SHOPPING LIST

3/4-in. x 4x8 sheet MDF-core plain-sliced maple veneer plywood (1)
10 bf 10/4 hard maple (for eight legs)
14 bf 4/4 hard maple, for 25 ft. of 7/8 x 1½-in. trim and 20 ft. of 3/4 x 3½-in. rail
2½ x 1⅜-in. cabinet hinges (4)
1½ x 2⅞-in. rule-joint hinges (2)
Table clips (10)

core sheet stock (see photo 1). Then cut them to final size on your table saw. (We used a 40-tooth blade on our circular saw and an 80-tooth blade on our table saw.) Try to cut the pieces so all four sides have freshly cut edges.

The leaves and tabletop are banded with 1½-in.-wide maple strips to conceal the edges. You have a couple of milling options when making the banding. The easier way is to plane and joint your banding stock so it's exactly the same thickness as the MDF stock. By using biscuits to align the banding strips, you should be able to get a pretty clean fit. But if you're a little more particular and you want to guarantee that your banding strips are exactly flush with the top and bottom surfaces of the MDF, mill the strips so they're slightly thicker than the MDF — about 7/8 in. Then after you attach them, trim them — either by sanding or by using a router and flush-trimming bit. We chose the latter approach. It turned out to be a bit cumbersome, but our effort resulted in nice, flush seams.

To trim the banding, first attach a tall auxiliary fence to your router table fence. The bottom of the auxiliary fence should be far enough above the surface of the router table to provide clearance for the banding (at least 1¾ in.). Mount a piloted flush-cutting bit in your router table — we used a 2-in. bit to trim our 1½-in. banding strips. Adjust the fence so it's aligned exactly with the outside edge of the bearing on the piloted bit. Then feed the panel through the bit after the

Make The Top And Leaves

To begin, cut the tabletop and leaves to rough size from heavy MDF-

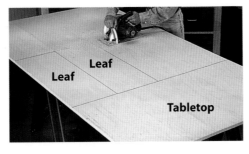

1 Lay out the tabletop and leaves on sheet stock. Cut them to rough size with a circular saw and then to final size on the table saw. The grain runs in the same direction on all parts.

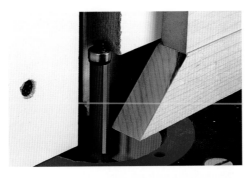

2 After mitering the corners of the 1½-in.-wide banding strips, attach two opposing strips with No. 20 biscuits; then trim the banding flush with the surfaces of the tabletop and leaves using a 2-in.-long flush-cutting bit.

3 Attach the second set of opposing strips as shown here, again using No. 20 biscuits and glue. Once the glue is dry, run this banding through the router table as before. Repeat the process until you have finished all three panels.

banding strip is attached, pressing the surface of the panel against the fence.

When framing a panel, trim each banding strip before the adjoining untrimmed strip is attached. Otherwise, the untrimmed strip will catch on the auxiliary fence, throwing off the cut. We cut all of our miters before flush-trimming, taping each banding strip in place once all the miters fit. Then we labeled and removed the strips. We attached two opposing strips to each panel using glue and No. 20 biscuits. Once the glue set, we ran the strips through the flush-cutting bit on both faces (see photo 2, page 297). Then we attached the second set of opposing strips and ran them through, repeating until all three panels were framed (see photo 3, page 297).

Once you've attached all the banding, cut the edge profiles and the rule joints. Start by mounting a piloted 1/2-in. roundover bit in your router. Cut a roundover in all four edges of the large tabletop, leaving a 1/8-in. lip at the top of each cut. Also round over the end and short edges of each leaf, leaving the longer edge that will mate against the tabletop uncut. You'll need to make a minimum of two passes on each cut, deepening the cut after each pass (see photo 4).

Make a 1/2-in. cove cut on the mating edge of each leaf (see photo 5). This cut should also leave a 1/8- to 1/4-in.-thick lip at the top edge. Make the cove cuts a little at a time, checking the fit of the coved edge against the mating roundover cut on the tabletop edge (see photo 6). Cut until the matching parts fit together perfectly, forming the rule joint.

Next, attach the rule-joint hinges to the tabletop and leaves. Use a pair of hinges at each joint, positioning the hinges so the near edge is 6 in. from the tabletop and leaf edges.

To lay out hinge locations, set the tabletop and leaves upside down on a flat surface. Press the rule joints together; then separate them by 1/32 to 1/16 in. to provide joint clearance. Position the hinges so they're parallel

with the joint and the hinge barrels are centered on the seam of the rule joint on the top side of the tabletop. Outline the hinge plates on the tabletop and leaves. Cut the mortises with a sharp chisel — note that the mortises for the short plates should start about 3/4 in. from the mating edges of the tabletop. You'll need to cut a shallow groove in the tabletop mortise to

4 With a piloted 1/2-in. roundover bit, cut the profile in all four edges of the tabletop and in all but the hinge edges of the leaves. Don't try to cut the entire profile in a single pass — you'll need to make at least two or three passes.

5 Cut cove profiles in the hinge edges of the leaves. Make test cuts on scrap wood first until the router is set up so the coved board fits snugly together with the roundovers on the hinge edges of the tabletop (see next photo).

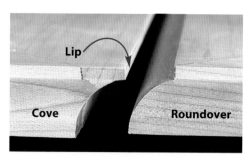

6 When cutting both the roundover and the cove (thus forming a rule joint), make sure the mating parts fit together snugly, with the tops and bottoms flush. Leave a lip (1/8 to 1/4 in.) at the top of each edge.

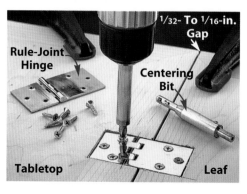

7 Cut mortises for the rule-joint hinges, remembering to allow for the hinge barrels. Use spacers between the tabletop and leaves to create a consistent 1/32- to 1/16-in. gap.

house the hinge barrel. Attach the hinges with 3/4-in. screws driven into pilot holes (see photo 7). Use a centering bit to drill the pilot holes.

Make The Legs

To begin making the legs, plane 10/4 maple to 2 in. thick; then rip it

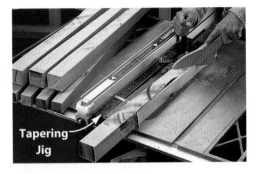

8 Cut tapers in two adjoining faces of each leg, starting 24 3/4 in. from the leg bottom. The bottoms of the legs should measure 1 1/4 x 1 1/4 in. after the tapers are cut. We used a tapering jig and table saw to make the taper cuts.

9 Using No. 20 biscuits and glue, attach a pair of legs to each end of each front/back rail. The outer face of each rail should be flush with the outer faces of the legs. Make sure the tapered faces of the legs meet at the inside corner.

10 Cut biscuit slots for joining the rail/leg assemblies to the end rails. (Remove the fence from the biscuit joiner to cut the slots for the legs.) Cut biscuit slots for the spreader that fits between the front and back rails as well.

11 Glue-up the table base assembly. Check to make sure the legs are square to the rails, and adjust as necessary. Clamp until dry.

into 2-in.-wide strips. (You could laminate thinner strips of maple into blanks if you prefer.) Cut all eight legs to a rough length of at least 30 in.

Lay out tapers in the two adjacent edges of each leg. The tapered legs will be 1 1/4 x 1 1/4 in. at the bottoms and gradually increase to the full 2 x 2-in. thickness 24 3/4 in. from the bottom. To cut the tapers (see photo 8), we used a table saw and taper-cutting jig. You could also use your jointer or a band saw.

Once you've cut the tapers, cut all eight legs to 28 3/4 in. long, resulting in 4 in. of untapered stock at the top of each leg. Then trim 1/8 in. off each end of four of the legs (the gatelegs). Making the gatelegs slightly shorter prevents them from touching the floor when the table leaves are down — otherwise, the table will rock.

Make The Table Base

Now that the legs are completed, you can begin the table base. Plane and rip stock to thickness and width; then cut the front/back rails, end rails, swing rails and spreader to length. Attach a fixed leg to each end of the front and back rails. The legs should be flush with the rail ends and tops. Make sure the legs and rails are perpendicular and the tapered faces meet in the inside corner. Join the legs to the rails with glue and No. 20 biscuits (see photo 9).

Position the end rails and spreader between the leg/rail assemblies. Cut slots for biscuit joints (see photo 10); then glue and clamp the joints, checking to make sure the assembly is square (see photo 11). For extra reinforcement, drive a pair of No. 8 x 2-in. flathead wood screws through the inside faces of the end rails into each leg.

Next, make the swing rails. Attach the gatelegs to the swing rails using glue and biscuits (see photo 12, page 300). The tops of the swing rails should be flush with the tops of the gatelegs, and the faces should be flush.

Cut mortises for your cabinet hinges in the free ends of the swing rails and in the inside faces of the fixed legs. Position the hinges so the bottom edges of the swing rails are flush with the bottom edges of the end rails, creating a 1/8-in. gap between the tops of the swing rails and the tops of the fixed rails. (This will provide clearance for the swing rails and allow you to level the leaves.) Screw the hinges to the swing rail ends and then to the fixed legs (see photo 13).

Attach The Tabletop

We used table clips to attach the MDF-core tabletop to the table base. We cut the grooves for the clips with a biscuit joiner. Once the grooves are cut, lay the tabletop and leaves upside down in an open position on a flat surface. Position the table base on the underside of the tabletop, adjusting so the overhang is equal at the front and back and on the ends. Attach the tabletop by driving 5/8-in. flathead wood screws through the guide holes in the table clips and into the underside of the tabletop (see photo 14). Do not use glue.

Adjust And Level

Set the assembly upright; then swing the gatelegs open. Use a framing square or straightedge to adjust the gatelegs until the swing rails are parallel with the front and back rails. Outline the position of the gatelegs on the undersides of the table leaves.

Bevel-rip a 2-in.-wide strip of maple so it's 1/4 in. thick on one edge and 1/8 in. thick on the other. Crosscut the strip so you have four 2 x 2-in. pieces to serve as leveling wedges for the leaves. Slip each wedge between the bottom of the leaf and the top of a gateleg, leading with the thin edge of the wedge. (Make sure the legs match up with the outlines you made on the tabletop.) Adjust the wedge position so the leaf is level with the tabletop. Trace a cutting line onto each wedge by following the edge of the gateleg (see photo 15). Trim each wedge along the cutting line; then glue the wedges to the undersides of the leaves. Test the fit when the glue is

dry: You may need to attach leveling feet to the gateleg bottoms, depending on how flat your floor is.

To prevent the gatelegs from swinging open too far, cut thin stopblocks and glue them next to the wedges, away from the direction of swing.

Finally, sand thoroughly and apply your finish of choice. We sprayed satin-finish waterborne lacquer with an HVLP sprayer.

12 With No. 20 biscuits and glue, attach the swing rails flush with the tops of the gatelegs. Make sure to trim 1/8 in. from the end of each gateleg first, and note that the swing rails are 1/8 in. narrower than the fixed rails.

13 Cut mortises for the swing rail butt hinges, making sure to center the hinge plate top-to-bottom on the swing rail. Use a centering bit to drill pilot holes for the hinge screws; then attach the hinges.

14 Use table clips to attach the tabletop to the table base. Drive 5/8-in. screws through the clips and into the tabletop. Make sure the top is centered on the base and that the leaves have clearance to swing.

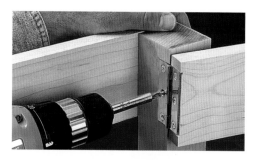

15 Open the table and adjust the level of each leaf by slipping a wedge between the top of each leg and the underside of the leaf. Adjust the wedge until the leaf is level. Mark the position of the wedge, trim it to size and glue it in place.

ROBUST BENCH
A Traditional Workbench Made Cheap And Easy

A woodworker's bench isn't just a work surface; it's a tool — maybe the hardest-working tool in any shop. Hardwood construction and elaborate joinery typically make these benches expensive, but you can build a lower-cost bench that works just as well as high-priced versions.

By stripping away unnecessary design details, we created a woodworker's bench that performs all of the functions of a traditional bench, but ours is made of less expensive materials and takes less time to build. Standard ¾-in. lumber and simple joinery keep the cost down and make this an attractive project for woodworkers with limited tools. Stack-laminating the base-frame mortise-and-tenon joints makes the joinery process quick and easy without sacrificing strength. Woodworkers of all skill levels can confidently build this rock-solid bench.

The Design

You can build this bench out of almost any wood. It's best to use a hardwood such as maple for the top, but the base can be made from any solid stock — we chose pine. To minimize wood movement and achieve a consistent appearance, select boards with a straight grain pattern and similar color. We bought all of the materials at a local home center.

The bench's footprint is 28 x 60 in., making it small enough to fit in almost any shop but large enough for most woodworking tasks. You can place it against a wall or in the center of the room, and it's easy to disassemble for moving or storage. We made

ours 38 in. tall because that is a comfortable working height, but you can adjust the leg lengths to suit your needs. You might consider making the height the same as or slightly lower than your table saw so the bench can act as an outfeed or side table.

This wouldn't be a woodworker's bench without vises. We chose a Veritas Twin Screw end vise and a Jorgensen woodworker's vise. Add bench-dog holes to further expand your vise's capacity and to hold work steady on the top.

Additional features include a tool tray to keep small tools and hardware within reach but off of the work surface. A shelf between the legs provides a place to put glue bottles, boxes of screws and nails, and a removable lower shelf is designed to hold toolboxes and cases.

This attractive and sturdy woodworker's bench is built with materials from a home center and employs simple joinery.

Workbench

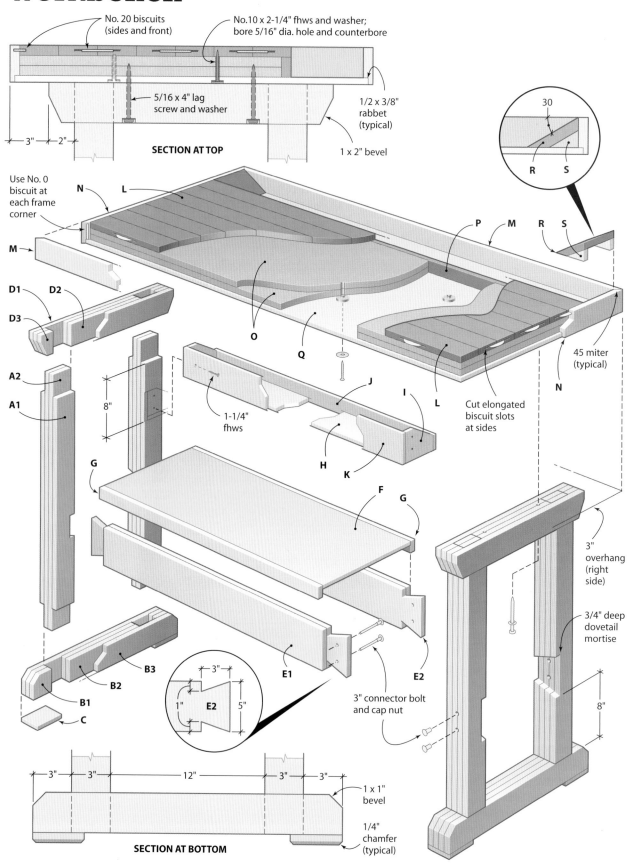

No. 20 biscuits (sides and front)

No.10 x 2-1/4" fhws and washer; bore 5/16" dia. hole and counterbore

5/16 x 4" lag screw and washer

SECTION AT TOP

3"   2"

1/2 x 3/8" rabbet (typical)

1 x 2" bevel

30

R   S

Use No. 0 biscuit at each frame corner

N   L

M

D1   D2

D3

A2

A1

8"

G

O   Q

J

1-1/4" fhws

H   K

I

P   M   R   S

N

45 miter (typical)

Cut elongated biscuit slots at sides

L

F   G

3" overhang (right side)

3/4" deep dovetail mortise

B3

B2

B1

C

3"

1"   E2   5"

E1

E2

3" connector bolt and cap nut

8"

3"   3"   12"   3"   3"

1 x 1" bevel

1/4" chamfer (typical)

SECTION AT BOTTOM

MATERIALS AND CUTTING LIST

KEY	NO.	DESCRIPTION	SIZE
BASE			
A1	8	Outer leg, pine	$3/4$ x 3 x $28^{1}/_2$ in.
A2	8	Inner leg, pine	$3/4$ x 3 x $34^{1}/_2$ in.
B1	4	Outer foot, pine	$3/4$ x 3 x 24 in.
B2	4	Center inner foot, pine	$3/4$ x 3 x 12 in.
B3	8	End inner foot, pine	$3/4$ x 3 x 3 in.
C	4	Foot pads, pine	$3/4$ x 3 x 4 in.
D1	4	Outer top rail, pine	$3/4$ x 3 x 22 in.
D2	4	Center inner top rail, pine	$3/4$ x 3 x 12 in.
D3	8	End inner top rail, pine	$3/4$ x 3 x 2 in.
E1	2	Outer stretcher, pine	$3/4$ x 5 x 43 in.
E2	2	Inner stretcher, pine	$3/4$ x 5 x 37 in.
SHELVES			
F	1	Lower shelf, Baltic birch plywood	$1/2$ x $15^{1}/_8$ x 37 in.
G	2	Lower shelf edging, pine	$3/4$ x $1^{1}/_2$ x 37 in.
H	1	Upper shelf bottom, Baltic birch plywood	$1/2$ x 5 x 36 in.
I	2	Upper shelf sides, Baltic birch plywood	$1/2$ x 4 x 5 in.
J	1	Upper shelf front, Baltic birch plywood	$1/2$ x 2 x 37 in.
K	1	Upper shelf back, Baltic birch plywood	$1/2$ x 4 x 37 in.
TOP			
L	7	Top, maple	$3/4$ x 3 x 59 in.*
M	1	Top frame front and back, maple	$3/4$ x $2^{3}/_4$ x 60 in.**
N	2	Top frame sides, maple	$3/4$ x $2^{3}/_4$ x 28 in.**
O	2	Substrate, MDF	$3/4$ x $20^{1}/_4$ x $58^{1}/_2$ in.
P	3	Top inside frame, maple	$3/4$ x $1^{1}/_2$ x $58^{1}/_2$ in.
Q	1	Top/bottom, Baltic birch plywood	$1/2$ x $27^{1}/_4$ x $59^{1}/_4$ in.
R	5	Tool tray ramps, maple	$3/4$ x $5^{1}/_2$ x $4^{3}/_8$ in.
S	6	Ramp cleats, Baltic birch plywood	$1/2$ x $1^{3}/_8$ x $2^{1}/_4$ in.

* Finished panel is 21 x $58^{1}/_2$ in.

** Length is from longest point to longest point.

SHOPPING LIST

1x4 x 8-ft. pine boards (10)
1x6 x 8-ft. pine boards (2)
1x2 x 8-ft. pine board (1)
1x4 x 8-ft. maple boards (10)
$3/4$-in. x 4x8 MDF (1)
$1/2$-in. x 5x5 Baltic birch plywood (1)
$1^{1}/_4$-in. brads or staples
No. 20 biscuits

3-in. connector bolts and caps
$1^{5}/_8$-in. flathead wood screws and finish washers
$5/16$ x 4-in. lag screws and washers
No. 10 x 2-in. screws and washers
Wood glue
Tung oil

SECURE YOUR WORK

A variety of bench dogs and hold-downs are available to keep your work in place. Bench dogs are inserted in the bench holes, extending the vise capacity to handle longer work-pieces. Hold-downs are friction-fit in the bench holes and tapped tightly into place to hold work down on the bench top.

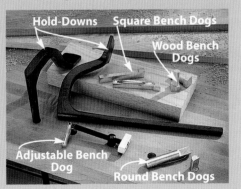

Hold-Downs   Square Bench Dogs   Wood Bench Dogs   Adjustable Bench Dog   Round Bench Dogs

The Base And Shelves

The look and strength of thick base stock was achieved by face gluing 1x stock to make the 1½- and 3-in.-thick legs, feet, top rail and stretchers.

Start the assembly with the legs. Center the two outer leg pieces over both sides of the two inner leg pieces to form the 3-in. tenons at each end of the leg. Glue and clamp the parts together. After the glue has cured, remove the excess glue with a scraper or chisel.

The stretchers and legs are assembled with a dovetail halving joint . We used a band saw to cut the dovetailed ends of the outer stretcher parts, but a jigsaw or handsaw will also work. Glue the stretcher parts together (see photo 1).

After the glue has cured, hold the stretchers against the legs as a template for you to mark the dovetail profile on the leg. Use a router to remove the material between the layout marks to a depth of ¾ in. (see photo 2).

Now assemble the foot parts around the bottom leg tenons (see photo 3). Do the same with the top rail parts and the upper leg tenons. Measure the leg assembly diagonally from corner to corner to ensure it is square. Then use the router to cut a ¼-in. chamfer on four edges of each foot pad, and attach the pads to the bottoms of the feet.

Finish the base assembly by fastening the legs to the stretchers with 3-in. connector bolts (see photo 4). Do not apply glue to this connection if you plan to disassemble the workbench in the future.

We used Baltic birch plywood for both shelves. One 5 x 5-ft. piece (a typical size for this type of plywood) is all you need. If it's not available in your area, you can substitute ½-in. AC-grade plywood. Fasten the upper shelf between the legs with screws, and rest the lower shelf on the stretchers.

1 Glue the stretcher parts together, lining up the ends of the inner stretcher with the dovetail shoulders that you cut on the outer stretcher. Spread a thin layer of glue on one face, and use a damp cloth to wet the mating face.

2 Cut dovetail mortises in the legs. Clamp straightedges to the leg, and remove ¾ in. of material in three passes.

3 Carefully line up the laminations when gluing the feet and top rails to the legs. Glue and staple one piece in place at a time, and then clamp the entire assembly.

4 Fasten the leg assemblies and stretchers together with connector bolts (see inset). Use glue to reinforce this joint if you don't plan to disassemble the bench.

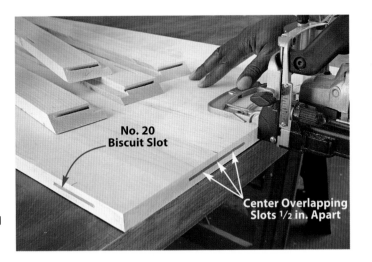

5 Cut three No. 20 biscuit slots in the side frames (see drawing for details), and then cut three overlapping biscuit slots to form elongated slots in the maple top side edges.

No. 20 Biscuit Slot

Center Overlapping Slots 1/2 in. Apart

The Top

A stable, flat work surface is essential for any bench. Traditional woodworking benches feature thick, solid tops, often made from 2- to 3-in.-thick quartersawn maple. We used 3/4-in.-thick maple for the top surface and two layers of 3/4-in. MDF as a substrate. The maple provides a hard work surface that can be sanded or planed when it becomes worn, and the MDF provides a stable and hefty backing. The bottom of the top is a 1/2-in. piece of birch plywood that also acts as the tray bottom.

The top assembly is designed to keep the maple top flat and still allow wood movement. The top is glued only to the MDF along the front edge of the bench, which keeps the front edge flush. Biscuits are glued in the top and are not glued in the elongated slots in the side frames. And, the center and back edge of the top are held in place by screws driven through oversize screw holes in the MDF.

Carefully select surfaced maple that is straight and has smooth edges. Cut No. 20 biscuit slots on the edges of the top panel pieces; then glue up the panel. When the glue has cured, plane, scrape or sand the top flat and trim the ends to final size.

Before cutting the frame pieces to their final lengths, use a table saw or router to cut 1/2-in.-wide x 3/8-in.-deep rabbets along the bottom edge of each frame piece. Then miter the pieces to final length and cut slots for No. 0 biscuits in each miter.

Next, line up and cut No. 20 biscuit slots in the front and side top frame and front edge of the top. Then cut elongated slots in the side edges of the maple top (see photo 5).

We found it easiest to assemble the top upside down. Spread glue on the first few inches along the front edge of the maple top. Then place one of the MDF pieces on the top, keeping it flush against the front. Now spread glue over the exposed MDF surface, wet the face of the second sheet of MDF and place the second MDF piece on top. Clamp the three pieces, using cauls to distribute pressure over the entire surface.

While the panel assembly is curing, glue biscuits into the side frames. Gluing these biscuits in advance will prevent them from accidentally adhering to the maple top during the final assembly.

Finally, attach the frame parts to the top assembly (see photo 6) and

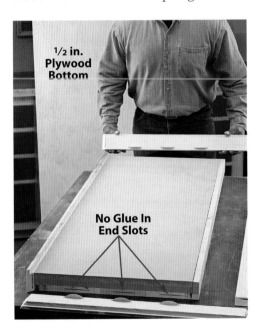

1/2 in. Plywood Bottom

No Glue In End Slots

6 Glue the front and inner frame pieces to the top assembly. Apply glue only to the miters of the side frame pieces.

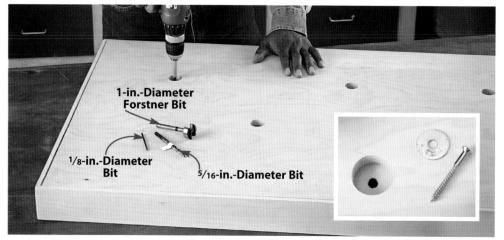

7 Three bits are used to create the countersink and pilot holes in the top assembly. First, bore the countersink with a 1-in.-dia. Forstner bit. Next, bore the oversize pilot hole with a $5/16$-in.-dia. bit. Finally, bore a $1/2$-in.-deep pilot hole in the maple top with a $1/8$-in.-dia. bit.

then spread a layer of glue over the bottom MDF surface and in the rabbets, and position the $1/2$-in. plywood bottom. Clamp the top assembly together. When the glue has cured, remove the clamps and drill six countersink and pilot holes through the top assembly. Stop the pilot holes before you bore into the maple top. Secure the top with No. 10 x 2-in. screws and washers centered in the oversize holes (see photo 7).

Small ramps in each end of the tool tray make cleaning it easier. Bevel cut the 30- and 60-degree ends in each tool tray ramp (see photo 8). Attach the cleats and ramps; then you're ready to mount the top to the base.

Attach the top with two countersunk $5/16$- x 4-in. lag bolts and washers through each top rail/leg assembly. If you intend to leave the bench permanently assembled, apply glue between the top and base.

Finishing Touches

Apply a few coats of tung oil to the bench and it's ready to use as is, but adding a couple of vises greatly increases its utility (see photo 9).

Mounting the vises can be a project in itself. For example, the hefty Twin Screw end vise we chose required very precise hardware positioning. For specific instructions, refer to the vise's installation manual.

The final step is to drill $3/4$-in.-dia. bench-dog holes in line with each vise. Space the holes apart half the distance of the vise's total capacity. Now you're ready to put the bench to work on your next project.

8 Use a scrap board as a carrier to safely cut the steep 30-degree ramp angles on a table saw. Cut the 60-degree bevel on the other end using a compound miter saw.

9 Fasten the vises to the underside of the bench with lag screws. Use shims to position the top of the vises flush with the top of the bench.

TOP-SHELF BOOKCASE

Add Storage And Style To A Room Or Hallway With A Built-In Unit

Whether you fill it with first-edition novels, art pottery or your favorite DVDs, a bookcase is a useful and versatile piece of furniture in any home. Freestanding and wall-mounted bookshelves offer the benefits of portability and easy installation. But by making a little extra effort you can greatly increase storage capacity and architectural interest with a built-in unit.

Built-in bookcases can be elaborate, but they are not necessarily hard to build. We designed an elegant cabinet that even a beginning woodworker can complete; the most difficult aspect might be handling the plywood and finding the space to assemble the large cabinets.

Bookcase

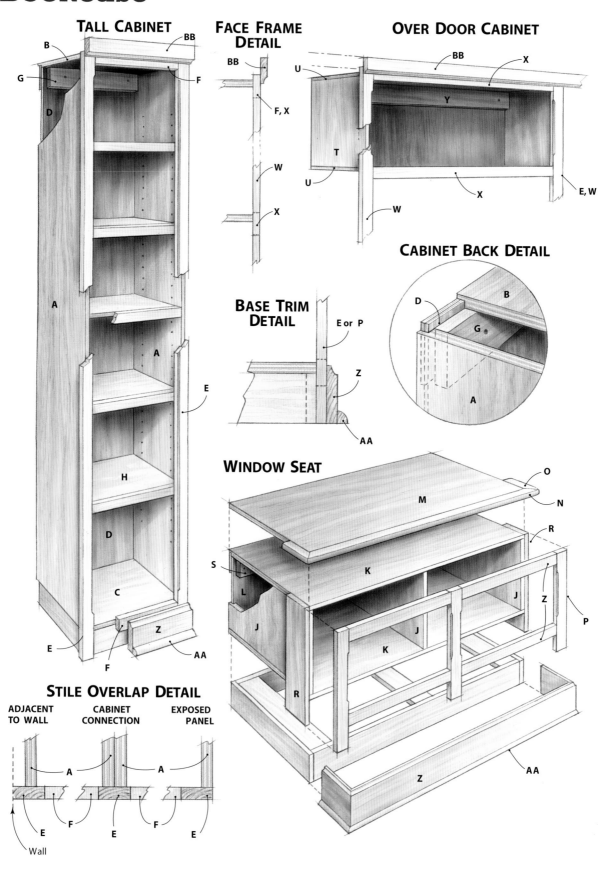

TALL CABINET

FACE FRAME DETAIL

OVER DOOR CABINET

CABINET BACK DETAIL

BASE TRIM DETAIL

E or P

WINDOW SEAT

STILE OVERLAP DETAIL

ADJACENT TO WALL   CABINET CONNECTION   EXPOSED PANEL

Wall

MATERIALS AND CUTTING LIST

*Editor's note: Dimensions in **bold** may be modified for larger or smaller cabinets*

KEY	DESCRIPTION	SIZE
24-IN.-WIDE TALL CABINET		
A	Side panels	3/4 x 11 1/2 x 91 in.
B	Top panel	3/4 x 11 1/2 x **24 in.**
C	Bottom panel	3/4 x 11 1/2 x **22 1/2 in.**
D	Back panel	1/4 x **23 1/2** x 90 1/2 in.
E	Face frame stiles	3/4 x 2 x 94 in.
F	Face frame rails	3/4 x 2 x **20 in.**
G	Wall cleat	3/4 x 2 x **22 1/2 in.**
H	Shelves	3/4 x 10 1/8 x **23 3/4 in.**
I	Shelf edging	3/4 x 1 1/4 x **22 3/8 in.**
48-IN.-WIDE WINDOW SEAT		
J	Side and center panels	3/4 x 16 x 12 in.
K	Top and bottom panels	3/4 x 16 x **48 in.**
L	Back panel	1/4 x 16 x **47 1/2 in.**
M	Seat board	3/4 x 16 x **48 in.**
N	Front seat board edging	3/4 x 1 1/4 x **50 1/2 in.**
O	Side seat board edging	3/4 x 1 1/4 x 5 3/4 in.

KEY	DESCRIPTION	SIZE
48-IN.-WIDE WINDOW SEAT (CONTINUED)		
P	Face frame stiles	3/4 x 2 x 17 1/2 in.
Q	Face frame rails	3/4 x 2 x **21 3/4 in.**
R	Side filler strips	3/4 x 3 3/4 x 17 1/2 in.
S	Wall cleats	3/4 x 2 x **22 7/8 in.**
36-IN.-WIDE OVER-DOOR CABINET		
T	Side panels	3/4 x 10 x 11 1/2 in.
U	Top and bottom panels	3/4 x 11 1/2 x **36 in.**
V	Back panel	1/4 x 11 x **35 1/2 in.**
W	Face frame stiles	3/4 x 2 x 12 in.
X	Face frame rails	3/4 x 2 x **32 in.**
Y	Wall cleat	3/4 x 2 x **34 1/2 in.**
TRIM		
Z	Baseboard	3/4 x 4 1/2 x **cut to fit**
AA	Base shoe	3/4 x 3/4 x **cut to fit**
BB	Top cap	3/4 x 2 1/2 x **cut to fit**

Customize The Design

You might think built-in bookcases are only for large rooms, but they also work well in very small rooms and even hallways. Tight spaces like these are often too small for furniture arrangements but offer enough space to accommodate a built-in cabinet.

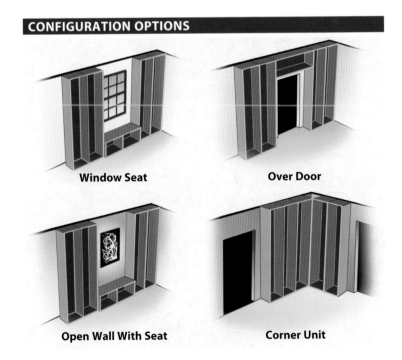

Window Seat

Over Door

Open Wall With Seat

Corner Unit

Bookcases are often installed on an empty wall, but you might consider building one around a door or window to make the unit seem more integrated with the room. This approach can also make the unit more functional — for example, the bookcase we built also serves as a nook and window seat. To incorporate a door opening into the unit, you can install a cabinet above the door that connects bookcases on both sides.

If you are planning to install a bookcase on an empty wall, consider breaking up the bookcase units with an opening instead of filling the entire wall with shelves. This approach can create a nook that adds dimension to the room and provides a place to hang a piece of art. Another option is to install bookcases on two adjacent walls, butting the inside bookcase corners together to create a corner unit.

Two additional design considerations are which type of shelving to use and whether you will integrate lighting into the bookcase. Plywood shelves are most common but require solid-wood edging as reinforcement to prevent them from bowing. Glass shelves should be used to support only lightweight decorative objects and should be made of tempered glass that's at least 1/4 in. thick and no wider than 30 in.

You can build integral lights into the unit or install them in the room and direct them toward the bookcase. The most common integral lights are small "pot" or "puck" lights. These lights are typically recessed in 55- to 60-mm holes that are drilled through the top of the cabinet. Install pot lights before attaching the face frame and trim. We installed recessed ceiling lights in front of the bookcase.

Once you have determined the space that you want the bookcase to fill, it is time to design the specific structural elements. This bookcase is simply a set of cabinet boxes with a face frame covering the seams. Determine the number and size of cabinets that will be required to fill the space, keeping in mind that no vertical cabinet should be more than 30 in. wide. For example, we combined three tall cabinets and one short cabinet to fit around a window. You might need to change the dimensions of the boxes to fit your space, but the construction will be the same.

The 2-in.-wide face will align with the cabinet side differently, depending on whether it covers an exposed end panel or the seam between two cabinets or it butts against an adjacent wall. The outside edge of the face frame should be flush with the outside face of an exposed end panel. The face frame should be centered on the seam between two cabinet side panels. And the face frame should overhang cabinet sides that butt against an adjacent wall by approximately 3/4 in. to allow for scribing. We designed our face frame in three sections to cover the large double cabinets on the left, the window seat and the single cabinet on the right side.

Build The Cabinets

Sheet goods such as plywood and medium-density fiberboard (MDF) are perfect for building a large book-

case. A unit made with such large panels of solid wood would not only take longer to build and cost more but also be more vulnerable to future structural problems such as warping and splitting. For a natural-wood finish, use hardwood-veneer plywood for the cabinets and shelves and a matching solid wood for the face frames and shelf edging. If you plan to paint the bookcase, consider substituting MDF for the cabinets and shelves, and use poplar or pine for the face frames and shelf edging. (Either way, use solid wood for the face frames because of its appearance, workability and durability.)

We used 1/4-in. shelf pins (available at home centers and hardware stores) to support the shelves. Once you've routed the rabbet for the back (see photo 1), bore the shelf-pin holes, using a piece of perforated hardboard as a template (see photo 2). Drill the holes 1 1/2 in. from the front and back edges, 3 in. apart and beginning and ending 8 in. from the top and bottom.

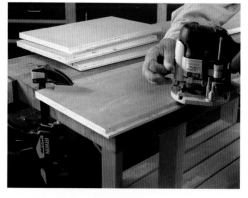

1 Rout a 1/2-in.-wide x 1/2-in.-deep rabbet in the back inside edge of the top, bottom and side panels. The depth of the rabbet is twice the thickness of the back panel.

2 Use perforated hardboard as a jig for drilling the shelf-pin holes in the side panels. Space the holes 3 in. apart and 8 in. from the ends of the panels.

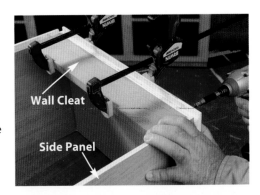

3 Assemble the top, bottom and side panels with glue and 2-in. coarse-thread screws. Then attach the wall cleat to the top and side panels with glue and 2-in. coarse-thread screws.

Wall Cleat

Side Panel

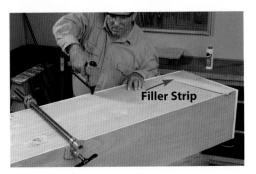

Filler Strip

4 Attach the back panel to the cabinet with glue and 1-in. crown staples. Then attach a 3-in.-wide strip of the back material to fill the gap left behind the wall cleat.

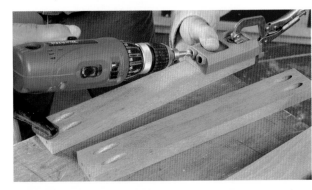

5 Use a stepped drill bit and pocket-hole jig to drill the pocket-screw holes in the rails.

The cabinet sides, top and bottom are joined with butt joints fastened with No. 8 x 2-in. wood screws (see photo 3) and concealed by trim. Fasten the back, which covers the wall and squares up the cabinet, with glue and 1-in. crown staples or brads (see photo 4). Then cut the shelves to size and attach a piece of solid-wood edging along the front edge of each shelf for reinforcement.

Mill The Trim

We used 2-in.-wide stock for the face frames, which are easy to assemble using pocket screws (see photos 5 and 6). However, these fasteners require a drilling jig and stepped drill bit to make an angled countersink hole for the pocket screw.

When milling the face frames, you can cut the profiles either after assembly or before you cut the stock to length. I cut the stopped cove profiles in the face frames after they were assembled, using a router with a bearing-piloted cove bit and stop blocks clamped at each end of the stile (see photo 7). We worked in reverse order on the trim stock, cutting the profiles

6 Glue and clamp the face frame together, and secure the joints by driving self-tapping washer-head screws into the pocket holes.

6-in. No. 2 Square-Drive Bit

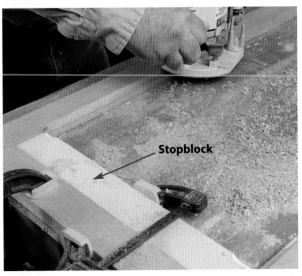

7 Rout the stopped cove profile in the face frame stiles with a bearing-piloted ¼-in.-radius cove bit. Clamp a 2-in.-wide stopblock to the rails to stop the cove cut at each end.

Stopblock

Safety note: Blade guard and splitter removed for photo clarity.

8 Create a bullnose edge on the seat board by first attaching the seat edging to the seat board with glue and biscuits and then routing a 3/8-in.-radius roundover on the edges.

9 To make the base shoe molding, first rout a 3/8-in.-radius roundover on a piece of trim stock lumber that is wider than the final base shoe width.

10 Next, rip the base shoe molding to its final 3/4-in. width. Repeat the routing and ripping process to create multiple pieces of molding. You can use the same technique with any thin stock molding.

in the trim stock on a router table before cutting it to final width and length (see photos 9 and 10). Cutting the profiles first allows for cleaner miter cuts and reduces tearout.

Apply The Finish

If you want a natural-wood look, apply the finish before installing the cabinets and trim — this keeps the mess out of the house. You can fill nail holes with matching wood putty after completing the installation.

If you choose to paint the bookcase, apply one coat of primer before installation. After you've completed the installation, you can caulk all of the seams, fill the nail holes with spackle and apply two coats of satin or semigloss interior paint.

Install The Case

A built-in bookcase should look like it is a part of the house and make flush connections with the surrounding surfaces. Achieving a clean and flush installation is not always easy because most homes do not have flat, square walls. Compensating for irregularities is one of the biggest challenges of installing any built-in project.

The easiest way to overcome variations in floor height is by installing the bookcase on a level base called a plinth. Before securing the plinth, check that the walls are plumb, and position the plinth so that the back edge is in line with the part of the wall that extends farthest into the room. Next, shim and level the plinth on the floor and screw it to the wall (see photo 11).

3/4-in. Spacer

11 Position, level and fasten the plinth to the wall studs with 2-in. screws. Leave a 3/4-in. space between the plinth and any adjacent side wall.

POSITIONING THE BASE

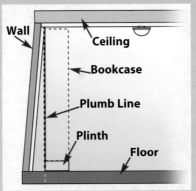

Use a 4-ft. level, laser level or plumb bob to check each wall for plumb (photo, above). Position and secure the base so that the back edge of the base is directly below the part of the wall that extends the farthest into the room (illustration, above right).

Large dips or variations in the wall's surface will be more apparent after the bookcase is installed. If variations in the surface are greater than 1/4 in., smooth them out with a skim coat of joint compound before installing the bookcase.

We used two methods to create a tight connection between the walls and ceiling. The first method, scribing, employs a compass or scribe to transfer the irregularities of the wall to the cabinet or face frame, which is then cut to match the profile of the wall. Our bookcase cabinets are designed with extra material to accommodate a small amount of scribing where the back meets the wall. The rabbet that holds the back panel is twice as deep as the back panel, leaving a 1/4-in.-wide x 1/4-in.-deep cabinet side extension beyond the back for scribing. If your walls will require more than 1/4 in. of scribing, you can cut a deeper rabbet for the back, but this may require you to make the shelves narrower to compensate for lost space inside the cabinet.

Position the cabinet and face frame so that it is plumb and touches the wall. Set the scribe or compass to match the widest gap between the wall and the face frame; then scribe the wall profile onto the face frame (see photo 12 and inset). Trim the face frame on the scribe line. When you attach the face frame to the cabinet, it will fit tightly against the wall, covering any gaps.

The second way to compensate for gaps is to cover them with trim pieces. This technique is easy, but it works best with flexible pieces of trim. For example, we used base shoe to conceal the gaps between the baseboard and floor.

12 Scribe the edges of the face frame to follow the wall profile using a compass. Trim to the line with a jigsaw or belt sander.

13 Fasten the face frame to the first cabinet with 2-in. finish nails. Secure the cabinet to the plinth with 1¼-in. screws and to the wall with 3-in. screws driven through the wall cleat.

14 Install the rest of the cabinets. Secure the cabinet sides to each other with 1¼-in. screws and to the wall by driving 3-in. screws through the wall cleat.

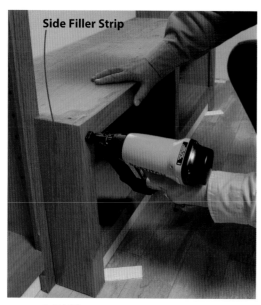

Side Filler Strip

15 Solid filler strips conceal the sides of the window seat cabinet. The window seat face frame is fastened with 2-in. finish nails.

16 Attach the window seat board with 2-in. finish nails. To prevent nails from popping through the top of the window seat cabinet, be careful to drive them into the face frame and cabinet sides.

The bookcase must be securely fastened to the wall. In order to ensure a flush fit against the side wall, I secured the scribed face frame to the first cabinet before securing it to the plinth and wall (see photo 13). I then fastened the first cabinet in place by driving 1¼-in. screws through the bottom into the plinth and by driving 3-in. screws through the wall cleat at the stud locations. Secure the remaining bookcase cabinets to each other with 1¼-in. screws and then fasten them to the plinth and wall (see photo 14). finally, attach the remaining face frame and trim to the cabinets with 2-in. and 1¼-in. finish nails (see photos 15 to 18). Fill the nail holes with putty to match the wood finish, or apply spackle and then paint.

Allow the finish to cure before installing the shelf pegs and shelves. When deciding what to put on each shelf, place the largest and heaviest items on the lower shelves, and work your way up with smaller or lighter-weight objects. This technique makes the bookcase more stable and enhances its visual appeal.

17 Miter the inside and outside corners of the base molding. Then position the base molding ¼ in. below the top edge of the bottom face frame rail and attach it with 1¼-in. finish nails. Next, conceal any gaps between the base molding and the floor by attaching the base shoe.

18 Finish the installation by attaching the top cap molding to the face frame. If there are gaps larger than ¼ in., scribe the top cap to match the ceiling. Otherwise, caulk any small gaps between the cabinet and walls or ceiling, and touch up with matching paint.

INDEX

D

Dadoes

with guide collar jig, 208
with router table, 176–177
stopped with straightedge routing, 160–161
straightedge routing, 159–161
with T-square or offset straightedge guide, 162
veneer tip, 160

Dado joints, 217–220
bit options, 217
description and usage, 217
housed, 217
machining options, 218–219
stopped, 217, 219–220

Dado-rabbet joints, 221–222
Decorative edge profiling, 17–18

Depth adjustment

fixed-based router, 32
plunge router, 38–39
professional vs. consumer-grade models, 54
trim routers, 45

Depth-setting controls, 13

Desk project

Wall Desk, 289–294

Detailing bits

characteristics and uses of, 100
essential bits for bit collection, 110
sampling of, 100

Dish-carving bit, 98

Door-building bits

characteristics and uses of, 100–101
sampling of, 101

Double-fluted straight bit, 99, 102
Double rabbet joint, 212

Double-sided tape

anchoring workpieces, 72

Dovetail bit, 97

Dovetail joints

half-blind, 252–255
sliding, 244–246

Downcut spiral bits, 102–103
Drawer lock joint bit, 96
Drop-leaf table bit set, 97
Dust collection, 51
plunge router, 41
Dust mask, 59–60
Dust respirator, 60

E

Ear protection, 58

Edge banding

flush-trimming with handheld router, 165

Edge guide routing, 153–155

feed directions, 155
mortises with edge guide and plunge router, 234–235
setting up, 154–155

Edge guides

for trim routers, 46

Edge jointing, 22
Electronic feedback circuitry, 49

End grain

profiling with router table and, 173

Eye protection, 59

F

Face frame flush-trim and V-groove bit, 95
Face shield respirator, 60
Featherboards, 67–69
making, 69

Feed direction

avoid overfeeding, 77
body position and router table techniques, 170–171
climb cutting, 66
edge guide routing, 155
for freehand routing, 65
for router tables, 66

Fence

bit guard, 129
characteristics of, 120–121
flat and square, 135–136
jointing with router table, 184–185
micro-adjustment provisions, 130
options for, 128–130
parallel to bit, 170
profiling with router table, 172–173
zero-clearance fence face, 169
zero-clearance inserts, 130

Fence project

Gateway to a Garden, 264–271

Finger joint bit, 97
Fixed-based router, 26–33
advantages of, 27–28
base of, 13
depth-setting controls, 13
disadvantages of, 28
handles, 27–28, 50
helical motor adjustment, 31–32
motor mounting and adjustment, 29–31
other motor adjustment systems, 33
overview of, 26
parts of, 9
vs. plunge router, 41
power issues, 29
professional vs. consumer-grade models, 54–55
router table and, 28
setting bit depth, 32

subbase, 27
zeroing out, 32

Floor mats, 76
Flush-trim bit, 98
pilot bearings, 92
Flush-trim insert bit, 98
Flush-trimming edge banding with handheld router, 165
Fluted straight bits, 90
Flutes, 87–88
Fluting bit, 94

Footing

providing sure footing under router, 74–75

Frame project

Stacked Mirror Frame, 272–276

G

Gateleg Table, 295–300
Gateway to a Garden, 264–271
Grind angle, 89

Grooves

with router table, 176–177
stopped with straightedge routing, 160–161
straightedge routing, 159–161
veneer tip, 160

Guide bushings, 195

Guide collar

advantages of using, 195
with guide collar jig, 208
hinge mortises with, 203–205
keeping guide collars tight, 197
length of, 198
straight lines with jig and guide collar, 207–208
subbase standardization, 51
template routing with, 195–200
types of, 196–197
understanding guide collar offset, 198–200

Guides

mortises with edge guide and plunge router, 234–235
offset straightedge guide, 162–163

H

Half-blind dovetail joints, 252–255
bit options, 252
description and usage, 252
dovetail jigs, 253
routing, 253–255
Half-lap joint, 227
Handheld router techniques, 139–165
circle routing, 162–164
edge guide routing, 153–155